THE FONTANA ECONOMIC HISTORY OF EUROPE

General Editor: Carlo M. Cipolla

There is at present no satisfactory economic history of Europe – covering Europe both as a whole and with particular relation to the individual countries – that is both concise enough for convenient use and yet full enough to include the results of individual and detailed scholarship. This series is designed to fill that gap.

THE FONTANA ECONOMIC HISTORY OF EUROPE

The Fontana
Economic History of Europe
Volume 5

The Twentieth Century – 2

Editor Carlo M. Cipolla

Harvester Press/Barnes & Noble
By agreement with Fontana Books

This edition first published in 1977 by
THE HARVESTER PRESS LIMITED
Publisher: John Spiers
2 Stanford Terrace
Hassocks, Nr Brighton
Sussex, England
and published in the U.S.A. 1977 by
HARPER & ROW PUBLISHERS, INC.
BARNES & NOBLE IMPORT DIVISION
10 East 53rd Street, New York 10022.

The Twentieth Century Part Two
This edition first published in 1977
by The Harvester Press Limited
and by Barnes & Noble
By agreement with Fontana

First published in paperback 1976
by Fontana Books

© Hermann Priebe 1976
© Angus Maddison 1974
© Carlo Zacchia 1976
© Fred Hirsch and Peter Oppenheimer 1976
© Benjamin Ward 1975
© Max Nicholson 1976

The Harvester Press Limited
ISBN 0 85527 809 9
Barnes & Noble
ISBN 0-06-492182-4

Printed and bound in Great Britain by
Redwood Burn Limited Trowbridge & Esher

Contents

8. The Changing Role of Agriculture 1920—1970

Hermann Priebe

Since the end of the First World War, European agriculture has undergone greater structural changes within five decades than it had previously in the course of centuries. This rapid transformation must be considered to be a precondition as well as a consequence of the general realignment in social and economic life which with ever-increasing intensity and speed is altering every aspect of human life and continuously spreading farther in space.

On the one hand, trigger factors must be looked for inside the farming sector. Biological and technical innovations, above all the mechanical energy replacing animal draught power, have exerted a decisive influence on production techniques. On the other hand, changes in the social and economic fields have had manyfold repercussions. They have made for new ways of thinking and behaviour in the rural population, have offered new job opportunities, and have thus pushed ahead the process of rural modernisation.

The increase in productivity not only improved income from farming but at the same time enabled a substantial transfer of labour to other sectors of the economy which contributed to overall economic growth. Again, the process of urbanisation spread into the rural areas, the village has become a dwelling place for people in all walks of life, and the traditional differences between town and country life have been levelled out to a great extent.

Yet it is true that considerable differences continued to exist between individual European countries. Partly they stemmed from historical roots, but also from the fact that the aims and methods of economic and agricultural policies varied distinctly.

In eastern Europe, traditional farming was the livelihood of the majority of the population even after the First World War, whilst the degree of industrialisation was still low. The USSR started collectivisation and the incorporation of agriculture into the government-planned economy in the late 'twenties. And it was only twenty years later that other east European countries followed this course. On the whole, eastern Europe requires special treatment because agriculture and farm policies developed along quite different lines from the west. For this reason we shall have to focus our attention on western Europe in the first place.

Here, national and group interests as well as agricultural methods and policies were at odds before the EEC started. Some sort of balance had to be achieved in the Common Market. Common Agricultural Policy is a great attempt at creating a system that would combine the two major goals of satisfying farmers' needs and meeting the food demand of consumers within a highly developed market-orientated economy. There are several reasons why the double task could not be performed satisfactorily. Not only did CAP begin just at the time when important structural changes in agriculture caused a considerable increase in production and in consequence led to a host of problems concerning foreign as well as domestic affairs. Moreover, the integration of general economic and currency policies lagged behind that of the agricultural policy of the EEC which proved rather awkward for the setting up of market organisations. And, of course, a certain lack of political strength in arriving at genuinely common decisions proved harmful to the functioning of agricultural policy too.

The development sketched above is a fascinating subject of research into recent European economic history and a preliminary analysis may help us to understand the problems which the Community of western Europe is confronted with in the middle of the 'seventies.

EUROPEAN AGRICULTURE BETWEEN
THE WORLD WARS

The period between the First and Second World Wars meant a time of transition in agricultural development. While this had been going on at a steady pace during the preceding hundred years, scope was given now to structural changes which, after 1950, set in on a large scale and thoroughly altered the economic as well as the social situation of agriculture.

A summary of events will make it clear how these major changes came about and what problems and new tasks were to follow from them in the long run.

A TRANSITIONAL PHASE IN AGRICULTURAL DEVELOPMENT

For many centuries, in the traditional agrarian society most people's lives had been hemmed in by narrow social confines while their modest livelihood mostly depended on subsistence farming. Only towards the end of the eighteenth century, the great social reforms in western Europe granted the peasants personal liberty and the right to make their own dispositions on their holding, thus giving them an incentive to exercise hitherto unwonted initiative. Also, the beginning of industrialisation meant rising demand for food while at the same time it made better tools and aids available to the farmers. All this was very much to the advantage of the farming community.

In the course of the nineteenth century, the ancient type of subsistence farming which comprised the production of almost every item of everyday use, gave way to a new system of specialisation and exchange of goods over the market. Economic development led to a growing mutual dependence between agriculture proper and the other industries. Tasks which up to then had fallen to the farming sector, such as the preparation of dress materials and other consumer goods or the processing of farm produce, were taken on by the manufacturing sector which in its turn began to provide more amply for the farmers' needs. Increased productivity in farming also allowed part of the farm population to take up work outside farming and those could now obtain their victuals from the market, while the increasing demand for industrial goods in the rural areas gave new impulses to domestic trade.

At the beginning of the twentieth century, farming was no longer the basic means of subsistence for three-quarters of the population, as it had been a hundred years before. Instead, in 1920, only 20 to 40% of the people made up the farming sector of western European countries, while the gross product per hectare of agricultural surface as well as per head of the labour force employed in farming had risen to three or even four times what it had been before. Thus, the greater part of the working population were then employed in other fields and the upshot was that, while value added in agriculture rose in absolute terms, the relative economic importance of farming had markedly declined.

Still, in spite of the great economic progress achieved, the traditional structure of agriculture was preserved even well into the twentieth century. Farm work continued to rely on human and animal muscle power while machinery could be put only to a very limited use. At this stage, the increase in productivity was for the most part brought about by biological progress in plant and animal genetics, in the techniques of manuring and animal feeding, more intensive methods of crop rotation, and a wider range of crops. This type of improvement could be carried through in holdings of any size, so that structural changes were not required in order to benefit from the innovations. Therefore, neither the number nor the average acreage of holdings needed to be altered and the absolute number of the farm population could remain constant. But its proportion of total population diminished sharply because the whole of the population increase was taken up by the growing industrial sector.

Meanwhile, in the second half of the nineteenth century, social concern centred on two great topics: the living conditions of the industrial labour force and the future of the rural population. Both were the subject of fierce controversy. Preserving the bulk of the farm population became the central aim of agrarian policies, and it was considered indispensable for any sovereign state to make sure of sufficient space for rural settlements in order to provide domestic food supply from the national soil and recruits for the armed forces from farm families.

Experience of undernourishment during the First World War roused a livelier interest in the state of farming. Even in Great Britain, where about three quarters of food demand had been met by imports before the war, domestic production was then enlarged to cover half of her needs.

The policy of nationalism as it was practised after the First World War provided a new argument in favour of the basic importance of the rural population as an element of national strength. All this led to the concept of rural settlements as a means of fortifying national unity, and many countries introduced special programmes for the expropriation of latifundia owned by the former landlords for the benefit of national groups.

While over much of the European scene traditional villages inhabited by genuine farmers were still to be found, the remains of former feudal systems had also survived into the twentieth century. In eastern Europe this ancient feudal élite was mostly of German descent. Even if land reforms in these regions in the first place aimed at cutting up the big estates into smallholdings, they meant at the same time that ownership of the land was transferred to subjects of the new nations.

A special role fell to the big estates in eastern Germany. They had been the economic foothold of a politically leading group and in the absence of a significant intermediate social class had been rather shut off from industrial development. Therefore it seemed desirable to counteract the threat of depopulation by settling as many smallholders as possible in this area. But exertions towards land reform met with heavy obstruction which was propped up by pseudo-economic reasoning. The importance of big estates in meeting food demand and their superior economic performance were contended for years. But the economic world crisis of the late 'twenties put these objections to shame: most of the big estates came to grief because of their obsolete labour conditions. It was the family holdings which, on the contrary, showed themselves surprisingly viable everywhere.

An aid programme for east German agriculture was started under the label of 'Osthilfe' which for the most part was a political sham to assure subsidies to the big landowners and save their estates. A new attempt at land reform in the interests of larger groups of the population was made in 1931 by Reichskanzler Brüning. But the programme initiated by him only hastened his political downfall. Finally, the idea of land reform was taken up again by the allied forces occupying western Germany – but only a very few of the bigger estates were to be found there, and besides in the meantime the whole question of farm size had come to be viewed somewhat differently because of recent developments in agricultural techniques.

In Nazi Germany, a last effort had been made by the 'Reichsnährstand' to form a conclusive concept of farm policy on the basis of traditional ideas. 'Blut und Boden' (blood and soil) had been one of the slogans summarising a set of exaggerated social values imputed to farm people, while that of 'Erbhof' (hereditary family holding) likewise overstrained the role of the farm in national life. The true nature of these anachronisms is revealed by the fact that at the same time the so-called battle for production ('Erzeugungsschlacht') was proclaimed in order to achieve food autarky by the most advanced production methods. These were scarcely felt to be contradictory claims. And it has in fact remained a characteristic feature of farm policies that on the one hand traditional ways of farming and farm life were to be defended, while on the other hand agriculture was to have its share in general economic growth.

In the meantime, however, the first tractors had arrived on the scene of agricultural development as harbingers of technical progress. It is true that they were still rather imperfect and employable in specified operations only. And they remained so for some time because their improvement and diffusion were delayed first by the economic crisis, then by the rearmament of the 'thirties, and finally by the Second World War. But in the post-war period, mechanisation and the use of engines in farming got going with a vengeance and thoroughly transformed farm work and farm life. It was also the root cause of structural changes in the rural areas which still continue with undiminished force.

DIVERGENCIES BETWEEN INDIVIDUAL COUNTRIES

Agricultural development started at different times and with varying intensity in the European countries. Innovations in farming are clearly connected with those in other sectors, the whole process being an integral part of social life. Still, as they take place within a framework of differing historical, political, demographic, and natural conditions, there is bound to be a variety of possibilities and obstacles to agricultural development according to national peculiarities.

In order to judge the performance of a national economy of which farming is one section, the distribution of gainfully employed persons by sector is a useful criterion. Generally, a low proportion of active persons in agriculture points to a highly developed national economy with not only a high degree of industrialisation but also a highly productive farming sector.

TABLE 1: Share of Agriculture in Active Population about 1920 (% of total active population)

Germany	31	Norway	37
France	42	Sweden	41
Italy	56	Switzerland	26
Netherlands	24	Austria	40
Belgium	19	Spain	57
Luxemburg	—	Portugal[b]	62
Great Britain	8		
Ireland[a]	52		
Denmark	—		

[a] 1926.
[b] 1930.

It is true that differences in statistical method somewhat impair the comparability of these data and moreover they have not been collected at exactly the same time in different countries. Still, the material available in this field is the most indicative of the order of magnitude of the problems involved.

Great Britain holds a special position with respect to economic development. She was the first among European countries to start industrialisation and in consequence the increase in non-farming population is to be noted at quite an early date. Around 1920 the proportion of active population occupied in farming had already dropped to 8%. Here, however, special factors have to be taken into account: Great Britain being a world power was able to assure her food supplies in exchange for industrial goods, especially from her own colonies. In effect, her domestic food supply did at one time drop as low as one quarter of domestic demand, although during the 'twenties and up to the Second World War it rose again to about one half. In 1930 about 50% of total imports still consisted of agricultural produce. Since then its share has dropped to just one quarter of total imports, as domestic production was raised. On the whole, for some decades farming has been of lesser economic importance in Great Britain than in other countries. This fact is confirmed by its contributing only 3% to total gross domestic product.

In *continental Europe* the share of farming in the economically active population mirrors to a great extent the respective national level of industrialisation (cf. Table 1). Belgium, the Netherlands, and Switzerland were the most highly industrialised countries and in consequence in 1920 the percentage of active population in farming was 19, 24, and 26% respectively. Germany with 31% comes next, while in the rest of the countries more than one third and in the case of Italy even more than one half of the active population still had to make their living from farming. Among the more important causes for these divergencies the aims and measures of national farm policies have to be mentioned. For already in the nineteenth century European countries had chosen different courses according to their particular interests and needs.

In *Germany* – with respect to the geographical situation of the country – the goal of keeping as many people as possible on the land and maintaining a high level of self-sufficiency in farm produce had been sponsored by wide circles of the population – and this in spite of advancing industrialisation. In 1878 the first grain tariff was established, followed by the elaboration of a system of protection for agriculture that raised farm prices above the world market level and gave home production preference on the domestic market. The conservatives got support for these efforts from the political concept of the society, but their success was also due to the fact that domestic production could not meet the growing demand and self-sufficiency only amounted to about 75%. It was this gap in food supply which made the import blockade during the First World War really dangerous, and the shock of war-time hunger was partly responsible for the people's consent to the Nazi government's exaggerated ideas on food autarky.

Agricultural policies in *Germany* and in *Great Britain* rested on opposite principles characteristic of the respective situation of each of these countries. While Germany tried to protect domestic production from the world market, England relied on her worldwide trade policy. Her liberalistic import policy connected consumers' prices for food to the world market level. British farmers, though, were no more able to subsist on these terms than were their German colleagues. Subsidies in England took the form of deficiency payments. Thus, in both countries producers' prices were far above world market level. The main difference being that price support in England came from the budget, i.e. the tax-payers, while in Germany the consumer had to bear the burden in much the same way as later on in the EEC. But with the low level of domestic supply in Great Britain, cheap food imports were certainly advantageous to the national economy.

As will be shown in due course, particular difficulties deriving from their respective farm policies had to be dealt with in both countries when they joined the EEC. After several decades of protection, the CAP was not easily acceptable to German farmers, at least from the psychological angle. The United Kingdom, in its turn, was compelled to face the necessity of importing farm produce at higher prices from other EEC countries and this is a controversial issue not only from the view-point of the national economy but also of individual consumers.

Farm policies in the *Netherlands* and *Denmark* might be considered to be antitypes of another kind to the German strife for self-sufficiency. Both these countries had been relying on a policy of world-wide trade, but they had turned the cheap world market prices to their advantage by building up an intensive low-cost animal production which put them into a favourable competitive situation. They were able to do so because they could boast of a well educated class of farmers and because their soils and climate made family holdings both efficient and prosperous. This made possible an aggressive export policy and the excellent marketing performance of Dutch and Danish farmers assured them an outstanding position in European agricultural markets.

The differences in the efficiency of farming in the four countries here mentioned are very instructive. On the average of the period 1934 to 1938 there were for instance the following yields p.a. to be observed:

	wheat 200 kg/ha	milk kg/cow
Great Britain	23	2,500
Germany	23	2,500
Netherlands	30	3,400
Denmark	30	3,200

In the densely populated *Netherlands* (1930: 231 persons/sq km) agricultural surface per head was just under 30 acres. Notwithstanding, the one fifth of the active population employed in agriculture succeeded in producing 50% of total exports. At one time, more than half of the butter production and one third of the meat could be exported.

Half the grain demand, it is true, had then to be met by imports.

Denmark was less densely populated (1930: 83 persons/ sq km) so that agricultural surface per head was about 90 acres. With domestic demand somewhat lower than in the Netherlands, the share of farm products in total exports was over 80%. Before the Second World War, Denmark's meat export almost equalled domestic demand. Butter exports even amounted to six times the figure of domestic demand. Between 1924 and 1928, 40% of the world market supply of bacon and 29% of the butter came from Denmark. Even at that rate of export, Denmark managed to meet about 85% of domestic grain demand. Farming was therefore among the most important economic sectors in Denmark, employing about 35% of the active population. It was only after the Second World War that industry began to overtake agriculture, so that the share of farming in the active population dropped to 11% in 1971.

In *France* domestic farming had for a long time to compete with that in the colonies and overseas territories of the country. But her industrial development, as compared to Great Britain, was lagging behind. Moreover, it was confined to the surroundings of Paris and a few other places. Population density on the whole was low (76 persons/sq km) and because of the great distances between her industrial centres, France could only exceptionally offer her population alternatives to farming. Therefore, the French provinces have for a long time remained agricultural areas. In consequence, the levels of sales and of producers' prices were low, and yields, too, rose reluctantly. During the period between 1934 and 1938, the average figures were only 1,600 kg of wheat per hectare and 1,850 kg of milk per cow. Even around 1920, 42% of the active population of France were still occupied in farming. And around 1960, at the start of the EEC, the figure was still 25%. These structural data offer an explanation for the special interest of French politics in the CAP, because they clearly show that in wide areas people still depended on market outlets for their produce.

Italy was facing particular problems deriving from the contrast between a highly developed northern part and the economically weak southern regions. For several centuries, the north of Italy, owing to its free cities, had been a cultural and political centre of Europe. Also it had begun to industrialise at an early period, whereas the Italian south remained an underdeveloped feudalistic area which even the social reforms of the nineteenth century could not really reach. The concentration of landownership into the hands of a few still coexists with rural pauperism even now. On the national average, in the Italy of 1920 there were still 56% of total active population engaged in farming. And still today a great many people in the south of Italy cannot see their way to improving their condition otherwise than by migrating to the north or even to other European countries. It may be recalled in this context that the Italian minority in the USA are descended from immigrants from southern Italy.

The one advantage of Italian agriculture is the climate. It favours the production of wine, fruit, vegetables, rice, and olives, all of which can be cultivated intensely on small plots. It is therefore understandable that Italy entered the EEC with great expectations, hoping for larger outlets for her special produce as much as for financial help with the economic improvement of her southern regions.

The other *western European countries* fit into the picture outlined above. Spain and Portugal show features similar to those of Italy, i.e. surviving traces of feudalism, namely significant contrasts between the life conditions of the landlords and the poor conditions for smallholders in big rural areas. The remaining countries had made better progress toward sound land tenure and distribution because of their old democratic traditions. In their case industrialisation too had started in good time. In Belgium and Switzerland e.g. the low proportion of agricultural employment in 1920 (19% and 26% respectively) testifies to their superior economic performance, whereas the figure for Austria, Sweden, and Norway was still 40%.

On the other hand, a large farming population could constitute a power reserve for economic growth. This was proved after the Second World War, when agricultural politics, aimed at fostering the increase in agricultural productivity, did succeed in releasing surplus labour from farming to the benefit of other economic sectors. It will be shown later on how the share of farming in the active population dropped drastically everywhere in the course of economic growth after 1950.

European agriculture and the development of the European national economies always have been far from uniform, as must be expected with her wide range of political, economic and cultural traditions. It will therefore be all the more interesting to follow up further developments in the different ways of thinking and the ensuing economical and political outlook which came to bear on the attitude of each country in the EEC.

GREAT STRUCTURAL CHANGES AFTER THE SECOND WORLD WAR

CAUSES AND EFFECTS

In the post-war period, major structural changes took place in the agriculture of each of the west European countries within two decades. New engines made mechanical energy available to farming and caused a genuine agrarian revolution. As compared to industrial production, there had been a time lag of several decades before electrical and internal combustion engines were adapted to farm operations. Steam engines and iron-wheel tractors had been of very limited use only. It was only when rubber tyres were fitted to the tractors and farming machinery that they could be employed for every kind of work on fields and pastures. At the same time, electrical equipment permitted a thorough change in animal husbandry and in the farmyard.

Already in the 'thirties, the new techniques had been foreshadowed, but after the war the use of engines and machinery spread at a rate unthought of in any previous innovation. The rapid growth of the rest of the economy and the change in thought and behaviour which then reached the villages, certainly helped to speed up the process. It only took one or two decades to firmly establish full mechanisation in west European farming, and in spite of the pride farmers had always taken in their horses, their number now dwindled at an astonishing rate, so that only a very small stock was left.

Engines and machinery made labour productivity rise at one great leap. This in turn made it necessary to invest much more capital and affected the man-land ratio too, the more so as the cost of labour was rising noticeably.

All this has important consequences which are, however, not the same for different types of holdings. The bigger farms reduce the number of farm hands, while family farms try to adjust the acreage to the working capacity of the family members which is, of course, much increased by the new technical equipment. Part of the family labour from smallholdings is transferred into other occupations while the farm is worked as a part-time job. All these different attempts at adjustment to changed conditions resulted in a decrease in the number of persons employed in farming and in the total number of holdings. Modern agriculture requires higher capital outlay per worker than most non-farming activities.

The change here outlined has its impact on the social situation in agriculture as well. There is no room any more for the unskilled farm hand of earlier times. It is true that the developed agricultural techniques mean new chances for the farmer, but it is equally true that a far higher level of education, vocational training, and responsibility in taking the appropriate decisions, is required to match the higher risk. In modern farming, the personal qualities of the farmer are of the utmost importance for a successful performance. And for this reason, the self-dependent family farms of west Europe and North America have proved to be far more viable economic units than the centrally planned giant farms of east Europe and the USSR.

The dynamics of all these technical and social changes taken together have been so strong that in the post-war period agriculture proved itself capable of overcoming within a relatively short time the damage wrought by the war. Notably, the pre-war level of production was reached again in western Germany already by 1950, in spite of the fact that important regions with favourable conditions for farming had been separated from what was now the German Federal Republic.

OUTLINE OF STRUCTURAL DEVELOPMENT

The decrease in the agricultural labour force and in the number of farms as well as the increase in production and turnover of goods of all kinds are indicative of the structural

TABLE 2 : Statistical Data on Agricultural Development 1950-70

		FGR	France	Italy	Netherl.	Gr. Britain
Ganfully Employed in Agric. (in 1,000 persons)	1950	5,114	6,348[a]	8,468[b]	747[c]	1,215[d]
	1971	2,234	2,787	3,652	319	665
	1950 = 100	44	44	43	43	55
Gainf. Empl. in Agr. persons p. 100 ha AS	1950	35·9	19·1[a]	43·3[b]	31·9[c]	6·2[d]
	1971	16·5	8·5	20·7	14·9	3·5
Holdings of 1 ha or more (in 1,000)	1950	1,648	2,091[a]	4,473[e] [f]	241	481[g]
	1970	1,083	1,421	2,175	164	308
	1950 = 100	66	68	49	68	64
Tractors p. 1,000 ha AS	1950	10	4	3	9	17
	1970	101	37	33	61	24
	1950 = 100	1,010	925	1,100	678	141
Average yields grain in 100 kg/ha	1950	23·1	15·9	15·7	27·9	23·9
	1972	38·2	42·2	29·2	39·8	40·7
	1950 = 100	165	265	186	143	170
milk per cow in kg p.a.	1950/51	2,560	1,900	2,262	3,715	2,729
	1971	3,856	2,900	2,912	4,440	3,490
	1950 = 100	151	153	129	120	128
Value of agr. prod. at curr. prices and exch. rates (million DM)	1950	13,563[h]	20,820[h]	17,159[d]	3,864	11,038[as]
	1970	35,729[j]	46,669[k]	37,076[l]	11,818[m]	23,226[h]
	1950 = 100	263	224	216	306	210

Average consumption p. head, kg p. a.		FGR	France	Italy	Netherl.	Gr. Britain
total grain[o]	1950/51	102	119	153	101	102
	1970/71	66	76	129	63	72
potatoes	1950/51	190	126	36	140	111
	1970/71	102	96	41	85	102
sugar[p]	1950/51	29	27	12	39	41
	1970/71	34	36	27	46	46
total meat[q]	1950/51	37	56	16	32	47
	1970/71	87	96	57	66	72
fats and oils[r]	1950/51	21	15	11	26	23
	1970/71	27[g]	26[g]	21[g]	32[t]	23
eggs	1950/51	8	11	7	5	13
	1970/71	16	13	11	12	13

Source: Official Statistics

a Average 1946–54.
b 1954.
c 1947.
d 1951.
e 1946.
f over 0·5 ha.
g 1953.

h 1950/51.
i Gross output of agriculture.
j total subsidies deducted.
k incl. tax on value added.
l incl. indirect taxes.
m excl. tax on value added.
n incl. subsidies and deficiency payments.

o flour equivalent.
p refined equivalent.
q incl. intestines.
r fat content.
s 1969/70.
t 1966/67–1968/69.

change in farming. But there is even more to it: villages have altered, and so have rural areas and the landscape.

The foregoing statistical breakdown of agricultural development in five representative countries may serve to make clear what has been going on for twenty years.

Table 2 shows the trend of development to be about the same in each of the countries:

> The number of persons gainfully employed in agriculture has declined in absolute figures as well as in relation to agricultural surface, by more than half; the only exception being Great Britain because of her lower initial figures.

> Holdings have diminished by one third. The higher rate of decline in Italy is explained by the vanishing of part of the smallest holdings in the southern provinces.

> Average yields of grain and milk have risen most steeply where the initial figures of 1930 were lowest. This applies above all to France and Italy.

> The tenfold increase in tractors demonstrates the rapid mechanisation of farming. The figures show Great Britain to have been foremost in this respect as early as 1950.

> The value of agricultural production has doubled or tripled everywhere, with the Netherlands as the main exporter of farm products taking the lead. Labour productivity augmented five to six times alongside of the strong decline in agricultural labour.

> Consumption per head, as a typical indicator of generally rising incomes, has considerably risen in regard of sugar and animal products, while demand for staple products like grain and potatoes, declined.

On the whole, these figures too point to the mutual dependence of farming and industry: not only the increase in agricultural production but also the transfer of workers has contributed to economic growth. On the other hand, the additional produce could be marketed at good prices only because of rising purchasing power and per head consumption. What does not become visible from the national averages is the variegation in agricultural development in the several regions of each country. But these are very important, because whereas traditional tools and animal power, and even the biological innovations could be used indiscriminately, the use of engines and machinery is dependent on a variety of factors which determine the structure of agriculture.

We may summarise the structural changes of the last two decades which have so thoroughly upset the foundations of agricultural policy:

(1) The peasant village, familiar throughout European history, does not exist any more. Farmers are nowadays a minority and the traditional values and living conditions are vanishing. The villages accommodate people of all vocations and have been drawn into the wake of increasing urbanisation.

(2) Traditional agricultural policies that had been conceived for the good of full-time farmers, cannot keep the bulk of the population on the land, but under modern conditions with low demand for farm workers it rather undermines the existence of rural populations and endangers soil cultivation. The bulk of rural families do not consist any more of farmers in the traditional sense. They are families who often own a few acres only and cultivate their gardens or small farms as a part-time occupation.

(3) The low population density which is the consequence of modern farming, makes it impossible for any rural area to survive as a purely agricultural region. The classical instruments of agricultural price and market policies are quite unsuited to solve the problems of today and so is the former type of structural policy. The future of the rural areas is inevitably dependent on the development of the industrial and service sectors.

In the face of all this, it is easy to understand why the agricultural policy of the EEC has run into tremendous difficulties and why some countries are laying strong emphasis on regional policy.

FARM POLICIES AT THE THRESHOLD OF THE EEC

A certain amount of disequilibrium in the grain markets, and for some time also in those of dairy products, was to be noticed already before the beginning of the EEC. Most countries had not succeeded in adjusting the structure of their agriculture to the general economic development. The general ideas of the market economy have never ruled unconditionally in the farming sector. On the contrary, there was not a single country which did not try to counterbalance certain disturbances in the relations between production and the market by the political expedient of market intervention. In order to keep up the guaranteed farm prices, surplus produce was bought, stored, and part of it exported, by the help of government subsidies. In consequence, other countries, seeing their own farm policy endangered by the cheap exports of their neighbours, took defensive measures. They set up import quotas or supported prices at a level they deemed desirable.

Already during the 'fifties this situation had become so bad that there was no true competition any more between the industrial nations, in so far as farming was concerned. One could rather term the state of affairs then prevailing a competition of subsidies, and this was very much like a secret war carried on apart from the lively exchange of industrial goods. It cannot be denied that each of the countries tried to shift its agricultural difficulties on to the others and to dump their surpluses on them. There was quite a wide range of possibilities: to grant subsidies, to bargain on the basis of compensation, or even to bring political pressure to bear on business partners. As a result of it all, relations between the countries of western Europe and North America had become complicated and sterile as regards agricultural trade.

It may be concluded from this short account that difficulties and tensions do not date from the creation of the EEC, but constituted a dismal heritage which individual member states brought into the Community. There were, moreover, difficulties and tensions over the concept of a future agricultural policy. In this context we may refer to the differences in the historical development of the nations involved which reach back into the nineteenth century, as has been shown above (see p. 405).

Around 1960, countries with an aggressive farm policy, like the Netherlands and Denmark, were confronted with the defensive, protectionist measures of others, amongst which Germany and Switzerland rank first. But Belgium and Austria also belong to this group, as does Great Britain which was no less protective in her agricultural policy although employing different methods.

The Netherlands had built up a strong competitive position for their animal products, and decided on an aggressive marketing policy. German farm policy, on the contrary, was of a defensive character. High prices for grain and sugar beet, which mostly came from the bigger farms, also meant costly animal feed. Thus, her total farm production could not hold its own in free competition but had to be protected from imports. And Germany was, with the single exception of Great Britain, the greatest importer of farm products in Europe, because she had never succeeded in attaining food autarky before the Second World War, and her total domestic supply only reached the relatively low level of 75%.

France, possessing nearly half of the agricultural surface of the original EEC, was therefore the more optimistic about her position in the Common Market. She had been cautious in her price policy and thus her agriculture had remained comparatively extensive, the level of yields relatively low. Therefore, her production reserves were considerable. In addition to this, the general economic structures of both these countries were quite different. In Germany, 49% of the gainfully employed held jobs in industry and scarcely 10% in farming, whilst in France the respective figures were 39% in industry and over 20% in farming. Naturally, France had a great interest in the CAP which promised to offer her a market for her rising farm production, which was of great importance to the population of her wide rural areas where access to industrial employment was still a difficult problem.

French agriculture had to fear no losses, but instead hoped for considerable gains from CAP, while German agriculture was apprehensive of the danger to its favourable situation which for a hundred years her national agricultural policy had taken great pains to defend.

Italy's was a peculiar situation. Her special products had no competition from the EEC so that a conflict of interests was to be feared only from the treaties of association with other countries, especially those on the Mediterranean.

To sum up, at the starting of the EEC there existed a multiplicity of agricultural interests and systems which had to be brought to a common resolution. Italy and France expected the EEC to bring them into a position which would allow of more active farm policies than they had hitherto been able to pursue, and which in turn would render their production reserves advantageous. The Netherlands, too, hoped for easier access to a larger market. But it is improbable that anybody could have anticipated the rapid increase in production which has really been achieved in the Common Market. It may also have been very unlucky for the EEC that the start of CAP coincided with such an overwhelming revolution in the productive capacity of farming.

AGRICULTURE IN THE EEC

From the view-point of economic policy, the Common Agricultural Policy in the EEC was a courageous step toward unification. By strengthening competition and abolishing any barriers to free trade, it was hoped to free agricultural trade of unproductive burdens and provide new incentives for the exchange of goods between the member countries.

The political weight of CAP was meant to be even more than that. Agricultural policy was to take on a leading role in European integration, and it was expected that every advance in CAP would be for the good of the European Community. In fact, the common agricultural system proved to be a bond which at certain moments prevented the Community from breaking apart.

But in the long run, the special political task assigned to it put rather too much strain on the CAP. Its proper functioning has been hampered by the influence of political reasoning which all too often has overruled rational argument. Decisions have been taken which, from the point of view of agricultural policy, have been mistakes, but could not be avoided when political integration was at stake. Important aims of the agricultural policy had then to be sacrificed. Therefore, market imbalances soon grew to be more disturbing than before, and the protection granted to agriculture within the EEC has become deeply harmful to world trade. Within a few years the CAP proved to be unsuitable as an instrument of European unification: rather it has created serious tensions.

THE AGRARIAN SYSTEM OF THE EEC

From the start of the EEC, there have been more difficulties in the field of agriculture than in others. The internal market for industrial goods could be extended by simply reducing tariffs and quantity regulations. This would not do in the agricultural sector: here, national market organisations and special arrangements had to be replaced by an entirely new and uniform system which could not be modelled on any precedent.

The Treaty of Rome, concluded in 1957, only provided general guide-lines for agricultural policy in Articles 38ff. Elaboration had been left to the executive organs of the Community. At the Stresa Conference, in 1958, a preliminary exchange of ideas had taken place. In 1960, the Commission of the EEC submitted to the Council of Ministers the first proposals for a system of common market regulations which can be said to have been of an almost ingenious simplicity. Free trade in agricultural products and competition within the Common Market were to be established on the basis of uniform prices. These would be fixed annually by the Council of Ministers, with a minimum level to be maintained not only in the member countries but also in regard to countries outside the EEC. Domestic production within the EEC was to be given preference, and besides, common financing of the market organisation was envisaged. So the main points were, first, internal free trade, second, Community preference in foreign trade, and, third, financial solidarity of European agriculture. These three principles were to play an important part in many of the dissensions on CAP which were to arise later on.

From 1960 on, market regulations for the most important agricultural products have been set up, and in 1962 the Agricultural Guidance and Guarantee Fund was agreed upon. The newly created system appeared to be by far superior to the former national regulations. The multitude of sometimes contradictory measures, the direct subsidies, quantity controls, bilateral arrangements, and all the other obstacles to trade, were done away with and so were the monopolistic practices which had been used in marketing arrangements in the Netherlands, in dairy production in Germany, and in the control of grain production in France.

The original idea was that the economic functions of

demand and supply were to be governed by the price mechanism, with the important provision, though, that a minimum level of domestic prices was to be supported by import levies. Inside the Common Market, on the other hand, intervention prices were fixed for the staple produce, grain and sugar, as well as for dairy products, in order to prevent any undesirable deterioration of prices. The price of grain had to be given a key position, cereals being both a staple food and a raw material for animal production, strongly influencing the prices of pigs, poultry, eggs, and, therefore in an indirect way, the price level of all animal products. Between 1967 and 1972, wholesale prices of wheat and barley were about 60% above world market level, and that of sugar even more than 100%.

In later years, the EEC system of market regulations has been severely criticised, it has been considered not only as protectionist and bureaucratic, but also as discriminating against 'outside' countries. This latter criticism is, however, unjust. The system is neutral as far as economic policy is concerned. Chances of access to the Common Market are equal for all countries. The real problem lies in the decrease in imports which is determined by the rise in domestic production to which some preference is given on the internal markets of the EEC. It cannot be maintained that any 'third country' is excluded from the Common Market, although this has been supposed for some time also in the USA.

But apart from this erroneous idea, it must be admitted that there is one weak point in the agricultural system of the EEC. Prices are fixed by political bodies and there is always the possibility that government intervention may be extended. Imbalances can arise when decisions are not taken in accordance with the sound criteria of market economics. This has been the case in several instances and has resulted in the accumulation of surpluses of several products. These have grown to be a heavy burden on the financial resources of the EEC and on its political relationships.

Politicians have been confronted with considerable difficulties in fixing prices and implementing market

regulations, although the general aims are generally agreed.
Common Agricultural Policy is to:

improve the income of producers
assure supply to consumers at adequate prices
help to balance production and sales
promote the exchange of goods with the rest of the world.

With such a comprehensive programme, a permanent
conflict of aims was bound to ensue from the measures
concerning price and market policies. While a balance
can be achieved in other sectors of the economy by the
workings of the market forces, political bodies should
certainly not be charged with this task.

The development in the agricultural sector under the
influence of decisions taken in Brussels during the first
decade of CAP is instructive. Looking back on the course
of events, one has to admit that bureaucracy has failed in
several respects and therefore one may feel inclined to
plead for the market economy. Besides, an analysis of the
past is likely to clarify the principles on which future
solutions might be based.

ANALYSIS OF A DECADE OF EUROPEAN FARM POLICIES

Readiness for compromise should have been a precondition for arriving at a genuine common policy. But there
have been decisions which showed a lack of political
strength. Negotiations have been left in the hands of experts
without strict guidance by government directions. Instead
of political concepts, technical details have been discussed
with surprising prolixity, and in the meantime politics
came to be influenced more and more by the agricultural
pressure groups.

The haggling over a common grain price went on for
years and it was by no means an edifying spectacle. At the
beginning of the EEC, corn prices had been highest in
Germany. If an economic community was to be created, a
compromise had to be brought about. But with the intransi-

gence of the Germans, valuable time and energy were
wasted and integration delayed. This was very much to the
detriment of the infant CAP.

When finally, at the famous night session of 15 December
1964, the grain price was agreed, agricultural policy had
already taken a wrong turn. As a result, the price level
began to rise by 20% above the previous average of the
EEC countries, and even by 32% above that of France,
which, as has already been shown, was rich in productive
reserves. There was even more harm done, because in
return for their compliance over the corn price other
countries sought compensations in other fields. Thus was
started a gradual extension of the system which once had
been planned as an instrument for dealing with a few key
products. Sales were guaranteed for a variety of other
products, and market regulations set up for produce which
nobody had ever dreamt of including in the regulations
system. The so-called, and at that time much praised,
pragmatical procedure made agricultural policy stray
from the original concept instead of heralding integration,
because the counter-demands of member countries caused
an escalation of protectionist devices.

Thus, the system of market regulations, having trespassed
on the liberal rules laid down in the beginning, developed
into a maze of bureaucratic perfectionism. Until 1972,
15,000 ordinances concerning agriculture – amounting to
97% of total EEC ordinances – were issued to make sure
that every detail was fixed with an ambition for exactitude
which expressed itself in several decimal places to each
figure. But the basically important economic data had got
out of hand. The fixing of guide prices was wreathed with a
kind of myth made up of ideas which had nothing in common
with the generally acknowledged theories on the formation
of market prices. Farmers' Associations as well as Ministries
of Agriculture and also the EEC Commission endeavoured
to vindicate themselves by the most sophisticated arguments
for agreeing on price increases in spite of growing surpluses.
Those who should have acted with political responsibility
were becoming prisoners of a bureaucracy dominated by

experts. Their fear of endangering integration made them give in to decisions which did not make any sense from the angle of economic and agricultural policy.

Whenever price increases were demanded, the old argument of agricultural income disparity was trotted out. But this has always been a moot question, partly because statistical data on agricultural income tend to be misleading. Besides, the available average figures are not very meaningful, because internal income disparity in the farming sector is much greater than any imaginable differential between farming and the other sectors. Moreover, it can be proved that since the end of the 'fifties the average income of farmers has increased more than that of most other people. E.g. the Agricultural Reports (Agrarberichte) of the German Federal Government show that average labour income from farming has risen to 796% between 1955 and 1974, while the figure for comparative wages in the industrial sector is only 591%.

As this could not very well be denied, Farmers' Associations and also some agricultural scientists then maintained that agricultural production is not dependent on prices but on technical progress. In reality, though, farmers have been quite shrewd in making their economic decisions. Price increases were recognised as signals for investing in modern technical equipment. This can be seen very clearly from the production trend in the EEC. Table 3 gives the indices for prices, production, and consumption from the

TABLE 3: Prices, production^a and food consumption^a in 1968/69 (1957–60 = 100)

	FGR	France	Italy	Neth.	B.Lu.	EEC
Prices	104	137	123	123	130	123
Production in grain equivalent	137	146	134	141	130	140
Consumption in grain equivalent	125	131	150	120	116	132

^{a} Total in grain equivalent based on computations by the Statistical Office of the European Communities, Luxemburg.

average of the period 1957–60 to 1968/69, that is during the first five years of common prices and market regulations.

It is true that the common grain price of 1966/67 meant a price decrease of almost 10% for Germany. This was, however, largely overcompensated by the subsequent price increase for animal products which account for about 80% of total sales proceeds. In all the other countries, an overall price increase was brought about, amounting to 123% on the average of the EEC. France, the country with half the agricultural surface of the EEC and most of the idle capacity, even attained 137%. As sales guarantees for cereals and dairy products were now unlimited, most of the farmers in the EEC have been much better off after a short time. They were quick in responding to the new possibilities for sales: On average, production has risen by 40%, in France by 46%. French farmers soon spent three times as much on mineral fertilisers than they had been used to, their wheat yields rising from 2,200 kg per ha to 3,600 kg per ha, and milk yields from 2,300 kg to 3,200 kg per cow and year.

The increase in agricultural production during the first decade of the Common Market therefore has been much higher than the increase in food consumption, with the exception of Italy, where consumption per head had been so low in the beginning that the increase was absorbed completely by the market. But in the other countries, production exceeded consumption all the more.

The degree of self-sufficiency in the EEC in regard of food under market regulations increased from 91 to 96% during this period. But this is only an average figure. The percentage of domestic supply by product has been as follows:

	1957–62	1968/69
Wheat	91	112
Total cereals	85	94
Sugar	103	104
Butter	101	113

Part of the wheat surplus in France had to be denaturalised, i.e. made unfit for human consumption, and to be sold as animal feed at a cheaper price. Total grain production in the EEC, initially about 55 million tons, increased to 80 million tons in 1972. Because grain demand for animal feed was still rising rapidly, the scope for imports remained at about 10 million tons. Thus, in the GATT negotiations of 1968, the position of the EEC was still relatively good. But in the 'seventies a series of record harvests appear to be indicative of an upward trend in yields rather than exceptions due to favourable weather. If this holds true, the import gap has been shrinking considerably, and in addition the animal products have also come near self-sufficiency. So there have been serious problems to be faced in the relations with the rest of the world, especially with the USA which are most interested in grain exports.

The level of domestic supply of dairy products had already been relatively high at the inception of the EEC. It has soon come to surpass demand, especially because the guaranteed butter price was instrumental in producing surpluses. The 'butter-mountain' was at one time as high as 44,000 tons, and as it could not be disposed of at normal market conditions, its storing and the subsidies for clearing the market by domestic sales and exports required costly governmental action.

There has been a continued and large increase in the financial burdens resulting from agricultural market regulations. The money is raised jointly and has to be obtained through the European Fund for Guidance and Guarantee. According to an estimation of the EEC Commission (included in the preliminary budget 1971) its volume of expenditure had reached the sum of 3·637 million m.u.a. (monetary unit of account. The value of 1 m.u.a. is equivalent to 0·88867 grammes of fine gold). All resources available are exhausted, further contributions are drawn from the member countries according to a special code. But the countries with the highest surplus production receive most of the money raised in this manner.

France had every reason to be contented with her share and this certainly strengthened her interest in common agricultural policy and common financing. Other countries had some cause to view this result with a more critical eye.

Regarding the agricultural foreign trade of the EEC, the increase in imports of products subject to market regulations had been very small at 10% up to 1969. Exports, however, increased by 30% because they were subsidised. Net import from third countries thus remained practically unchanged in absolute figures. To specify, since 1963 there had been a marked increase in net imports from countries with state-controlled trade, while imports from industrial countries dropped to 92% and those from developing countries even to 82%. As was to be expected, however, internal trade in agricultural goods within the EEC has increased considerably. While in 1963 it had amounted to 2,500 m.u.a., it was 5,800 m.u.a. in 1969. It is therefore understandable that all over the world the agricultural sector of the EEC came to be regarded as a closed area of preference. Even more uneasiness has been caused by the additional disturbance which the export subsidies of the EEC have been creating in the world trade. The World Trade conferences of 1969 and 1972 have made it clear that tension has been gathering.

Inside the EEC, evaluations and devaluations of currencies created more problems for agricultural policy. In order to fix common prices, members had agreed on the unit of account, which in 1962 was not only the equivalent of 0·888 g of pure gold, but also of one US dollar, so that for some time it was termed the 'Green Dollar'. The unit of account was a sort of sectoral currency and in a way anticipated the common currency unit envisaged for the EEC. It could, of course, work only if the purchasing power of the member countries' currencies did not change to any considerable extent and exchange rates remained constant.

But common policies had not yet been achieved in the realms of general economy, business cycles, and currency. So the artificial system was shattered for the first time by the evaluation of the German Mark and the devaluation of the French Franc. In consequence, the guide prices for agricultural products ought to have been raised in the case of France by the percentage of devaluation, and diminished in that of Germany by the percentage of evaluation. To avoid this, the Council of Ministers granted special concessions. In the interests of stabilizing prices, a gradual increase was allowed in France. In Germany, a compensatory amount was to prevent prices from falling all of a sudden. Later on, farmers were to be compensated for eventual losses by special aid.

The border adjustment virtually meant a partial split in the Common Market. It was extended to other countries because of subsequent changes in the rates of exchange. It is true that free trade in agricultural products has not been wholly obstructed within the Common Market. But national boundaries have gained in importance. And above all it has become obvious that CAP is but a makeshift so long as the European Community does not become an Economic and Currency Union.

It must, however, not be supposed that these currency problems have been at the root of the difficulties experienced in the EEC's agricultural policy. They have deepened them and brought them to general attention, but they are not the main reason why the EEC will have to reform its agricultural policy if it wants to reduce surpluses and the ensuing burdens on the national economies, to restore market equilibrium, and comply with the exigencies of foreign trade.

The key weakness of CAP has always been its price policy. The question is really whether it makes sense to insist on having prices which on the one hand are to achieve equilibrium between demand and supply, while on the other hand serving an income function. Experience has taught that neither of these goals has been attained. Probably the only way out of this dilemma will be to use other instruments in the income policy, while prices ought to be tuned to establishing market equilibrium and avoiding a chaotic production of surpluses.

The Commission in Brussels, though, has looked for an

expedient in quite another direction and proposes to intensify structural policy as a remedy to the above mentioned ills.

THE IMPACT OF STRUCTURAL POLICY

In December 1968, the Commission issued a 'Memorandum on the Reform of Agriculture in the EEC', known as the Mansholt Plan after Dr Mansholt who initiated it. Hardly ever before has the demand been made that the structure of agriculture should be changed in such a short time through so basic a reform. The principal aims of the Plan were a drastic reduction in the number of persons employed in agriculture and a spectacular improvement in the social situation of those farmers who were to be retained in the Common Market. The underlying idea was that market equilibrium could be brought about by the decrease in productive capacity.

Actually, structural policies had up to then largely been left within the competence of the several national authorities. Their different measures for the furthering of farming and marketing had only begun to be co-ordinated in 1962. Besides, certain aids had been distributed out of the EEC's Agricultural Fund.

At this stage, structural adjustment in the farming sector had still generally been viewed as an evolutionary process connected with overall economic growth. The rate of outmigration from farming had then been mostly dependent on job opportunities in other sectors. The picture to be gained from the pertinent statistics is quite impressive. From 1950 to 1972 farm labour decreased by about 62% while the volume of farm production doubled or tripled. Less efficient farms were abandoned, so that the total number of farms dropped by one third. This shows that the structural adjustment of European farming was already going forward with speed and vigour (see Table 2, p. 418).

But the suggestions of the Commission were aimed at hastening the process in a revolutionary manner. Over a period of ten years, one half of the farmers were to leave agriculture altogether, while big, specialised production units based on uniform technical norms were to be created for the remainder. Substantial subsidies were to be provided both to give the new enlarged holdings a successful start, and to give the other farmers an incentive to give up their activities and leave their land.

Of course, such a unique attempt at complete innovation has stirred European farmers and public opinion, in some cases to violent opposition. The Commission therefore put forward another set of proposals in 1970. These were more realistic and better suited to the economic differences between the various regions. But still, the creation of larger and more capital-intensive holdings and the corresponding encouragement to other farmers to give up farming were at the centre of the revised plan too. Parts of it were adopted by the Council of Ministers when, in 1972, they agreed on Common Guidelines for the implementation of structural policy in the member states.

It has been a positive result of this discussion on structural policies that many traditional ideas had to give way and the immense possibilities of structural change as well as their far-reaching consequences have been brought to public attention. The major problems to be considered in the context of their impact on economic and social life can best be summarised as follows:

(1) If the creation of larger, more capital-intensive farms is pushed ahead forcefully, more capital will be substituted for labour. In the end, productive capacity will then be increased. This kind of structural policy would be more likely to raise production increases than to attain market equilibrium.

(2) In most of the economically developed countries, the actual development of agricultural structure already tends to make full-time farmers enlarge their holdings, but it has also given incentives to combine farming with other activities. In the GFR, three quarters of all farmers were already drawing incomes from other sources as well as from farming in 1972. A multi-functional agrarian structure with mixed farms, varying farm acreage and the combina-

tion of several occupations and incomes offers greater scope for adaptation to changing economic conditions. Above all, the risk inherent in structural change is less in such a community and the economic and social resources of rural regions can be more easily mobilised.

(3) If adequate incentives are to be given to farmers who are to give up their farming activity and if the creation of modern farms is to be fostered by all means, high costs and losses to the national economy become inevitable. Capital formerly invested in the farms would lose its value if it could not be used any more in the modern units. And high subsidies would have to be paid to the retiring farmers who would not be able any more to find new and more profitable jobs. In the GFR, in Belgium, and in the Netherlands, difficulties of this kind could certainly be overcome because here the number of farmers is already low and industry is decentralised. But far more serious problems would be presented in countries with high agglomeration of industry, and correspondingly vast rural areas, like France and Italy where respectively 17 and 25% of the active population are still engaged in farming. On the whole, making about five million farmers in the EEC of the Six move out of farming would already have meant a thorough change in the conditions of life of about 20 to 25 million people. The order of magnitude increases with the enlargement of the EEC.

(4) When contemplating these aspects, the draw-backs of a one-sided structural policy appear very considerable. If the larger full-time farms were to be given high preference, landed estates would be concentrated in big enterprises, the distribution of income would become more unequal, and the size of the land-owning population would diminish. Another consequence would be to reinforce the differential between agricultural regions because in some of them conditions are unfavourable to large-scale, specialised farming. It would be preferable if types of farming appropriate for those areas were developed and additional activities provided as well. Otherwise farming might be given up altogether, the hitherto cultivated landscape

would decay and this in turn would lessen its value for recreation as well as for housing. Finally, such a process would be detrimental to the control of pollution. The harm to the northern regions of their country which might be done by such a structural policy may have been one of the reasons why the Norwegians objected to accession to the EEC.

It can therefore be concluded that a rapid revolution of agricultural structure would be bad for the future development of rural regions. Nor would it offer a solution to the problems of farm policy proper. With agricultural production rising at a rate of 3 to 4% while consumption is increasing only by 1 to 2% p.a. at the outside, surpluses would certainly remain a problem. Support for structural innovations and also the price policy should therefore be cautious.

As indeed only a small number of farmers is needed in modern agriculture, it cannot be any more the task of agricultural policy to assure a desirable rural population density. Great problems have already arisen in some sparsely populated areas when people have left the farms. In a broad range across the middle of France and down to the Pyrenees, there are even now less than 50 inhabitants per sq km, for Scotland the figure is 66, and for western Ireland only 25. This is surely disquieting.

On the whole, agriculture has lost much of its importance for employment and economic growth. But with respect to political and social development it has gained added significance. For this reason, structural policy in the agricultural sector today ought not to be conceived of as a separate project but as an intrinsic part of regional economic policy.

As this has gradually come to be realised, interest in regional policy has grown in the EEC. It may be recalled that a preliminary conference on regional economic policy was held in Brussels as early as in 1961. And when in 1967 the Direction Générale was reorganised, a General Directorate of Regional Policy was also created. Italy has always taken a most lively interest in regional policy because of the problems of her southern regions, but now the new member states Great Britain an⟍ Ireland are also setting great store by a common European regional policy. This is truly one of the challenges the EEC will have to deal with in the 'seventies.

AGRICULTURAL PROBLEMS IN THE LARGER EEC

Agricultural policy has played a large part in negotiations about the accession of other countries to the EEC, and also in the Agreements on Association. The interests of each of the countries involved have of course been different.

Already in the Treaty of Rome of 1957, association had been envisaged for the former French colonies and for the overseas territories of EEC member countries. In this respect, the most important stipulations of the treaty were that their trade with the Community was to be fostered, and development aid to be granted out of the EEC Development Fund. Details were arranged when in 1962 the Treaty of Jaunde was signed by eighteen African States. In 1962, there was also an Agreement of Association with Greece, and in 1964 Agreements with Israel and Turkey followed. With their industrial sectors still economically weak, the chief interest of these countries was in agricultural exports to the EEC. If these were facilitated, it was hoped that they would earn the foreign exchange needed for building up their national economies. Conflicts were not really to be feared from the production of general farm produce in both the Associated and the EEC countries. But it was to be expected that the several countries on the Mediterranean would have to compete with one another in the markets for their special produce, such as olives, vegetables, wine, and citrus fruit. The preference granted to Italy in this respect has already been mentioned. But the absorptive capacity of the European market, too, had to be regarded as a limiting factor.

In 1960, seven European countries outside the EEC had founded the EFTA which was to be a region of free trade

440   *The Twentieth Century*

in all goods with the exception of agricultural products.
The EFTA members, Great Britain, Denmark, Norway,
Sweden, Switzerland, Austria, and Portugal, had deliberately renounced a common agricultural policy. But as
early as in 1961, Great Britain, Denmark and Ireland, and,
in 1962, Norway too, had considered accession to the EEC.
The agrarian system of the EEC could, of course, not be
overlooked in this context. Considerable difficulties were
to be expected from taking part in it, especially so in the
case of Great Britain. The 50% of her agricultural imports
which came from Commonwealth countries had been
assured by long term agreements, such as the Commonwealth Sugar Agreement, or the contracts with New
Zealand concerning dairy products. Otherwise, they rested
on traditional trade relations of long standing. It would
scarcely have been feasible to cancel the existing obligations, while, on the other hand, an increase in the flow of
imports from the EEC countries with their elevated
producers' prices would have resulted in higher food
expenditure, and in a strain on the foreign exchange balance.
It is easy to understand that Britain then tried for special
provisions regarding her agricultural trade agreements and
even hinted at the possibility that the agricultural policy
of the EEC should adopt, to some extent at least, the British
system of deficiency payments.

No tangible results had been reached as yet in these
negotiations, when, in June 1965, France decided to stand
aloof to a certain degree from the EEC and followed a
policy of 'the empty chair' in the political organs of the
EEC until February 1966. Any talk about accession was
then interrupted, to be taken up again only at the Summit
Conference at the Hague in the end of 1969.

Conditions had changed when in 1970 the topic of
accession was re-approached. Agricultural policy in the
EEC had been consolidated by then and it was not possible
any more to question it. In principle, therefore, the agrarian
system of the EEC has then been accepted by Great Britain
and the other three countries, with the reservation that
transitional measures be provided for an initial period.

The Treaties of Accession, drafted in the summer of 1971, were signed in January 1972.

In Norway, though, accession to the EEC was turned down by a plebiscite, because of the special situation of the country's economy. The future of middle and northern Norway was thought to be in danger from the EEC policies regarding fishery and agricultural structure.

Great Britain, on the contrary, was by then prepared to agree with the principle of CAP, so that she could take part with the full right of vote in the decisions which then lay ahead. Thus she has been able to join immediately in the opposition against further increases in prices and surpluses. And as regards structural policy, Britain has at once voiced a particular interest in an aid programme for the hill farmers and in the creation of a common fund for regional policy.

Agricultural policy will by no means cease to be a field of tension in the larger EEC. It is true that the market has grown wider with the increase of total EEC inhabitants from 190 million to 255 million. But high prices and guaranteed sales are bound to result in mobilising productive reserves in the new member states too, and this will probably make market equilibrium an even more distant aim than it had been before.

Regarding external relations of the EEC with the Third World as well as with the USA, agricultural policy will grow to be a source of even more problems if the EEC is going to develop into an enlarged zone of preference for well-to-do nations with high domestic food supply.

Internally, western European countries will have to reckon with a further decrease in agriculture as a gainful employment and a decline in its share in the national product. But they will have to direct their attention so much the more to the importance of farming for the economic structure of rural regions, and for landscape and environment. In these fields, agriculture will certainly continue to hold a key position.

9. Economic Policy and Performance in Europe 1913–1970

Angus Maddison

The average European in 1970 had a real income three times as high as in 1913, but the improvement in living standards was by no means steady over the six decades. From 1913 to 1950, output per head rose by only 1 per cent a year. Since 1950 the rise has been four times as fast. Experience varied from country to country, but the marked acceleration of the post-war period was felt everywhere, as is obvious from Table 1. This chapter attempts to explain the reasons for these variations in economic performance with particular reference to the role of government policy. The analysis is concentrated on experience in the capitalist countries, but the statistical material covers the whole of Europe.

Growth in output per head does not necessarily mean an equivalent increase in consumption per head. The latter has increased somewhat more slowly for two reasons; (a) certain European countries receive a smaller income from the rest of the world than they did in 1913 when they had large overseas Empires; (b) a bigger proportion of output is devoted to investment.

France, Germany, the Netherlands and UK now receive less in real terms from overseas investments than in 1913 because of wartime losses of foreign assets and inflation.[1] In the UK, income from abroad added 10 per cent to domestic product in 1913 and a negligible amount in 1970. French income from abroad probably added

1 In 1913 overseas assets were about $18·3 billion for the UK, $8·7 billion for France, $5·6 billion for Germany and about $2 billion for the Netherlands. Russia was a debtor to the tune of $4 billion. Figures for first three countries from H. Feis *Europe The World's Banker*, Norton, New York, 1965. Russia from P. A. Khromov, *Ekonomicheskoye Razvitiye Rossie*, Moscow, 1967. The Netherlands figure is my estimate derived by capitalising the income flow at 5%: income figures from *1899–1959 Zestig Jaren Statistiek in Tijdreeksen*, Zeist, 1959.

about 7 per cent to GDP in 1913 and was negligible in 1970. Germany's foreign income added 2·4 per cent to domestically produced resources in 1913, but in 1970 Germany was making payments to others. On the other hand, in some of the East European countries, e.g. the USSR and Hungary, there were substantial remittances to foreign investors in 1913 which had disappeared by 1970. In 1913 Hungary remitted almost 10 per cent of its GDP abroad for such payments.[2]

Private consumption has increased less than output because of the increased proportion of income devoted to investment and government expenditure. In 1913 private consumption was typically about 80 per cent of national product, in 1950 about 70 per cent and in 1970 about 60 per cent in Western Europe. However, levels of private welfare are affected by government expenditure, some of which is a form of collective consumption. This is particularly true of publicly provided education and health services which have increased rapidly. Public expenditure on these two items probably averaged about 10 per cent of national product in West European countries in 1970. In 1970, about half the population aged 15-19 was being educated in these countries compared with 5 per cent in 1913. About 12 per cent (4 million) of the relevant age group were getting higher education in 1970 compared with 1 per cent in 1913.

In terms of consumption patterns the main difference between the two epochs were better housing, greater urbanisation, widespread use of motor transport and electrical appliances which have reduced domestic drudgery, universal use of radio and television, and much better facilities for health and education.

There has been a big change in type of job. In 1913, 37 per cent of people in Western Europe worked in agriculture, in 1970 only 14 per cent. In Eastern Europe

2 See A. Eckstein, 'National Income and Capital Formation in Hungary 1900–50', in S. Kuznets, ed., *Income and Wealth*, Series V, London 1955, p. 171.

TABLE 1: Growth of Per Capita Real Output

	annual average compound growth rate	
	1913–1950	*1950–1970*
Austria	0·2	4·9
Belgium	0·7	3·3
Denmark	1·1	3·3
Finland	1·3	4·3
France	1·0	4·2
Germany	0·8	5·3
Greece	0·2	5·9
Ireland	0·7	2·8
Italy	0·8	5·0
Netherlands	0·9	3·6
Norway	1·8	3·2
Portugal	0·9	4·8
Spain	−0·3	5·4
Sweden	2·5	3·3
Switzerland	1·6	3·0
UK	0·8	2·2
Average, Western Europe	1·0	4·0
Bulgaria	1·0	5·9[a]
Czechoslovakia	1·5	3·3[a]
East Germany	0·8	4·8[a]
Hungary	0·7	4·1[a]
Poland	n.a.	3·3[a]
Rumania	n.a.	4·8[a]
USSR	2·2	4·4[b]
Yugoslavia	1·1	4·1[a]
Average, Eastern Europe	1·2	4·3

[a] 1950–68; [b] 1950–69.

Source: Appendices A and B: see pp. 493 and 497.

agriculture occupied three-quarters of the labour force in 1913 and only 30 per cent in 1970.

An average person born in 1913 in West Europe would have lived only 52 years had 1913 health conditions prevailed over his lifetime. By 1970 life expectation had risen to 72 years. The fall in death rates was due to both lower infant and adult mortality. In 1913 about one child in ten died either at birth or in the first years of life, by 1970 it was one child in 50. The drop in death rates was due to cheap and successful drugs and better medical facilities, but there was also a drop in fertility, so the domestic life cycle of women became considerably easier than it had been. People also had easier working lives because of the large drop in weekly working hours and the big extension of holidays. The average work week in 1913 was around 54 hours and by 1970 had fallen by more than 10 hours. In 1913 Saturday work was normal practice, but by 1970 it had virtually disappeared in industry. In most countries workers had about 30 days' holiday with pay in 1970, whereas their 1913 holidays had been half as long and were something of a mockery because time off was then unpaid.

There has been a marked increase in the role of government in the past half-century. In 1913, British Government current expenditure represented 10·5 per cent of GDP at factor cost. In 1969 the ratio had risen to 38·6. In Germany the comparative figures were 12·1 per cent in 1913 and 36·7 per cent in 1970.[3] In the other countries where evidence is available, the magnitudes have changed in similar fashion. Government spending on goods and services is now typically 15 per cent of GNP, i.e. two or three times the 1913 proportion; official spending on transfers and subsidies is about 20 per cent of GNP and was negligible in 1913.

In Western countries, governments engage in much bigger transfer activities to support low incomes than in 1913, and levy higher taxes on high incomes. Society has therefore become more egalitarian. However, the degree of equality in 1970 was by no means homogeneous even in Western countries (with France, Italy, Portugal and Spain having the most inequality and Scandinavia the least). Furthermore, there has been little significant change in the unequal distribution of property in Western countries. In Eastern Europe, by contrast, virtually all means of produc-

3 For UK, see *The British Economy: Key Statistics 1900–1970*, LCES, London. For Germany 1913, see S. Andic and J. Veverka, *Finanzanchiv*, January, 1964.

tion are now publicly owned and property income has largely disappeared. State transfers are smaller than in the West, but pre-tax earnings are much more egalitarian than in Western countries.

The growth of government spending is not the result of a grand design or articulate policy but is a by-product of war, inflation and economic growth. Governments pushed taxes up in wartime, and reduced them afterwards, but never to pre-war levels. Furthermore, as tax structures are progressive, the claim of governments on resources is automatically increased by inflation and growth. The redistributive impact of government transfers is relatively mild. The most striking effect of 'bigger' government is the promotion of consumption of certain public goods beyond the point which would exist as the result of market forces. Governments have become interventionist in favour of all sorts of pressure groups, not all of them contributing to welfare.

The history of the period can be divided into two main parts. The first, from 1913 to 1950, was characterised by two wars and a world economic crisis. In this period 67 million Europeans were killed in wars or died as a result of war. In the 37 years 1913 to 1950, European output and living standards were well below what they could have been. For Western Europe as a whole, 20 of the 37 years 1913 to 1950 were ones in which output was below some previous peak. Since 1950, by contrast, there has been a continuous boom in economic activity, with output and living standards rising at an unprecedented pace. Investment has been high and rising, unemployment has been low, trade has flourished.

THE 1914–18 WAR

The destructive impact of the First World War was concentrated on a narrow band of territory in Belgium and France. Italy, Yugoslavia and Russia also suffered material damage but it was less intensive. All of Scandinavia, the Netherlands, Switzerland, and Spain remained neutral. About 9 million soldiers died, and very large numbers received wounds which left a lifetime of misery and reduced working capacity. Very few civilians were killed as the direct result of military activities – some sources put the loss as low as 100,000. However, 'abnormal' civilian mortality in the war and immediate post-war period was about 5 million (outside Russia). A good deal of this was due to disease. Typhus killed many, and the great influenza epidemic of 1919 killed millions whose resistance was weakened by war, though a good many of the latter may well have died anyway. A good many civilian deaths were due to malnutrition because the Allies continued to blockade food supplies to Austria, Germany and Hungary after the war at a time when food supplies were desperately short. In Russia, food supplies were better maintained than in Germany during the war but losses in the revolution were very high because of civil war, disease and famine. Total Russian losses from 1914–23 were 10 million dead on top of the 1·7 million soldiers killed from 1914 to 1917. Total 'abnormal' loss of life was therefore about 25 million from 1914 to 1923, of which about 12 million deaths were directly due to war. This compares with 174,000 soldiers killed in the Franco-Prussian war of 1870–71 and 42 million people killed in the Second World War.[4]

TABLE 2: Military Deaths Due to First World War 1914–1918
in thousands

Austro-Hungarian Empire	1,200	Poland	250
Belgium	40	Portugal	8
Bulgaria	100	Rumania	250
France	1,320	Russia	1,700
Germany	2,000	Serbia	365
Greece	100	UK	744
Italy	700	Total	8,777

Source: C. Clark, *Population Growth and Land Use*, Macmillan, London, 1967, p. 121.

4 Sources for this paragraph are C. Clark, *op. cit.*, and E. Kirsten, E. W. Buchholtz and W. Köllman, *Raum und Bevölkerung in der Weltgeschichte*, Ploetz, Würzburg, 1956.

Apart from massive suffering from loss of life and physical injuries, the war caused a very big cut in normal consumption levels and reduced the growth potential by reducing capital formation and the stock of productive assets.

The war had its most direct impact on living standards in belligerent countries, but the neutrals suffered from blockade and interruption of normal supplies. Belgium was subject to military occupation with part of the population evacuated, part compelled to work in Germany and continuous fighting over the Southern part of its territory. France suffered a sharp decline in both agricultural and industrial output, both as a direct impact of war and through loss of manpower to the army. Though no fighting took place in Germany, its wartime output fell substantially. Over-mobilisation at the beginning of the war reduced the labour supply and dislocated production, and the Allied blockade cut down supplies of raw materials. German agricultural output declined by a quarter because the labour force and fertiliser input fell by more than half, and imports of barley and maize were not available for feeding stuff.[5] The UK fared much better. Conscription was introduced only in 1917, civilian manpower was reduced less, and imports of food were better maintained. In fact it would appear that the war had a less adverse effect on British living standards than it did on those in Holland which was neutral.[6]

There was a substantial destruction of factories, farms and dwellings in France and Belgium, and heavy losses of British merchant shipping sunk by submarines. All the belligerent countries experienced a drastic cut in the normal pace of civilian investment. The capital stock was therefore considerably lower at the end of the war than it would otherwise have been.

Keynes estimated war damage to capital stock (at pre-

5 See League of Nations, *Agricultural Production in Continental Europe during the 1914–1918 War and Reconstruction Period*, Geneva, 1943.

6 During the war British food consumption was much nearer to pre-war levels than that on the continent, see W. H. Beveridge, *British Food Control*, 1928.

war prices) at £150 million in Belgium, £500 million in France, £260 million in the UK (mostly shipping), and between £50–£100 in Italy. He did not express the figures in relation to pre-war capital stock except for Belgium where the loss appears to have been about 12 per cent.[7] Germany lost no domestic assets during the war, but most of her pre-war foreign investments (£1·2 billion) were either sold or seized as reparation, and the same is true of her merchant marine which Keynes valued at £120 million. France lost about two-thirds of her pre-war foreign assets because of default (mainly by Russia) and inflation. The net foreign investment position of the UK did not change much in money terms. From 1914 to 1918 she sold only £236 million of her pre-war assets and her losses through default and inflation were much less than those of France. She received substantial war gifts from Canada and India and accumulated large war debts. She borrowed £1,285 million, mainly from the USA but this was more than offset by lending £1,688 million to her allies.[8] These war debts were frozen in the 1930s, and later written off.

There were important geographic changes after the war involving the creation of new countries – Finland, Czechoslovakia, Poland, Yugoslavia, the Baltic States – out of the ruins of the Austrian, German and Russian Empires. The new Austria which emerged after the war had only a third of the income and a quarter of the population in the pre-war German part of the old Dual Monarchy of Austria–Hungary. The economy of Imperial Hungary was also cut to a third of its former size. The division of the old area led to new tariff barriers, upset traditional transport routes and created massive problems of adjustment to new market situations. Austria did not surpass its 1913 per capita income level until 1950. Poland had to forge a national economy out of three different currency and fiscal areas. Germany lost her pre-war colonies and about 9 per cent of

7 See J. M. Keynes, *The Economic Consequences of the Peace*, Macmillan, London, 1920.

8 See E. V. Morgan, *Studies in British Financial Policy 1914–1925*, London, 1952.

her population – 7 million inhabitants. The Saar and Alsace–Lorraine went to France, North Schleswig to Denmark, Eupen and Malmedy to Belgium, Memel, Danzig, Posen, West Prussia and Upper Silesia were lost to Poland. Ireland was separated from the UK and there were geographic changes in the Balkans. Civil war and the war of intervention in Russia, and Soviet confiscation of foreign assets were major factors bringing a sharp reduction in trade with the East. In the 1920s, because of the power vacuum in Central and Eastern Europe, the dominant powers in international economic policy in Europe were France, the UK and USA.

1918–1929

Although the post-war period was one of political instability and a rather poor degree of international co-operation, the performance of the European economies was not too bad in the 1920s. There was a sharp recession in the UK, Italy and Scandinavia in 1921 when the post-war inventory boom ended, but this recession was not felt everywhere and in most countries the 1920s were a period of rapid growth and fairly buoyant demand. Output grew by 3·9 per cent a year from 1920 to 1929 in the capitalist countries, and unemployment averaged only 3·3 per cent. Some of the output growth represented recovery but even after discounting for this, the growth performance was reasonably respectable. Trade expanded much faster, at nearly 10 per cent a year, but a good deal of this represented recovery and the ratio of trade to output was lower in 1929 than in 1913.

There were, in fact, a number of problems which accumulated in the 1920s and made their impact only in the 1930s. These were the destruction of the international monetary system and failure to find a workable substitute, fundamental payments disequilibrium of some of the major countries, lack of international co-operation, and pursuit of traditional pre-war policy objectives which no longer had a rational relation to economic welfare.

International economic relations were made acrimonious by the effort to extract large reparations from Germany and the existence of large Inter-Allied debts. The French had been invaded twice by the Germans (in 1870 and 1914), and they paid an indemnity of about $1 billion to

TABLE 3: Rate of Growth of Total Output 1913–1938

	annual average compound growth rate		
	1913–1929	*1920–1929*	*1929–38*
Austria	0·3	5·2	–0·5
Belgium	1·5	3·5	0·0
Denmark	1·9	3·9	2·0
Finland	2·2	5·3	3·8
France	1·4	4·9	–0·5
Germany	1·1	4·5	3·9
Italy	1·7	3·0	1·4
Netherlands	3·4	4·2	0·3
Norway	2·8	2·7	2·9
Spain	2·2	1·6	–3·0a
Sweden	2·3	2·6	2·6
Switzerland	2·8	3·7	0·6
UK	0·7	1·9	1·9
Average Western Europe	1·9	3·6	1·2
Czechoslovakia	2·7	6·0	–0·2b
Hungary	1·2	(5·2)	1·1
USSR	0·9	9·4	6·1
Yugoslavia	2·1	4·5	1·3
Average, Eastern Europe	1·7	6·3	2·1
Total, Europe excluding USSR	1·9	3·9	1·1

b 1929–1937; a 1929–1940.

Source: See Appendix B, p. 497.

Germany in 1871–3 without great strain. To them it seemed quite natural to make Germany pay heavily. They and the Belgians were so confident of achieving this that they paid large compensation to the war victims in their countries and followed fiscal policies based on the assumption that Germany would pay. However, French demands

TABLE 4: Unemployment as a Percentage of Labour Force 1920–1938

	average for years cited	
	1920–1929	*1930–1938*
Austria	6·0	13·4d
Belgium	1·5a	8·7
Denmark	4·2	6·6
France	1·8b	3·3e
Germany	3·9	8·8
Italy	1·7c	4·8f
Netherlands	2·3	8·7
Sweden	3·2	5·6
Switzerland	0·4c	3·0
UK	7·5	11·5
Average	3·3	7·5

a 1921–9; b 1921 and 1926; c 1929; d 1930–37; e 1931, 1936 and 1938; f 1930–34 and 1937–8.

Source: A. Maddison, *Economic Growth in the West*, Appendix E, except for Austria which is from *Osterreichs Volkseinkommen 1913 bis 1963*, OIW, Vienna, 1965, and UK which is from C. H. Feinstein, *National Income, Expenditure, and Output of the U.K., 1855–1965*, Cambridge, 1972, p. T126. Lundberg has suggested that my estimates for this period may be too low, see E. Lundberg, *Instability and Economic Growth*, Yale, 1968, but the alternative figures he provides are much too high because they show unemployment as a percentage of industrial employment only.

were extreme, and were backed by threats and humiliations which were counterproductive. The British and Americans took a milder view and were more interested in German reconstruction, if only as a bulwark against Bolshevism. The conflicts are clearly delineated by Keynes whose writings did a good deal to stiffen German resistance. Bitterness between the French and British was strong in the 1920s, when Montagu Norman, the Governor of the Bank of England and a major arbiter of British policy, entertained much closer relations with Schacht at the Reichsbank than with his French colleague.

At the Paris Peace Conference no exact amount was fixed for reparation but in 1921 the Reparation Com-

TABLE 5: Rate of Growth in the Volume of Exports 1913–1938

	Annual average compound growth rate		
	1913–1929	*1921–1929*	*1929–1938*
Belgium	0·4	n.a.	–0·5
France	2·4	7·4	–5·2
Germany	0·1	15·8	–5·2
Italy	2·4	8·9	0·5
Netherlands	2·4	9·0	–2·2
Sweden	2·3	13·5	0·8
Switzerland	0·1	6·1	–2·6
UK	–0·8	7·3	–3·9
Average	1·2	9·7	–2·3

Source: A. Maddison 'Growth and Fluctuation in the World Economy. 1870–1960,' *Banca Nazionale del Lavoro, Quarterly Review*, June 1962. Figures refer to customs area of each year cited.

mission fixed Germany's obligation at $31·5 billion.[9] In the period 1919–22 Graham estimated that Germany transferred resources equal annually to about 4–5 per cent of her income in reparations, occupation costs etc.[10]

Germany found the claims excessive and was in no mood to pay; (a) because of the obvious disagreement amongst the Allies; (b) because the financial demands were accompanied by other humiliations such as the forced cession of parts of Upper Silesia to Poland which had voted by plebiscite to stay German, and the fact that the Reparation Commission expected to some extent to dictate internal German policy; (c) because the German Government did

9 At that time the US Government's war debt claims on Allied countries were about $11 billion and British claims were £1·8 billion ($8.7 billion at the 1925 parity). See J. M. Keynes, *A Revision of the Treaty*, London, 1971, pp. 154-5. French claims were about $1·9 billion.

10 H. G. Moulton and C. E. McGuire, *Germany's Capacity to Pay*, McGraw Hill, New York, 1923, estimated that Germany paid about 26 billion gold marks (about $6 billion) under various reparations headings up to the beginning of 1923 in addition to occupation costs.

not have sufficient internal political power to transfer resources on the scale demanded.

When it became evident that Germany would not fulfil her obligations, France and Belgium, anxious for funds to finance reconstruction, occupied the industrial area of the Ruhr and tried to extort payment in kind. The Germans retaliated by passive resistance and widespread strikes. German national income fell by about a sixth in 1923 because of the disruption. The fall in output further reduced the already inadequate tax receipts of government which was subsidising the Ruhr strikers, and printed money on an unparalleled scale, causing hyperinflation in 1923. When the mark was stabilised in 1924, the new unit was worth 1 trillion old marks, and all savings in the form of bonds, insurance policies and money were made virtually worthless.[11]

In spite of these disputes about debts and reparations, the actual course of international lending was stabilising. In the immediate post-war period, the USA and UK provided relief supplies to Europe. From 1919 to 1929 the US exported $12·9 billion of capital – mostly private – a good deal of which went to Europe. The financial instability and inflation of the 1920s were regarded with horror by contemporary pundits, but were less harmful than the stabilisation policies pursued in the UK During the inflation, Germany enjoyed a rapid growth of output and had high rates of investment.[12]

11 The German inflationary experience was not unique – Austria, Hungary, Poland and Russia also had hyperinflations.

12 See the analysis of F. D. Graham, *Exchange, Prices and Production in Hyper-inflation in Germany 1920–23*, Princeton, 1930, who concluded that the inflationary policy was the one best fitted to promote the development of real income in Germany and to minimise the burden of reparations. Unfortunately this scholarly work is less well known than that of Bresciani-Turroni, who managed to discuss the problem without considering what happened to real income. During the inflation Germany rebuilt her merchant marine and railway system, strengthened her road network and carried out a good deal of industrial investment. Graham argues that the wasteful character of investment in the inflation period has been exaggerated. Furthermore Germany's loss on terms of trade by selling cheap exports was outweighed by capital gains at the

After the German inflation and stabilisation of the mark in 1924, the UK and the USA persuaded the French and Belgians to leave the Ruhr, reparation liabilities were scaled down and Germany received a $200 million stabilisation loan in 1924 under the Dawes agreement. Reparations were further scaled down in 1929 under the Young Plan, the Reparation Commission was abolished, and the Bank for International Settlements was created to try to develop a more co-operative approach to government indebtedness. From 1924 onwards, Germany paid $1·8 billion on reparation account, but this was more than offset by a $4 billion inflow of foreign capital.

The economic experience of the 1920s differed considerably from country to country. In Belgium, France and Italy it was a period of rising prices, expansionary monetary and fiscal policy, reasonably rapid growth and low unemployment. In Germany the 1920s were a period of high investment and rapid expansion, only temporarily interrupted in 1923. The Scandinavian countries followed rather deflationary policies, but not as extreme as that of the UK which was the only really stagnant economy of the 1920s.

Until the mid-1920s most European countries had floating exchange rates, and there was considerable concern, particularly in the UK, to end this situation and return to the previous system of fixed parities. The international currency system was patched up after 1925 when Churchill put the UK back on a fixed parity for sterling. In 1927, Poincaré fixed the parity for the franc, and thereafter all countries were back on fixed parities. This return to the pre-war international monetary system reflected in part a reasonable judgment that fixed parities would make for faster growth in world trade, but there was a failure to recognise that fixed parities would require more elaborate arrangements for international liquidity than in the period 1870–1913 when the UK had dominated the international capital market and confidence in existing exchange parities

---

expense of foreigners who had bought large quantities of marks in the expectation that the pre-war parity would be restored.

was firmly established. Furthermore, the new parities over-valued sterling appreciably and undervalued the franc. The precarious equilibrium of the 1920s involved large reserve accumulations by France, and forced the UK to maintain deflationary policies. Germany balanced her payments and paid reparations only because of massive US foreign investment.

The poor UK performance centred on its export trades which were extremely depressed. Her exports were tradi-tionally directed outside Europe, her economy was heavily dependent on trade, and the depreciation in the real value of foreign assets meant that she had to increase exports to finance the pre-war level of imports. Her old markets were damaged by wartime growth of exports by the USA and Japan and by the third world's effort (e.g. India and Latin America) to replace traditional imports (textiles) by domestic output. Many writers have stressed these structural problems and the stagnation of the coal and textile indus-tries. But the structural problems of the UK were smaller than those of Germany which enjoyed faster growth. In truth, most of the UK's problems were self-inflicted – the result of monetary and exchange-rate policies which re-pressed domestic demand and depressed exports. The effort to regain the pre-war parity for sterling was recommended by the Cunliffe Commission in 1919, and although this was not formally achieved until 1925, policy was basically oriented towards this goal from 1919 onwards. This meant that British exports were very uncompetitive. Furthermore, the authorities continued to foster export of British capital because Imperialists like Churchill, who was Chancellor of the Exchequer, felt that it cemented the Empire.

The attempt to sustain the pre-war exchange parity and to maintain British capital exports led the government to follow a policy of extreme deflation, in the attempt to force down wages. After the return to pre-war sterling parity, there was a general strike in 1926 which was crushed within 9 days by the government, but which kept the miners out of work for 6 months. As a result of these policies, 1·5 million British workers were without jobs throughout the 1920s and many skilled workers experienced years of continuous unemployment eking out a miserable existence on the meagre 'dole' which they got from the Labour Exchange. For many years workers who had jobs worked a four-day week because of inadequate demand. Thus production potential was greatly underutilised and investment was low.

To some extent the deficiencies of British policy in the 1920s were due to weaknesses in economic analysis which were general in the period.[13] The more expansionary policies of Belgium, France and Germany were due more to political inability to establish 'sound' financial policies, than to substantial analytical differences from those who inspired British policy. Everywhere there was a feeling that balanced budgets, price stability and restoration of the gold standard were the prime aims of policy. The major error peculiar to the UK was the insistence on returning to the exact pre-war parity for sterling.

1929–1938

The expansion of the 1920s was brought to an end by the world crisis of 1929–33, which originated in the financial collapse and fall in demand in the USA but had drastic effects in Europe.

From 1929 to 1933, US output fell by almost a third, and the average fall in European GDP was about 10 per cent from peak to trough (see Table 6). This was the biggest peacetime cyclical disturbance ever to hit Western Europe, and its biggest economy, Germany, experienced a fall in output of 16 per cent. In Austria, Czechoslovakia and Poland, which were closely linked to Germany, the fall was even bigger. France was also very heavily hit. The repercussions in Germany and France were particularly severe because of

13 The extraordinary indifference of some economists to unemployment is analysed by K. Hancock, 'Unemployment and the Economists in the 1920s', *Economica*, November, 1960. Gregory argued that it was 'useless to allow working-class sentiment to govern monetary policy.' For him unemployment was a price worth paying in order to do justice to the rentier.

their links to the US via capital flows and reparations. Amongst the big countries, those least affected by the depression were the USSR, Italy and the UK. After 1933, there was an incomplete recovery, so that aggregate growth performance in the 1930s was poor – on average, output grew by only 1·1 per cent a year and unemployment averaged 7·5 per cent. Trade was even worse hit and never recovered. In 1938 European exports were a quarter below those of 1929. Europe was not significantly affected by the US recession of 1937–38 because the interdependence of the economies had been reduced by protectionism and the disappearance of reparations and Inter-Allied debt payments.

The 1929-33 crisis was transmitted to Europe in several ways. The decline in US imports reduced demand for European goods, withdrawal of American capital reduced

TABLE 6: Magnitude of GDP Fall Within the Period 1928–1935

		per cent difference between peak and trough	
Austria	−22·5	Netherlands	−9·1
Belgium	−7·9	Norway	−7·8
Bulgaria	−12·7	Poland	−20·7
Czechoslovakia	−18·2	Rumania	−5·5
Denmark	−2·0	Spain	−10·0
Finland	−6·5	Sweden	−11·9
France	−11·0	Switzerland	−8·0
Germany	−16·1	UK	−5·8
Greece	−6·5	USSR	−1·1
Hungary	−11·5	Yugoslavia	−11·9
Italy	−6·1	Average	−10·1

Source: Appendix B, see p. 497.

European activity and damaged the balance of payments – particularly in Germany. The slump had a depressing psychological impact on the stock markets, entrepreneurs, central bankers and politicians of Europe.

In order to explain the origins of the crisis we must make an excursus into US economic history.

In the two decades preceding 1929, the output of the

US economy doubled. The US had clearly overtaken the major European countries and had become the world's dominant political power. It was an era of American optimism. In 1929, investment was almost one-fifth of GNP and a major stock market boom was in progress. However, the USA had always had a more volatile economy than that of European countries. From 1907 to 1908 its GDP had fallen by 8·2 per cent, and a sensible observer might well have anticipated a recession this size again in 1929, because nothing had been done in the field of policy to make the economy less volatile. In the event, the depression of 1929-33 was much bigger and more prolonged than anything which had occurred earlier.

The reason for the extreme severity of the recession was the collapse of confidence and credit. The stock market boom was based on speculative fever, margin trading and shady business practices which were unregulated by government. Once the market turned down, credit crumbled and the forces which had accelerated the boom, accelerated recession (i.e. they acted as built-in destabilisers).

Stock market prices fell by three-quarters from 1929 to 1932 and did not regain the 1929 level until 1954. This financial weakness was compounded by the precarious banking structure. In 1929 there were 25,000 independent banks. In this small-scale and largely unregulated system, failures were normal, and the number of suspensions had risen ominously in the 1920s. In the 1908 recession 155 banks were suspended, but in 1929-33 almost 10,000 banks failed. Many Americans either lost their money or had no access to it for long periods.

The stock exchange and banking collapse caused widespread bankruptcies and froze business activity. Investment fell by almost 90 per cent from 1929 to 1933. Private consumption fell by 19 per cent, and exports by about half.

The severity of the crisis was probably mainly attributable to the fact that the USA was trying to run a major capitalist economy with the financial institutions of a rural frontier society. Furthermore, the government did nothing very sensible to offset the deflationary forces in the private sector. Some theorists, such as Alvin Hansen, explained the severity of the recession by suggesting that the USA had exhausted its investment opportunities due to the disappearance of the frontier and the slowing down of population growth. In retrospect, this seems an excessively pessimistic view. But there certainly was an unusually severe concentration of negative factors to reinforce the colossal decline in productive investment – including the sharp downturn in demand for housing, and the end of the boom in consumer demand for automobiles.[14]

Germany was the European country most directly affected by the US depression. It was heavily dependent on the inflow of US capital to finance reparation payments and had enjoyed a boom economy in the 1920s. In 1929 German investment was equal to 18 per cent of the GNP. The American slump led to a massive outflow of capital from Europe (mainly Germany) as well as causing a fall in German exports. This created very severe payments problems and led Germany to default on its reparations obligations and foreign debt in 1931. The attempt by US President Hoover to mitigate the problem by declaring a temporary suspension of payment on war debt and reparations in 1931 was welcomed by Germany and the UK, but was bitterly resented by the French, who were net losers from the moratorium.[15] Furthermore, the French were then in a powerful bargaining position as they had accumulated large exchange reserves. They sabotaged efforts to stave off the collapse of major financial institutions in Austria and Germany (the *Kreditanstalt* in Vienna and the *Darmstädter und Nationalbank* in Germany).[16] When these banks collapsed there was a financial panic in Ger-

14 For interpretations of the US depression and its causes, see J. Schumpeter, *Business Cycles*, McGraw Hill, New York, 1939; J. K. Galbraith, *The Great Crash 1929*, Penguin, London, 1961; and T. Wilson, *Fluctuations in Income and Employment*, Pitman, London, 1948.

15 Service of Inter-Allied indebtedness ended for good in 1931.

16 France also sabotaged the effort to establish a customs union between Austria and Germany at this time.

many. The authorities took effective measures to prevent the bank collapse going as far as in the USA, but because the inflationary experience of 1919-1923 had had such a traumatic effect, the German authorities were not willing to let their exchange rate float, or risk inflation, but tried to reach payments equilibrium by deflationary policies. Schacht at the Reichsbank restricted credit and raised interest rates, the Brüning government made cuts in public expenditure, increased taxation substantially and cut wages. These policies pushed unemployment up to 17 per cent of the labour force but were not sufficient to restore German competitiveness. Germany was finally forced to defend its exchange rate by detailed exchange and price controls. German policy was more deflationary than that of the USA, but the German depression was not quite as big. Gross domestic product fell 16 per cent, investment 70 per cent and exports 44 per cent. The fall in private consumption was negligible compared with that in the USA.[17]

The collapse in German activity and imports sent shock waves throughout central Europe. Countries like Austria, Czechoslovakia, Hungary and Yugoslavia which had close trade and investment ties to Germany were very badly affected.

France, which had a strong payments position, was affected more slowly, but quite severely. In France, too, the policy reaction was highly deflationary. The policy package introduced by Laval in 1935 being rather similar to that of Brüning in Germany in 1931. In 1936, the Popular Front government of Leon Blum attempted to stimulate expansion by raising wages and to spread employment by cutting working hours. However, these measures made France less competitive, provoked a capital flight and had an adverse effect on domestic investment, so they did not succeed in promoting expansion.

In the UK the recession was much less severe partly because the initial level of activity was already low. Investment fell by a third, but the 1929 level was only about 10

17 See R. Erbe, *Die nationalsozialistische Wirtschaftspolitik 1933-1939 im Lichte der modernen Theorie*, Polygraphischer Verlag, Zurich, 1958.

per cent of the GNP – i.e. about half of the US level. British consumption of durables like cars was very small in 1929 and housing had been depressed in the 1920s so there was not much scope for a fall in these items. Total consumption actually rose from 1929 to 1933. UK internal policy was deflationary enough, with Chancellor Snowden cutting unemployment benefits, but the UK was able to activate a defensive mechanism of Empire trade preferences, so that its foreign trade fell somewhat less than that of other countries. Furthermore the UK devalued in 1931 which strengthened its competitive position, because the USA did not devalue until 1933, and Belgium, Italy, Switzerland and France not until later.

The restrictive internal policies by the major countries reinforced the direct impact which the fall in demand had had on international trade, but the fall in trade was much greater than the fall in demand because of the universal resort to protectionist devices intended to transfer the impact of recession to neighbouring countries. The US introduced the Hawley-Smoot tariffs in 1930, and the UK abandoned free trade and introduced tariffs with Empire preference in 1932. By 1931 the average European tariff level was close to 50 per cent, and new kinds of trade restrictions had been invented. Germany erected a complex series of exchange controls and quantitative restrictions, France had import quotas. Most countries introduced measures to support inefficient domestic farm output. The impact of these European and US policies was disastrous for the export earnings of primary producers who experienced a sharp decline in an already weak market for primary commodities. Latin American countries intensified their protectionism by increasing tariffs, introducing quantitative restrictions and import controls and defaulting on foreign debt. These trade restrictions were intended to dampen the impact of recession in each country, but because they were used by all countries, they did not have the intended effect. They simply accentuated the problem by producing a vicious circle of mutual immiseration.

TABLE 7: Ad Valorem Incidence of Import Duties in 1931

			percentages
Austria	36	Italy	48
Belgium	17	Poland	68
Bulgaria	97	Rumania	63
Czechoslovakia	50	Spain	69
Finland	48	Sweden	27
France	38	Switzerland	26
Germany	41	Yugoslavia	46
Hungary	45	Average	48

Source: W. S. and E. S. Woytinsky, *World Commerce and Governments*, New York, 1955, p. 277.

As a result of these policies which were piled on top of a weak demand situation, financial instability and falling prices, there was a drastic fall in world trade from 1929 to 1933. The volume of West European exports fell 40 per cent and although there was some recovery thereafter, the 1937 European export level was more than a fifth lower than in 1929 and 13 per cent lower than in 1913.

There were attempts to achieve a restoration of world trade on an expansionary basis, e.g. in the World Economic Conference in London in 1933. But disagreement between the major European powers was too great and the USA sabotaged the Conference by an unnecessary devaluation of the dollar.

Behind the protective walls there was some recovery in output after 1933, most notably in Germany and the UK. But in the capitalist economies the average growth rate for the 1930s was only 1 per cent a year and the average unemployment rate was 7·5 per cent of the labour force. Apart from the loss of output represented by unemployed resources, the trade barriers and other devices led to substantial misallocation of employed resources.

Germany had considerable success in raising output and eliminating unemployment in the 1930s because of government spending on public works and rearmament. However, the Nazi government's economic policy record was not particularly brilliant. The increased taxes imposed by the Brüning government were maintained, and the government preferred exchange controls to devaluation. Industry was subject to detailed controls operated through corporate organisations. Agriculture and agricultural marketing were tightly regulated. Trade unions were destroyed and a *dirigiste* system of price and wage controls enforced. The consumer got virtually no benefit from increased output which went largely into armaments production, the creation of expensive substitutes for imports of oil and rubber for strategic reasons and the building up of the military forces. By 1939 Germany was on a virtually complete war footing with 25 per cent of GNP going to government current spending.

In the UK, growth in the 1930s was about the same as in the 1920s,[18] but the margin of unused resources was bigger. From 1930 to 1938 unemployment averaged 2·6 million. Although government policy leaned in a more expansionist direction than in the 1920s, the policy performance was poor and involved considerable efforts to promote monopolistic restrictions. In 1931 the UK abandoned the policy of supporting the overvalued exchange rate and for a few years the pound was devalued against some other currencies (though the dollar rate returned to the 1931 level in 1933). It also embarked on a policy of tariff protection[19] and discriminatory trade arrangements with Commonwealth countries, and the British payments situation was eased by the big fall in export prices of primary commodities which reduced the

18 This conclusion is based on the output figures shown in Appendix B. Other analysts, basing themselves on older data or different periodisation, have taken a more sanguine view of the 1930s in the UK, see A. J. Youngson, *Britain's Economic Growth 1920–1966*. Allen and Unwin, London, 1968, p. 135.

19 The free trade policy was first abandoned during the First World War when McKenna (wartime Chancellor of the Exchequer) imposed duties (1/3 *ad valorem*) on luxuries. The number of items covered by

cost of British imports. The expansion of output was helped by low interest rates which sparked off a housing boom, and consumption levels rose because the fall in the price of imported food liberated income for other purchases. At the end of the 1930s there was the added stimulus of rearmament, capital exports were reduced and home investment rose.

In Belgium, Italy, the Netherlands and Switzerland, however, the 1930s remained a period of severe depression, and in Austria, Czechoslovakia and France, output in 1938 was still well below that in 1929. In Scandinavia output in the 1920s increased more than in most continental countries, but the margin of unused resources was bigger than in the 1920s.

If one looks at Western Europe as a whole, all the indicators: growth of output, level of unemployment, level of trade, and rate of price increase, show the 1930s as a much worse period than the 1920s. In most countries even the latter half of the 1930s was worse than the 1920s. The causes of this regrettable situation were threefold; (a) the fact that international economic relations were organised on an acrimonious beggar-your-neighbour basis; (b) the fact that the economic analysts at that time had not devised policies adequate for the major disequilibria which were the consequence of the war. They and the governments they advised were usually striving vainly and nostalgically to restore the world as it was in 1913. Many of the things governments did in the crisis made the situation worse. Most advisers were astonishingly indifferent to unemployment;[20] (c) poor quality of economic intelligence. The

---

these duties was expanded in 1921. The 1932 act imposed a 10 per cent duty on most other items.

20 Lundberg summed it up as follows: 'in the 1920s and the crucial first years of the following decade, there were various policy aims that today would largely be considered as either intermediate, secondary, irrelevant, or irrational targets, such as the restoration or preservation of a specific exchange rate, the annual balancing of the government budget, and the stability of the price level.' See E. Lundberg, *op. cit.*, pp. 37–8.

economic statistics of those days reflected the policies pursued. They were mainly concerned with prices, interest rates and exchange rates. No government made estimates of national income, there were few official indices of industrial production, and even data on unemployment were scarce. For this reason no government knew very accurately what the impact of its policy was or was likely to be.

THE 1939–1945 WAR AND ITS AFTERMATH

By 1939 the dominance of Germany in Europe was greater than in 1913. The Saar (population 0·9 million) was recovered in 1935, Austria (6·8 million) became the German Ostmark in March 1938, part of Czechoslovakia (3·6 million) became the German Sudetengau in 1939, Memel, Danzig and a large part of Poland were incorporated in 1939 (10·5 million), bringing the population of the Reich to 90 million compared with 40 million in France and 48 million in the UK.[21] Furthermore, output per head was higher and the degree of unemployment lower in Germany than elsewhere.

After a few months of 'phoney' war in the West, the German blitzkrieg was highly successful. By mid-1940, Germany controlled Poland, Czechoslovakia, Norway, Denmark, Belgium, Holland and France, and had added Eupen and Malmedy, Luxemburg, Alsace and Lorraine to the Reich. The German victories were achieved without a great deal of damage to economic potential or capital stock. Germany had taken over three million prisoners. In 1940 Italy entered the war as a German ally. Later Yugoslavia and Greece were conquered after a struggle. Bulgaria, Finland, Hungary and Rumania became German allies. Germany's leverage on the strategically most

21 These comparisons leave colonial territories out of account. One could argue that Britain's possession of large colonial areas to some extent offset Germany's strength in Europe, but these overseas ties were also a burden and involved the UK in large military commitments outside Europe in areas where she piled up most of her war debts.

important neutral, Sweden, was bigger than that of the UK, and Sweden provided Germany with iron ore on a large scale – 46 million tons in the course of the war.

When Germany attacked Russia in 1941 she controlled a compact area of 250 million people with a higher per capita output than Russia's 175 million. In 1941 the Wehrmacht had only lost 200,000 men and it seemed that the Russian campaign would be another cheap victory, but in fact it was the beginning of the most destructive phase of the war.

The Germans claimed to be establishing a 'New Order' in Europe but in practice their economic policy internally and in the occupied countries was incoherent and inefficient. The type of administration varied according to political considerations. Areas incorporated in the Reich were in the German customs and currency area. Countries such as Denmark, Finland, Hungary, Rumania, Bulgaria, Vichy France and Slovakia were more or less autonomous, but Belgium, the occupied zone in France, the rump of Poland, and occupied Russia were under German military government. Norway and the Netherlands were under German commissars, and the protectorate of Bohemia and Moravia – a fief of the SS – was a German colony with German currency. Greece and Yugoslavia were first under Italian and then under German military government. Police duties in occupied countries were exercised by the SS, which also had substantial economic interests. Economic administration was handled partly by the army, partly by General Thomas' Wehrwirtschafts und Rüstungsamt, which belonged to the OKW (successor agency of the War Office), partly by Rosenberg's Ministry for occupied territories, partly by the Foreign Office, partly by the SS, partly by Sauckel as head of forced labour and partly by Speer, who was Armaments Minister. Goering also interfered both in his capacity as head of the Four-Year Plan and as the most rapacious looter of the Reich.

The autonomous countries were relatively lucky but had to grant Germany foreign exchange credits which were subject to exchange-rate manipulation in Germany's favour. The areas under German military rule had a further heavy burden of 'occupation costs', unrecorded levies in kind, and drafts of forced labour to work in Germany. Germany also used prisoners of war as part of its domestic labour force (these were mainly French and Russians; the Norwegians, Danes, Dutch and Dutch-speaking Belgians were released). Occasionally assets were taken over by German settlers or by 'mixed' companies under German control. More often, big local enterprises were made subordinate parts of German companies – being transformed into branches, agencies or subsidiaries of firms like I. G. Farben or Reichswerke Hermann Goering.

In total, German occupation levies and credits received from occupied countries amounted to 104 billion Reichsmark ($42 billion) and these levies added about 14 per cent to German GDP from 1940 to 1944. Most of these funds were provided via Central Bank allocations in national currencies in occupied territories which were used for local purchases. Including the contribution of foreign forced labour, it would seem that the Reich added about a quarter to its domestically produced resources from foreign conquests. In addition there were seizures of gold, foreign exchange assets, works of art and raw materials. Most of the useful resources from abroad were from the West – about half from France and a good deal of the rest from Belgium and Holland. In the East, German policy was so destructive that there was little economic benefit from the occupation of Poland or Russia.[22]

By the end of the war Germany was using about 7.5 million foreigners in its domestic economy (of whom very

22 Figures on foreign levies from an unpublished document of the US Strategic Bombing Survey, *Gross National Product of Germany 1936–44* (by W. C. Haraldson and E. F. Denison available in Library of Congress, Washington D.C.). Figures on geographic origin of foreign levies from B. S. Klein *Germany's Economic Preparations for War*, Harvard, 1959. Klein presents some downward revisions of the Bombing Survey estimates of foreign levies by Germany, but Klein's figures contain internal contradictions and his calculations are not presented explicitly. Furthermore Klein only covers the period to the end of 1943.

few were volunteers). These constituted over a fifth of its civilian labour force. Many of the prisoners and slave workers were debilitated by a deliberate policy of starvation. In some cases they would have made a bigger contribution to Germany's war effort if they had been kept at home. In 1943, Speer, the German Minister of Armaments, attempted to cut down the inflow of labour from France and made a deal with the Vichy Minister of Production, Bichelonne, whereby levies on French labour would end in factories making deliveries to Germany. This agreement was also applied in principle to Holland, Belgium and Italy.

During the war, the Germans deliberately murdered 20 million civilians (mostly Poles and Russians) and 4 million Russian prisoners of war. Many perished from hunger or maltreatment as slave labourers or in concentration camps, but even more were deliberately exterminated in Vernichtungslagern like Auschwitz, or by S.D. Einsatzgruppen in Poland and Russia. Total loss of life during the Second World War was about 42 million – three and a half times as many as during the First World War. Most of the slaughter was concentrated in Eastern Europe. In general there seems to have been less loss of life through disease than during the First World War because of advances in medical technology. In terms of people killed, the damage done by the war was equal to about 160 atom bombs of the type dropped on Hiroshima.

Wartime living standards in Western Europe fell much more relatively than they had in the First World War. In France, the level of output during the occupation averaged less than two-thirds of that in 1938 and occupation levies (for troop support, military construction and transfers to Germany) took a third of this, so French wartime consumption levels were only about 45 per cent of those in 1938.

Belgian and Dutch experience was similar to that in France. Norway was fortunate in that output fell only about 8 per cent, but with half a million occupation troops added to its small population, occupation costs took

TABLE 8: Loss of Life Through War in Europe 1939–1945

	Military	Civilian		in thousands Military	Civilian
Austria	230	104	Italy	175	80
Belgium	7	100	Netherlands	6	200
Bulgaria	10	10	Norway	1	—
Czechoslovakia	150	220	Poland	320	4,200
Finland	50	—	Rumania	200	260,
France	167	400	UK	298	100
Germany	3,760	3,090a	USSR	10,000	15,000
Greece	50	500	Yugoslavia	410	1,280
Hungary	140	280	Total	15,964	25,814

a includes 1,400 Volksdeutschen who had lived beyond the 1933 borders of the Reich (mainly in Poland and Czechoslovakia).

Source: Western Europe from C. Clark, *Population Growth and Land Use*, Macmillan, London, 1967, p. 121, and Kirsten, Buchholz and Köllmann, *op. cit.* for Germany and Eastern Europe. USSR from W. Eason in A. Bergson and S. Kuznets, *Economic Trends in the Soviet Union*, Harvard, 1963, p. 52.

a third of Norwegian income, so wartime standards were less than two-thirds of those in pre-war years.[23] Denmark probably fared best amongst the occupied countries. Experience was worst in Greece, Poland, the USSR and Yugoslavia, because their inhabitants were regarded by the Nazis as subhuman. In these countries wartime living standards fell below subsistence levels and large numbers died from malnutrition. In Germany itself the wartime reduction in living standards was small, because of heavy levies on the rest of Europe and the use of foreign workers to maintain domestic food output.[24] In the UK, per capita

23 Occupation costs in France taken from A. S. Milward, *The New Order and the French Economy*, Oxford, 1970, p. 273 related to our Appendix B figures of wartime output. Norwegian figures from O. Aukrust and P. J. Bjerve, *Hva Krigen Kostet Norge*, Oslo, 1945, p. 45.

24 Germany's experience in this respect was much more favourable than in the First World War as she then had no conquered territory to exploit, the Allied blockade was more effective, and she had only

civil consumption levels fell on average by less than 10 per cent, distribution of supplies was more equitable than anywhere else and health standards actually rose during the war.[25] The UK was able to use resources (about $50 billion) 20 per cent above its GDP by running down foreign assets, accumulating debt and receiving US and Canadian aid. This permitted a very high degree of mobilisation and cushioned the fall in living standards.

Damage to the European capital stock was much more extensive than in the First World War. There was fighting in France, Germany, Greece, Italy, the Netherlands, Poland, the USSR and Yugoslavia which did extensive damage. The USSR followed a scorched-earth policy to deny resources to Germany. The Allies dropped 2 million tons of bombs on the Continent (mostly on Germany) and the Germans attacked the UK with bombs and rockets. Submarines sank a great deal of merchant shipping, and livestock was destroyed on a large scale. Wartime levels of investment were low, though in both the UK and Germany wartime investment in armaments production turned out later to be useful for civilian production. The biggest losses to capital stock were probably in Poland[26] and Yugoslavia. The second largest were probably in the USSR and UK.

The UK accumulated very large war debts to Commonwealth countries and sold foreign investments during the war. Then in 1946, before Marshall Aid started, it borrowed about $4·6 billion from the USA and another $1·3 billion from Canada. As a result its net foreign asset position

---

400,000 foreign workers and prisoners to add to her labour force. See H. Mendershausen, *The Economics of War*, Prentice-Hall, New York, 1940.

25 For UK wartime real consumption levels and size of civilian population, see *Statistical Digest of the War*, HMSO, 1951.

26 An official Polish estimate put losses as equal to a third of the pre-war capital stock, but this may be an exaggeration of net losses when allowance is made for gains of assets in former German territories ceded to Poland after the war. See T. P. Alton, *Polish Post-war Economy*, Columbia, New York, 1955, pp. 31-32.

TABLE 9: Loss of Capital Assets in Europe Through War 1939–1945

| | Percentage of immediate pre-war stock lost (excluding land) | | |
	Domestic	Foreign	Total
Austria	16	0	16
France	8	2	10
Germany (FR)	13	−1	12
Italy	7	0	7
Norway	6	−3	3
UK	3	15	18
USSR	25	0	25

Source: Austrian estimates were supplied by Dr. Anton Kausel: France derived from *Dommages Subis par La France et l'Union Française du fait de la Guerre et de l'Occupation Ennemie*, Presidence du Conseil, 1948–1951; Germany from W. Kirner, *Zeitreihen für das Anlagevermögen der Wirtschaftsbereiche in der Bundesrepublik Deutschland*, DIW, Berlin, 1968; Italy from G. Fuà, *Notes on Italian Economic Growth 1861–1944*, Giuffré, Milano, 1965; Norway from *Nasjonalinntekten I Norge 1935–1943*, Statistisk Sentralbyra, Oslo, 1946; UK, W. K. Hancock and M. M. Gowing, *British War Economy*, HMSO, London, 1949, p. 551 quote a figure of 10 per cent for physical destruction and internal disinvestment (I have excluded the latter); USSR, R. Moorsteen and R. P. Powell, *The Soviet Capital Stock*, 1966, p. 75.

declined from a positive balance of $21 billion[27] in 1938 to a negative one of $2 billion in 1947. Unlike the situation after the First World War these debts were honoured in full and have been a very heavy burden for the UK. By 1947 France's pre-war net asset position of $3·9 billion had been reduced to zero. The Netherlands had lost about half of its pre-war $4·8 billion assets by 1947 and lost more later. The net foreign assets of Belgium declined only slightly.[28] In 1938 Germany had been a net debtor by about $2 billion. She acquired assets illegally and accumulated more debt during the war. She made no service payments on pre-war debt until 1953, and in that year her pre-war

27 This excludes UK claims for war debts of its allies during and after the First World War.

28 See C. Lewis, *The United States and Foreign Investment Problems*, Brookings, 1948.

and post-war debts were scaled down. She was therefore a net gainer on foreign account because of the war.

After the Second World War there were major frontier changes, mainly affecting the USSR, Poland and Germany. Germany was divested of its territorial acquisitions of 1938–40. In addition it lost East Prussia and other territories of the Weimar Republic east of the Oder-Neisse which had had a pre-war population of 9·4 million. Until 1957 the Saar was treated as part of France. Germany was also split into three areas – the three Western zones of occupation which became the Federal Republic, and the Soviet zone which became the DDR, with Berlin sandwiched in the middle. After 1945 there was a large forced migration of Germans from Poland and Czechoslovakia. Most of them went to the Federal Republic which (together with West Berlin) had a 1970 population of 60·7 million compared with about 42 million in the same area in 1939; East Germany (together with East Berlin) had about 17·3 million people in 1970, virtually the same as in 1939. Politically, the biggest changes brought by the war were the addition of 13·7 million people to the Soviet population, the incorporation of Eastern Europe (102 million people in 1970 – or 122 million including Yugoslavia) into the Soviet sphere of influence, the establishment of a communist economic system there, and the division of Germany.

Because of the overriding significance of the political split between East and Western Europe,[29] the post-war rivalries *between* West European countries have not been a very serious impediment to economic growth and co-operation has been relatively close. Furthermore, US co-operation in rebuilding the West European economy and in promoting West European co-operation has been massive. In Eastern Europe, too, most of the ethnic minority problems which were so important in inter-war

29 For the whole post-war period, European military forces have been very substantial. In 1971 there were about 4·6 million in the armed forces of Eastern Europe and about 2·9 million in the West, but the figures were bigger in earlier years. See *The Military Balance 1971–72*, International Institute for Strategic Studies, London, 1972.

years were eliminated by wartime extermination, post-war migrations, and frontier changes.

Although the damage done by Germany to other countries was greater than in the First World War, Western efforts to secure reparations were much less ambitious. Germany's rather small foreign assets were seized, and a good deal of German merchant shipping, but these were less important than after the First World War. Most of Germany's post-war reparation payments were made on a voluntary basis.[30] Germany had to bear the costs of occupation troops until 1953, but since then she has had $17 billion foreign exchange receipts from military expenditures on troops stationed in Germany. East Germany and Germany's wartime allies in East Europe were not so lucky. The Soviet Union received about $15–20 billion of reparations mostly from East Germany, but from Austria, Hungary and Rumania as well.[31]

Another big improvement compared with the period after the First World War was the absence of a serious problem of international indebtedness – with the marked exception of the UK

At the beginning of the European war, the USA was prevented by the Neutrality Act from lending to the belligerents as it had in the First World War. War supplies were sold to the Joint Franco-British Purchasing mission for cash. But from March 1941 to mid-45 the US Government transferred $43·6 billion of Lend Lease Aid to its allies (about 4·75 per cent of US national income in the period), ($30 billion to the UK and British Empire, $10·7 billion to the USSR and $2·9 billion to others).[32] This aid was virtually all on a grant basis and meant that

30 B. J. Cohen, 'Reparations in the Post-war Period: A Survey', *Banca Nazionale del Lavoro Quarterly Review*, September 1967, suggests that foreign assets seized in the Federal Republic were worth $300 million. In addition the Federal Republic paid $5·2 billion in reparations to individuals and to Israel.

31 See *New Directions in the Soviet Economy*, Joint Economic Committee, US Congress. 1966, p. 900.

32 Reciprocal British aid to the USA, Russia etc. was $7·6 billion.

TABLE 10: US Government Loans and Grants (Economic and Military) to Europe mid-1945 to mid-1971

	Gross Lending	Loan Repayment (including interest)	$ million Grants
Austria	137	100	1,195
Belgium-Luxemburg	282	289	1,739
Denmark	54	49	867
France	2,132	2,433	7,470
Germany (FR)	1,330	1,501	3,759
Greece	366	264	3,587
Italy	1,218	894	5,209
Netherlands	468	486	2,079
Norway	166	130	1,138
Spain	1,042	453	1,375
UK	5,199	2,760	4,493
Other Western Europe	701	471	705
West European Total	13,095	9,831	33,616
East European Total	1,217	624	2,733
Regional Organisations	212	162	2,381
Grand Total	14,524	10,617	38,729

Source: US Overseas Loans and Grants, July 1, 1945–June 30, 1971, AID, Washington, May 1972.

the recipients did not pile up war debts. Canada also made the UK a wartime grant of $1 billion.

Immediately after the war, US foreign aid was switched from a grant to a loan basis, but Soviet expansionist policies in Greece, the putsch in Czechoslovakia and the blockade of Berlin converted the US to a more generous posture, with the creation of Marshall Aid in 1947 which was a model for successful reconstruction and co-operation.

Marshall aid enabled Europe to re-equip its industry quickly and restock with raw materials – giving a major boost to recovery. This early growth momentum has never been seriously checked since. From 1945 to 1971 US aid to Europe (military and civilian) amounted to $53 billion gross, and $43 billion net, of which $39 billion in grants. The distribution of this aid is shown in Table 10.

In most Western countries, fiscal and monetary policy was more successful in restraining price inflation in the second than during the First World War, and the greater post-war supply of foreign aid, together with currency reforms to eliminate excess liquidity, made for smoother adjustment to peacetime conditions. There was no period of extreme deflation as in 1921 – indeed prices have never fallen. There were, however, two cases of hyper-inflation – in Hungary and Greece. In Germany the currency system collapsed in 1946 and 1947, but it was not hyper-inflation. Overt inflation was suppressed by price controls and rationing, and black market trading was largely done on a swap basis. The currency reform of June 1948 reduced the value of private monetary assets to one-fifteenth of their former level, wiped out the tremendous liquidity and abolished controls.

TABLE 11: Percentage Rate of Increase in Cost of Living

	1914–20	1920–29	1929–38	1938–50	1950–60	1960–70
Belgium	26·0	7·9	−0·7	35·0	2·0	3·0
Denmark	17·3	−4·5	0·7	5·0	3·0	5·5
France	23·0	5·5	2·9	29·0	5·7	3·6
Germany	48·0	3·8^a	−2·2	2·5	1·9	2·6
Italy	28·0	2·4	−0·2	38·0	3·0	3·9
Netherlands	14·1	−3·0	−2·1	7·4	3·1	4·1
Norway	20·0	−6·4	0·4	4·3	4·5	4·5
Sweden	19·3	−5·0	−0·2	4·1	4·6	4·0
Switzerland	14·4	−5·7	−1·8	4·0	1·4	3·3
UK	17·0	−3·8	−0·6	5·6	4·1	4·0
Average	22·7	−0·9	−2·6	13·5	3·3	3·9

^{a} 1924–29

Sources: Statistical Yearbooks of the League of Nations and United Nations, UK from *The British Economy: Key Statistics*.

1950–1970 THE SECULAR BOOM

Since 1949, when pre-war output levels were regained, the European economy has experienced a secular boom. The early post-war period was understandably one of rapid growth because most countries were able to exploit a double recovery effect from the war and the wastes of the 1930s. American aid helped a good deal to launch the European economy into a high growth orbit. But what has been so surprising is that the growth momentum of most countries did not slacken when recovery was over. The boom has been self-propelling – nurtured but not basically propelled by policy.

In Western Europe the average growth of output in the 1950s was 4·4 per cent a year, which was substantially better than the 1920s. Unemployment averaged 2·9 per cent – roughly the same level as in the 1920s. The decade of the 1960s was even better, with an average growth rate of 5·2 per cent and an unemployment average down to 1·5 per cent of the labour force. The 1960s performance was more homogeneous than that of the 1950s. Austria, Germany and Italy grew at a more normal pace, as their recovery phase was over and their labour force grew more slowly, but all other countries had faster growth and in some countries the pace was considerably accelerated particularly in Belgium, Ireland, Scandinavia and Southern Europe. The only real laggard was the UK, but even there, performance was better than in pre-war years, and marginally better than in the 1950s (see Table 12).

The period 1950–70 was remarkably free of cyclical disturbance. There was an absence of serious business fluctuations with virtually no loss of output because of recession.[33] The stability of financial institutions was much stronger than in the inter-war period.

There has been a continuous rise in prices since 1950, averaging 3 per cent in the 1950s and 4 per cent in the 1960s. This has frequently caused anxiety and has occasionally led governments to take up mildly deflationary policies, but the downward inflexibility of prices has played an important role in sustaining profit expectations, and the downward inflexibility of wages has been an even bigger support to demand.

33 See M. Bronfenbrenner, ed., *Is the Business Cycle Obsolete?* Wiley, New York, 1969, for an analysis of the post-war situation.

TABLE 12: Rate of Growth of Total Output 1950–70

	annual average compound growth rate	
	1950–1960	1960–1970
Austria	5·8	4·7
Belgium	2·9	4·9
Denmark	3·3	4·8
Finland	5·0	5·1
France	4·6	5·8
Germany	7·8	4·8
Greece	5·9	7·5
Ireland	1·7	3·9
Italy	5·8	5·7
Netherlands	4·7	5·1
Norway	3·2	5·0
Portugal	3·9	6·2
Spain	5·2	7·5
Sweden	3·4	4·6
Switzerland	4·4	4·5
UK	2·7	2·8
Average for Western Europe	4·4	5·2
Bulgaria	6·7	6·9a
Czechoslovakia	4·9	3·2a
East Germany	5·7	2·9a
Hungary	4·6	4·6a
Poland	4·6	4·9a
Rumania	5·8	6·3a
USSR	6·6	5·3b
Yugoslavia	5·7	4·7a
Average for Eastern Europe	5·6	4·9

a 1960–1968; b 1960–1969

Source: Appendix B, see p. 497.

To some extent the post-war acceleration of growth was due to luck rather than positive policy action.[34] But the

34 Some observers suggest that the greater stability and faster growth experienced in post-war years is due in substantial part to changes in business structure, i.e. concentration of output in large firms whose corporate planning eliminates uncertainty. J. K. Galbraith argues that the 'technostructure' which runs modern business can be safely left to guarantee our material needs, see his *The New Industrial State*,

TABLE 13: Unemployment as a Percentage of the Labour Force

	1950–1960	*1960–1970*
Austria	3·9	1·9
Belgium	4·0	2·2
Denmark	4·3	1·2
France	1·3	1·4
Germany	4·2	0·8
Italy	7·9	3·3
Norway	1·0	1·0
Netherlands	1·9	1·1
Sweden	1·7	1·7
Switzerland	0·2	0·0
UK	1·2	1·6
Average	2·9	1·5

Source: OECD *Labour Force Statistics*, various issues, 1950–60 for Denmark, Sweden and Switzerland from A. Maddison, *Economic Growth in the West*, page 220.

basic policy objectives of governments have been appreciably different from those in the inter-war years. There was no nostalgia for pre-war methods, and the importance of social security systems is such that there is an automatic degree of protection of demand which did not exist in pre-war years.

As government policy has been continuously active, it is difficult to disentangle the rhythm of the private sector from that induced by governments. Governments keep fluctuations within a much narrower range than would otherwise occur: hence government action has been the proximate cause of most of the very mild fluctuations in activity which have occurred in the post-war period. However, government demand has not been the basic source of the boom.

H. Hamilton, London, 1967 (although he does attach importance to the high level of government spending and the self-stabilising character of the tax structure). The planning function of business is also strongly stressed in A. Shonfield, *Modern Capitalism*, Oxford University Press, 1965.

After the war, most governments formally committed themselves to maintaining full employment and with the development of Keynesian analysis, they felt they had adequate tools to attain this – though their capacity to do so has not really been fully tested. In general, governments have been much less worried about inflation and less willing to sacrifice growth for price stability – though there have been exceptions. At an early stage – in 1949 – most of Europe devalued against the dollar and established fixed exchange rates. In most countries there has not been the same problem of choice between maintenance of sacred exchange parities and economic prosperity that there was in the inter-war period – though here again there have been some exceptions. The economies have therefore been kept very close to the full employment threshold.

In France, acceleration of economic growth was an explicit goal of policy earlier than in other Western countries. It adopted official growth targets, promoted high rates of public investment and encouraged population growth. However, in the course of the 1950s, economic growth became a proclaimed aim of policy in all Western countries.

The most important statistical indicators in the post-war period have been unemployment figures and the national accounting aggregates – a more sophisticated armoury than in pre-war years.

In fact there has not been much need for governments to promote demand. In the main, they have operated to prevent demand outrunning production potential in order to curb the rise in prices. Government policy has generally acted as a safety net rather than as a propulsive force. Its virtue has been to avoid the worst mistakes of the inter-war period.

There is considerable disagreement amongst economists concerning the causes of the post-war acceleration in European growth. The main difficulty is the lack of a generally accepted and articulated growth theory. The most elaborate attempt to 'explain' European growth rates is that of Edward Denison, which I have criticised in detail elsewhere.[35]

My own feeling is that accelerated growth can be reasonably explained in terms of the increase in capital formation, greater efficiency in resource allocation because of the openness of the economies, and faster growth of labour input. However, these are only approximate causes which are themselves explained by the buoyancy and stability of demand. The change in the approach to economic policy and the improved climate of international economic relations are probably the ultimate causes.[36] The fact that international co-operation has been so productive and so successful is due only partly to good will and intelligence on the part of Western governments. A good part of it was simply a defensive reaction against the Stalinist challenge – which had unexpected by-products.

THE INTERNATIONAL ENVIRONMENT

The most striking feature of this period compared with 1918–39 has been the high degree of international co-operation. The USA fostered West European co-operation by making its aid conditional on removal of quantitative trade restrictions via the OEEC Code of Liberalisation, and elimination of payments barriers via EPU. It also initiated several rounds of tariff reduction in GATT. Within Western Europe, trade barriers have virtually disappeared in the Common Market and EFTA. The USA tolerated discrimination against US imports without retaliation, and continued to aid Europe when its own exchange reserves were falling and those of Europe rising. From 1950–70 European exchange reserves rose from $10

35 See E. F. Denison, *Why Growth Rates Differ*, Brookings, 1967, and A. Maddison, 'Explaining Economic Growth', *Banca Nazionale del Lavoro Quarterly Review*, September 1972.

36 See R. C. O. Matthews, 'Why has Britain had Full Employment Since the War?', *Economic Journal*, September 1968, for a brilliant historical analysis of the role of policy and circumstance. See also my book, *Economic Growth in the West*, for a detailed analysis of economic policy and its impact on growth in the 1950s.

billion to $47 billion, whereas US reserves fell from $23 billion to $14 billion (see Table 14).

There has been an unparalleled boom in international trade with an average increase in the volume of exports of 8 per cent from 1950 to 1960 and 9 per cent in 1960–70 compared with less than 1 per cent from 1913 to 1950 (see Table 15). This has increased efficiency and stimulated demand.[37] There was some instability in exports in the 1950s, mainly during the Korean boom, but in the 1960s the only country to suffer a drop in export earnings was the UK (see Table 16). The great buoyancy of international trade and payments have played a major role

TABLE 14: Changes in International Liquidity 1928–1970

	1928	1937	$ billion at end of period 1950	1970
France	2·54	2·78	0·79	4·96
Germany	0·78	0·00	0·27	13·61
Italy	0·58	0·21	0·60	5·35
UK	0·75	4·14	3·67	2·83
Other Western Europe	1·24	3·66	4·47	20·31
Total Western Europe	5·89	10·79	9·80	47·06
USA	3·75	12·79	22·82	14·49

Source: *International Reserves and Liquidity*, IMF, 1958, *International Financial Statistics*, IMF, January 1951 and June 1972.

in reducing macro-economic risk. International co-operation has provided a safety net ensuring business men that they operate in an expanding system. With few exceptions governments have not felt constrained to check output because they lacked liquidity; the exceptions were Belgium and Denmark in the 1950s and the UK throughout the post-war period.

In spite of the generally encouraging picture there have been some persistent and deep-seated payments dis-

37 The impact of trade liberalisation on efficiency is a matter of controversy, see the discussion in A. Maddison, 'Explaining Economic Growth', *op. cit.*

TABLE 15: Increase in Volume of Exports 1913–1970

		annual average compound growth rate	
	1913–1950	*1950–1960*	*1960–1970*
Belgium	0·2	7·4	10·7
Denmark	1·5	6·9	7·1
France	1·1	7·3	8·6
Germany	–2·4	16·0	9·6
Italy	1·4	11·9	13·1
Netherlands	1·2	9·9	10·1
Norway	2·7	5·4	8·9
Sweden	1·9	5·6	7·9
Switzerland	0·3	5·4	8·7
UK	0·2	1·8	4·8
Average	0·8	7·8	9·0

Source: 1913–1960 from A. Maddison, 'Growth and Fluctuation in the World Economy,' *Banca Nazionale del Lavoro Quarterly Review*, June 1962. 1960-70 from *Monthly Bulletin of Statistics*, UN, New York. Danish figure for 1913-50 derived by dividing export values by national income deflator from Bjerke and Ussing, *op. cit.* Norway from *National Accounts, 1900–1929*, p. 129.

TABLE 16: Experience of Recession in Exports

	Maximum Cyclical Percentage Fall in Dollar Value of Exports from Peak to Trough		
	1921–1938	*1950–1960*	*1960–1970*
Belgium	53·5	15·0	0·0
Denmark	52·9	0·0	0·0
France	64·1	7·4	0·0
Germany	57·4	0·0	0·0
Italy	56·5	15·9	0·0
Netherlands	57·4	0·0	0·0
Norway	49·2	17·9	0·0
Sweden	64·2	16·9	0·0
Switzerland	62·0	1·3	0·0
UK	64·0	3·6	1·9
Average	58·1	7·8	0·2

Sources: A. Maddison, 'Growth and Fluctuation in the World Economy,' *Banca Nazionale del Lavoro Quarterly Review*, June 1962. 1950–70 from *Monthly Bulletin of Statistics*, UN, New York, various issues.

equilibria of which the most serious have been the substantial surplus of continental Europe (particularly Germany) to which the counterpart has been the deficit of the UK and the much bigger deficit of the USA.

A good deal of the problem has arisen from payments on government and capital account. US government aid to Europe amounted to $43 billion net, and there have been big payments on military and private capital account as well. In the twenty years 1950–70 Germany has had receipts of almost $17 billion on military account, because most of the 300,000 US troops in Europe are stationed there. The US deficit on military account was about $53 billion (on a world-wide basis).[38] The UK has had a net deficit on military account of over $7 billion.

The USA and the UK have also been major capital exporters to other developed countries. After the establishment of convertibility and the Common Market in 1958 there was a flood of US private capital to Europe (about $20 billion). The UK was also a major capital exporter to developed countries in the sterling area like Australia and South Africa – investments which had a poor yield.[39]

The existence of this basic payments disequilibrium made economic growth easier for the continental countries. The flows from the USA freed European countries from payments constraints, reduced their military burden and speeded technical progress. Nevertheless it is obvious that a payments disequilibrium of this size (which has some parallels in the situation of the 1920s) cannot last forever, and at the end of the 1960s it became clear that some of the corrective measures might endanger progress. They have already led to a fairly substantial tightening of exchange controls and some mild reversal of the liberal trends of the 1960s, though, so far, they have not led to trade restrictions.

Another related problem which has emerged since

38 See *Statistics of Balance of Payments 1950–61*, OECD, Paris, 1964; and E. Merigo and S. Potter, *Invisibles in the 1960s, Economic Outlook, Occasional Studies*, OECD, July 1970.

39 See W. B. Reddaway, *Effects of UK Direct Investment Overseas*, Cambridge, 1967.

European currencies became convertible in 1958, is the volatility of short-term capital movements. These flows have reached massive proportions, undermined earlier confidence in currency stability, and have brought the post-war system of fixed exchange rates to the point of collapse. No clear alternative international monetary system had emerged. There has been experimentation with a floating exchange rate system, but with a considerable degree of government manipulation of rates, which have not been left genuinely free. Here again we find a strengthening of restrictive practices to make the present system work, and an increase in political tensions over the kind of international payments system which is desirable. The major difference between the present situation and that in the inter-war years is the existence and active stabilisation role of the IMF, the monetary Committees of OECD and the Common Market. The BIS also plays a bigger role than in pre-war years and there have been several occasions on which central bankers have mobilised massive funds for international stabilisation purposes.[40]

One of the major forces promoting growth in the 1960s (particularly in the smaller countries) was the abolition of trade barriers within the Common Market and EFTA. The split of West Europe into these two blocs in itself did little to hinder growth but was a source of political tension which threatened the spirit of international co-operation. The UK tried to tack an industrial free trade area on to the Common Market in 1958 but was rebuffed and instead sponsored the foundation of EFTA. Then the UK, having rather belatedly decided to join, was twice rebuffed. In 1972, the situation changed with the agreement of the six original Common Market countries to widen their scope. Now that the UK has been admitted there will be problems of policy adjustment within the Common Market, because the original agreement was weighted in France's favour – a price Germany was willing to pay. The main

40 For pre-war years, see S. V. O. Clarke, *Central Bank Co-operation 1924–31*, Federal Reserve Bank of New York, 1967.

significance of widened membership is probably political rather than economic.

THE INVESTMENT BOOM

Since 1950 there has been a secular investment boom sparked off by the prospects of rising demand, the absence of depression and constantly rising prices. For the business man the risk of not investing has been greater than that of investing, and the rate of investment has not only been high but has risen steadily. In the 1950s, gross fixed investment (excluding housing) averaged 15 per cent of national product as compared with only 10 per cent from 1920 to 1938, and in the 1960s the ratio rose further to 18 per cent (see Table 17).

The acceleration in growth of capital stock was even bigger than the rise in the investment ratio. In the first place, the growth of capital stock is determined by the growth of net rather than gross investment, and the proportion of gross investment needed for depreciation was smaller in 1950–70 than earlier. Secondly, the national product was growing faster than before because of faster growth of labour inputs and greater efficiency of resource allocation due to international trade.

On average, it seems probable that the capital stock was growing more than twice as fast from 1950 to 1970 as from 1913 to 1950.[41] Although figures excluding housing

41 In the UK for instance, the capital stock has been estimated to have grown at 3·1 per cent a year from 1950 to 1969 and at 1·2 per cent a year from 1913–1950. See *The British Economy: Key Statistics 1900–1970*, LCES, Table 1, p. 12. In France the capital stock was estimated to have grown at 1·3 per cent a year from 1913 to 1954 and 4 per cent from 1950 to 1966, see J.-J. Carré, P. Dubois and E. Malinvaud, *La Croissance Française*, Seuil, Paris, 1972, pp. 189 and 204. In Norway the capital stock was estimated to have grown by 2·4 per cent a year from 1913 to 1950 and by 4·2 per cent a year from 1950 to 1961, see *National Accounts 1865–1960*, Central Bureau of Statistics, Oslo, 1965, pp. 362-3. The growth of capital stock can vary according to measurement conventions, however, the weight of the evidence for great acceleration in the growth of capital stock is overwhelming, see A. Maddison, 'Explaining Economic Growth', *op. cit.*

are not available for Eastern Europe, it seems certain that the investment effort there has been even bigger than in the West since 1950.[42]

TABLE 17: Non-Residential Fixed Investment as Percent of GNP at Current Prices

		average of ratios for years cited	
	1920–1938	*1950–1960*	*1960–1970*
Austria	6·1a	16·4	20·2
Belgium		12·4	15·5
Denmark	8·9	14·0	16·9
Finland		19·6	20·0
France	11·8	13·7	17·4
Germany	9·7	16·1	19·3
Greece	7·5b	11·7	18·2
Ireland		13·1	15·1
Italy	13·6	15·1	14·5
Netherlands		18·0	20·3
Norway	12·4	23·7c	23·8c
Sweden	10·5	15·5	17·3
Switzerland		14·1	20·0
UK	5·7	11·6	14·2
Average for Western Europe	9·6	15·4	18·1

a 1924-37; b 1929-38; c includes some elements of repair and maintenance excluded by other countries.

Sources: 1913–49 Austria, Greece and Sweden from sources cited in Appendix B (with an adjustment of 18 per cent of fixed investment to eliminate housing investment in Austria and Greece). For other countries see sources cited in A. Maddison, 'Explaining Economic Growth,' *Banca Nazionale del Lavoro Quarterly Review*, September 1972. 1950–70 from *National Accounts 1950–68*. OECD, Paris, 1970, and *National Accounts 1960–70*, OECD, Paris, 1972.

42 See figures on total fixed investment given in T. P. Alton, 'Economic Structure and Growth in Eastern Europe', *Economic Developments in Countries of Eastern Europe*. Joint Economic Committee, US Congress, 1970, pp. 59-60.

TABLE 18: Rate of Growth of Non-Agricultural Employment

	annual average compound growth rate	
	1913–1950	*1950–1970*
Austria	0·8	0·5
Belgium	0·3	1·0
Denmark	1·5	2·0
Finland	2·3	3·2
France	0·0	1·6
Germany	1·0	2·4
Greece	0·6	2·3
Ireland	0·3	0·4
Italy	0·9	2·3
Netherlands	1·7	1·4
Norway	1·2	1·4
Portugal	1·1	1·1
Spain	1·3	2·5
Sweden	1·5	1·2
Switzerland	0·8	1·8
UK	0·6	0·5
Average for Western Europe	1·0	1·6
Bulgaria	2·4	4·3
Czechoslovakia	0·1	2·2
East Germany	1·1	0·7
Hungary	1·8	2·5
Poland	0·8	3·3
Rumania	1·9	3·5
USSR	2·6	3·2
Yugoslavia	0·9	4·4
Average for Eastern Europe	1·5	3·0

THE LABOUR SUPPLY

Mainly because of the high pressure of demand there has
been a more rapid growth of labour input since 1950 than
in previous years. In the early 1950s there were still structural
employment problems in Germany and Italy (because of
lack of capital). In Belgium and Denmark government
policies failed to achieve full use of resources. In the 1950s
therefore average unemployment – whilst low – was little

better than in the 1920s. In the 1960s unemployment was lower in all countries – an average of only 1·5 per cent and the structural unemployment of Germany and Italy was eliminated.

There has been a substantial flow of immigrants to Western Europe and from Southern to Northern Europe, i.e. an exodus of workers from Italy, Spain, Portugal, Greece and Yugoslavia.[43]

The industrial labour supply has been substantially augmented by a large flow of labour from agriculture. In general, labour is used less efficiently in agriculture than elsewhere in the economy and shifts of farm labour from low productivity jobs to other parts of the economy have been regarded as an important source of economic growth by several authors,[44] who have treated this kind of labour movement as providing some sort of free bonus to the economy. Table 18 therefore shows growth in non-agricultural rather than in total employment. It can be seen that labour inputs rose considerably faster in 1950-70 than 1913-50 in both Western and Eastern Europe. In Western Europe, the acceleration in growth of labour supply was greatest in France, Italy and Germany. In the UK by contrast, labour supply actually grew more slowly.

The high level of labour utilisation in the post-war period and the high level of investment are not autonomous supply factors stimulating growth. They have been induced by high levels of demand.

OTHER FACTORS STIMULATING GROWTH

Another factor which played a role in the acceleration of post-war growth was an increase in the rate of technical progress. The rate of innovation is influenced considerably by the rate of capital formation in the world as a whole,

43 For an analysis of the impact of migration on post-war growth, see C. P. Kindleberger, *Europe's Post-war Growth: The Role of Labour Supply*, Harvard, 1967.

44 See N. Kaldor, *Causes of the Slow Rate of Economic Growth of the United Kingdom*, Cambridge, 1966

which has been bigger than before the war. It has also been influenced by the sharp rise in government spending on research and development. The transmission of ideas has been speeded by removal of trade barriers, growth of air travel and international investment. It is not possible to measure the overall pace of technical progress, but the fact that the life of capital assets has been reduced in many countries would suggest that technical progress is faster than it used to be.

Many governments have attempted to promote growth by active policies of government intervention. Thus there was some early post-war nationalisation of industry in the UK and France which was partly motivated by the idea that government ownership would promote faster growth. Governments have done a good deal to promote research and development – most notably in the UK, which has put large research resources and subsidies into the aircraft industry, atomic energy, and computers. In the 1960s governments did a good deal to promote industrial training, and the Swedish Government promoted an active labour market policy. The Labour Government in the UK from 1964 to 1970 represented the interventionist approach in a somewhat extreme form. The government had a National Plan, set up the Industrial Reorganisation Corporation to help particular private industries on a large scale, promoted industrial mergers, industrial training and consultancy and introduced the Selective Employment Tax and regional employment premia to secure reallocation of labour.

My own feeling is that policies to promote 'structural' adjustment and improve supply potential have made only a modest contribution to the post-war acceleration of growth,[45] and some of them have been rather wasteful examples of technological chauvinism. The big acceleration in economic growth has been due largely to better macro-economic policy and to international co-operation.

45 Similarly I feel that Svennilson exaggerated the structural problems of the 1920s and 1930s and understated the importance of macro-economic policy. See I. Svennilson, *Growth and Stagnation in the European Economy*, ECE, Geneva, 1954.

EASTERN EUROPEAN EXPERIENCE

Eastern Europe has also enjoyed high rates of growth since 1950. The average growth performance of the communist countries being roughly comparable with that of Western Europe, though the achievements in the 1960s were generally below those of the 1950s.

In Eastern Europe the post-war period has been one of very high investment, probably somewhat higher than in the West. In all the Eastern countries except Eastern Germany the growth in the non-agricultural labour supply has been rapid, and higher than in the West. Trade has also expanded rapidly.

In view of the higher input of labour and capital, one might have expected a higher growth performance in Eastern than in Western Europe, but economic efficiency was probably hindered by the devotion of a higher proportion of resources to military purposes, the inadequate use of the price mechanism to allocate resources, and the greater difficulty in transfer of technology, because of the virtual absence of foreign investment, strategic limitations on trade, and the bilateral character of trade controls.

Appendix A

POPULATION AND LABOUR FORCE

Population figures for 1913 are derived from various national sources and I. Svennilson, *Growth and Stagnation in the European Economy*, ECE, Geneva, 1954. Employment statistics for 1913 are derived from sources cited in A. Maddison, *Economic Growth in the West* and from P. Bairoch, *The Working Population and its Structure, International Historical Statistics*, Vol. I, Brussels University, 1968. In several cases the estimates of the agricultural employment proportion in 1913 involved adjustments to census figures around 1910 to ensure better comparability in definition to those for later years. Figures for Western countries for 1950–70 are derived from OECD sources and for Yugoslavia from the UN *Monthly Bulletin of Statistics* and Yugoslav yearbooks. Figures for 1950–68 for Bulgaria, Czechoslovakia, East Germany, Hungary, Poland and Rumania are to be found in *Economic Developments in Countries of Eastern Europe*, Joint Economic Committee, US Congress, Washington, 1970, and these were extrapolated to 1970. USSR from *Narodnoe Khoziastvo SSSR*, various issues with assumptions about agricultural labour on private plots similar to those described in A. Maddison, *Economic Growth in Japan and the USSR.*

TABLE 19: European Population at Mid-Year, 1913–1970

	1913	1913	1950	in thousands 1970
	1913 Frontiers		1970 Frontiers	
Austria	29,193	6,767	6,935	7,391
Belgium	7,605	7,665	8,639	9,676
Denmark	2,833	3,000	4,270	4,921
Finland	—	3,017	4,009	4,616
France	39,790	41,825	41,836	50,768
Germany[a]	66,978	37,210	49,989	60,670
Greece	2,728	5,425	7,566	8,793
Iceland	87	87	143	205
Ireland	—	3,110	2,969	2,944
Italy	35,192	36,640	47,105	54,459
Luxemburg	265	265	297	340
Netherlands	6,144	6,144	10,114	13,032
Norway	2,447	2,447	3,265	3,879
Portugal	5,973	5,973	8,405	8,949
Spain	20,300	20,300	27,868	33,646
Sweden	5,621	5,621	7,017	8,046
Switzerland	3,865	3,865	4,694	6,267
UK	45,860	42,750	50,363	55,812
Western Europe	274,881	232,111	285,484	334,414
Bulgaria	4,497	4,794	7,251	8,501
Czechoslovakia	—	13,245	12,389	14,497
East Germany[b]	—	14,624	18,388	17,117
Hungary	21,325	7,840	9,338	10,333
Poland	—	26,710	24,824	32,777
Rumania	7,353	12,527	16,311	20,394
USSR	165,700	159,200	180,050	242,770
Yugoslavia	3,032	13,591	16,346	20,370
Eastern Europe	201,907	252,531	284,897	366,759
Total Europe	476,788	484,642	570,381	701,173

[a] includes West Berlin
[b] includes East Berlin

TABLE 20: European Employment at Mid-Year, 1913–1970

	(*adjusted to refer to equivalent 1970 territory throughout*) *in thousands*		
	1913	*1950*	*1970*
Austria	3,398	3,347	3,100
Belgium	3,457	3,371	3,842
Denmark	1,333	1,980	2,373
Finland	1,255	1,984	2,183
France	21,307	19,006	20,974
Germany[a]	16,625	21,080	27,204
Greece	2,018	2,600	3,718
Ireland	1,278	1,220	1,066
Italy	16,084	16,985	19,162
Netherlands	2,367	3,835	4,678
Norway	1,047	1,455	1,545
Portugal	2,550	3,196	3,130
Spain	7,613	10,617	12,539
Sweden	2,578	3,390	3,854
Switzerland	1.837	2,147[b]	2,960
UK	19,520	23,229	25,081
Western Europe	104,267	119,442	137,409
Bulgaria	2,397	4,114	4,408
Czechoslovakia	5,854	5,972	7,103
East Germany[c]	6,534	8,477	8,496
Hungary	3,285	4,379	5,194
Poland	14,049	12,718	16,893
Rumania	6,877	9,710	11,807
USSR	68,600	77,570	115,600
Yugoslavia	6,863	7,568	9,158
Eastern Europe[d]	114,459	130,508	178,659
Total Europe	218,726	249,950	316,068

[a]Federal Republic and West Berlin.
[b]December 1st.
[c]Democratic Republic and East Berlin.
[d]Figures for Eastern Europe refer to the labour force and not employment.

TABLE 21: European Agricultural Employment at Mid-Year, 1913–1970

	1913	1950	1970
	(adjusted to refer to equivalent territory throughout) in thousands		
Austria	1,685	1,078	577
Belgium	795	368	181
Denmark	520	555	265
Finland	868	912	486
France	7,969	5,800	2,865
Germany[a]	5,645	5,041	2,406
Greece	1,001	1,350	1,743
Ireland	639	496	291
Italy	9,007	7,250	3,683
Netherlands	608	533	330
Norway	401	433	208
Portugal	1,464	1,569	1,001
Spain	4,286	5,217	3,662
Sweden	1,060	(600)	314
Switzerland	487	355[b]	220
UK	1,698	1,262	707
Western Europe	38,133	32,819	18,939
Bulgaria	1,918	2,982	1,782
Czechoslovakia	2,306	2,250	1,314
East Germany[c]	2,287	2,069	1,199
Hungary	2.102	2,121	1,479
Poland	9,834	7,113	6,131
Rumania	5,474	6,914	6,229
USSR	51,450	32,800	32,000
Yugoslavia	5,490	5,676	(4,680)
Eastern Europe	80,861	61,925	54,814
Total Europe	118,994	94,744	73,753

[a]Federal Republic and West Berlin.
[b]December 1st
[c]Democratic Republic and East Berlin.

Appendix B

OUTPUT[46]

Wherever possible the figures in this appendix refer to gross domestic product (GDP) and in every case they are adjusted throughout to refer to the territory of 1970. I have tried to cover as many years as possible, so that those who wish to analyse growth or cycles can use a different periodicity from that which I chose to use in the text of the chapter. In most cases, the estimates of war output are very rough. I have attempted to select figures which conform as closely as possible to the OECD standardised system of national accounts.

WESTERN EUROPE

For 1950–70 for Western Europe, all figures were derived from OECD national accounts publications. For 1913–50 the sources were as follows:

AUSTRIA: 'Osterreichs Volkseinkommen, 1913–63,' *Monatsberichte des Osterreichischen Institutes für Wirtshaftsforschung*, 14th Sonderheft, Vienna, August 1965.

BELGIUM: estimates derived from C. Carbonnelle, 'Recherches Sur l'Evolution de la Production en Belgique de 1900 à 1957,' *Cahiers Economiques de Bruxelles*, No. 3, April 1959, p. 353. Carbonnelle gives GDP figures for only a few benchmark years but gives a commodity production series for many more years. I have made interpolations for the service sector to arrive at a figure for GDP for all the

---

46 In preparing this appendix I received help from a number of national accounts statisticians who were kind enough to answer my queries. I would like to thank T. P. Alton, P. J. Bjerve, R. C. Geary, S. Geronymakis, Dan Grindea, A. Kausel, O. E. Niitamo, K. H. Raabe and I. Vinski for their courtesy in this regard. I did not always follow the advice I received, so responsibility for the procedures used, and for any errors, lies with me.

years for which Carbonnelle shows total commodity production.

DENMARK: GDP at factor cost from K. Bjerke and N. Ussing, *Studier over Danmarks Nationalprodukt, 1870–1950*, Copenhagen, 1958, p. 147. The figures were adjusted to eliminate the effect of the cession of North Schleswig to Denmark in 1920.

FINLAND: figures for GDP supplied by O. E. Niitamo, figures for 1913–26 based on estimates of material product; 1926–48 from E. H. Laurila, 'Suomen Kansantulo Vuosina 1926–1949,' *Tilastokatsauksia* 11-12, Helsinki, 1950; 1948–50 official estimates of the Central Statistical Office.

FRANCE: gross domestic product from J.-J. Carré, P. Dubois and E. Malinvaud, *La Croissance Française*, Seuil, Paris, 1972, p. 35 with the 1913 figure adjusted upwards 4·6 per cent to include Alsace-Lorraine. Interpolation betweeen 1939 and 1946 was based on A. Sauvy's report on national income to the Conseil Economique, *Journal Officiel*, 7th April, 1954.[47] Interpolation between 1913 and 1920 based on figures for industrial and agricultural output shown in J. Dessirier, 'Indices Comparés de la Production Industrielle et Production Agricole en Divers Pays de 1870 à 1928,' *Bulletin de la Statistique Générale de la France, Etudes Speciales*, October-December 1928; service output was assumed stable in this period, and weights for the three sectors were derived from Carré, Dubois and Malinvaud, *op. cit.*

GERMANY: 1913–25 net domestic product from W. G. Hoffmann, *Das Wachstum der deutschen Wirtschaft seit der Mitte des 19. Jahrhunderts*, Springer, Berlin, 1965, p. 455. Hoffmann's figure for 1925 was adjusted upwards by 8·3 per cent to offset the impact of changed boundaries. (The

47 I have checked Sauvy's estimates by rough calculations based on figures for wartime agricultural and industrial output and Sauvy's figures seem reasonable. For agriculture, see M. Cépède, *Agriculture et Alimentation en France durant le IIe Guerre Mondiale*, Génin, Paris, 1961; for industry, see *Annuaire de Statistique Industrielle 1938-1947*, Ministère de l'Industrie et du Commerce, Paris, 1948.

territorial adjustment was derived from F. Grünig, 'Die Anfänge der Volkswirtschaftlichen Gesamtrechnung in Deutschland,' *Beiträge zur empirischen Konjunkturforschung*, Berlin, 1950, p. 76 further adjusted by me to include the Saar). 1914–24 pattern of movement in individual years derived from Dessirier, *op. cit.*, on similar procedure as for France. 1925–38 from *Statistisches Jahrbuch für die Bundesrepublik Deutschland, 1961*, p. 544. 1939–44 from US Strategic Bombing Survey, *The Effects of Strategic Bombing on the German War Economy, 1945*, Special Paper No. 1, *The Gross National Product of Germany 1936–1944*. 1945–47 figures are my guesses. 1938–48 link and figure for 1949 from OEEC, *Europe and the World Economy*, OEEC, Paris, 1950, p. 116.

GREECE: 1913–29 real product in international units from C. Clark, *Conditions of Economic Progress*, 3rd edition, Macmillan, London, 1957. 1929–38 figures for GNP at factor cost from *Ekonomikos Tachidromos* 22 May 1954. 1938–50 from *Europe and the World Economy*, OECD, Paris, 1960, p. 116.

IRELAND: 1913–38 from C. Clark, *op. cit.* 1938–50 from *Europe and the World Economy*, OEEC, Paris, 1960.

ITALY: Gross domestic product from G. Fua, ed., *Lo Sviluppo Economico in Italia*, vol. III, pp. 402–3, Angeli, Milan, 1969.

NETHERLANDS: 1913–17, 1921–39, and 1948–50 net domestic product at factor cost derived from *1899–1959 Zestig Jaren Statistiek in Tijdreeksen*, Centraal Bureau voor de Statistiek, Zeist, 1959. 1917–20 national income from *op. cit.*; 1939–47 real product in international units interpolated from C. Clark, *Conditions of Economic Progress*, 3rd ed. Macmillan, London, 1957, p. 166–7.

NORWAY: Gross domestic product at market prices. 1913–50 from *National Accounts 1865–1960*, Central Bureau of Statistics, Oslo, 1965. The original figures of gross fixed investment were adjusted downwards by a third to eliminate repairs and maintenance. 1939–44 movement in national income (excluding shipping and whaling operations carried out from Allied bases 1940–44) from O. Aukrust and P. J. Bjerve, *Hva Krigen Kostet Norge*, Dreyers, Oslo, 1945, p. 45. 1945 assumed to be midway between 1944 and 1946.

PORTUGAL: 1913–38 from C. Clark, *op. cit.* 1938–50 from *Europe and the World Economy*, OEEC, Paris, 1960.

SPAIN: 1913–50 net national product at factor cost from *La Renta Nacional de España 1940–64*, Consejo de Economica Nacional, Madrid, 1965, pp. 112 and 164.

SWEDEN: gross domestic product at market prices from O. Johansson, *The Gross Domestic Product of Sweden and its Composition 1861–1955*, Almquist and Wiksell, Stockholm, 1967, p. 153.

SWITZERLAND: 1913–44 real product in international units from C. Clark, *Conditions of Economic Progress*, 3rd edition, Macmillan, London, 1957, pp. 188-9. 1948–50 from *La Vie Economique*, September 1965.

UK: gross domestic product at factor cost (compromise estimate) from C. H. Feinstein, *National Income Expenditure and Output of the United Kingdom 1855–1965*, Cambridge, 1972, pp. T19–20. Post-1920 figures are increased by 3·8 per cent to offset the exclusion of output in the area which subsequently became the Irish Republic.

EASTERN EUROPE

BULGARIA: 1913–50 from C. Clark, *op. cit.* 1950–68 from T. P. Alton, 'Economic Structure and Growth in Eastern Europe,' in *Economic Developments in Countries of Eastern Europe*, Joint Economic Committee, US Congress, 1970, p. 46. Figures for 1926–39 from N. Spulber. *The State and Economic Development in Eastern Europe*, Random House, New York, 1966.

CZECHOSLOVAKIA: 1913–37 GDP (inter-war territory) from F. L. Pryor, Z. P. Pryor, M. Stadnik, and G. J.

Staller, 'Czechoslovakia Aggregate Production in the Inter-war Period,' *Review of Income and Wealth*, March 1971, p. 36. 1937–68 from T. P. Alton, *op. cit.*

EAST GERMANY: from T. P. Alton, *op. cit.*

HUNGARY: net domestic product 1911–13 to 1938 from A. Eckstein, 'National Income and Capital Formation in Hungary, 1900–50,' in S. Kuznets, ed. *Income and Wealth*, Series V, Bowes and Bowes, London, 1955, p. 171 (1920–38 data refer to fiscal years). 1920 is based on Eckstein's figure for national product growth from 1920 to 1924 (he gives two series; domestic, and national product). 1938–68 from T. P. Alton, *op. cit.*

POLAND: 1929–38 national income from N. Spulber, *The State and Economic Development in Eastern Europe*, Random House, New York, 1966 linked to postwar years via 1937 from T. P. Alton, *op. cit.*

RUMANIA: Data for 1926–38 are available in N. Spulber, *op. cit.* 1950–68 from T. P. Alton, *op. cit.*

USSR: 1913–50 from sources given in A. Maddison, *Economic Growth in Japan and the USSR*, Allen and Unwin, London, 1969. 1920 is a crude estimate based on the Soviet index of agricultural production and Nutter's indices of industrial output. 1950–69 derived from S. H. Cohn's estimates in *Economic Performance and the Military Burden in the Soviet Union*, Joint Economic Committee, US Congress, Washington, 1970, p. 17. I have given agriculture a lower weight than Cohn for reasons discussed in Maddison, *op. cit.*, pp. 153-6.

YUGOSLAVIA: 1913–50 GDP at market prices from I. Vinski, 'National Product and Fixed Assets in the Territory of Yugoslavia 1900–59,' in P. Deane, ed., *Studies in Social and Financing Accounting, Income and Wealth*, Series IX, Bowes and Bowes, London, 1961, p. 221. 1950–68 from T. P. Alton, *op. cit.*

TABLE 22: Movement in Total Volume of Output (1913=100)

	Austria	Belgium	Bulgaria	Czechoslovakia	Denmark	Finland	France	Germany	Greece	Hungary	Ireland
1913	100·0	100·0	100·0	100·0	100·0	100·0	100·0	100·0	100·0	100·0ᵃ	100·0ᵇ
1914					105·7	92·9	94·4	92·9			
1915						91·0	86·9	86·6			
1916						95·6	83·2	85·9			
1917						81·0	80·7	85·7			
1918						63·9	76·4	85·2			
1919						75·3	75·2	74·7			
1920	66·4	92·5		90·4	95·0	88·7	81·8	80·6		(77·2)	
1921	73·5	94·1		97·7	97·1	92·0	80·5	88·6			
1922	80·1	103·3		95·1	103·9	103·0	93·1	95·7			
1923	79·3	107·0		103·0	117·7	109·1	98·1	79·9			
1924	88·5	110·5		113·7	120·4	115·2	108·2	92·2		89·9	
1925	94·5	113·1		127·1	117·2	122·2	109·4	101·7		107·6	
1926	96·1	116·9	102·6	126·6	120·9	126·7	110·7	104·6		106·0	
1927	99·0	121·3	109·0	136·1	125·1	137·4	109·4	115·0		112·7	
1928	103·6	127·6	107·4	148·1	130·1	142·0	115·7	120·2		120·3	
1929	105·1	126·5	105·8	152·2	134·1	141·2	125·8	119·6	170·2	121·9	99·9
1930	102·2	125·3	116·9	147·2	140·0	139·3	122·0	118·1	166·1	119·7·	
1931	94·0	123·1	134·2	142·2	142·3	132·8	117·0	108·9	159·2	113·3	
1932	84·3	117·5	134·2	136·5	139·5	135·2	112·0	100·8	172·7	107·9	
1933	81·5	120·1	137·4	130·7	141·5	144·7	117·0	106·9	182·8	117·3	
1934	82·2	119·1	124·7	125·7	146·9	162·9	117·0	116·5	187·3	118·5	
1935	83·8	126·4	120·0	124·5	150·4	166·8	113·2	127·0	195·1	123·7	
1936	86·3	127·3	145·3	134·7	154·9	178·5	114·5	138·0	195·8	131·2	
1937	90·9	129·0	153·2	149·8	160·1	196·1	120·8	153·6	223·6	128·3	
1938	100·0	126·1	157·0		160·5	197·5	120·8	168·8	218·0	134·3	109·4

ᵃ 1911–13
ᵇ 1911

Italy	Netherlands	Norway	Portugal	Spain	Sweden	Switzerland	UK	USSR	Yugoslavia	
100·0	100·0	100·0	100·0ᵃ	100·0	100·0	100·0	100·0	100·0	100·0ᵇ	1913
99·0	99·1	102·2		103·6	97·6		101·0			1914
110·8	100·8	106·6		96·5	101·3		109·1			1915
122·5	105·3	110·0		105·7	114·3		111·5			1916
126·5	97·7	100·0		110·3	104·3		112·5			1917
127·5	92·5	96·3		107·3	97·5		113·2			1918
107·8	115·7	112·6		107·7	99·7		100·9			1919
100·0	118·3	119·7		122·7	113·5		94·8	51·9	93·6	1920
98·0	122·7	109·8		117·5	100·0		87·1		95·9	1921
103·9	127·5	122·6		114·7	94·8		91·6		98·7	1922
109·8	131·9	125·3		120·8	102·6		94·5		103·6	1923
111·8	136·3	124·7		119·3	110·4	119·2	98·4		110·5	1924
119·6	142·8	132·4		127·5	121·0	127·8	103·2		115·9	1925
120·6	146·2	135·3		125·4	126·1	134·2	99·4		123·4	1926
117·6	154·2	140·5		133·8	132·0	141·5	107·4		122·2	1927
126·5	158·5	145·1		127·0	132·3	149·3	108·7	113·2	132·1	1928
130·4	166·5	158·6		141·8	143·4	154·5	111·9	116·2	138·7	1929
123·5	168·2	170·3		135·6	148·3	153·6	111·1	123·1	136·5	1930
122·5	162·6	157·1		135·2	134·1	147·2	105·4	125·6	133·0	1931
125·5	157·0	167·6		145·1	130·7	142·2	106·2	124·2	122·2	1932
125·5	152·9	171·6		130·5	132·3	149·2	109·3	129·3	125·5	1933
125·5	154·3	177·1		147·1	145·2	149·5	116·5	142·0	129·7	1934
137·3	158·3	184·7		142·3	152·4	148·9	121·0	163·4	128·1	1935
137·9	161·3	196·0			163·3	149·4	126·5	176·4	143·1	1936
146·1	170·0	203·0			174·2	156·5	130·9	194·3	145·6	1937
148·0	171·6	208·1	145·3		180·7	162·6	132·5	197·8	156·4	1938

ᵃ1914; ᵇ1909-12.

TABLE 22 (Contd.): Movement in Total Volume of Output (1913=100)

	Austria	Belgium	Bulgaria	Czechoslovakia	Denmark	Finland	France	Germany	Greece	Hungary	Ireland
1939			159·5		170·3	192·1	125·8	186·8	218·6		
1940					145·1	169·2	103·8	188·1			
1941					131·5	179·5	82·3	200·1			
1942					134·0	187·7	73·6	202·9	134·2		
1943					148·0	204·6	69·8	206·8			
1944					162·2	200·8	61·0	212·2			
1945					150·1	171·1	66·2	106·1	79·5		
1946	58·4				170·1	193·3	100·6	110·0	119·1		
1947	64·4				183·9	206·1	109·5	115·0	153·7		
1948	82·0	134·0			189·7	219·5	125·8	124·9	161·4		
1949	97·5	139·4			198·7	228·8	134·5	145·1	170·0		
1950	109·6	147·1	219·3	156·3	216·1	243·0	144·6	177·2	167·9	127·8	123·9
1951	117·2	155·5	264·5	159·1	215·6	265·7	153·3	196·5	182·5		125·6
1952	117·5	154·2	252·4	164·4	218·5	275·1	157·3	214·2	183·3		129·3
1953	122·1	159·2	280·7	163·7	231·5	275·3	162·0	231·2	208·1		133·1
1954	132·6	165·3	275·4	170·4	238·0	300·6	169·8	247·6	215·2		134·4
1955	147·3	173·3	295·2	185·0	239·1	323·7	179·6	276·9	228·6	166·4	137·1
1956	154·9	178·3	295·4	195·9	244·4	329·7	188·6	296·0	247·3	158·9	135·3
1957	164·0	182·8	326·7	207·9	256·8	334·7	199·9	312·7	267·7	172·1	136·0
1958	170·8	181·6	355·1	223·8	263·7	334·3	205·0	322·8	275·3	183·5	133·4
1959	178·4	186·0	383·4	233·6	281·9	359·1	210·8	345·4	285·7	191·0	138·9
1960	193·1	196·3	419·7	251·4	299·5	394·8	225·8	375·9	297·8	201·0	146·3
1961	203·9	206·1	447·2	261·4	317·5	426·3	237·5	396·4	331·3	211·2	153·6
1962	209·2	217·7	483·8	264·9	335·3	444·2	254·1	412·3	343·1	220·0	158·8
1963	217·0	227·3	505·9	259·9	337·8	454·8	268·8	426·6	371·1	232·0	165·9
1964	231·4	242·9	545·7	272·1	368·1	484·2	286·5	455·0	405·0	245·1	172·2
1965	239·3	252·1	578·5	282·1	385·7	508·9	300·0	480·3	437·5	246·9	176·9
1966	251·2	259·5	626·3	297·1	395·3	520·5	316·8	494·4	469·3	262·2	179·4
1967	258·0	269·9	666·5	311·5	411·3	533·3	332·3	493·5	494·4	274·2	189·2
1968	269·7	279·4	714·3	323·7	429·1	545·7	347·8	529·1	527·2	287·9	204·5
1969	286·3	298·3			464·2	602·6	374·5	571·2	569·4		212·1
1970	306·6	316·3			478·7	650·5	397·1	602·2	615·0		215·3

Italy	Netherlands	Norway	Portugal	Spain	Sweden	Switzerland	UK	USSR	Yugoslavia	
158·8	178·2	218·0			190·6	162·3	133·8	210·0	164·6	1939
159·8	160·0	198·6		101·7	188·7	164·0	147·2	208·4		1940
157·8	162·8	203·4		101·4	185·2	162·9	160·6			1941
155·9	148·7	195·5		108·4	185·8	158·8	164·6			1942
141·2	144·6	191·6		113·9	198·2	157·4	168·2			1943
114·7	97·7	181·6		117·4	209·3	161·2	161·6			1944
89·8	99·1	203·5		98·7	228·1		154·5	165·5		1945
117·6	173·2	225·3		123·2	251·8		147·8	165·0		1946
138·2	200·0	251·1		117·8	266·8		145·6	183·4	147·6	1947
146·1	221·4	271·1		113·7	281·3	204·1	150·2	208·5	173·6	1948
156·9	235·5	276·4		114·3	293·1	196·9	155·8	231·0	190·4	1949
169·6	243·0	291·5	195·8	123·3	315·6	211·1	160·8	253·1	180·7	1950
182·5	249·4	300·3	204·4	144·9	319·4	228·2	164·5			1951
190·6	254·5	311·9	201·5	151·5	328·1	230·0	163·7			1952
205·0	276·7	324·2	215·4	146·6	339·0	240·3	171·4			1953
212·4	295·7	339·4	227·4	165·7	359·6	253·9	178·1			1954
226·5	317·6	346·4	235·6	174·3	371·6	267·4	183·6	343·7	223·1	1955
237·3	329·6	364·1	243·8	186·8	383·1	283·5	187·3		218·0	1956
250·1	338·9	366·9	254·7	194·8	394·9	291·6	191·2		254·3	1957
262·3	.337·9	371·2	258·6	203·6	405·1	286·3	192·8	426·5	264·6	1958
279·7	354·5	383·8	272·8	199·7	427·6	306·9	200·1	452·8	297·2	1959
297·2	384·2	397·7	288·4	204·3	442·7	324·8	209·7	479·1	315·9	1960
322·0	397·2	423·0	303·8	228·6	469·3	348·6	217·0	509·2	330·2	1961
342·2	412·2	443·1	323·8	249·9	486·2	366·3	219·8	531·3	336·4	1962
360·7	427·6	466·6	342·8	271·8	511·0	383·2	228·9	550·5	371·5	1963
371·1	465·7	489·1	367·1	288·5	550·1	402·6	241·3	591·2	406·9	1964
384·6	490·9	517·4	394·3	309·3	573·8	420·1	247·5	630·0	417·9	1965
407·3	503·5	539·9	409·5	334·3	593·3	432·1	252·8	669·2	440·4	1966
435·1	532·6	570·5	442·3	348·5	608·0	439·9	258·1	706·4	448·0	1967
462·8	567·7	593·7	475·0	368·2	627·6	458·2	265·8	737·5	457·4	1968
490·3	600·3	623·7	490·8	396·2	664·1	485·5	271·1	762·8		1969
515·4	633·7	646·9	527·7	423·0	694·5	506·0	276·5			1970

TABLE 23: Growth of Output in Selected Years 1937–1970
(1950=100)

	E. Germany	Poland	Rumania
1937		97·1	
1950	100·0	100·0	100·0
1960	173·9	156·6	176·0
1968	218·3	230·3	286·5

TABLE 24: Growth of Output in Selected Years 1926–38 (1938=100)

	Poland	Rumania
1926		87
1927		87
1928		87
1929	87	83
1930	83	89
1931	77	91
1932	71	86
1933	69	90
1934	70	91
1935	71	93
1936	73	94
1937	87	90
1938	100	100

BIBLIOGRAPHY

For the period between the wars the best book is W. A. Lewis, *Economic Survey 1919–1939*, Allen and Unwin, London, 1965. I. Svennilson *Growth and Stagnation of the European Economy*, ECE, Geneva, 1954, is an invaluable reference book although it advances a structuralist approach to inter-war problems with which I disagree. A. Maddison, 'Growth and Fluctuation in the World Economy 1870–1960' *Banca Nazionale del Lavoro Quarterly Review* June 1962 gives a brief description of the interrelations between trade and income in the inter-war and post-war period, and A. Maddison, *Economic Growth in the West*, Allen and Unwin, London 1964 gives a comprehensive coverage of post-war economic performance and policy up to the end of the 1950s. E. Lundberg, *Instability and Economic Growth*, Yale, 1968 is a good analysis of cyclical movements and policy problems in individual countries. Economic analysis of the war experience and its consequences is as yet inadequate. There is a massive collection of volumes on all belligerents for the First World War edited by J. S. Shotwell for the Carnegie Foundation, but most of the volumes are descriptive and not analytical. J. M. Keynes, *The Economic Consequences of Peace*, Macmillan, London, 1920 is still the most useful study of the consequences of the First World War. On the Second World War there are a number of individual country studies but no general survey of the European economy. The best of the country studies is the one by the US Strategic Bombing Survey, Overall Economic Effects Division, *The Effects of Strategic Bombing on the German War Economy, 1945*. This was written by a bevy of stars including Galbraith, Kaldor, Scitovsky and Denison but is now a rare book. More accessible and based on the same material is A. Speer, *Inside the Third Reich*, Weidenfeld and Nicolson, London 1970. On the 1920s, F. D. Graham, *Exchange, Prices and Production in Hyper-Inflation in Germany 1920–23*, Princeton 1930, helps considerably to demystify the German inflation. The article by K. Hancock, 'Unemployment and the Economists in the 1920s', *Economica*, November 1960 is a useful study of British economic thought. The article by R. C. O. Matthews, 'Why has Britain had Full Employment Since the War,' *Economic Journal*, September 1968 is a short but penetrating analysis with historical perspective. On French economic history the best book is by J.-J. Carré, P. Dubois and E. Malinvaud, *La Croissance Française*, Seuil, Paris 1972.

10. International Trade and Capital Movements 1920-1970

Carlo Zacchia*

MAIN FEATURES AND POLICY LINES

MAIN FEATURES

For a review of the foreign trade and capital movements of
the European countries from 1920 to 1970, a number of
sub-periods – each of them with specific features – can be
distinguished: the expansion during most of the twenties,
the Great Depression, the short recovery of the thirties in a
policy framework quite different from that of the previous
decade, the Second World War, the continuous period of
expansion following it, the first signs of an acceleration of
inflation at the end of the 1960s also for import and export
prices.

During the First World War the level of output and
foreign trade fell in Europe as a whole and in most individual
countries.[1] The decline was bigger for trade than for output
and it affected more seriously intra-European trade than
trade flows between Europe and the other regions. A part
of the European overseas investment was sold (to finance
the war effort) or was confiscated. Therefore, the investment income accruing to Europe was smaller in 1918
than in 1913. These are obvious consequences of a war
which was fought mainly among European countries and
the sequence of events was largely the same during the

* The author is a member of the Secretariat of the United Nations
Economic Commission for Europe (ECE) but the views expressed in
this paper are his own and they do not necessarily reflect those of the
Organization.
He wishes to thank Mr. N. Marian and Mr. R. Notel who read part of
a previous draft and made useful suggestions.

1. When not otherwise specified, the word 'output' is used in this
study to denote gross national product (GNP); similarly, when not
otherwise specified, changes in trade (or in output) refer to changes in
real terms (that is at constant prices).

Second World War. After the socialist revolution, the contribution of Russia to European and world trade fell drastically for a number of years in comparison with the pre-revolution levels.

It is customary in economic and monetary histories to split the twenties into two periods: a first one going from the end of the war up to 1923 and characterized by political tensions, monetary instability and, in some countries, by run-away inflation; and a second one going from 1924 to 1929, and characterized by much more stable conditions in the political as well as in the monetary field. In the second half of the twenties, the deep-felt goal of 'going back to normal' seemed to be reached. True, the two periods present profound differences in many respects, but when the attention is focused on medium- and long-term trends in real terms rather than on short-term monetary vicissitudes most of the twenties appears as a period of rapid growth in output and foreign trade. As far as can be judged from fragmentary data, foreign trade rose virtually at the same rate as output at least for the most important European countries (at near five per cent per year). Foreign lending was resumed on a large scale and short-term capital movements – partly connected with the problem of German war reparations – took dimensions quite unknown before the war. In the field of long-term capital movements, direct investment (as opposed to portfolio investments) started to be of an increasing importance – a shift which was associated with the emergence of the United States as a major creditor country.

The great depression was, in the fields of commercial policies, foreign trade and capital movements, perhaps even more than in other fields, the end of an epoch. Trade fell as abruptly as output in volume and even more severely in value since prices dropped dramatically for most internationally traded commodities. As usually happens in periods of depression, intra-European trade – which at that time was largely concentrated among a small number of already industrialized countries – fell in volume more than trade between Europe and overseas regions. The depression was further aggravated by hectic (mainly short-term) capital movements until foreign lending came virtually to a standstill. All the attempts to cope with the crisis on the basis of a broad international approach failed under the urgency of immediate national difficulties. Each government felt that it had no choice but to safeguard the immediate (and often dramatic) needs of his own country. Thus, in 1933 the European landscape of commercial policies had little in common with that of 1928. The previous multilateral system of trade and payments had been replaced by bilateral agreements, clearings and quotas.

The recovery in output and foreign trade which started in 1933-4 was short-lived; it was interrupted in 1939 by the Second World War. It took place in a framework of protectionist and, in some cases, autarkist policies; it is therefore not surprising if foreign trade grew less than output for Europe as a whole and for most individual countries. The equilibrium of the national trade balances was (precariously) reached at much lower trade levels than those prevailing before the great depression. The trade of the major European countries was further concentrated into preferential areas (the British trade within the sterling area and the French trade within the franc area). In Germany commercial policies and trade agreements were made increasingly dependent upon political and military considerations and various agreements were concluded with Italy and the central and south-eastern European countries for an exchange of raw materials and agricultural foodstuffs against manufactures.

On the eve of the Second World War, the level of industrial output was higher than in 1913 in Europe as a whole and probably in all European countries, but, for Europe as a whole, the export volume was lower. The overall decline was essentially due to the three major western European countries (the United Kingdom, Germany and France), to the Soviet Union and to Switzerland. In 1938 the export level was lower than in 1913 by probably ten to twenty per cent in the United Kingdom, France and Switzerland, by no less than 25 per cent in Germany and by a wider margin in the Soviet Union. In most other countries it was higher but the increase lagged behind the output increase recorded in the same period by the individual countries. The import volume was higher in 1938 than in 1913 in Europe as a whole and in most individual countries (during the late thirties imports were swelled by stockpiling for military purposes). The financing of exports was made possible by an improvement in the terms of trade which may perhaps be estimated at twenty per cent for the period.

During the Second World War, both output and foreign trade fell again in most individual countries and in Europe as a whole and, as was the case in the First World War, the decline was sharper for trade than for output. However, the recovery was more rapid than after the First World War. For the western European countries combined, the 1938 level of industrial production was already reached in 1948, that is only three years after the end of the war while the 1913 level had been reached again only in 1924 (that is six years after the end of the war). The lag witnessed by foreign trade in respect of the output during the First World War was not recaptured during the twenties when, as we have seen, output and trade volume expanded virtually *pari passu*. By contrast, the lag witnessed by trade in respect of production during the Second World War had been made good already at the beginning of the fifties. In 1950, both industrial production and *exports* were nearly thirty per cent above their 1938 level for the OECD countries combined. True, the rapid recovery was partly due to the Korean war but even when that occasional factor subsided, the underlying trend remained strongly upward. On the other hand, aggregate *imports* of the western European countries were in 1950 only ten per cent higher than in 1938. Since then, the growth rate of exports and imports was very similar to each other (about eight per cent per year). Technological and structural factors had brought about a change in the relative pre-war level of imports and exports which remained a lasting feature of the European foreign trade with the other regions. After the Second World

War, merchandise exports have contributed more, and factor income has contributed less than before the war to the equilibrium of the current balance of payments of the western European countries combined.

Albania, Bulgaria, Czechoslovakia, Hungary, Yugoslavia, Poland, Rumania and the eastern part of Germany underwent after the Second World War a political and social revolution which affected deeply the development and especially the pattern of their foreign trade. In these countries – as in the Soviet Union – the pre-war level of output and trade was reached only at the beginning of the fifties but thereafter expansion was quite fast. Most of the pre-war commercial links were discontinued and foreign trade was largely concentrated inside the group of the socialist countries, where it became part and parcel of the planned economic system. Since the late forties, therefore, the split of Europe between 'market economies' and 'centrally planned economies' was fully reflected in the trade field. Trade relations between the two groups of countries (the so-called east-west trade) became insignificant in comparison with the volume of trade which was taking place inside the two groups. However, starting from a very low basis, east-west trade grew fast in the fifties and in the sixties and indeed at a faster rate than most other major intra-European trade flows.

On the whole, the post-war period has been characterized in Europe by an unprecedented rate of growth for both output and foreign trade; in volume terms, trade expanded at a considerably higher rate than output (a distinct novelty in comparison with the previous period).[2] However, Europe's trade with the other regions rose only slightly more than did output in Europe. The very rapid expansion of foreign trade was mainly due to intra-European trade

2. In value terms, the difference between the growth rate of output and trade was quite small since prices rose much more rapidly for output than for foreign trade. This is hardly surprising since the basket composition of 'output' (that is of GNP) is quite different from that of foreign trade and contains a large share of services; in this sector prices rise faster (and productivity less fast) than in the commodity-producing

whose development has been a typical feature of post-war Europe. It is mainly constituted by an exchange of manufactured products against other manufactured products and it takes place among countries having not too different levels of output per head and an increasingly similar industrial structure. Disregarding short-term vicissitudes and special national cases, the growth rate of foreign trade has been rather steady during the two decades for Europe taken as a whole and for its major groupings. Foreign lending, too, rose fast in the post-war period. In the field of long-term capital movements three main flows can be noticed: first, the flow of direct investment from the United States to western Europe; second, the flow of portfolio investment from Europe to the United States; and, third, the flow of capital towards the developing countries. Short-term capital movements were relatively unimportant during the fifties when administrative controls were still in force in this field; but they took a new dimension in the sixties and particularly towards the end of the period.

COMMERCIAL POLICIES, INTER-WAR PERIOD

The deep-felt wish for 'a return to normality' (that is to the pre-war world) which was a typical feature of the first post-war years was fully reflected in the interrelated fields of monetary system, foreign trade, and international capital movements. For trade and capital movements, the return to normal essentially meant the removal of the administrative controls and other obstacles imposed in virtually all countries during the war, and the re-establishment of the philosophy of *laissez-faire*. For the international monetary system, the goal was to go back to the 'gold standard' which had been established over a large part of the world by 1914. Closely associated with the desire

---

sectors. Foreign trade includes by definition only commodities. If a comparison is made between export and import prices on the one hand and the domestic prices of only the commodity-producing sectors on the other hand, the difference becomes much smaller but still foreign trade prices rose (slightly) less than domestic prices until the end of the sixties in most European countries.

to go back to a system of 'gold standard' was the widespread belief that the depreciation of most European currencies vis-à-vis the US dollar was a temporary phenomenon. The national economies were supposed to be sufficiently flexible to allow for a restoration of the old currency parities without putting an excessive burden on the level of output and employment. The deep changes which had taken place during the war in productivity, cost and price levels were not fully grasped; neither was their lasting nature.

The hard conditions prevailing in Europe in the first half of the twenties prevented any stabilization; in that period the general practice was that of fluctuating exchange rates and changes in parities were often used by governments as an instrument of commercial policy. The general impoverishment caused by the war and the troubled social conditions (not to speak of the political complications) were powerful inflationary factors which prevented not only the return to the pre-war parities but also the fixing of any lasting parity whatsoever. As extreme cases of this general climate, suffice here to recall the sweeping inflation which plagued Germany, Austria, Hungary and Poland. Monetary stabilizations took place only later – in 1924 and 1925 – when the most dramatic legacies of the war on the political as well as the economic field had subsided. The German mark was stabilized in 1924 and the British sterling in 1925: the Italian lira in 1926: but it was only in 1927 that a *de facto* stabilization took place of the French franc.[3] Looking at the situation *expost*, it clearly appears that the currency stabilizations of the mid-twenties were the effect of the (relative) stabilization which in the meantime had taken place in the economic and political sphere, even though the opposite view was prevailing in those years when the stabilization of the currency was often considered as a pre-condition for the stabilization of the economy.

3. In fact, the system officially recommended – at an international conference held in Genoa in 1922 under the auspices of the League of Nations – was a system of 'gold exchange standard'. See League of Nations, *International Currency Experience* (Princeton 1944) for a detailed account of the monetary vicissitudes in the inter-war period.

The currency stabilization affected international trade of the individual countries in quite a different way depending essentially on the rate of exchange which was chosen. Thus, the exchange rate chosen in 1925 for sterling (4.96 dollars per one pound sterling, that is the pre-war exchange rate) was too high in relation to the price level in the United Kingdom and put a brake on the expansion of the British exports which declined in 1926 and rose only modestly in the following three years. In 1929, the volume of British exports was only nine per cent higher than in 1925. Very much the same happened in Italy with the currency stabilization of 1926. By contrast, the French franc was stabilized (in 1927 as already mentioned) at a very low rate and exports continued to grow rapidly until the end of the twenties. In 1929, they were eighteen per cent higher than in 1925. Since this chapter deals with trade flows and capital movements, the monetary vicissitudes will not be illustrated in detail. Two points, however, are worth recalling for their direct impact on trade. First, the potential benefits of the stabilization were partly frustrated because the exchange rates did not always closely reflect the relative price levels in the various countries. Second, the belief that national price levels would adjust themselves to the new currency parities without serious consequences on the development of output and exports proved wrong.

If the exchange rate policy did not provide a firm basis for a generalized and lasting development of international trade, it was fairly obvious – and it was generally recognized – that at the end of the war by far the major obstacle to the expansion of international trade lay in the thick network of quantitative controls established by the countries during the war, and their dismantling was the main concern of a series of international conferences (most of them held under the auspices of the League of Nations).[4] The repeated

4. The major international conferences held in the twenties with the main goal of dismantling trade barriers were the following:

(1) The *Brussels Financial Conference*, October 1920. This was the first international conference convened by the League of Nations. The conference adopted a resolution stating *inter alia* that commerce should

attempts to remove administrative controls were only partially successful. In the most industrialized European countries including the United Kingdom, the Netherlands, Belgium and the Scandinavian countries, such controls had been very largely removed by the end of 1919 but in the other European countries the return to relatively unrestricted trading conditions was somewhat slower. In Italy and Spain a large amount of control remained in force even after the introduction of new and higher tariffs in 1921 and 1922 respectively. In France there was some

---

as soon as possible be freed from control, and impediments to international trade removed.

(2) The *London Congress of the International Chamber of Commerce*, 1921. The conference stressed in particular the importance of moderating and stabilizing the level of customs tariffs – a point to which no direct reference had been made in previous conferences.

(3) The *Genoa Conference*, May 1922. The conference was convened by the Supreme Council of the League of Nations and made recommendations in the field of administrative controls and tariff levels, dumping, differential prices, and related matters like customs formalities, unfair competition and double taxation.

(4) The *'prohibition conferences'* of 1927–29. These were held in Geneva under the auspices of the League of Nations and were prepared by its Economic Committee. There were three conferences, which were held respectively in October 1927, in June 1928 and in December 1929. At the first conference (October 1927) an international convention was adopted whereby the participating countries took the commitment to abolish within a period of six months most of the existing import and export prohibitions or restrictions. In the second conference (held in June 1928) it was agreed that the convention would come into force if ratified by 18 States before September 30, 1929. By that date, however, only 17 ratifications had been deposited. By a special arrangement, the convention was brought into force beginning January 1930 by only a few countries (in fact by those countries whose administrative controls had already only a very limited range). By the middle of 1934, it had been denounced by all of them.

(5) *The world economic conference*, May 1927. The conference was decided in 1925 and it was hoped that by the time it was scheduled to meet, administrative controls to foreign trade would have completely disappeared. This, in fact, was not the case. The conference centred its attention on the problem of tariff levels and tariff structures but there were on the whole very limited practical results. (See, for a detailed account: League of Nations, *Commercial policy in the inter-war period: international proposals and national policies*, Geneva 1942).

relaxation in 1919 but a large number of sensitive commodities remained subject to administrative controls. Switzerland dropped most of its war-time controls in 1919 but reintroduced a permit system for sensitive imports in 1921.

The removal of the quantitative restrictions proceeded much more slowly in the central and south-east European countries where trade had practically ceased at the end of the war and was only gradually resuming, first on the basis of intergovernmental barter and later on the basis of the clearing systems. In view of the appalling situation prevailing in this area at the end of the war, the goal of a rapid return to 'free trade' could not claim high priority; but the establishment (or the restoration) of sizeable trade flows took more time than was generally expected, because of lack of timely and adequate reconstruction plans on the one hand and nationalistic rivalries on the other hand.[5] The peace treaties of 1919 contained a number of provisions in the field of commercial policies concerning the defeated and the newly created countries. Thus, Germany, Austria, Hungary and Bulgaria were ordered to grant the 'allied and associated powers' unconditional most favoured nation treatment, for a certain number of years. These were punitive measures and could not be expected to provide a contribution to the economic reconstruction of these countries. In a more positive mood, Austria and Hungary were permitted to enter into a special (preferential) custom regime with each other and/or with Czechoslovakia for a period not exceeding five years, but this clause was never implemented by the interested countries. In 1921 an international conference was held in Portorose (Yugoslavia) where the succession States of the Austro-Hungarian empire agreed to re-establish 'as soon as possible' free trade among them; but this convention was not ratified by any of the participating countries. It was only later – when the most dramatic consequences of the war on the internal political and economic life of these countries

5. For some indications about the reconstruction plans in the first post-war period, see section 3 of this chapter (capital movements).

subsided – that the administrative controls on foreign trade were loosened or abolished in this region. Thus, Hungary abolished her whole system of export and import provisions in the course of 1924; Austria established free dealings in foreign exchanges in March 1925; in 1925 Germany too abolished the licensing system but in the same year the system was reintroduced in Poland.

The gradual dismantling of the quantitative controls brought to the forefront the problem of the customs tariffs. On *a priori* ground it could have been expected that the dismantling of the administrative controls would have been paralleled (or followed) by a reduction and consolidation of the tariff barriers. In fact, this did not happen. The United States was among the first to raise a large range of customs tariffs (in 1921-22) to offset the (real or alleged) increased competition of the European goods due to the currency depreciation in European countries, particularly in Germany. But in the first half of the twenties, most European countries replaced the pre-war tariffs with new ones. Though comparing the level of two tariffs is by no means a simple exercise (mainly because of difference in classification and degree of detail), there is a' fairly general consensus that most of the post-war tariffs contained higher duties than the pre-war ones. Furthermore, modification of the basic duties were mostly in the upward direction from the beginning of the twenties up to the great depression (when administrative controls were re-established). Up to about 1925 the main increases in tariffs referred to industrial goods but after 1925 a number of countries (in particular, Italy, Germany and France) raised the tariff levels also for agricultural commodities.[6] True, the tariffs as approved by governments and parliaments were not in fact applied as such. They contained the maximum tariffs which were often lowered in country-to-country agreements. This was already the pre-war practice. But most of the post-war agreements were of a short-term nature and,

6. For a detailed review of the tariff policies in Europe in the twenties see H. Liepman, *Tariff levels and the economic unit of Europe,* London 1938.

furthermore, the contracting parties retained the right to increase specific duties in certain circumstances. No general *international* agreement could be reached to peg the national duties at a certain level without limit of time. Custom duties thus became – as the exchange policy – an instrument of the commercial policy (in some cases, it would be more correct to say 'of the commercial warfare').

The downturn in output and foreign trade started in most European countries towards the end of 1929 or the beginning of 1930. Yet, in 1930, commercial policies remained generally quite liberal. Only a few countries introduced physical controls for the imports of selected agricultural products. (As is well known, prices of most agricultural products fell dramatically at the beginning of the great depression and Governments were faced with the problem of defending domestic production and the level of the farmers' income against foreign competition). Thus, in 1930 Spain prohibited the import of wheat and Czechoslovakia imposed a licensing system for imports of rye and barley. The massive wave of import controls for foodstuffs came in 1931 when the economic situation – and the situation of the agricultural sector in particular – deteriorated further in Europe and in the United States. The years 1932 and 1933 saw a fairly general reimposition of controls also on industrial products.[7] Slowly, three major trading areas emerged in Europe on the ashes of the defunct multilateral system of trade and payments. One commercial area had the United Kingdom as leader and was mainly constituted by the sterling area (that is, by non-European countries). Sterling was devalued in 1931 (and made inconvertible into gold) and the system of the imperial preferences was reinforced. Within this system, trade and capital movements continued to develop with relatively few physical controls. A second area had France as its leader. France and other countries (Belgium, Netherlands, Switzerland, Italy and Poland) did not follow the devaluation of the sterling and formed the so-called 'gold

7. For a detailed analysis, see: League of Nations, *Quantitative trade controls*, Geneva 1943.

bloc'. The overvaluation of these currencies – further amplified by the devaluation of the dollar in 1933 – forced the respective governments to follow a severe deflationary policy which prevented – especially in France – any revival in output and trade. The 'gold bloc' area was short-lived: France devalued in 1936 and Italy had already attached itself to the German area. The third commercial area had Germany as its leader. Germany too refused to devalue but at the same time the then Nazi government took virtually complete control of foreign trade and capital movements. Imports and exports were increasingly conducted on the basis of clearing agreements, and of exchange of products against other products. In these conditions, the level of the exchange rate had little practical significance. Most of these 'agreements' were concluded with the other central European and Danubian countries.

COMMERCIAL POLICIES, POST-WAR PERIOD

Commercial policies of the socialist countries and of the market economy countries differ considerably (for the instruments more than for the goals) and it is therefore convenient to examine separately the two regional sub-groupings.

For the *market economies*, the basic philosophy underlying commercial policies after the Second World War was not fundamentally different from that of the First World War. In fact, the two basic principles that had shaped the commercial and exchange rate policy after the First World War were retained after the Second World War, that is, the dismantling of administrative and other barriers for foreign trade and capital movements on the one hand, and stable exchange rates on the other hand. But the objective conditions as well as the practical implementation of the guiding principles had little in common in the two periods. First, there was a difference in the political landscape of Europe. After the First World War the national rivalries among the European countries constituted a severe obstacle to the framing and even more to the implementation of a co-ordinated economic policy at international level. After the

Second World War, the political and ideological differences between the two European sub-groups (socialist countries and market economy countries) operated as a cohesive factor for the market economy countries. Furthermore, most of the remaining market economies were constituted by industrialized countries with rather similar levels of income per head and a similar industrial pattern – and, therefore, with rather similar needs and problems. A second difference was to be found not in the field of commercial policy but in the management of the domestic economy. Full (or near full) employment was accepted by all countries as a priority target. The so-called 'Keynesian revolution' provided a new insight into the operation of market forces and made possible a control of the cyclical fluctuations which was quite unknown in the inter-war period. Third, the bitter experience of the twenties and the thirties provided a telling lesson for policy-makers: in particular, it made it clear that commercial policies were to be integrated much more closely than it was the case after the First World War with domestic economic policies and that a much stronger institutional basis was needed. Fourth (but probably this is the most important factor though it is linked with the previous ones), in the post-war period commercial policies operated in an atmosphere dominated by the aim of economic growth and in fact output rose much faster than in any past period of similar length and shortage of resources became an overriding preoccupation for governments.[8] In this new political and economic climate, seemingly identical principles took a different tinge and led to quite different results than after the First World War.

After lengthy discussions about the virtues of stable and fluctuating exchange rates, a system of fixed exchange rates was chosen (at the Bretton Woods conference) and the dollar and the pound sterling were considered as reserve currencies. The dollar was convertible into gold and the system became *de facto* a system of dollar standard.

8. See below (p. 549) for a brief discussion about the relevance of this new situation on the expansion of foreign trade.

A new international organization was created, the 'International Monetary Fund' to which the fixed parities should be communicated. The Fund was charged with important operative tasks. It was agreed that in case of 'fundamental' disequilibria in balance of payments, the currency in question had to be devalued (or revalued) while 'temporary' imbalances had to be corrected with appropriate fiscal and monetary policies – and with the assistance of the Fund which was authorized to grant short-term credits. But in order to get the financial assistance of the Fund the country concerned had to submit its own programme which had to be accepted by the Fund. Most of the European currencies in fact stabilized fairly soon after the war (in 1947–48). The major changes in parities up to the end of the sixties were the following: in 1949, the British pound sterling was devalued and in its wake most other European currencies devalued too. A new devaluation of the pound sterling took place in 1967 and was accompanied by devaluations in Denmark, Finland, Ireland and Spain. In Germany a new currency (the Deutsche Mark) was introduced in 1949 which was revalued in 1961 and 1969.[9] France devalued in 1958 and in 1968.

This system (the Bretton Woods system) remained virtually in force until the beginning of the seventies and it collapsed when the dollar convertibility into gold was discontinued and most west European countries adopted a floating exchange rate in respect of the dollar and, in some cases, also among themselves.

For the dismantling of trade barriers and in particular for the lowering of the customs tariffs another organization was set up (in 1948) the GATT. This organization, as the IMF, operates at world level but, as in the case of IMF, its activity is of particular relevance for the industrialized countries with a market economy system. The GATT has convened a series of tariff negotiations among all the participating countries the first of which took place in 1949. The tariff negotiations continued during the fifties and were

9. The revaluation of the DM in 1961 was accompanied by a similar revaluation of the Dutch florin.

generally conducted on an item-by-item basis of the national tariffs (each including thousands of items). Towards the end of the fifties, the need was felt for a bolder approach. The creation of the regional sub-groupings in western Europe aroused anxieties in the United States as to the likely effect of the newly established discrimination on their export trade with Europe. Thus, the United States government took the initiative of a new round aiming at an *overall* tariff reduction. A major tariff negotiation took place in 1964–67 (the so-called Kennedy round) and the results were quite substantial for the tariff levels of the industrial products (of primary importance for the industrialized countries).[10]

At the European level, the Organization for European Economic Co-operation (OEEC) was set up in 1948. Its primary task was to elaborate and implement a reconstruction programme and, in this framework, to allocate the financial help provided by the United States. This programme known as the European Recovery Programme (ERP) lasted from 1948 to 1951.[11] The actual results fell short of the ambitious targets which foresaw, among other things, a close co-ordination of the national policies and in particular of investment plans. Yet, in comparison with the policies followed after the First World War (when no comprehensive programme of reconstruction was implemented) it was a conspicuous success. Simultaneously, OEEC started to be active in the two inter-related fields of commercial policies and balance of payments. In these two fields, IMF and GATT operate – as we have seen – at world level while OEEC carved out a more specific programme for the European member countries. In the field of trade policies, its major target in the late forties was the gradual dismantling of the quantitative controls. The results in this field were quite satisfactory while an ambitious

10. They were much more modest for the hard core of quantitative restrictions and for agricultural products (of special interest for the developing countries).

11. It is also known as the 'Marshall plan' after the name of the United States State Secretary who launched the programme.

scheme of creating a customs union in western Europe failed. Within western Europe, trade and payments liberalization proceeded rather rapidly but it was purposely postponed vis-à-vis the United States. As had been the case in the First World War, the American economy had recorded a rapid output expansion also during the Second World War while the European economies declined. The ensuing imbalances in the trade flows between the two areas gave rise to the so-called 'dollar shortage' – a problem which seemed intractable at that time to many observers but which in fact disappeared during the fifties (because the European reconstruction was more rapid and more lasting than most observers thought it would be). In the field of international payments, OEEC set up in 1950 the European Payments Union (EPU) which gave a considerable contribution to soften the effects on economic growth of short-term imbalances in the current accounts of the OEEC member countries. Under the EPU arrangements, automatic lines of credit were granted (within limits) by the surplus to the deficit countries. The EPU lasted until 1958 when convertibility of the European currencies was re-established vis-à-vis the dollar. In 1960, the OEEC was replaced by the OECD (Organization for Economic Co-operation and Development) of which the United States and Canada are full members (subsequently Japan and Australia also joined). The replacement of OEEC by OECD marks in a sense, the end of the reconstruction period for western Europe.

Projects for sub-regional customs unions started early in the post-war period but (except for the special case of the customs union between Belgium, Luxemburg and the Netherlands) no practical result was reached until 1958 when – on the basis of the Rome Treaty of 1957 – the European Economic Community was created. The original member countries were the Benelux countries, France, western Germany and Italy. The European Economic Community intends to be much more than a customs unit but it is in this field that so far the major progress has been achieved. By 1968, intra-trade in commodities was free of duties and a common external tariff had been put into effect. A much more complicated mechanism was established for agricultural products with a view of unifying national agricultural markets of EEC countries and protecting these markets against foreign competition (with a system of customs duties and export subsidies). On the whole, the agricultural policy of the Common Market presents strong protectionist features and is still the subject of lively debates.

The creation in 1958 of the Common Market was followed in 1959 by the creation of the European Free Trade Area. The participating countries were Austria, Denmark, Norway, Portugal, Sweden, Switzerland and the United Kingdom. Finland became an associate member in 1961. The goals of the FTA are much more modest than those of the European Economic Community and the institutional set-up much less impressive. Agricultural products were excluded but some of them have been reclassified as industrial products. As it has been the case for the Common Market, the abolition of duties and of the remaining administrative controls proceeded more rapidly than foreseen. Quantitative restrictions had virtually disappeared (with some exceptions for Finland and Portugal) by 1965 and customs duties had been completely abolished already by 1964. In 1970, Denmark and the United Kingdom (and Ireland) became members of the enlarged European Economic Community and the Free Trade Association includes at present Austria, Norway, Sweden, Switzerland, Finland and Portugal.

In sum, the process of dismantling trade barriers for industrial goods inside western Europe has proceeded quite rapidly in the post-war period. This process has been powerfully helped by more skilful domestic policies for the control of aggregate demand, by a better realization than after the First World War of the close inter-dependence of the various western European economies and – last but not least – by the rapid pace of technological progress and the associated economies of scale. In turn, trade liberalization became one of the major factors behind the unprecedented growth of output in western Europe in the post-war period.

Commercial policies of the *east European countries* are part and parcel of their centrally planned system. Immediately after the war, there were hopes that the east European countries could participate in the new international organizations set up (largely at the initiative of the United States and the United Kingdom) to frame and implement international economic policies. But this hope rapidly vanished. Thus, the eastern European countries did not become members of IMF, GATT or OEEC when these institutions were set up (with the exception of Czechoslovakia for GATT). Their non-participation reflected not only a refusal to accept, *de facto*, a minority role on these organizations but also deeply different views about the guiding principles embodied in their statutes. At present (1974) the situation has partly changed for GATT as Poland, Rumania and Hungary are full members of this institution. Rumania became at the beginning of the seventies a member also of the IMF (and of its sister organization, the International Bank for Reconstruction and Development).[12]

In early 1949 the eastern European countries established their own organization for economic co-operation, the 'Council for Mutual Economic Assistance' (CMEA) which at that time could be considered as being in some respects a parallel of OEEC. In assessing the activity of this organization and, more generally, the commercial policy of the east European countries, their institutional set-up has to be kept in mind. By 1949, all the eastern European countries had introduced central economic planning including a State monopoly for foreign trade. Under this system 'each State trading enterprise has the exclusive right to trade with other countries in its particular field of activity in accord-

12. For details about the protocols of accession to GATT of Hungary, Poland, and Rumania, see ECE, *A review of east-west commercial policy developments, 1968 to 1973*, in 'Economic Bulletin for Europe', vol. 25, 1973. This article also provides (as the title indicates) a general review of policies in the most recent years.

ance with the State foreign trade plan defining the quantities and values of product groups to be imported or exported by each enterprise in the plan period, with a varying degree of specification by geographical or currency area. This system does not allow any direct competition between domestic producers and traders on foreign markets; nor is there any direct competition with foreign producers and traders on the domestic market.'[13] Though the basic institutional set-up has not been changed radically, its practical function has been made considerably more flexible in recent years. In particular foreign trade enterprises have been empowered to set up export or servicing agencies in foreign markets, major producing enterprises or associations of producers have been authorized to participate directly in foreign trade operations, and in some cases, domestic producers have been allowed to retain part of the receipt of their exports in order to finance the import of necessary producer goods. The earlier prevailing system of item-by-item price differentials between foreign trade and domestic prices is being increasingly replaced by uniform foreign trade coefficients which fundamentally implies a transition from differential towards more uniform foreign exchange rates. These modifications, even if they still do not permit *direct* competition between domestic and foreign producers, leave an increasing scope for some kind of *indirect competition*.

In the framework of this general institutional set-up, bilateral trade agreements were (and are) the main instruments for conducting foreign trade – inside the group of the socialist countries and with the market economies as well. The two trade flows, however, cannot be put entirely on the same footing. Foreign trade inside the socialist group is closely linked with the overall process of economic planning and specialization which takes place among the

13. ECE, *Analytical report on the state of intra-European trade* (New York 1970), p. 42. This report reviews in some detail the commercial policies and practices governing east-west trade (and also intra-east trade) in the post-war period. For the most recent developments see the ECE publication quoted in footnote 12.

socialist countries.[14] Three periods can be distinguished in this context. In the years up to 1953 a major effort was made for putting in motion and carrying on a process of rapid industrialization, the priority being given to heavy industry and to capital goods. The planning technique which was generally used – following the example of the Soviet Union – was that of the so-called 'material balances'. In this period, the almost exclusive role of foreign trade was to provide a given country with the necessary raw material and/or capital goods which was not possible to produce at home or not in sufficient quantities.[15] In the years following 1953 a second period started in which more attention was given to the problem of inter-country specialization in output, in some cases by means of a co-ordination of the national medium-term plans. In May 1956 twelve permanent commissions were established at the CMEA to promote plan co-ordination and specialization of production among the member countries in various sectors of industry and agriculture.

While in the previous period the emphasis was almost exclusively put on import substitution, in the second phase more consideration started to be given also to imports and exports as an instrument of reducing costs and therefore to the possibilities of judging import and export policies on the basis of efficiency and relative productivity. Foreign trade was no longer only seen as a means of supplementing domestic resources but also as an engine of growth *via* a more efficient allocation of resources. But the extensive use of efficiency criteria proved difficult to reconcile with the domestic cost and price structure. The third phase, which started in the second half of the 1960s, was associated with the process of economic reforms in national planning and can be considered as an accentuation of the tendencies

14. For an analysis of planning techniques for foreign trade in the socialist countries of eastern Europe up to 1963–64, see UN/ECE, *Economic Planning in Europe* (Geneva, 1965) especially chapter iv.

15. For more details on the concentration of foreign trade on 'essentials', imported as far as possible from other countries of the area see UN/ECE, *Economic Bulletin for Europe*, vol. 11, no. 1, 1959, p. 39 ff.

already noticeable during the second phase. There were no radical changes in the guiding principles of the commercial policies, but there was a considerable and growing role assigned to foreign trade in the overall system of economic planning. The 'Comprehensive programme of further intensification and improvement of co-operation and development of socialist economic integration of CMEA member countries', adopted in July 1971, provided a more flexible framework for planning intra-area exchanges.[16] Although the situation is by no means identical in the various socialist countries, on the whole economic criteria of efficiency and competition are given an increasing importance, especially in more recent years when it has become increasingly apparent in all countries of the area that they are gradually engaged in a more 'intensive' type of economic growth (mainly based on productivity increases).

East-west trade relations are also carried on mainly on the basis of bilateral agreements, and, as is the case for trade among the socialist countries, the system is moving towards a gradual liberalization. In the late forties, trade relations between socialist and market economies were in a lamentable situation. Political considerations added to the difficulties stemming from differences between the two social and economic systems. At the end of 1947 the United States put an embargo on exports of strategic materials to the eastern European countries and this principle was subsequently applied also by the western European countries. The United Nations Economic Commission for Europe (ECE) considered since its establishment the promotion of east-west trade as a priority task of its activity but for some years the results were anything but encouraging. In 1949, the 'Committee for the development of (east-west) trade' was set up but the political situation was so unfavourable that it was only in 1954 that the Committee was convened again. However, slowly, things started to change for the better. The list of strategic materials was reduced in 1954 and 1958 and after this second revision it no longer constitutes a serious obstacle to east-west trade

16. For details see *Economic Bulletin for Europe*, vol. 23, no. 2, p. 32.

relations. The dismantling of the administrative controls which, as we have seen, was relatively rapid inside western Europe, is proceeding more slowly for imports from the eastern European countries. Still, at the end of the sixties, liberalization covered as a rule 50 to 90 per cent of the value of imports of western from eastern Europe. Beginning in the sixties, three major factors made possible a rapid development of east-west trade. First, the multilateralization of payments: since early in the sixties, an eastern country can settle a deficit with a western country by utilization of a credit with another western country. This mechanism does not work on the other side but on the whole the process of payment multilateralization, partly with the help of the International Bank for Economic Co-operation (IBEC) has proceded further than laid down in the original rules.[17] Second, the increasing demand on the part of the eastern European countries for western products with a high technological content; and third, the stipulation of long-term agreements replacing the previous one-year agreements. The new role assigned to foreign trade in the over-all planning system with the 'intensive' pattern of growth and the increased attention paid to meeting consumer requirements have been leading to a very fast rise of CMEA's trade with the outside world, especially with developed market economies, in recent years. Its dynamism is, however, limited by the unfavourable structure of CMEA's exports concentrated on raw materials and agricultural products. The attempts at present under way to intensify the industrial co-operation between the western and the eastern European countries, aim *inter alia* at facilitating exports of manufactures from the eastern towards the western European countries and, in this way to enhance the possibilities for increasing eastern Europe's export earnings and thereby their capacity to import.[18]

17. The IBEC was set up in 1965. Its seat is in Moscow.
18. See UN/ECE, *Analytical report on industrial co-operation among ECE countries*, Geneva 1973.

FOREIGN TRADE

MAJOR TRADE FLOWS

A broad view of the relative development of international trade in current prices from 1913 to 1930 is provided by Table 1, where four trade flows have been singled out, that is, intra-European trade, exports from Europe to the other regions, imports into Europe from the other regions, trade among the non-European countries.[19] Unfortunately, such breakdown, for so long a period is not available at constant prices and therefore changes in the proportions or differences in growth rates may reflect changes in volume and/or in prices.

Statistical information on changes in terms of trade for individual European countries or for Europe as a whole before the Second World War is very deficient. It would appear anyhow, that between 1913 and 1929 the terms of trade improved sharply for the United Kingdom as a consequence of its export pattern (essentially constituted by manufactured goods) on the one side, and of the revaluation of sterling in 1926 on the other side. Terms of trade improved, but only slightly, for Germany, Sweden and Switzerland, while in France there was virtually no change (for most of the twenties, the French franc was undervalued in respect of the dollar and many other European currencies). In the other countries terms of trade deteriorated largely because of an unfavourable export pattern. Terms of trade turned sharply in Europe's favour during the great depression, because of the dramatic fall in most imported raw materials and agricultural commodities. Obviously, this improvement did not apply to all the European countries. The less developed, prevalently agricultural countries – and in particular those of the Balkan region – fully shared the terms of trade losses of the overseas primary exporting countries. A new deterioration for Europe started with the output

19. These four trade flows add up to total world trade.

revival and price stabilization in 1933; this was very mild up to 1938 but took large proportions during the Second World War. In fact, the deterioration of the thirties offset only a minor part of the improvement recorded during the great depression. After the Second World War, terms of trade remained relatively stable until 1948 but they deteriorated again for Europe in 1949 because of the wave of the European monetary devaluations, and in 1950 for the impact on the commodity markets of the Korean war. Since mid-1951, terms of trade turned again (gradually and slowly) in Europe's favour and this trend continued – disregarding cyclical vicissitudes and special national cases – until the beginning of the 1970s.[20]

Keeping these qualifications in mind about changes in terms of trade, Table 1 shows that, for the period as a whole, trade among the non-European countries grew faster than the other three trade flows: it accounted for only 15 per cent of total world trade in 1913 and for 30 per cent in 1970. At the other extreme are the two flows representing European exports to the other regions and European imports from outside Europe which grew less than either the trade among the non-European countries and intra-European trade. Intra-European trade grew less than trade among the non-European regions but more than trade between Europe and the other regions. It accounted for about one-third of total world trade in 1913 and for about 40 per cent in 1970. Over the period as a whole, there has been an increase in the share of both intra-European trade and of trade among the non-European countries (in relation to total world trade), while the trade flow between

20. A new deterioration in Europe's terms of trade started in 1972–73 when prices of most raw materials and agricultural products underwent an unprecedented price increase. The massive price increase for oil (1973) contributed further, of course, to the deterioration of Europe's terms of trade. But this is to enter the history of the seventies. For developments in terms of trade up to 1950, see UN/ECE, *Economic Survey of Europe since the war*, Geneva 1953. Terms of trade for subsequent years can be easily followed in national publications and in the 'Yearbooks of international trade statistics', prepared by the United Nations Secretariat.

Europe and the other regions represented a declining proportion of world trade.

The changes in the·proportions of the world trade which took place between 1913 and 1970˙and which have been just outlined conceaℓ the specific features of the sub-periods. The following major swings can be singled out: (i) It was in the first period shown (1913 to 1928) that trade among non-European countries made a big jump, its share in total world trade virtually doubling. This extremely rapid increase reflected rapid economic growth in the United States, Canada, Japan and the coming into the network of world trade of a large number of other (mainly colonial) countries which before the First World War had not yet reached the threshhold of exchange economies. After 1928, this fraction of the world trade fluctuated in both directions but in 1970 its share was not sizeably higher than in 1928.

In this period (1913 to 1928) the share of intra-European in total world trade declined only slightly and the increased share accounted for by trade among the non-European countries was mainly reflected in a relative decline of Europe's trade with the other regions. (ii) Between 1928 and 1938, the weight of 'trade among the non-European countries' in total world trade was considerably reduced partly because of the severity of the 'great depression' in the United States. Its decline was completely offset by a relative increase of the trade flows between Europe and the other regions while the intra-European share in world trade remained virtually unchanged. Therefore, intra-European trade that was equal to 70 per cent of the European trade (exports plus imports) with the other regions in 1928 fell to only 62 per cent in 1938. These two trade flows are of quite different nature: intra-European trade is constituted mainly by manufactured products and by agricultural products of temperate area, that is, broadly speaking by 'competitive' products in the sense that imports compete with domestic European production. It bears therefore the full impact of restrictive (or liberal) commercial policies. European imports from other regions are mainly constituted by raw materials and agricultural products from the tropical countries. They are, broadly speaking, non-competitive imports and their level is mainly dictated by the level of European output. In other words, the particularly severe decline of intra-European trade during the thirties was due to the fall of European output on the one hand and to restrictive policies on the other. The decline of European imports from the other regions was less severe because it stemmed essentially from the fall in European output (European exports to the other regions are mainly a function of their exports to the developed countries).[21]

(iii) The Second World War brought about a repetition of the sequence already experienced during the First World War, that is a rapid (relative) decline of intra-European trade in favour of European trade with the other regions and, especially, of the trade among the non-European countries. In 1950, intra-European trade was equal to only 50 per cent of European trade (exports plus imports) with the other regions against, as already mentioned, a ratio of 62 per cent in 1938 and of 70 per cent in 1928.

(iv) The two decades from 1950 to 1970 saw a dramatic reversal of the previous trends. As a consequence of an uninterrupted and extremely rapid growth, intra-European trade accounted in 1970 for about 40 per cent of world trade as against about 20 per cent in 1950 and was 30 per cent higher than the trade (exports plus imports) between Europe and the other regions. In previous periods, intra-European trade had remained constantly below the level of European trade with the other regions. The trade flows between Europe and the other regions (and in particular European imports) continued to lose in relative importance not only in respect of intra-European trade but also in respect of trade among the non-European countries.

So far Europe has been considered as a trading unity. Tables 2 and 3 provide some information about the foreign trade position of the individual European countries. The left side of Table 2 shows the percentage share of each

21. Towards the end of the thirties, European imports from other regions were swollen by stockpiling for military purposes.

European country in total European exports in selected years from 1913 to 1970; the right side of the table shows the percentage of national exports directed towards other European countries (the rest is directed towards countries outside Europe). Table 3 shows the same percentages for imports. In 1913, the United Kingdom and Germany were by far the two major exporting European countries; together, they accounted for nearly 50 per cent of total European countries. France accounted for about 12 per cent and Russia for about 7 per cent; Austria-Hungary, Italy and the Netherlands for about 5 per cent. The participation of the other countries was smaller. As could be expected, the situation was fairly similar for imports. However, for the United Kingdom the import share was higher than the export share because this country was (and still is) a large exporter of invisibles (transports, factor income). For the Netherlands too, the import share was considerably higher than the export share because of a large inflow of factor income consequent to capital exports.

The changes in the share of the individual countries over time have been considerable. The biggest change was recorded by the United Kingdom whose share in total European exports dropped from 24 per cent in 1913 to about 12 per cent in 1970. Apparently most of the decline took place in the fifties and the sixties but this may partly be a statistical illusion. At the beginning of the fifties, the defeated and occupied countries of the Second World War were only at the beginning of their recovery and the level of their foreign trade unduly low (this was particularly true of western Germany). Thus, the British decline probably started before. Some decline in the share of the United Kingdom was in the nature of things since this country was the first to industrialize and had been for many years the main exporter of manufactured products; but some special factors had a special relevance for the United Kingdom in the post-war period.[22] Suffice here to

22. The literature in this field is quite abundant indeed! For a major empirical investigation covering the pre-war period and the fifties, see A. Maizels, *Industrialization and world trade*, CUP, 1965.

remember only two points: first, in the pre-war period, the United Kingdom had a *de facto* monopoly in her colonies and dominions – which was gradually lost during the fifties and the sixties. Second, in this period trade expansion has been particularly rapid within western Europe, which traditionally was not the most important market for the United Kingdom (the share of Europe in total British exports was – and still is – much lower than for the other European countries).

Among the other major European countries, the share of France too declined (though only moderately) from 1913 to 1970, but in contrast with the United Kingdom, France's share rose from 1938 to 1970. The share of Germany fluctuated sharply from period to period but in 1970 the aggregate share of the Federal Republic and of the German Democratic Republic was virtually identical to the share of the German Reich in 1913. It has to be kept in mind however that the level of foreign trade in relation to the level of output is inversely correlated to the size of the country: the smaller (larger) the country, the higher (lower) is the ratio of foreign trade to domestic output. Therefore, the apparent stability may in this case conceal some decline (because the split of Germany into two countries has operated in the sense of raising the ratio 'foreign trade – output level').

The ground lost by the United Kingdom and (to a much less extent) by France has been gained by most of the remaining countries.[23] These countries – in spite of the differences in size and in the level of economic development – have one point in common as against the United Kingdom, France and Germany: their industrialization took place later than in the three countries just mentioned. Empirical research has shown that the rate of growth of industrial production has been in Europe negatively correlated to the level of GNP per head: the higher is the income level the lower is the growth rate of industrial

23. In percentage points particularly large has been the improvement recorded by Italy, the Netherlands and Sweden.

production.[24] The same phenomenon can be observed for foreign trade. Of course, special factors have variously affected individual countries. For instance, the discontinuation of most foreign trade relations in the Soviet Union after the revolution of 1918 resulted in relatively low trade flows until 1938. It was only at the beginning of the fifties that the level of 1913 was reached again. But the general principle of a relative loss on the part of the countries which were the first to industrialize and of a relative gain on the part of the other European countries (which industrialized later) seem difficult to disprove.

So far in this section, exports and imports have been considered at current prices. For the period going from 1913 to 1950 very little information is available on development of exports and imports at constant prices; and furthermore the international comparability of the national sources is very dubious. However, such fragmentary information as is available shows that in that period the development of foreign trade at constant prices was quite modest. Annual growth rates for exports have been estimated at 2 per cent for Sweden, between 1 and 1½ per cent for France, Italy and the Netherlands, 0·2 per cent for Belgium, Switzerland and the United Kingdom. For Germany, there was a net decline.[25] Exports rose more than output probably only in France – not so much because of a particularly high export development but rather because of a very low output increase (less than 1 per cent per year).

After the Second World War the situation has changed completely as can be seen from Table 4 which shows for the period 1950–52 to 1967–69, the growth rate for exports and imports at constant (1963) prices. The table also shows the growth elasticity of exports and imports in respect of

24. See UN/ECE, *Structural trends and prospects of the European Economy* (Economic Survey of Europe in 1969, part 1), Geneva 1970.

25. These figures have been taken from A. Maddison, *Economic growth in the west*, London 1964. For other empirical investigations in this field see A. Maizels, *Industrialization . . . op. cit.*; League of Nations, *Inaustrialization and foreign trade* 1945; H. B. Lary, *The United States in the world economy*, Washington 1943 (this last volume contains data not only for the United States but also for a group of European countries).

GNP. Finally, on the right side, the level of exports (of goods and services including factor income) is compared with the level of GNP in 1950 and 1970 at current prices. This part of the table refers only to the market economies since the centrally planned economies do not publish data on their current balance of payments. The growth rate for exports and imports has been around 7 to 9 per cent for most of the industrialized western European countries; it was higher for Austria, western Germany and Italy where the initial level was depressed by quite special factors. The growth rate of both exports and imports was, on the whole, higher in southern and in eastern Europe than in the industrialized western European countries taken together.[26]

Between 1950–52 and 1968–70, most of the growth elasticities for exports and imports in respect of GNP ranged between 1·5 and 2. Higher elasticities were recorded by Austria, Belgium, Ireland, Italy and Bulgaria and these reflect special factors in each country. Thus, in Austria and Italy, the trade level was in 1950 even more depressed than the output level because of the vicissitudes of the war; in Belgium the sharp expansion of exports is partly linked with the establishment of foreign enterprises in the fifties and the sixties which have introduced there lines of production for the whole European market. In all these countries the export expansion has been associated with a market diversification of the original commodity structure. By contrast, in the United Kingdom, the export increase has

26. Prices rose only moderately (and less than domestic prices) for exports and imports in most European countries after the Second World War and growth rates in current and constant prices differ only marginally (especially in the socialist countries). The annual growth rates for exports and imports at current prices from 1948 to 1970 for the western and eastern European countries (including the countries not listed in table 4 because no data at constant prices are available) are as follows:

	Exports	Imports
—western European countries[a]	9.7	8.3
—centrally planned countries	10.8	11.2

a includes the south European countries

Source: United Nations, Statistical Yearbook 1971.

been not only weak in comparison with the other European countries but also in comparison with the expansion of output in that country. Foreign trade elasticities in respect of the output growth have been relatively low also in the Soviet Union where, owing mainly to the size of the country, foreign trade still plays a less important role than in the other European countries. Up to the end of the sixties there have been no indications of a clear tendency for trade elasticities to decline. There have been upward and downward changes in elasticities for individual countries and individual commodity groups but no overall tendency for a change in the basic trends.[27]

The rapid growth of the foreign trade of the European countries in the post-war period has been accompanied by considerable changes in its geographical distribution as well as in its commodity structure. Geographically, there has been a gradual concentration of trade of the European countries inside Europe – a shift which has been already mentioned before. The changes in the commodity composition of trade are closely linked with its geographical changes. Its concentration inside Europe has meant, to an increasing extent, an exchange of manufactured products against other manufactured products. At the end of the sixties, manufactured products accounted for about 90 per cent of total European exports and for no less than 50 per cent of total European imports (intra-trade is included in both cases). Inside the manufacturing sector, exports and imports of engineering and chemical products rose fastest.

27. For a detailed analysis of foreign trade developments and trade elasticities in the post-war period in Europe, see UN/ECE, *Trade dependence in European countries*, in Economic Bulletin for Europe, vol. 21, no. 1, New York 1970. See also UN/ECE, *The European economy from the 1950s to 1970s*, (Economic Survey for Europe in 1970, part 1), especially chapters 2 and 3. The trade problems of the southern European countries have been examined in particular in UN/ECE, Economic Bulletin for Europe, vol. 20, no. 2, New York 1968 (*Foreign trade developments in the southern European countries*) and, with special reference to the manufacturing sector, in UN/ECE, Economic Bulletin for Europe, vol. 23, no. 2, New York 1972 (*Some aspects of manufacturing development in southern Europe: production, trade and transfer of technology*).

The commodity structure of exports and imports still differs (of course) from country to country depending on the level of economic development, factor endowment and historical vicissitudes: but the prevailing tendency in the period following the Second World War has been towards an increasing inter-country similarity at least in terms of industrial branches if not in terms of individual products and component parts. The less industrialized countries, which at the beginning of the fifties had a less favourable export structure (large share of primary products in total exports and, in the field of manufactures, predominance of textiles and other technologically simple products) exhibited, broadly speaking, a better export performance than the already more industrialized countries with a more favourable export structure; and their progress was particularly rapid in those branches which were very under-represented (or not represented at all) in their export structure.

INTRA-EUROPEAN TRADE

It was seen in the previous section that before the Second World War intra-European trade accounted for 60 to 70 per cent – depending on the years – of Europe's trade with the other regions while at the end of the sixties it had become larger than the European external trade flows (exports plus imports). This section reviews the major features of intra-European trade, its area and commodity pattern and the major changes which occurred in the period under review; and briefly discusses the major factors behind its rapid expansion in the fifties and the sixties.

The Inter-War Period

The country and commodity pattern of intra-European trade in the inter-war period has to be seen, of course, in the frame of Europe's economic structure in that period when a large number of countries were still prevalently agricultural or at the first stage of their industrialization process. The gap between countries in terms of level of economic development and degree of industrialization was much larger at that time than at the end of the sixties. This aspect of recent European economic history is not examined in this chapter; suffice it here to remember that in the thirties the share of population engaged in agriculture accounted for about 80 per cent of total active population in Bulgaria, Rumania, Turkey, Yugoslavia and Poland while it was no more than 7 per cent in the United Kingdom and about 15 per cent in Belgium; but it was no less than 20 per cent in the Netherlands, 30 per cent in Germany and more than 40 per cent in Italy. Though the distinction between industrialized and non-industrialized countries is to some extent always arbitrary, it seems convenient to follow the classification adopted in the economic reports of the League of Nations where the following ten countries were considered as industrialized, that is, the United Kingdom, Germany, France, Belgium-Luxemburg, Netherlands, Italy, Sweden, Switzerland, Czechoslovakia and Austria. (Inside this group, the United Kingdom, Germany and France occupied a dominating position not only because of their size but also because of the degree of industrialization.) All the other countries were considered as 'mainly agricultural countries'. However, the USSR, because of its size, its rapid pace of industrialization, and its socialist system was considered as a special case. Inside the group of the 'agricultural countries', Denmark, Norway and to a certain extent Finland, stand in a group apart in terms of living standard; their income per head was much higher than in the other 'agricultural' countries and, indeed, higher than in some industrialized countries. Still the ten 'industrialized' countries had one point in common of direct relevance for the problem here examined, that is, all of them (and only them) were net exporters ·(again to a various degree) of manufactured products.[28] Thus, for the problem here

28. Again, the distinction between manufactured and other goods in total commodity éxports and imports is to some extent arbitrary. For the pre-war period, the available statistical sources – and in particular the studies prepåred by the League of Nations – are generally based on the so-called '*Brussels classification*' of 1913 where all exports and imports

under consideration (intra-European trade) the European countries may be arranged in three groups; that is, first the United Kingdom, Germany and France; second, the other seven 'industrialized' countries (by the pre-war standard), that is Austria, Belgium-Luxemburg, Czechoslovakia, Italy, Netherlands, Sweden and Switzerland, and third all the other (mainly agricultural) countries.

The Soviet Union, as already mentioned, cannot be included in any of these groups. True, the industrialization process was at its beginning in the twenties and the share of agriculture in total employment was still as high as 55 per cent on the eve of the Second World War. The Soviet Union was – as it is at present – a net exporter of raw materials and a net importer of manufactured products. But, partly because of its size and partly for political reasons, the volume of foreign trade was not only quite marginal in respect of domestic output but also quite small in comparison with the foreign trade level of the major European countries. Furthermore, foreign trade was

---

were classified under five major groups, that is: 1. live animals; 2 articles of food and drink; 3. materials, raw or partly manufactured; 4. manufactured articles; 5. gold and silver. In the text, for brevity's sake, the word 'food' indicates exports or imports of classes 1 and 2; 'raw materials', exports or imports of class 3, and manufactures, exports or imports of class 4. For the post-war period, trade statistics are generally based on the so-called Standard International Trade Classification (SITC), prepared by the Statistical Office of the United Nations Secretariat (see *Standard International Trade Classification*, United Nations Statistical Papers, Series M, no. 10, 2nd edition). In the SITC, all commodity imports and exports are classified in 10 groups. According to the usual practice, imports or exports of manufactures include the SITC number 5 to 8 [chemicals (5), manufactured goods classified by materials (6), machinery and transport equipment (7), miscellaneous manufactured articles (8)]. The (pre-war and post-war) classifications present several differences but still they allow a broad comparison for all the major groups considered here. Food manufactured products are excluded from the manufactured goods both in the old and new classification.

For historical series about the value of exports and imports of manufactured products (on the basis of the 1913 Brussels nomenclature) for a number of European countries from the end of the nineteenth century to 1936 38 see, League of Nations, *Industrialization and foreign trade*. 1945.

conducted on the basis of principles and criteria which differed deeply from those applied by all other (non-socialist) countries.

The commodity composition of exports and in particular the share of the manufactured products in total national exports – largely reflecting the degree of industrialization – has played a dominating role in determining the share of total European exports of the individual countries, though the geographical location and historical vicissitudes also played a role. The less industrialized countries exporting mainly agricultural products and raw materials found their natural outlets in the neighbouring more industrialized states. Thus, traditionally, Ireland and, to a lesser extent, Denmark were major exporters of agricultural produce to the United Kingdom and the Scandinavian countries were major exporters of wood and paper towards the same market. Similarly, the agricultural countries of central Europe and of the Balkan area have been major exporters of agricultural products and raw materials to Germany. It can be seen from Table 3 that in 1928 European outlets absorbed about, or more than 80 per cent of total exports from Bulgaria, Denmark, Finland, Ireland, Greece, Hungary, Poland, Yugoslavia and Rumania. This proportion was even higher for the three small Baltic states not shown in the table (Latvia, Lithuania, Estonia). It was somewhat lower (around 70 per cent) for Portugal and Spain owing to their geographical proximity to Africa and their traditional links with Latin America. For Portugal furthermore, a sizeable trade flow was taking place with the colonies.

In the group of the small (or medium-sized) but relatively industrialized countries, the share of Europe was about 70 per cent of their total exports for Belgium, Netherlands, Sweden and Switzerland but it was still as high as 80 per cent for Austria and Czechoslovakia partly because of their geographical position at the heart of Europe and partly (probably) as a consequence of historical vicissitudes and previous economic and political links.

A very small proportion of Italian exports went to Europe: in 1928 (as in 1913) only the United Kingdom displayed a lower ratio. A latecomer in the group of the industrialized countries, Italy had tried to diversify the geographical destination of its manufactured products and find new outlets in a number of overseas markets. This process of geographical diversification has been made easier by the commodity composition of exports where the weight of the primary products always remained quite modest.

The geographical distribution of exports varied greatly in the group of the 'big three' (the United Kingdom, Germany and France). The European share was exceptionally low for the United Kingdom (less than one third) because a large part of British trade was traditionally directed towards her colonies, dominions and the United States. By contrast, about 70 per cent of the German exports were directed to Europe; therefore, though total British exports were higher than the German ones, Germany and not the United Kingdom was the major supplier of industrial products to Europe. The position of the two countries differed also in two other aspects. First, the United Kingdom had a deficit trade balance with most European countries and Germany had a surplus trade balance. Second, the commodity composition of the exports of the two countries in the European markets showed considerable differences: the United Kingdom ranked first for textiles (in 1928 the British exports of textile products to Europe amounted to 339 million dollars as against 270 million dollars coming from Germany) but Germany ranked first for metals, machinery, chemicals and miscellaneous manufactured products.[29] On the European markets, the British exports were in 1928 (as in 1913) even lower than the French exports though total British exports are much higher than the French ones. The commodity composition of French exports was more similar to the British than to the German ones.

29. Britain ranked first also in the (small) sector of transport equipment. However, in 1928 exports of machinery from Germany to Europe were nearly three times higher than those from the United Kindgom. See, for details, ECE, *Growth and Stagnation in the European Economy*, cit. Geneva 1954.

The share of Europe in total imports of the individual European countries follows broadly speaking the export pattern but with some sizeable differences for major countries. The United Kingdom was sending to Europe (as already mentioned) less than one third of her total exports but the imports coming from the other European countries accounted (in 1928) for nearly 40 per cent of total British imports. The situation was the opposite for Germany and France. These two countries sent to Europe more than 60 per cent of their total exports but received from Europe less than 50 per cent of their total imports. The United Kingdom was exporting the bulk of its manufactured products to the overseas markets while Germany was at that time – as it is now – the major supplier of industrial goods to Europe. The United Kingdom, Germany and France were the major markets for the other European countries. The United Kingdom was in that period by far the largest European importer and the British market was of vital importance for a number of small countries which delivered to the United Kingdom 50 per cent or more of their exports and indeed a quite sizeable proportion of their commodity production. According to an estimate made by the ECE Secretariat, exports to the United Kingdom absorbed in 1938 about 35 per cent of Ireland's commodity *production*, 29 per cent for Denmark, 20 per cent for Finland, 14 per cent for Norway, 11 per cent for the Netherlands and 9 per cent for Sweden.[30] Germany's total imports were considerably lower than the British ones (by 22 per cent in 1913 and by 33 per cent in 1928) and also the imports coming from Europe were smaller though in this case the difference was not so large. The difference in the import bill of the two countries was largely due to a much smaller import of foodstuffs and agricultural products in Germany, partly because of a lower level of consumption per head and partly because of a higher domestic agricultural production in turn due to a larger territory and a bigger share of total labour force employed in agriculture. Still Germany was by far the largest outlet for Austria, Czecho-

30. *Ibid.*

slovakia and the prevalently agricultural countries of Central Europe and the Balkan area. It absorbed (in 1298) nearly 40 per cent of total Polish exports (as against a share of 6 per cent going to the United Kingdom) and about 20 per cent of exports from Austria and Czechoslovakia. Germany was also the major outlet for the Dutch exports (24 per cent as against 22 per cent going to the United Kingdom). French imports were considerably lower than either the British or the German ones but still France was the major market for Belgium and Spain.

In short, before the great depression the inter-European trade can be split into two major parts. More than half of it was formed by intra-trade among the ten 'industrialized' countries already mentioned and in this trade flow manufactured products predominated though trade in raw materials was also quite developed (coal from the United Kingdom, food products and iron ore from France, wood from Sweden). Inside this group, intra-trade among France, Germany and the United Kingdom was predominant before the First World War but it gradually lost its relative importance as the other seven countries proceeded in their industrialization process and developed their foreign trade relations. The second big part of intra-European trade (more than 40 per cent) was constituted by trade between the ten industrialized countries and the other (prevalently agricultural) countries. This trade flow was mainly constituted by an exchange of manufactures against primary products. There was very little intra-trade (no more than 5 per cent of total intra-European trade) among the less industrialized countries.

The protectionist policies of the thirties and the deteriorating political climate not only brought about a deeply fall in the level of intra-European trade but deeply affected its structure; and had in particular a disruptive effect on intra-trade among the three major industrial countries, that is the United Kingdom, Germany and France. The intra-trade among these three countries which accounted for about 15 per cent of total intra-European trade in 1928 declined to a share of 9 per cent in 1938. The reorientation of the foreign trade of the major countries was partly the effect of the protectionist policies which were introduced but, on the other hand, it was also purposely aimed at by the Governments on the basis of political and military considerations. Thus, the United Kingdom authorities tried to concentrate further the foreign trade of the country within the Commonwealth and the sterling area (largely overlapping). The share of imports coming from Europe declined from 40 per cent in 1928 to 32 per cent in 1938; and all this decline was due to her trade with the major European 'industrial' countries whose share declined from 22 to 13 per cent. The trade share with the other European countries (Scandinavian countries and non-industrial countries) remained virtually unchanged. For Germany on the other hand, the share of her total imports coming from Europe rose (though slightly) between 1928 and 1938, but the share coming from the European industrial states declined from 31 to 24 per cent in the same period; however this decline was more than offset by a sharp increase in trade with both the Scandinavian and the Balkan States. The diversion of traffic from potential enemies to probably neutral or satellite states was largely determined by governments. Furthermore, the protectionist policies operated in the same direction since the replacement of imported with domestic products had much larger scope in the field of manufactured than in that of raw materials. For France, the share of Europe in total imports declined from about 43 per cent in 1928 to 34 per cent in 1938 as France purposely followed the policy – like the United Kingdom – of concentrating her imports from her over-seas territories. For Italy (as for Germany) the European share in total imports rose between 1928 and 1938 and there was a dramatic reorientation of Italian exports and imports towards Germany. These swings are typical of that particular historical period and of little value for assessing long-term trends and projections.

Largely because of the First World War, the great depression and the ensuing restrictive policies, intra-

European trade did not show any increase – in volume – between 1913 and 1938. In fact, according to a (necessarily) rough estimate, in 1928, it had just recovered the 1913 level and in 1938 it was 10 per cent lower than in 1928. It recaptured the 1913 level only in 1950.[31] Its commodity composition is available only for the group of the more industrialized countries; for Europe as a whole, it may be estimated that trade in manufactures (class 4 of the Brussels Classification) probably accounted for no more than 60 per cent of total trade. Within this field, trade in textiles occupied a dominating position making up 30 per cent of total trade in manufactures; metal products accounted (probably) for about 15–16 per cent; machinery for 12 per cent, chemicals for 9–10 per cent and transport equipment (largely ships) for no more than 4 per cent; the remaining share (about 30 per cent) was contributed by all the other manufactured products. Outside the field of the manufactured products, trade in basic metals (iron ore, steel), in coal and in forestry products was probably nearly double the trade in food products.

The Post-War Period

The development and the pattern of intra-European trade in the years following the Second World War have to be seen in the frame of two basic factors: first, the unprecedented pace of economic development recorded by the region as a whole and the associated spread of industrialization and, second, the establishment of two regional sub-groupings (each numbering about 350 million persons) with different political and economic systems. One group is composed of the socialist countries of eastern Europe (the Soviet Union, Albania, Bulgaria, Czechoslovakia, the German Democratic Republic, Hungary, Poland and Rumania) and the other group by the remaining countries – which, for brevity will be called (following the usual

31. *Ibid.*

practice) 'market economy countries' or 'western European countries'[32]. Yugoslavia stands however in a rather special situation[33].

Because of the establishment in Europe of two groups of countries with different political and social systems three major trade flows can be detected, that is, the trade among the west European countries, the trade among the east European countries and the trade between the two groups (the so-called east-west trade). Each of these three trade flows has some specific features. In the socialist countries of eastern Europe, foreign trade is a State monopoly and it is closely integrated with the overall process of economic planning. In the western countries the decisions to import and to export fall primarily on the individual enterprises and, with the dismantling of the administrative controls and customs duties, governments may affect (or better, may hope to affect) the overall level of foreign trade only *via* the management of domestic demand and changes in

---

32. The expression 'western European countries' is surely not very precise in geographical terms since Turkey for instance is also included in this group. The market economy countries are usually arranged in three groups, that is: 13 industrialized western countries (Austria, Belgium, Denmark, Finland, France, Germany FR, Ireland, Italy, Netherlands, Norway, Sweden, Switzerland, and the United Kingdom); five 'southern European countries' (Greece, Portugal, Spain, Turkey and Yugoslavia) and the peripheral very small countries or at least with very small population, like Iceland, Malta and Cyprus, etc. Partly for insufficient statistical data and partly because of the special features of their economies, this third group of countries is not taken into consideration in the present chapter.

33. Yugoslavia adopted in 1945 a socialist system and most of its foreign trade was re-directed towards the other socialist countries of eastern Europe. But in June 1948, because of political divergencies, the Yugoslav Communist Party was expelled from the 'Communist Information Bureau' and the other socialist countries of eastern Europe discontinued most of their commercial relations with Yugoslavia The blockage obliged the Yugoslav government to a new dramatic re-adjustment of its foreign trade direction. Foreign trade with the socialist countries of eastern Europe was resumed only slowly but towards the end of the sixties it accounted for about 35-40 per cent of its total trade. Yugoslavia is associated in certain works of OECD (located in Paris), particularly that of the Economic and Development Review Committee.

exchange rates[34]. However, in spite of institutional differences, some prevailing features are common to all three trade flows: in particular, a growth rate higher than the output growth, a stronger dynamism for trade in manufactures than in raw materials and an increasing similarity in the commodity composition of national exports and imports.

The relative importance of the three trade flows in 1955 and 1969 – separately for manufactures and other commodities – can be grasped from the following text-table where each trade flow is expressed in percentage of total intra-European trade, at 1963 prices:

Shares in intra-European trade, 1955 and 1969, at 1963 prices[a]

(PPs = primary products; Mf = manufactures; Tot = total trade)[b]

(percentages: total intra-European trade = 100)

Exports to Exports from		Western Europe		Eastern Europe		Total Europe	
		1955	1969	1955	1969	1955	1969
Western Europe	PPs	26·3	17·5	1·7	0·7	28·0	18·2
	Mf	46·8	57·2	2·4	4·3	49·2	61·5
	Tot	73·1	74·7	4·1	5·0	77·2	79·7
Eastern Europe	PPs	3·4	2·9	8·0	4·2	11·4	7·1
	Mf	1·6	2·0	9·8	11·2	11·4	13·2
	Tot	5·0	4·9	17·8	15·5	22·8	20·3
Total Europe	PPs	29·7	20·4	9·7	4·9	39·4	25·3
	Mf	48·4	59·2	12·2	15·5	60·6	74·7
	Tot	78·1	79·5	21·9	20·5	100·0	100·0

a No comprehensive data are available for the period before 1955.
b Primary products include all products except manufactures.
Source: ECE, *The European Economy from the 1950s to the 1970s* (Economy Survey of Europe in 1971, part 1), Geneva 1972.

As can be seen from the above figures, at the end of the sixties intra-western European trade accounted for about 75 per cent of total intra-European trade, intra-eastern

34. Agricultural products are still subject to a considerable degree of control in most countries In the Common Market countries, national controls are gradually replaced by Community controls.

European trade accounted for about 15 per cent and trade between the two sub-regional groups for the remaining 10 per cent. The share of intra-east European trade declined (slightly) between 1955 and 1969 and the share of the other two trade flows rose correspondingly. The table also brings to light the increasing share of the manufactures in all the three trade flows. For instance, inside the eastern European group, trade in primary products was in 1955 nearly as important as trade in manufactures but by 1969 it amounted to no more than 37 per cent of trade in manufactures. Primary products were in 1969 more important than manufactures only in the exports from east to west European countries (though less so than in 1955).

The Soviet Union is obviously the major partner for the eastern European countries though its share tends on the whole to decline. Towards the end of the sixties, it accounted for about 55 per cent of intra-eastern European trade on the export as well as on the import side. In the field of intra-western European trade, the Federal Republic of Germany occupies a leading position but, again, the place of the three major countries (Federal Republic, the United Kingdom and France) is declining because of the rapid expansion of trade among the other countries. East-west trade accounts for a relatively small (though rising) share of the total trade of the western European countries (about 4·5 per cent at the end of the sixties) but for a quite considerable part (more than 20 per cent) of the total trade of the eastern European countries[35].

The changes in the share of intra-west, intra-east and east-west trade which took place between 1955 and 1970 reflect of course differences in the growth rate. Exports from western to eastern Europe grew by 11 per cent per year and exports from eastern to western Europe by 9·3 per cent. Intra-western European trade grew by nearly 10 per cent per year and intra-east European trade grew

35. Detailed information on the geographical distribution of the eastern European countries foreign trade is regularly published in the *Surveys* and *Bulletins* prepared by the UN/ECE. See, for instance the Economic Bulletin for Europe, vol. 23, no. 2 (New York 1972).

by 8·4 per cent. Part of the differences in these growth rates are due to the different proportion of manufactures and primary products in total trade, the former displaying a greater dynamism than the latter in all the major trade flows. However, exports of manufactures from western to eastern Europe grew considerably faster than the opposite, smaller, flow (14 as against 10·6 per cent)[36]. The rapid process of industrialization in the eastern European countries needed a large amount of capital goods and especially of technology intensive products – only partly producible at home. On the other hand, exports of manufactures from east to west European countries have been so far mainly hampered by shortage of supply and to a less extent by differences in technical standards and import controls on the part of western European countries[37].

The impression a higher dynamism displayed by intra-western than by intra-eastern European trade – already emerging from the growth rates referred to above – is reinforced by a comparison between growth in trade and output. If intra-eastern European trade rose somewhat more slowly than intra-western European trade, output rose faster in eastern Europe and the import elasticity with respect to GNP growth was of 2·2 in western and 1·2 for eastern Europe (for manufactures the corresponding elasticities are 2·5 and 1·5). Two reasons may largely explain the smaller dynamism of intra-east European trade. First, the role of policy: as already mentioned, in these countries imports and exports were considered for many years mainly as a bottleneck-freeing instrument. Second, in the eastern countries, output diversification has not reached the proportions prevailing in western Europe.

In western Europe, trade growth was particularly

36. These growth rates are calculated on the basis of constant prices For more detail, see ECE, *The European economy from the 1950s to the 1970s, cit.*

37. For a detailed discussion of post-war developments and prospects of 'east-west' trade see ECE, *Analytical report on the state of intra-European trade,* New York 1970.

rapid among the countries of the European Economic Community (13 per cent per year). The growth rate was higher for manufactures alone but even in primary products it approached 10 per cent per year. Indeed one of the fastest rates of expansion was witnessed by intra-EEC trade in foodstuffs which increased by 11·5 per cent per year and accounted in 1969 for 40 per cent of total intra-European trade in foodstuffs against 22 per cent in 1955. Trade grew less rapidly among the EFTA countries. This relatively modest growth was due to the United Kingdom's trade with the rest of EFTA. Among the other members of EFTA intra-trade increased by 11·5 per cent per year, that is almost as much as intra-EEC trade. A major reason was the rapid development of trade among the Nordic countries, in which industrial co-operation and sub-contracting played a significant part.

The impact of ECE and EFTA on foreign trade has been the subject of extensive research in economic literature in past years though more recently the question has somewhat subsided – especially after the entry of the United Kingdom into the Common Market and the further liberalization of trade among the two areas. The main point was whether and eventually to what extent the creation of ECE and EFTA produced an intensification of trade among the member countries (the so-called trade creation) or rather a shift in the origin of imports (the so-called trade diversion). On the whole it is fairly clear that a process of trade creation did take place and on a large scale – while opinions differ about the importance (and even the existence at all) of trade diversion[38]. The following text-table, though it cannot (obviously) set out the question, provides some information about the actual trade flows in manufactures:

38. For a general review of the literature see J. W. Williamson and A. Bottrell, *The impact of Customs Unions on trade in manufactures*, in 'Oxford Economic Papers'. Nov. 1971. See also, with specific reference to the European Free Trade Association: EFTA, *The effects of EFTA on the economies of member States*, Geneva 1969.

Imports of manufactures as a percentage of consumption

A. Intra-trade as per cent of consumption[a]
B. Imports from the other group as percent of consumption[a]

| | ECE | | EFTA | |
	A	B	A	B
1955	6·5	3·0	3·5	7·0
1959	9·0	4·0	4·0	8·5
1965	12·0	3·5	5·5	10·5
1970	16·5	4·0	7·5	12·0

[a] Gross output minus exports plus imports.
Source: ECE, *The European economy from the 1950s ...*, cit., chapter 2.

The commodity composition of intra-west, intra-east, and 'east-west' trade at the end of the sixties is shown in some more detail in Table 5. The table shows that at the end of the sixties trade in engineering products and transport equipment taken together dominated both intra-west and intra-east trade as well as exports from west to eastern Europe. Trade in 'food, beverages and tobacco', crude materials and 'minerals and fuels' surpassed the share of 10 per cent only in exports from eastern to western Europe. On the whole, there is a striking similarity in the commodity pattern of intra-west and intra-east European trade; by contrast, western Europe's exports to eastern Europe differ considerably from the reverse flow. In particular, western Europe is a big net exporter to eastern Europe of engineering and chemical products and of miscellaneous manufactures and a net importer of foodstuffs, crude materials, fuels and minerals.

Obviously the commodity pattern of intra-European trade differs considerably as among countries because of differences in factor endowment, stage of economic development and historical vicissitudes. Thus, in eastern Europe the Soviet Union is still a net exporter of primary products and a net importer of manufactured goods. Czechoslovakia and the German Democratic Republic are the major net exporters of manufactures. In western Europe, Finland, Sweden and Norway are big exporters of pulp and paper and the first two countries also of wood. Norway exports large quantities of food products and of non-ferrous metals (especially aluminium) while Sweden has become a net exporter also of engineering products[39]. Agricultural products predominate in Irish exports and at the end of the sixties they still accounted for more than one third of Danish exports. Wood, paper and steel taken together accounted at the end of the sixties for nearly 30 per cent of total Austrian exports. The exports of the (less industrialized) southern European countries are still mainly concentrated on such 'traditional' fields as agricultural products, textiles and clothing (but Spain is a net importer of agricultural products). Some old industrial countries like the United Kingdom, France and Belgium still were at the end of the sixties net exporters of textile products. The Federal Republic of Germany and the United Kingdom are the major European exporters of engineering products though German exports in this field largely outstrip the British ones (the prevalence of Germany as a supplier of engineering products to the other European countries is not a novelty of the post-war period, as it was mentioned in the previous section). The Netherlands is a big net exporter of chemicals and electrical products. France, by contrast, is still a net importer of engineering products in intra-European trade (though of course, is a net exporter in some specific branches and for vehicles). Italy is a large net importer of agricultural products and a net exporter of textiles and many engineering products (in the field of the consumer goods).

However, the point of relevance here is that inter-country differences in the commodity composition of exports and imports exhibited a tendency to narrow rather than widen. For the market economies of western Europe, this increasing similarity among countries in the commodity composition of exports and imports came somewhat as a surprise. Fears were expressed that the rapid liberalization of foreign trade and subsequently the creation of the

39. A country is said to be *net* exporter in a given branch if its exports in that branch are higher than the corresponding imports. The same terminology is used on the import side.

Eurpean Economic Community and EFTA would have reinforced existing comparative advantage. It was thought, for instance, that the predominance of the Federal Republic of Germany and the United Kingdom in the exports of engineering goods (and of the investment goods in particular) would have been reinforced and that similar (but less powerful) industries in the other countries would have not been in a position to withstand their competition. In fact, rather the contrary happened. Broadly speaking, in each country exports developed more rapidly in those branches which were relatively underrepresented at the beginning of the period[40]. Thus, the Federal Republic of Germany still keeps a dominating position in the exports of capital goods but its share of the European market has (slightly) declined and not increased during the sixties.[41] This (admittedly slow) process of structural convergence among countries is not limited to the commodity composition of foreign trade but it holds also for the production structure and it is associated with a more rapid output growth in the less industrialized countries of the region.

The second feature of intra-European trade was its extraordinarily rapid development – not only in comparison with past experience but also in comparison with the output growth. It might be worth remembering in this context (i) that intra-European trade is mainly constituted by an exchange of manufactures against manufactures; (ii) that virtually all countries are exporters and importers in the same branch (food products, textiles, machinery, etc.) and in many cases for apparently similar products (steel, machine tools, plastic materials); (iii) that trade expanded more for intermediate and capital products than for consumer goods; (iv) that the largest part of the intra-European trade takes place among countries at rather similar levels

40. See for some statistical information, ECE, *The European economy from the 1950s to the 1970s, cit.*, chapter 3.

41 For detailed information on engineering industry see GATT, *International Trade* 1967, Geneva 1968; for more summary data by major manufacturing branches in selected West European countries, see INSEE, *Fresque historique du système productif* (Les collections de l'INSEE), Paris 1974.

of economic development; and (v) that there has been a process of convergence among countries in the commodity composition of exports and imports[42]. These features do not fit easily within the dominant theory of international trade. The theory states that the sources of national comparative advantages – the basis for international trade – are essentially determined by 'factor endowment', that is the relative abundance of factors of production which, in turn, have been normally identified for long in labour and capital. In the economic literature of the fifties and the sixties, numerous attempts have been made to take into consideration other factors and, in this context, the prominent role played by the level of technology was emphasized. Since a different pattern of factor endowment – in terms of labour reserves, capital stock and technology – is normally associated with a different level of economic development, it is not surprising if most of the empirical research inspired by the doctrine of 'factor proportions' was concerned with trade among countries at different levels of economic development and if it was – implicity if not always explicitly – assumed that there was more scope for division of labour – and therefore for trade – among countries at different stages of economic development than among countries having similar industrial structures[43]. True, research carried on already before the Second World War had shown the existence of a flourishing trade in manufactures among industrial countries and, also, that industrialization is associated with an increase – and not a decrease – in

42. The process of convergence (or increasing similarity in the commodity composition of national exports and imports) is by no means universal. Many exceptions can be noticed but on the whole it seems fairly clear that the prevailing tendency has been towards inter-country convergence and not divergence.

4?. On the basis of this theory warnings were expressed – which in fact proved to be wrong – that the industrialization of a hitherto prevalently agricultural country was likely to reduce its imports of manufactures because the country in question – as a consequence of becoming industrialized – would have produced at home some at least of the previously imported manufactured goods (see some quotations in A. Maizels, *Industrial growth and world trade* (CUP 1965), pp. 2–6.

imports of manufactures[44]. But this line of investigation lacked – and lacks – the support of an authoritative theoretical framework[45]. On the other hand, the traditional theory of factor proportions clearly is not of great help in explaining the very rapid growth of intra-European (and especially of intra-western European) trade which took place after the Second World War.

Some reasons which may help towards explaining it have already been mentioned: in particular the prevalence of full employment in most countries, the liberal commercial policies and a quite abnormal starting position because of the protectionist policies of the thirties and of the Second World War. In the inter-war period, attempts to liberalize foreign trade were resisted – by governments, the business community and labour – because of the fear that increased imports would depress even further domestic output and the employment level. The favourable effects to be expected on output and employment from higher exports (because of the other countries import liberalization) obviously carried less weight than the expected negative import effect. Lip service was paid to the benefit of free trade and the ensuing international specialization but policies were mainly dictated by the immediate (nearly day-to-day) needs of the domestic situation – in particular by the employment situation. In the condition of full employment prevailing in the industrialized western European countries after the Second World War, foreign trade became a central factor for fostering productivity increase and therefore output growth. It may be remembered in this connection that increase in output per man contributed to 90 per cent of the output increase in manufacturing industry for the 13 industrialized western European countries combined. Thus, if the growth policies pursued after the Second World War were a pre-requisite for the rapid

44. See, for instance, League of Nations, *Europe's trade*, *cit.*, and League of Nations, *Industrialization and foreign trade*, by F. Hilgerdt, 1945.

45. An attempt to build a theory for trade among countries at a similar level of income per head has been made by F. Lindner, *An essay on trade and transformation*, Stockholm 1961.

expansion of foreign trade and of intra-European trade in particular, the trade expansion became, in turn, a major factor behind the output growth[46].

But liberal commercial policies and full employment are in the nature of general premises rather than of specific factors. It is likely that two other forces (of a more technical nature) played an important role, that is, economies of scale and output diversification (including the increasing complexity of many production processes). The role played by economies of scale and output diversification in fostering trade in manufactures among industrialized countries is being often mentioned in recent publications but a comprehensive analysis is still missing. Clearly, the measurement of their role and their specific *modus operandi* poses a number of extremely difficult problems. Here we will limit ourselves to recalling that output diversification is an inherent feature of industrial development and that in all likelihood it reached large proportions in Europe after the Second World War (though more in western than in eastern Europe) in the field of consumer goods as well as for capital and intermediate products. On the other hand, the output diversification which can be obtained in each enterprise is limited by cost considerations (economies of scale). Indeed, rapidly changing technological conditions have considerably lifted – and are still lifting – the threshold below which production becomes uncompetitive[47].

46. Of course there is also the other side of the coin. In western Europe, the dismantling of the administrative controls and of the customs tariffs and the increasing integration of the European economies make it much more difficult to insulate a national economy from the cyclical swings of the other countries.

47. It is not implied here that because of output diversification prices do not play any role in international trade in manufactures. Price competition remains but prices are – in present conditions even more than in the past – only one element in the buying decision of enterprises and households.

EUROPE'S TRADE WITH THE OTHER REGIONS[48]

Because of its prominent position in world trade, and of the interdependence of the major trade flows, a detailed account of Europe's trade with the other regions, of its development, of its commodity and country pattern would in fact amount to a review of the network of the world trade at large. This is an unmanageable task in the present context. Therefore this section briefly concentrates on some basic (and elementary) issues, that is the commodity composition of Europe's overseas trade, the question of the 'European' trade balance, and the relative position of Europe and the United States in the world markets and in their mutual trade relations.

The size of the trade flow between Europe and the other regions was shown in Table 1 and its development from 1913 to 1970 was briefly commented upon on pp. 510-20 of this Chapter. Let us simply recall here that at the end of the sixties it accounted for about 30 per cent of the total world trade (including intra-European trade) and was of the same dimension as trade among all the non-European countries. The participation of the individual European countries in this overseas trade can be derived from Tables 2 and 3 (respectively for exports and imports). Until 1938, about 40 per cent of Europe's overseas trade was conducted by the United Kingdom alone whose share in 1970 had dropped to about 25 per cent. The participation of Germany

---

48. 'Other regions' include such disparate countries as the United States on the one hand, and the least developed of the developing countries on the other. In the trade studies referring to the period following the Second World War, it has become usual practice (especially in the United Nations reports) to make a distinction between the overseas developed countries and overseas developing countries. The overseas developed countries include Canada, the United States, Japan, Australia, New Zealand and South Africa. All the others are normally considered as developing countries. Within this last group, the petroleum exporting countries were normally singled out as a special sub-group even before the massive increase in oil price introduced in October 1973. It may be worth recalling that some of the overseas developed countries (Australia, New Zealand and South Africa) are still mainly exporters of primary products.

and France has not changed very much while the participation of a number of other countries which industrialized later, witnessed an increase. The United Kingdom, Germany and France taken together accounted for about 70 per cent of Europe's trade with the other regions in 1913 and for a full 55 per cent in 1970[49].

Though the overseas regions include such highly industrialized countries as the United States and Japan, no less than 70 per cent of European imports were still constituted by raw materials, fuels and agricultural products towards the end of the sixties, while European exports have always been mostly manufactured products. The commodity composition of Europe's exports and imports in 1967 is shown in the following text-table, separately for western and eastern Europe.

The commodity composition of Europe's trade with the other regions, 1967
(percentages)

	Western Europe		Eastern Europe	
	Imports	Exports	Imports	Exports
Food, beverages, tobacco	24	9	41	12
Raw materials	20	3	34	11
Fuels	20	2	1	7
Chemicals	4	11	3	5
Machinery and transport equipment	13	39	4	32
Other manufactures	18	39	16	22
Misc. commodities	1	1	1	11
TOTAL { percentages	100·0	100·0	100·0	100·0
{ million $	32,710	28,390	2,980	4,530

Source: ECE, *Analytical report on the state of intra-European trade*, (Geneva 1970), p. 103.

49. The share differs somewhat for exports and imports: the percentages given in the text refer to the average for both flows. For 1970, both the Federal Republic of Germany and the German Democratic Republic have been taken into account.

As can be seen, western Europe contributed in 1967 86 per cent and eastern Europe 14 per cent to total European exports overseas. The table also shows that manufactures accounted in 1967 for 85 per cent of western Europe's exports to the other regions, but the actual proportion is higher since most of the commodities listed under the heading 'food, beverages and tobacco' consist of processed products (that is products of the food industry). The category 'machinery and transport equipment' (where all the capital goods are included) accounted by itself for no less than 40 per cent of western European exports overseas. The share of manufactures was lower (and the share of food, raw materials and fuels, higher) in eastern Europe's overseas exports. Overseas exports of manufactured products from eastern Europe amounted only to 12 per cent of similar exports from western Europe while for primary products the ratio was about one third. The different proportion of manufactures and primary products in exports of eastern and western Europe reflects differences in the industrialization level (which is still higher in western Europe) and in availability of materials (which is bigger in eastern Europe mainly because of the vast natural resources existing in the Soviet Union). On the import side, too, the share of manufactured products is lower in eastern than in western Europe since by far the largest proportion of imported manufactured goods into eastern Europe comes from western Europe (and is therefore included in intra-European trade).

In the long run the share of manufactures in total European imports from overseas has increased, partly because of the rising exchange of manufactures between Europe (especially western Europe) on the one side and the United States and Japan on the other side. However, still at the end of the sixties, the trade dependence of Europe on other regions was quite small in sheer quantitative terms. It has been calculated that in 1969 imports of manufactures accounted for no more than 3 per cent of European manufacturing production. European exports of manufactures to the other regions accounted in the same year for 6 per cent of European manufacturing output. These ratios rose only fractionally from 1955 to 1970[50]; they are *average* ratios and conceal large inter-sectoral differences.

Table 1 also shows that Europe's trade balance with the overseas regions always closed with a deficit on the European side though the deficit – in relation to the level of imports and exports – gradually declined. Exports 'covered' only 75 per cent of imports in 1913 but around 92 per cent in 1970. It is important to stress that such ratios are the 'arithmetic' result of disparate national situations and therefore have to be interpreted with caution. National surpluses and deficits are not automatically transferable and countries in deficit might find little satisfaction in learning that others are in surplus. However, basically, Europe's trade balance with the overseas regions closed persistently with a deficit because the invisible items of the current account balance (transport, insurance, factor income, etc.) closed persistently in surplus and for the whole post-war period the surplus of the invisible items was bigger than the deficit of the trade balance The higher share of imports covered by exports in recent years in respect of 1913 and 1928 finds its basic explanation in the shrinking of the 'invisible receipts'. Those imports which could not be paid for with the invisible items had to be paid for with exports of commodities[51]. The trade balance of the socialist countries of eastern Europe with the overseas countries closes normally with a surplus largely because the net receipts of the service balance are virtually non-existent.

Europe's trade with the overseas regions may be split into two major flows. A first flow is constituted by trade with the developing countries whose capacity to import is essentially determined first by their exports to the developed

50. See, ECE, *The European economy from the 1950s to 1970s, cit.*, chapter 2. See also for more detailed data concerning the European Economic Community, UNCTAD, *Handbook of international trade and development statistics* 1972 (New York, 1972), part VII.

51. See the next section for a brief survey of the current balance developments between Europe and the overseas countries.

world and second by capital inflow[52]. A second flow is constituted by trade among the major industrial areas, that is, Europe, the United States and Japan. These three areas compete not only in their respective markets but also on the 'third markets' (which are mainly constituted by the developing countries). In the following pages the foreign trade position and development of Europe and the United States are briefly compared[53].

The level of European exports to the United States and of American exports to Europe in selected years is shown below, together with the percentage ratio between the two variables:

Trade between Europe and the United States

	Europe's exports to the United States	US exports to Europe	Percentage ratio between Europe and US exports
	(millions current dollars)		
1913	585	1,436	41
1928	938	2,281	41
1938	518	1,250	41
1950	1,305	3,230	40
1960	4,208	7,255	58
1970	11,370	14,620	78

Source: Table 1 and A. Maizels, *Industrial growth, cit.*

52. In turn the level of imports of the developed from the developing countries is mainly determined by the rate and pattern of growth in the former group.

53. Japan's foreign trade grew extremely fast after the Second World War but, obviously, the level of its exports is considerably lower than that of the United States and Western Europe. In 1970, Japan's exports (nearly 20 million dollars) amounted to 45 per cent of the United States total exports and to 42 per cent of Europe's exports overseas. In that year Japan had an active trade balance both with the United States and Europe. Japan's trade with the United States was much larger than with Europe. For a succinct review of Japan's foreign trade developments in the fifties and sixties, see GATT, *Japan's economic expansion and foreign trade 1955 to 1970*, Geneva 1971.

As can be seen, there has been a striking constancy in the relative level of the two trade flows until 1950, when European exports to the United States amounted to 40 per cent of the reverse trade flow. Obviously, the European deficit reached larger proportions immediately after the First and Second World Wars but as the reconstruction process advanced, the 'old equilibrium' was restored. Since the beginning of the fifties, European exports towards the United States grew much faster than the American exports towards Europe[54]. This was partly due to the commodity composition: the share of primary commodities still bulked large (about 50 per cent) in American exports to Europe at the beginning of the fifties while European exports to the United States are essentially constituted by manufactured products; and, as it was shown above, foreign trade in manufactures was particularly dynamic in the fifties and sixties. But even in the field of manufactures, the trade balance turned gradually in Europe's favour. The United States retained a dominating position for some products with a high technological content but lost ground for a large number of already 'standardized products' (from cars to textiles) which account for the largest share of manufactured products and are more sensitive to price relations[55]. In contrast with *total* trade balance, trade balance in *manufacturing* normally closed in Europe's and not in the United States's favour. In the period following the Second World War, a surplus in Europe's favour started to appear as early as the first half of the fifties[56]. If the over-evaluation of the dollar was one reason behind the relative weakness of the American exports to Europe·

54. From 1955 to 1970, European exports to the United States rose by 10·8 per cent per year while United States exports to Europe rose by 7·1 per cent per year (in volume).

55. These trade developments – and similar developments in trade between the United States and Japan – are at the root of the dollar devaluations at the beginning of the seventies. For a description of American trade in the post-war period, see, for example, GATT, *Trends in United States merchandise trade, 1953–1970*, Geneva 1972.

56. See A. Maizels, *Industrial Growth*, cit.

after the Second World War, another (partly related) factor is constituted by the activity of the American multinational corporations which localized in Europe an increasing share of their overall production capacity.

Europe and the United States are competing for a large number of products not only between themselves but also on the third markets. Their exports to these regions are summarized below:

Europe and the United States on the third markets[57]

	Exports from Europe:	Exports from the US: to the third markets[a] (million current dollars)	Percentage ratio between Europe and US exports
1913	3,490	590	592
1928	4,488	1,809	248
1938	3,453	1,345	257
1950	8,437	5,021	168
1960	17,472	9,415	186
1970	32,170	19,160	168

Source: As for Table 1.
a See footnote 57 for the definition of this term.

As can be seen by comparing the two text-tables, Europe's exports to the 'third markets' (in the main constituted by the developing countries) have always been much larger than European exports to the United States (and the same is true for imports). However, after the Second War, there has been a shift in favour of the exports towards the United States which in 1970 accounted for 35 per cent of Europe's exports to the 'third markets' as against 15 per cent only in 1938. The reasons behind the rapid increase of European

57. The expression 'Third markets' denotes the following regions in this section. For the United States: total exports less exports to Europe and to Canada. For Europe: total overseas exports (thus intra-European trade is excluded) less exports to the United States and Canada. This last country has been omitted from the comparison because its foreign trade with the United States presents some special characteristics (as does intra-European trade).

exports to the United States have been already briefly mentioned while Europe's exports to the other overseas markets have been hampered not only by the import possibilities of the developing countries but also by the intense competition from the United States and Japan. The United States exports towards the 'third markets' were very modest before the First World War, largely because of the commodity composition of American exports – the manufacturing products accounting for only 20 per cent of total exports. The dominance of food and raw materials explains the large share of their total exports shipped to Europe. However, the United States emerged from the First World War as a major industrial country and they also became net exporters of capital. These two features made possible a large expansion of American exports – both absolute and in relation to European exports – to the developing world. The relative position of Europe improved somewhat in the thirties (because of the protectionistic policies described earlier), fell (obviously) during the war and recovered somewhat in the fifties; but at the end of the sixties, it had fallen back to the relative position of 1950.

Thus, the United States proved to be a tougher competitor for Europe on the third markets than on their own market. The reasons have not been explored in detail so far in economic literature but the commodity composition of exports has probably played a role. The United States are big exporters of agriculture products and of capital goods (especially heavy equipment). The concentration of imports on capital goods on the part of the developing countries is well known. Furthermore, owing to urbanization, to the 'demographic explosion', a higher living standard and an only modest increase in agricultural production, the developing countries taken as a whole witnessed a rapid increase of agricultural imports which were largely provided by the United States. Finally, American exports to these areas have been helped – in a measure that it is impossible to quantify – by the large outflow of American capital.

CAPITAL MOVEMENTS

It is perhaps worth recalling at the outset that international capital movements may take various forms. The commonly accepted terminology speaks of public and private capital, long-term and short-term capital, direct investment and portfolio investment – just to mention only the major categories[58]. A credit is usually called 'short-term' when its maturity does not exceed one year. When short-term credit is provided by the banking system to exporters and importers to finance foreign trade, its functions are very similar to the domestic short-term bank credit. However, international short-term capital is also granted to permit the receiving country to overcome temporary balance-of-payment difficulties. Furthermore, liquid funds (that is short-term capital) move from one country to another, depending on differentials in interest rates, expectations of currency devaluations or revaluations and political considerations. When a loan is provided by a government or by a public institution, we are in the field of public capital movements (which may be long-term or short-term). A particularly important category of long-term capital is constituted by direct foreign investment which is defined as investment in an enterprise located in one country but 'controlled' by foreign capital. For that purpose, foreign capital has to reach a certain proportion of the total capital of the enterprise;[59] if it is lower, we remain in the category of portfolio investment. Finally, the reader may wish to remember an expres-

58. For a definition of the concepts see IMF, *Balance of payment yearbook*, vol. 16, 1964 and IMF, *Balance of payment manual*, third edition, 1961.

59. Effective control of a company is obviously difficult to determine: it can be obtained even if the proportion of the foreign capital is lower than 50 per cent of the total share capital. For statistical purposes, some guidelines have been put forward by the International Monetary Fund (see the publications quoted in the previous footnote). For a short summary see ECE, 'International direct investment by private enterprises in western Europe and North America' in 'Economic Bulletin for Europe', 1967, vol. 19, no. 1.

sion that is by now in common use, that is, the flow of financial resources to developing countries – an expression which denotes capital movements plus the grants (unilateral transfers) made by developed to developing countries.

For foreign trade there is plenty of statistical information, at least at current prices, and the major problem consists in rearranging and regrouping them so as to disentangle and bring to light the major trends and the most significant features. Nothing comparable is available in the field of capital movements. There are no international publications showing regularly capital movements by category *and* by country of origin and destination. This statistical deficiency is particularly serious for intra-European capital movements. Most of the information about capital movements between western Europe and the United States is based on American sources. Obviously, more information is available for the period following the Second World War than for the inter-war period. Because of this insufficient statistical basis, the review of capital movements will, of necessity, be less comprehensive and more episodical than the foregoing account of foreign trade. However, an attempt will be made to provide some information not only on the flow of capital movements but also on the position (or stock) in selected years, at least for some categories of international capital.

CURRENT BALANCE OF PAYMENTS

The current balance of payments, usually defined as including the trade balance and the balance of the so-called invisible items or services, is an essential link between trade balance and capital movements.[60] In national accounting, the surplus or the deficit of the current balance of payments is by definition equal to the difference between domestic savings and domestic investment. Therefore a surplus in

60. As mentioned, the international standard source for statistics on balance of payments is the International Monetary Fund. See also OECD, *Balance of payments surpluses and deficits: definition and meaning of different concepts*, in 'Occasional Studies', July 1975.

the current balance means that a country is a net exporter of real resources; and a deficit, that it is a net importer. A deficit normally entails foreign borrowing.[61] In principle, at least, a deficit can be financed by selling gold or official reserves, when available. In fact, current deficits have usually entailed both some reduction in official reserves and borrowing abroad. Foreign borrowing has in many cases reached higher proportions than was justified by the deficit because fears of devaluation led to a flight of liquid funds (that is, export of short-term capital) from the deficit country. Similarly, a surplus in the current balance was usually associated partly with an increase of official reserves and partly (or, rather, mainly) with capital exports.

For the period following the Second World War, there is solid documentation on the situation of the current balance of payments of the west European countries. In addition to national sources, the IMF regularly publishes internationally comparable statistics. By contrast, neither the IMF nor national sources provide information on the current balance for the socialist countries of eastern Europe. For the inter-war period, the concepts and the definitions are much less precise and inter-country comparability of scanty national data is, at best, only approximate for all countries.

Europe has traditionally been a net exporter of capital; this is tantamount to saying that Europe's current balance of payments has traditionally been in surplus. The United States, too, has been a large net exporter of capital since the end of the First World War. This is hardly surprising if one remembers what has been said before, namely that the current balance of payments equals the difference between savings and domestic investment. With the exception of a few special cases, only high-income countries generate a volume of savings higher than their investment

61. For the inter-war period, direct data on capital movements are not available for most countries; such movements have been estimated by making them equal to the current balance plus or minus changes in the gold stock.

needs. The relation between the level of development and the level of domestic savings may help to explain why only a few European countries closed their current balance in a surplus in the twenties while most of them had a surplus in the sixties.[62]

In the fifties, the aggregate current balance of payments of western Europe witnessed, on average, a yearly surplus of nearly half a billion dollars equal to about 0·2 per cent of gross national product of the region in that period. No data are available for the east European countries but it can be estimated that their current balance was only slightly in deficit. In the sixties, the aggregate surplus of the west European countries was considerably higher than in the fifties: it reached an annual average of about 2·5 billion dollars equal to about 0·5 per cent of the gross national product of the region. The aggregate balance of payments of the east European countries remained in deficit, which, towards the end of the decade, started to widen (see below in this section). Both in the fifties and the sixties, the highest surplus was recorded by the Federal Republic of Germany – a sharp contrast to the situation prevailing in the twenties. Italy, too, recorded in the sixties an exceptionally high surplus in her current balance of payments in spite of the relatively low income per head. The current balances of payments of the south European countries were in deficit both in the fifties and the sixties.

It is not possible to quantify the aggregate European surplus for the inter-war period. It is quite safe to say, however, that this was very modest. In the twenties, the current balances of payments of France and the United Kingdom showed comfortable surpluses but Germany was a net capital importer on a large scale. In addition to France and the United Kingdom, Switzerland, the Netherlands and Czechoslovakia closed their current balances in surplus in the twenties. In the thirties, the German deficit disappeared but the French and British surpluses were sharp-

62. The income level is, of course, not the only factor determining the balance between the domestic savings and domestic investment, but it is, probably, the most important one.

ly reduced in some years and became deficits in others. An international capital market hardly existed in that decade.

CAPITAL MOVEMENTS, INTER-WAR PERIOD

Before the First World War, international capital movements were largely confined to long-term capital and, in this field, portfolio investments were much larger than direct investment. The major part of (long-term) foreign loans were utilized by foreign governments or private corporations for expensive works of infrastructure (railways, harbours), plantations, etc. True, direct investments in industrial activities were present but – partly because the industrial sector was quite small in most of the receiving countries – they constituted only a minor part of the total capital exports of the lending countries. At that time the United Kingdom was by far the largest capital exporter and most of its capital was exported to the Empire and the United States. This kind of capital flow was associated, broadly speaking, with emigration of population from the capital-exporting to the capital-receiving country.[63]

Up to 1914, the transfer of liquid funds from one country to another in response to differentials in interest rates, political considerations or other special factors was the exception rather than the rule. Of course, movements of this kind did take place before the First World War but they

63. The approximate value of long-term foreign investment by the major capital exporting countries in 1913–14 was estimated to be as shown in the following figures:

	Billions US dollars
United Kingdom	18·0
France	9·0
Germany	5·8
United States	3·5
Belgium, Netherlands, Switzerland	5·5
Other countries	2·2
Total	44·0

The approximate distribution of this sum among continental areas was estimated to be as follows:

remained within modest dimensions. The international capital market in the twenties differed from the situation prevailing before the First World War in at least three major ways, that is, first, the rapid and disorderly growth of short-term capital movements; second, the increasing importance of direct investment in comparison with port-folio investment in the field of long-term capital; and, third, the emergence of the United States as a major capital exporting country (until 1914 it had been a net capital importer).

At the end of the First World War, a number of European countries, especially in central Europe and the Balkanic area, were not in a position to finance the imports even of primary necessities including food: the immediate problem was to avoid starvation rather than to elaborate long-term economic programmes. Even in countries where conditions were less dramatic, the pent-up demand provoked an upsurge of imports. It is therefore not surprising if all the European countries were net importers of capital in that period except the United Kingdom whose current balance of payments closed with a surplus in 1920. In 1919 and 1920 taken together, capital exports from the United States reached the exceptionally high figure of about 6 billion dollars, of which United States Government loans and advances accounted for about 2 billion. In addition to privately-floated capital issues, there were large withdrawals of funds deposited in the United States during or before the war by a number of European countries (in particular, the United Kingdom, France, the Netherlands, Sweden

	Billions US dollars
Africa	4·7
Asia	6·0
Europe	12·0
North America	10·5
Latin America	8·5
Oceania	2·3
Total	44·0

Source: United Nations, *International capital movements during the inter-war period*, New York 1949.

and Switzerland). Credits to Europe were granted also by some primary exporting countries like Argentina.

The relief programmes came virtually to an end in 1920 and capital exports from the United States dropped to less than one billion dollars in 1921. A number of traditional European creditor countries (France, the Netherlands, Switzerland) again became capital exporters. But the period 1921 to 1923 was characterized by political tensions and runaway inflation and was not conducive to large capital movements – with the exception of 'hot money' seeking refuge in the countries considered as more secure. With the political and monetary stabilization of 1924, international capital movements were resumed on a large scale. British capital continued to be mainly directed towards the dominions and colonies but the size of the outflow remained well below the pre-war level in real terms. French long-term investment was directed partly towards the overseas territories and partly towards Central Europe and the Balkans. However, the largest flow of international capital moved towards Germany and came mainly from the United States. A considerable part of it was at short-term maturity. The other Central European countries (except Czechoslovakia) and the Balkan countries were also net importers of capital.

The slowing down of the flow of United States capital towards Europe and especially Germany started already in 1928, that is before the outbreak of the Great Depression and was provoked by a considerable rise of interest rates on the American market. The Great Depression was accompanied and rendered more dramatic by hectic and large-scale movements of international short-term capital. The precipitous withdrawal of foreign capital from Germany will be briefly reviewed below in this section. The other Central European and the Balkan countries were also severely affected by the cessation of capital inflow and large withdrawals. However, direct investments were much less affected than either portfolio or short-term investment. In 1930, the accrued liquidity of some important financial centres like London, Paris and New York facilitated the issue of foreign loans for a number of non-European countries but this was a short-lived phenomenon. Capital movements were subject to more severe regulations and controls in all countries than was foreign trade.

In the protectionist atmosphere of the thirties, three major aspects can be noted in the field of international capital movements. The first concerns the 'compartmentalization' of capital movements. A similar feature was noted for foreign trade. The web of administrative controls reduced severely the possibilities of multilateral settlements and capital movements (as foreign trade) were further concentrated into some preferential areas, for instance the sterling area and the French colonies. A second aspect concerns the increasing flow of capital from Europe to the United States after the dollar devaluation of 1933 and dictated by a combination of economic and political reasons. Obviously, the political causes become gradually more important as one approaches the outbreak of the Second World War. The third aspect concerns a somewhat paradoxical result of the administrative controls affecting trade and income transfers. The autarkic policies in the trade field and the difficulties in the way of exporting investment income, gave an involuntary push to foreign direct investment which declined less or increased more than could be expected at first sight.[64]

A few summary indications of net capital movements from 1924 to 1934 for France, the United Kingdom,

64. For a summary review of capital movements in the inter-war period see United Nations, *International capital movements during the inter-war period*, 1949. A more detailed description up to the end of the Great Depression is contained in *The problems of international investment*, a report by a study group of members of the Royal Institute of International Affairs, London 1937. Capital movements from and to the United States are examined by H. B. Lary in *The United States in the World Economy*, Department of Commerce, Washington 1943. The vicissitudes of short-term capital movements in the twenties and during the Great Depression, with particular reference to Germany, are examined by M. Fanno, in *Normal and abnormal international capital transfers*, Minneapolis 1939 (translation from the Italian edition *I trasferimenti anormali dei capitali e le crisi*, Torino 1935.)

Germany and the United States, are given in the text-table on page 578.

France appears to have been a large capital exporter for most of the twenties. This country witnessed a fast economic development during the twenties and for most of the period the current balance of payments was largely in surplus. Economic expansion was however associated with a relatively high rate of inflation which provoked a flight of short-term capital mainly to London and New York. In 1919 and 1920 there had been a massive inflow of short-term capital into France which was gradually withdrawn in the subsequent years when the stability of the French franc began to falter. In 1925 and 1926 there was also a large outflow of French capital. During the Great Depression the tide changed direction. The French franc became the leader of the gold bloc and attracted large masses of hot money. A new outflow of short-term capital started in 1936 when a left-wing government took power. Long-term capital movements followed a less erratic course. Investment in overseas territories continued but never recovered its pre-war volume. Probably more important than capital flows overseas, were, during the twenties, the flow of long-term capital towards some central and Balkan countries. Before the First World War, there was a considerable amount of French investment in Russia, which was favoured by the French Government for political reasons. Such investments were lost in the Soviet revolution but the French policy of favouring a flow of private investment, and the granting of public loans to actual or potential allied countries, continued between the two wars.

The unique position of London as the world banking centre before the First World War has been mentioned already. In the inter-war period, overseas lending never regained the importance of the pre-war period, though the level in current sterling of new capital issues on overseas account was higher in some years of the twenties than in the peak period of 1910–13. Net income from overseas investment which amounted to 135 per cent of net capital exports in 1910–13 jumped to 265 per cent in the years 1922 to

Capital movements, net: millions of US dollars

(— denotes net exports; + net imports)

	France[a]	United Kingdom	Germany Long-term[b]	Short-term[c]	United States Long-term	Short-term
1924	−535	−380	+238	+227	−672	+119
1925	−450	−261	+289	+543	−543	−106
1926	−483	+126	+346	−170	−696	+419
1927	−504	−386	+424	+613	−991	+585
1928	−236	−569	+426	+541	−798	−348
1929	+ 20	−574	+157	+375	−240	− 4
1930	+257	−112	+266	−137	−221	−279
1931	+791	+313	+ 43	−583	+225	−637
1932	+917	+179	+ 3	−106	+257	−446
1933	+ 39	—	− 15	−153	+ 78	−419
1934	+172	+ 35	..	..	+200	+222

Source: United Nations, *International capital movements during the inter-war period*, October 1949.

  a Includes the French overseas territories.
  b Incomplete.
  c Mainly short-term

1928 reflecting a decline of the outflows in comparison with the total amount of foreign investment. This decline was the outcome of a number of interrelated factors, notably the impoverishment of the country provoked by the war and the consequent larger needs of the national economy, the emergence of New York as a second world-wide financial centre, and the high interest rates prevailing in London for most of the twenties in an attempt to defend the exchange rate of sterling.

Still, the United Kingdom remained the largest exporter of long-term capital among the European countries in the inter-war period. The figures shown in the above text-table indicate that capital export from France was bigger than from the United Kingdom; but, as already mentioned, such figures include long and short-term capital; and short-term capital movements differed in the two countries not only in intensity but also in direction. Sterling was a reserve currency and strenuous efforts were made to prevent its devaluation. A considerable amount of short-term funds was normally held in London by foreign countries, partly as working balances and partly for confidence reasons. The United Kingdom was therefore for a good part of the twenties a net importer of short-term capital (as was to be the case of the United States in the thirties and still more so after the Second World War). A significant part of the foreign funds was of French origin. This policy of 'lending long and borrowing short' was not without risk. Already in 1929 sterling went under pressure because of large withdrawals of French funds. The outflow on the part of most foreign countries holding balances in London continued in 1930 and reached its peak in 1931; but after the devaluation of sterling (in September 1931) a new inflow began. After 1933, following a pause in 1931 and 1932, there was again a net outflow of long-term capital but it was of modest proportions. The share of Europe remained very modest in total long-term capital exports from the United Kingdom (10 per cent or less).

In contrast with France and the United Kingdom, Germany in the twenties was a big, in fact the biggest, capital importer. The need to import capital was a direct consequence of the war and of the defeat and it was further enhanced by reparations. National needs, reparations, capital imports, abrupt withdrawals of funds since 1930, the banking and financial crisis, are just a few interrelated aspects of the economic and political vicissitudes of that period.[65] The literature on the financial and monetary developments which saw Germany at their centre, is immense.[66] Only a few points will be recalled briefly here, strictly in the field of capital movement.

After the monetary stabilization of 1924, it was an easy

65. For a suggestive interpretation of the major economic developments, see H. W. Arndt, *The Economic Lessons of the Nineteen-Thirties*, London 1944.

66. The publications quoted in footnote 64 contain a number of bibliographical references.

task for Germany to borrow from the international markets and particularly from the United States; because of the basic strength of the German economy, of the high interest rates which were offered, and of apparently sound fiscal and monetary policies. From 1924 to 1930 the net inflow of foreign long-term capital into Germany has been estimated at about 2 billion dollars. About 55 per cent of it came from the United States, and nearly 25 per cent from the United Kingdom and the Netherlands together. (The Dutch share was slightly higher than that of the United Kingdom.) The remaining part was scattered among a number of countries. About 40 per cent of this debt had been contracted by private borrowers (mainly banks and enterprises) and the remaining part by the central government and local authorities. The inflow of short-term funds was even bigger than that of long-term capital. In 1930, the outstanding German debt with short-term maturity may have amounted to about 3 billion dollars and it was mainly of American origin. The reparation payments in the period 1924 to 1930 were much lower than the volume of imported capital: they may be estimated at about $2\frac{1}{2}$ billion dollars. It is therefore fairly clear that the major part of the foreign capital was used for fostering domestic investment and consumption. A rapid reimbursement of the outstanding debt was out of the question for Germany since its current balance of payments was heavily in deficit and most of the imported foreign capital had been spent on capital or current expenditure by enterprises and public authorities. Already in 1929 the inflow of foreign capital into Germany slowed down, mainly because of the high interest rates prevailing in New York. In 1930, the depression led foreign investors to withdraw part, at least, of their credits. This action provoked a sharp decline in the gold reserves of the German Central Bank and a wave of bankruptcies ensured. In 1931, the German Government froze existing debts.

In the meantime, the extremely severe depression combined with administrative controls, had transformed the deficit of the German current balance of payments into a surplus. Payment of debts was thus facilitated, but, for various reasons, it took place only partially and very gradually. The Nazi Government took power in 1933 and foreign capital – under government control – was largely used as an instrument for creating a German preferential area in the central and Balkan areas.

Heavy borrowing by Germany in the twenties was not an isolated case. Austria, Hungary, Poland, Rumania, Bulgaria and Greece were also net capital importers in that period and some of them, like Austria, continued to import capital in the first half of the thirties. The economies of these countries had been shattered by the war and, in some cases, by post-war vicissitudes. Hungary, Poland and Yugoslavia were newly-created states. Everywhere there was an urgent need for foreign assistance, not only for economic development, but also, in part, to cope with the most basic needs of the population. Czechoslovakia was the only central European country to record a surplus in her current balance of payments in the twenties.[67]

The Austrian situation was perhaps the most serious. Immediately after the war, Austrian banks had great recourse to foreign capital, mainly in the form of short-term borrowing. In 1922, the intervention of the League of Nations was requested, and a plan was drawn up for the financial rehabilitation of the country. As part of this plan, a long-term loan was granted to Austria, and it was guaranteed by the Austrian Government. The central aim of the loan was financial and foreign exchange stability, rather than economic development. In the wake of the League of Nations programme, Austria was able to continue to borrow abroad, mainly at short-term. But the withdrawal of short-term funds in 1929 and 1930 made necessary the granting of a second long-term loan in 1930 and of a third in 1933. After the apparent success of the Austrian re-habilitation programme, rather similar reconstruction schemes were prepared by the League of Nations for Hun-

67. See R. Nötel, *International Capital Movements and Finance in Eastern Europe, 1919–1949,* in 'Vierteljahrschrift für Sozial-und Wirtschaftsgeschichte', Wiesbaden 1974.

gary and Bulgaria also. By and large, about 50 per cent of the foreign capital received by these two countries was utilized to buy imports; about 10 per cent for the purchase of gold, and the remaining 40 per cent for interest and dividend payments.

The world crisis of 1929 found the central European and Balkan countries in a highly vulnerable position. During the crisis, the long-term capital inflow was gradually discontinued, and payments for amortization, interests and dividends became a very heavy burden. It was, therefore, necessary to shift from a position of import surplus to one of export surplus for goods and services taken together, and this implied not only the establishment of import controls but also a severe restrictive policy to reduce domestic demand.[68] This painful process of adjustment for these countries was not followed by the reintegration into a system of international capital transfers. It was followed rather by a period of German hegemony where capital movements were dictated by the political and military pressure.

CAPITAL MOVEMENTS, POST-WAR PERIOD

The history of capital movements in the post-war period starts with the large-scale public programmes for assistance and relief essentially financed by the United States Government.[69] These programmes took a variety of forms and were handled by a number of organizations (partly created *ad hoc*) but they presented an important common feature: they were for the most part constituted by grants and not

68. Some relief was obtained by postponing debt repayments by agreement or by unilateral measures. However, the most important factor in the thirties, to lessen the burden of debt repayment was the devaluation of the US dollar and the pound sterling; but, in turn, the devaluation of the major currencies increased the difficulties of the debtor countries' export trade.

69. The whole approach followed after the Second World War for war reparations and treatment of the defeated countries differed sharply from that followed after the First World War.

by loans as was the case after the First World War.[70] Both in 1946 and 1947, unilateral transfers from the United States to European governments or public organizations amounted to about 2 billion dollars. The year 1948 is a landmark in Europe's post-war economic history. There was not only a shift from mainly humanitarian assistance to economic aid but the major policy orientations were laid down which were briefly reviewed in the first section of this chapter and which shaped the economic landscape of Europe in the fifties and sixties. In 1948 the Organization for European Economic Co-operation (OEEC) was set up and a massive programme of economic aid was launched: it was the celebrated 'European Recovery Programme' (ERP)[71]. This programme was financed by the United States; it consisted mainly of grants and lasted until 1951. The east European countries did not participate in the venture and, in 1949, they set up an economic organization of their own, the Council of Mutual Economic Assistance. The division of Europe into two blocs had started. The unilateral transfers which took place from the United States to Europe under the ERP amounted to about eight million dollars.

After the vicissitudes of the Korean war (1950) and the uncertain economic situation of 1951 and 1952, the year 1953 saw a sharp recovery of output in the west European economies. The expansion of output was associated with an improvement in the foreign accounts of the region which was more rapid than expected. By 1954 the current balance of the west European countries taken together was again in surplus. The rapid economic growth lasted virtually up to

70. In 1947, there was however a loan of 2,850 million dollars from the United States to the United Kingdom mainly in connection with the abortive attempt to re-establish the convertibility of sterling.

71. The full list of the European members of the OEEC is given in the publications of that organization. The literature on the ERP is voluminous. The OEEC reports provide a detailed account of the sums concerned and of their use. For a summary view and bibliographical references, see N. S. Buchanan, *International Investment*, in 'A Survey of Contemporary Economics', vol. II, pp. 307 *et seq.* (published by the American Economic Association, 1952).

1973. What were the major flows of international capital movements in that period?

Resumption of international capital movements took place only slowly during the fifties, when administrative controls were strict in most countries. The European Payments Union (EPU), set up in 1950, proved to be rather efficient machinery for preventing the disorderly movement of hot money. Towards the end of the decade, the situation started to change. The balance of payments of the major west European countries was in a comfortable surplus and virtually all national currencies were made convertible into dollars (the much-discussed dollar gap had disappeared). The continuing rapid economic expansion in Europe and the creation of the European Economic Community stimulated American direct investment in the region. The need to assist developing countries became a major policy issue. Finally, in the wake of a better political situation, economic relations between eastern and western Europe took on a new dimension and capital movements – mainly linked with the import of 'technology' into eastern Europe – played a significant role.

With some over-simplification, capital movements in the post-war period can be arranged in the following major categories: (a) short-term capital movements, due partly to inter-country differentials in interest rates but mainly to confidence factors; (b) long-term capital movements between the west European countries and the United States. In this field, the central and most controversial issue concerns direct American investment in European industry; (c) direct investment as between west European countries; (d) capital exports from Europe to the developing countries; and (e) capital movements between west and east (socialist) European countries.

(a) Short-term capital movements did not reach, in the post-war period, the dimensions of the twenties, neither did they produce such disruptive effects. However, this statement has to be qualified in two respects. The first concerns the United Kingdom. Sterling was a reserve currency in the fifties and sixties and capital movements were virtually free inside the sterling area. Furthermore, the United Kingdom had not been in a position to pay cash for all the imports she needed during the war. Foreign countries, and especially the countries of the sterling area, had thus accumulated in London a large amount of credits known as 'sterling balances'.[72] On the other hand, the gold and foreign exchange reserves of the United Kingdom were too low to provide a solid basis for a reserve currency. Therefore, any cyclical worsening in the current balance of payments of the United Kingdom undermined the confidence of creditor countries in the capacity of the United Kingdom to honour its commitments and provoked a withdrawal of short-term funds from the London market. This withdrawal weakened sterling further and compelled the authorities to take more severe deflationary measures than would otherwise have been the case (the much discussed 'stop go' policy).[73] Speculative withdrawals of short-term funds took place, for instance, at the end of 1950, in 1956, 1961, 1963 and 1967. These cyclical vicissitudes were superimposed on a steady flow of long-term capital towards the sterling area countries.

The second qualification concerns the dollar. Towards the end of the sixties and the beginning of the seventies, an increasing malaise affected the world's leading currency. The current balance of payments of the United States had deteriorated sharply in the second half of the sixties and its gold reserves had been considerably reduced. A change in parity between the dollar and the currencies of most west European countries was considered more and more likely

72. At the end of 1945, the holdings of the sterling area countries amounted to about 2,400 million sterling and the holdings of the non-sterling area countries amounted to about 1,170 million sterling. During the fifties, the sterling holdings of the non-sterling area countries declined sharply, while the sterling holdings of the sterling area countries rose, albeit modestly. (See R. A. Conan, *The Rationale of the Sterling Area*, London 1961.)

73. For a discussion of these developments, see, for instance, ECE, *Economic Survey of Europe in 1958*, chapter III. On the working of the sterling area, see Ph. W. Bell, *The Sterling Area in the Post-War World*, Oxford 1956 and R. A. Conan, *Capital Imports into Sterling Countries*, London 1960.

(and this, in fact, took place). In anticipation of the devaluation of the dollar, there were repeated outflows of liquid funds from the United States to Europe. Most of the 'hot money' which left the dollar was invested in German marks or Swiss francs, thus reinforcing basic market forces operating for a revaluation of these currencies. International movements of short-term funds towards the end of the sixties and the beginning of the seventies took place largely through the euro-dollar market.[74]

(b) At the beginning of the fifties, the outstanding amount of private long-term investment in the United States, by the combined west European countries, exceeded the amount of the United States's private long-term investment in Europe: 5·3 as against 3·1 billion dollars. There was a difference in Europe's favour both in the field of portfolio and in that of direct investment. The participation of European (mainly British) capital in United States's industrial and commercial activities was a feature going back to the nineteenth century. At that time, as mentioned, the United Kingdom was by far the largest net exporter of capital and most of it was directed towards the colonies and North America. However, already in 1950, more than 50 per cent of European long-term private investment in the United States was constituted by portfolio investment (mainly corporate stocks). In all likelihood, most of it had crossed the Atlantic in search of security against political risks and inflation.[75]

74. An account of the euro-dollar market's vicissitudes can be found in the annual reports of the Bank for International Settlements, Basel.

75. The amount of United States private long-term investment in western Europe (A) and of western Europe private long-term investment in the United States (B) is given below for selected years and separately for direct and other (mainly portfolio) investment.

(millions of dollars)

A	1950	1958	1965	1970
Direct	1,733	4,573	13,894	24,516
Other	1,371	2,332	5,707	5,118
B				
Direct	2,228	4,070	6,105	9,554
Other	3,071	7,319	12,237	22,191

Source: United States Department of Commerce, *Balance of Payments,*

In 1958, the amount of the European and of the United States reciprocal investment had more than doubled in comparison with 1950 and a feature became known which assumed much larger proportions during the sixties: on the American export side, the most dynamic category was constituted by direct investment, while on the European export side the fastest increase was recorded by portfolio investment. At the end of 1970, United States direct investment in western Europe had reached about 24·5 billion dollars. Europe's portfolio investment in the United States was not much lower but direct investment did not reach 10 billion dollars.

The factors behind the rapid expansion of American investment in western Europe have been the object of extensive examination by economic literature: differences in labour costs, the prospects offered by a booming European market, transport costs, the possibility of circumventing the external tariffs of the Common Market, have been generally considered as significant factors in this respect. Much more controversial is the question of the effects of American investment on western Europe. Economic and political considerations are strictly inter-related here and the question of foreign direct investment fades into the more complex problem of multinational corporations – a problem that falls outside the scope of the present chapter.[76] It may be noted however that the controversy centres not so much on the principle of foreign direct investments

_____

revised edition 1963 and *Survey of Current Business*, September 1966 and October 1972.

76. The bibliography on foreign direct investment and on multi-national corporations is quite large. We will limit ourselves to quoting three articles, partly bibliographical, dealing with the specific problem here discussed, namely United States direct foreign investment in western Europe. See Bela Balassa, *American Direct Investment in the Common Market*, in Banca Nazionale del Lavoro Quarterly Review, June 1966; ECE, *International Direct Investment by Private Enterprises in western Europe and North America*, in 'Economic Bulletin for Europe', vol. 19, p. 1, 1967; and *Rapport sur la capacité concurrentielle de la Communauté européenne* (by a working group set up by the Commission), Brussels, November 1971.

(they are generally considered a major vehicle for importing technology) but rather on some side effects (risk of a sudden transfer from one country to another, relations between the government of the host country and foreign enterprises, the desire to protect national enterprises in some key sectors etc.).

The share of western Europe in total foreign direct investment of the United States increased sharply in the post-war period: it was about 15 per cent in 1950 and more than 30 per cent in 1970. Most of the increase took place between 1958 and 1965 – those were the central years of western Europe's 'economic miracle' and the first years of the European Economic Community. What proportion of industrial enterprises located in Europe is 'controlled' by American capital, is a question that cannot be settled on the basis of available statistical information. A number of investigations have been carried out especially in the sixties by most west European countries but the methods used are too heterogeneous to allow inter-country comparison.[77] By and large, it may perhaps be said that towards the end of the sixties the share of manufacturing industry controlled by American capital approached 10 per cent in Belgium and the United Kingdom, in terms of output, while it was considerably lower in the other countries, especially in the Scandinavian ones. American investment in British manufacturing industry was already rather high before the Second World War while its participation in Belgian industry has risen sharply since the second half of the fifties. However, these average ratios are not very significant. The degree of participation varies a great deal from branch to branch and it tends to be concentrated on dynamic industries like computers and some sub-branches of chemicals and electrical engineering.[78] It is the large American participation in science-based industries which is a matter of concern for some European governments.

77. The United Kingdom is the only country which provides specific information on this matter in the industrial censuses of 1963 and 1968.

78. The American participation in the car industry is a notable exception to this statement.

(c) Unfortunately, very little can be said about long-term capital movements and, in particular, about direct investments as between the individual west European countries. The national investigations carried on in this field in a number of countries do not permit, for the reasons mentioned above, anything like a comprehensive picture. This lack of information, as well as being unfortunate for the present paper, may appear surprising, since liberalization of capital movements was, and still is, a major objective both for the OECD and the European Economic Community. In fact, the United States has so far remained the major partner of the individual west European countries in the field of capital movements. Going by broad generalizations, it is probably correct to say that European enterprises have found it more useful to seek partnership with American, rather than with other European, enterprises, because the former were better equipped to offer modern technology and 'know-how'. Developments in the capital field were thus at variance with developments in the field of international trade: at the end of the sixties, the largest trade partner of most west European countries was a west European country; by contrast, in the field of capital movements, as far as can be judged from admittedly fragmentary data, the United States is still the most important partner.

Yet the network of reciprocal foreign direct investment as between the west European countries is by no means negligible. National investigations suggest that towards the end of the sixties, the share of non-European capital (mainly of United States and Canadian origin) accounted for about 50 per cent of total foreign capital in the industry of Belgium, the Federal Republic of Germany and Italy. The participation of foreign capital of non-European origin appears to be lower than 50 per cent in Austria, France and the Scandinavian countries. The participation of British capital amounted to about 10 per cent of total foreign participation in a number of west European countries and reached 20 per cent in Sweden. The participation of Dutch capital amounted to more than 10 per cent of total foreign capital in the Federal Republic of Germany, France, Italy and Sweden. The United Kingdom was the only country where United States and Canadian capital, taken together, accounted for an overwhelming part (nearly 80 per cent) of total foreign participation.[79]

(d) Capital flow from Europe and other developed countries towards the developing countries, is just one facet of the policies which have been adopted by the former group to contribute to the economic development of the latter. The role of foreign capital cannot be assessed in isolation: for instance, a more liberal commercial policy on the part of the industrialized countries, by facilitating exports of manufactured goods from the developing countries could reduce the amount of foreign assistance in terms of grants and loans.[80]

As mentioned, the expression 'flow of resources' from developed to developing countries includes both grants and loans. In view of the heavy burden that the debt service represents for developing countries (amortization, interest and dividends), attempts were made not only to ease the loan conditions but also to increase the share of grants in the total resource flow. For the developed market economies, the development assistance programme was organized in the framework of a special OECD Committee. Total flow may be classified in three major categories: official development assistance, other official flows and private capital. The first category accounted at the end of

79. An attempt to assess the reciprocal participation of foreign capital of European origin in a number of west European countries has been made by the ECE, *Economic Survey of Europe in 1970*, part 2.

80. No attempt will be made here to quote the literature dealing with the various interrelated aspects of the economic development of the developing countries. On the strict field of the flow of financial resources from the developed to the developing countries, see United Nations Conference on Trade and Development, third session, Santiago de Chile, in particular vol. III, *Financing and invisibles*, New York 1973; OECD, *Development co-operation*, (annual review); United Nations, *The external financing of economic development, 1963–67*, New York 1969. Summary figures and a clarifying presentation of them can be found also in the United Nations Statistical Yearbooks (see, for instance, the edition for 1973, p. 709 *et seq.*).

the sixties for about 45 per cent of the total flow, and was constituted by grants for about 60–65 per cent. It should be 70 per cent according to the established norm. However, the actual share varies a great deal as among countries: broadly speaking it is highest (80–90 per cent) for the Scandinavian countries and no more than 50 per cent for the Federal Republic of Germany and the United Kingdom. In spite of the efforts made to concentrate the flow of resources into the official programmes, the most rapid growth in the sixties was witnessed by private capital, which expanded at a rate of 8·4 per cent per year as against 7·2 for total flows. Towards the end of the sixties, the annual net flow of resources from western Europe to the developing countries amounted to about 6 billion dollars. The development assistance programme of the socialist countries of eastern Europe is organized within the framework of CMEA and it is mainly constituted by credits. For 1970, bilateral commitments by these countries taken together amounted to about 1·3 billion dollars.

(e) Capital movements between the market economies of western Europe and the socialist countries of eastern Europe have to be seen in the context of their respective political and economic systems. As mentioned, foreign trade is conducted by state organizations in the socialist countries and the same principle applies to capital movements. On the western side, capital exports to the socialist countries can be made either by public or private organizations, eventually under state guarantee. Precise data on east-west current balance of payments and capital movements are not available but an attempt to estimate rough orders of magnitude has been made recently in a publication of the United Nations Economic Commission for Europe, for the period 1965 to 1974.[81] For most of these years, both the trade balance and the service balance closed in surplus for western Europe. The surplus of the service balance has always been very modest (100 million dollars per year or less). The two major items of the service balance have been the touristic balance which regularly

81. ECE, *Economic Bulletin for Europe*, vol. 27, 1975.

showed a surplus on the eastern Europe side and income payments, which regularly showed a surplus on the western Europe side. This latter account consists essentially of receipts for interest and earnings for leasing, licences and patents. The trade surplus of western Europe has been much bigger than the service surplus. From 1965 to 1974, the cumulated surplus of the current account balance between west and east European countries amounted to about 4·5 billion dollars in favour of the former. This surplus was mainly due to the import of capital goods by east European countries from west European ones. The east European deficit was, to a minor extent, financed by unilateral transfers (indemnities, pensions and private and official donations especially for the Federal Republic of Germany to the German Democratic Republic). Perhaps half of the remaining east European deficit was financed by western credits – most of them of medium or long-term maturity. The remaining part of the deficit was financed by multilateral settlements, sales of gold and operations on the euro-dollar market. The widening of the deficit in recent years is a source of concern for the future development of east-west economic relations and calls for more manufactured exports from eastern to western Europe.

TABLES

TABLE I:
World and Europe's trade (millions of current dollars and percentages; f.o.b. values)

	1913	1928	1938	1950	1960	1970
	(a) million current dollars					
World trade	19,159	32,615	21,917	61,000	128,000	312,700
Intra-European trade	6,278	9,630	6,393	13,152	41,810	123,400
European exports to other regions	4,255	5,656	4,101	11,478	22,670	45,300
European imports from other regions	5,819	8,253	6,241	14,790	25,200	49,700
Trade among the non-European countries[a]	2,807	9,076	5,182	21,580	38,300	94,300
	(b) Percentage composition					
World trade	100·0	100·0	100·0	100·0	100·0	100·0
Intra-European trade	32·8	29·5	29·2	21·6	32·7	39·5
European exports to other regions	22·2	17·4	18·7	18·8	17·7	14·5
European imports from other regions	30·4	25·3	28·5	24·2	19·7	15·9
Trade among the non-European countries[a]	14·6	27·8	23·6	35·4	29·9	30·1

a Obtained by difference.

Sources: World exports: Lamartine Yates, *Forty years of foreign trade*, London 1959; League of Nations, *The Network of World Trade*, Geneva 1942; UNCTAD, *Handbook of International Trade and Development Statistics*, New York 1972.
Other cols: UN/ECE, *Growth and stagnation in the European economy*, Geneva 1954; W. L. Woytinsky, *Die Welt in Zahlen*, Berlin 1927; UNCTAD, *op. cit.*

TABLE 2:
Europe's exports by countries, 1913 to 1970
(Percentages based on dollars at current prices and current exchange rates; f.o.b. values)

Exporting countries	Exports of individual countries as percentage of total European exports						Exports of individual countries to Europe as percentage of their total exports					
	1913	1928	1938	1950	1960	1970	1913	1928	1938	1950	1960	1970
1. Albania	—	..	..	..	0·1	0·1	..	..	..	100·0	97·4	..
2. Austria	5·3[a]	2·0	1·7	1·3	1·7	1·7	80·3[a]	86·5	83·7	80·0	81·2	85·3
3. Belgium-Luxemburg	6·5	5·6	6·9	6·7	5·9	6·9	79·2	69·9	69·1	67·4	68·9	81·1
4. Bulgaria	0·2	0·3	0·6	0·5	0·9	1·2	83·3	91·1	92·6	96·6	94·3	91·3
5. Czechoslovakia	—	4·1	3·4	3·2	3·0	2·2	—	84·4	70·1	83·0	79·8	79·2
6. Denmark	1·6	2·9	3·2	2·7	2·3	2·0	95·4	93·9	93·1	83·4	78·3	79·2
7. Finland	0·7	1·0	1·7	1·6	1·5	1·4	68·8	82·3	84·0	81·7	82·3	85·1
8. France	12·6	13·4	8·4	12·3	10·6	10·5	66·6	62·5	54·2	44·2	47·4	68·1
9. Germany R.F.	22·8 }	18·8	20·6	8·0	17·7	20·2	66·3 }	69·9	65·1	66·7	65·3	71·6
10. Germany D.R.				1·3	3·1	2·7				86·6	89·0	91·6
11. Greece	0·2	0·5	0·9	0·4	0·3	0·4	78·3	78·2	75·6	79·7	78·4	79·0
12. Hungary	[b]	1·0	1·5	1·3	1·4	1·4	[b]	96·5	88·4	86·5	86·6	91·0
13. Ireland	—	1·4	1·1	0·8	0·7	0·6	—	98·2	99·2	94·1	82·6	82·0
14. Italy	4·6	5·0	5·3	4·9	5·7	7·8	58·7	57·4	48·7	59·3	60·4	68·7
15. Netherlands	4·6	5·1	5·4	5·7	6·2	6·9	65·2	74·3	69·0	67·7	73·7	80·7
16. Norway	1·1	1·2	1·8	1·6	1·4	1·5	73·9	69·2	81·9	73·1	75·5	77·7
17. Poland	—	1·8	2·1	2·6	2·1	2·1	—	92·2	85·0	48·4	83·0	85·7
18. Portugal	0·3	0·3	0·5	0·8	0·5	0·6	59·4	69·8	69·4	46·4	46·0	56·1

19. Rumania	1·3	1·1	1·5	1·0	1·1	1·1	87·0	89·4	86·4	90·8	88·0	82·3
20. Sweden	2·1	2·8	4·4	4·5	4·0	4·0	83·6	74·9	77·4	75·6	75·8	79·6
21. Switzerland	2·5	2·7	2·9	3·7	2·9	3·0	69·3	69·2	69·4	59·2	64·0	66·5
22. Spain	2·0	2·7	0·9	1·6	1·1	1·4	69·4	69·7	73·5	60·4	64·8	57·1
23. Turkey	—	··	··	1·1	0·5	0·3	—	··	··	72·7	71·3	73·1
24. United Kingdom	24·2	22·9	21·7	24·7	15·8	11·4	30·1	31·6	32·1	35·0	35·0	46·0
25. Yugoslavia	—	0·7	1·1	0·7	0·9	1·0	—	95·6	88·9	77·8	78·1	79·9
26. USSR	7·4	2·7	2·4	7·0	8·6	7·6	··	··	··	68·2	73·4	70·9
Total Europe percentages	100·0	100·0	100·0	100·0	100·0	100·0	59·6	63·0	61·3	53·4	64·8	73·1
million dollars	10,533	15,286	10,494	24,630	64,450	169,040	6,278	9,630	6,393	13,152	41,810	123,400

Sources: See Table 1.
a Austra-Hungary
b Included in Austria.
Note: The figures have not been adjusted for the changes in national frontiers.

TABLE 3:
Europe's imports by countries, 1913 to 1970
(Percentages based on dollars at current prices and current exchange rates; c.i.f. values).

Importing countries	Imports of individual countries as percentage of total European imports						Imports of individual countries from Europe as percentage of their total imports					
	1913	1928	1938	1950	1960	1970	1913	1928	1938	1950	1960	1970
1. Albania	—	..	..	0·1	0·1	..		..	..	97·2	97·0	..
2. Austria	5·4ᵃ	2·4	2·1	1·7	2·0	1·9	65·8ᵃ	83·6	74·7	78·5	82·3	88·7
3. Belgium-Luxemburg	6·8	4·6	5·6	6·7	5·6	6·2	58·6	65·2	54·8	60·2	65·7	71·8
4. Bulgaria	0·3	0·3	0·4	0·7	0·9	1·0	80·6	94·1	93·3	97·2	95·0	92·0
5. Czechoslovakia	—	2·9	2·1	2·2	2·6	2·0	—	82·9	66·1	84·4	82·6	89·1
6. Denmark	1·8	2·4	2·6	3·0	2·6	2·4	73·5	71·3	83·3	86·5	82·7	78·6
7. Finland	0·7	1·0	1·3	1·3	1·5	1·4	71·6	78·2	82·5	80·2	85·0	84·2
8. France	12·7	10·9	9·7	10·5	8·9	10·3	46·5	42·7	33·7	32·0	41·2	63·7
9. Germany F.R.	20·1	17·3	16·3	9·3	14·4	16·4	40·7	47·1	50·3	53·6	57·7	65·0
10. Germany D.R.				1·3	2·8	2·7				87·8	88·5	93·0
11. Greece	0·2	0·8	1·0	1·5	1·0	1·1	71·0	62·7	73·3	71·5	68·3	72·5
12. Hungary	ᵇ	1·1	0·9	1·4	1·4	1·4	ᵇ	93·4	89·3	89·0	81·4	87·9
13. Ireland	—	1·5	1·5	1·5	0·9	0·9	—	86·3	66·8	72·3	71·3	75·6
14. Italy	5·5	6·0	4·3	5·2	6·7	8·2	58·2	47·0	60·0	60·9	52·2	59·3
15. Netherlands	6·4	5·6	5·7	7·1	6·5	7·4	47·0	61·4	58·7	59·0	63·0	71·1
16. Norway	1·2	1·4	2·1	2·4	2·1	2·0	84·5	74·7	77·1	76·5	77·0	73·5
17. Poland	—	2·0	1·8	2·3	2·1	2·0	—	75·6	62·8	90·2	83·0	89·1
18. Portugal	0·7	0·6	0·8	0·9	0·8	0·9	75·0	74·2	64·4	57·8	62·2	64·2

19. Rumania	0·9	1·0	1·0	0·7	0·9	1·1	89·5	90·8	89·1	93·1	90·5	88·8
20. Sweden	1·8	2·4	3·8	4·1	4·1	3·9	81·5	74·0	75·2	71·7	72·0	76·8
21. Switzerland	2·8	2·6	2·7	3·6	3·2	3·6	79·1	72·5	73·3	69·5	76·0	80·0
22. Spain	2·0	3·0	1·1	1·3	1·0	2·6	58·9	49·5	66·4	53·0	42·5	53·6
23. Turkey	—	··	··	1·1	0·7	0·5	··	··	··	71·1	65·0	71·0
24. United Kingdom	25·4	27·0	30·4	24·5	18·0	12·0	37·5	38·9	31·0	33·9	34·4	44·2
25. Yugoslavia	—	0·7	0·8	1·0	1·2	1·6	—	88·4	84·2	56·6	70·9	81·2
26. USSR	5·3	2·5	2·0	4·9	8·0	6·5	··	··	··	68·4	55·9	80·4
Total Europe percentages	100·0	100·0	100·0	100·0	100·0	100·0	49·4	53·6	50·4	46·1	0·62	0·71
million dollars	12,779	19,334	13,677	28,889	70,289	181,547	6,313	10,363	6,893	13,320	43,579	128,900

Sources: See Table I.
a Austria-Hungary.
b Included in Austria.

TABLE 4:
Imports and exports growth rates, relation with output growth, and share of goods and services in GNP, by countries

	Growth rates (annual compound) at 1963 prices, 1950–52 to 1967–69, for		Growth elasticities in respect of GNP for[a]		Goods and services (including factor income) as a share of GNP at current market prices. Percentages			
					Credits		Debits	
	Exports (goods only)	Imports (goods only)	Exports (goods only)	Imports (goods only)	1950	1970	1950	1970
Industrialized western European countries								
—Austria	11·0	10·6	2·2	2·1	15·2	30·5	19·5	30·3
—Belgium	8·6	8·3	2·5	2·4	29·4[b]	48·2	29·1[b]	45·1
—Denmark	6·8	8·1	1·7	2·0	27·4	29·1	31·2	32·1
—Finland	7·1	7·2	1·6	1·6	20·1	27·5	19·4	28·8
—France	7·3	8·7	1·5	1·7	16·4	17·0	15·6	16·6
—Germany F.R.	12·0	12·6	1·9	2·0	11·6	22·0	12·9	20·2
—Ireland	6·7	4·8	2·7	1·9	35·6	37·0	46·0	45·0
—Italy	13·1	11·1	2·4	2·1	12·0[c]	20·2	13·4[b]	19·6
—Netherlands	9·3	8·8	1·9	1·8	43·1	52·2	49·6	53·4
—Norway	7·3	7·8	1·8	1·9	47·4	42·4	45·9	43·9
—Sweden	6·8	6·7	1·7	1·6	24·2	24·4	23·5	24·9
—United Kingdom	3·1	4·4	1·1	1·6	26·9	22·6	24·6	21·8

Southern European countries							
—Greece	9·4[a]	1·6	1·4	6·1	10·2	21·1	22·2
—Spain	8·0	1·3	2·3	5·6[c]	17·0	7·3[c]	18·3
—Yugoslavia	10·0[e]	1·6	1·5	14·8[f]	17·5	16·1[f]	22·3
—Portugal	7·0	1·4	1·6	15·6	22·2	20·0	27·7
Centrally planned economies							
—Bulgaria	16·8	2·4	2·2	..	..	..	∞
—Czechoslovakia	8·5	1·6	1·8	..	..	..	..
—Poland	9·3	1·5	1·6	..	..	..	..
—USSR	10·1	1·3	1·2	..	..	..	..

Note: No comparable data are available for Albania, German Democratic Republic, Hungary and Rumania.

a Rate of growth of exports (or imports) divided by the corresponding rate of growth of GNP at constant prices. The growth rates for output (not shown here) have been taken from ECE, *The European economy from the 1950s to the 1970s* (New York 1972), table 1.2, p. 4.

b 1953.

c 1951.

d 1951–52 to 1967–69.

e 1951–53 to 1968.

f 1956.

Sources: Commodity exports and imports at constant prices, United Nations, *Yearbook of International Trade Statistics* and, United Nations, *Monthly Bulletin of Statistics*, various issues.

Goods and services: OECD national accounts.

Output: see footnote a.

Commodity composition of intra-European trade, 1969
(percentages and millions of US dollars)

	Intra-West	Intra-East[a]	West→East[b]	East→West[c]
Engineering and transport equipment	30·9	38·1	37·3	9·6
Chemicals	9·1	4·7	12·3	5·6
Iron and steel	8·1	7·9	9·9	7·8
Non-ferrous metals	3·8	2·1	3·4	4·2
Textiles	5·5	1·1	4·7	2·1
Clothing	2·8	3·1	2·2	2·0
Other mf. products	16·4	11·9	13·9	8·7
Food, beverages, tobacco	11·2	8·5	8·4	16·5
Raw materials	7·3	8·7	6·3	16·5
Minerals, fuels	4·1	8·3	0·9	18·0
Misc. commodities	0·8	5·6	0·7	9·0
Total { Percent	100·0	100·0	100·0	100·0
{ mill. $	91,850	14.480	5,840	6,120

a Partly estimated
b Exports from western to eastern Europe.
c Exports from eastern to western Europe.

Source: UN ECE, *Analytical report on industrial co-operation among ECE countries*, Geneva 1973, p. 72.

11. The Trial of Managed Money: Currency, Credit and Prices 1920-1970

Fred Hirsch and Peter Oppenheimer

The period 1920–70 spans the age of Keynesianism broadly conceived. In a retrospective interpretation, Keynesianism as a general policy approach reaches back to the aftermath of World War I with Keynes's plea for managed money in his *Tract on Monetary Reform* (1923), and extends forward through the 1960s to the high water mark of faith in the capability of technical budgetary and monetary management to achieve and sustain universally benign economic growth. Yet the period saw highly divergent movements in money, credit and prices. The early phase witnessed exceptionally rapid falls in prices and in money supply, notably during the collapse of the post-World War I boom and in the great depression of 1929–33. This was succeeded from the late 1930s onwards by secular inflation, which continued through the remainder of the period and ultimately took on virulent form in the early 1970s.

MONEY, DOMESTIC AND INTERNATIONAL

I

Internationally, the period had a distinct unity as the half century of world monetary reform – or at least attempted reform. The optimum monetary standard had been a subject of almost continuous nineteenth-century debate; it now came on to the agenda of intergovernmental negotiation. The period begins with committees of both national monetary authorities and the newly formed League of Nations considering urgently the means by which Europe could 'return to gold'. Because the shifts in economic structure and financial strength brought about by World War I made restoration of the pre-1914 gold standard far more difficult, it became evident even to those who greatly underestimated the extent of those changes, that a number of expedients and special supports would be needed in order to achieve the restoration. Consideration of such expedients, referred to at the time in such low-key phrases as the need to economise on gold, marked the beginning of a deliberate and internationally orchestrated search for a new monetary standard. That search has continued, with some intermissions, through to the end of our period and beyond. As at early 1976, international monetary reform remains unfinished business, still formally on the official agenda but not, for the time being, as a well-defined policy objective.

The two aspects of uniform experience, the full run-through of the attempt at Keynesian economic management and the uncompleted saga of international monetary reform, are loosely connected. World money, and the world economy with it, broke free in this half century of their golden chain. But the deliberately regulated levers that were intended as a superior replacement did not emerge as precise or powerful instruments, though they were worked hard enough.

As a result, the financial base of the world economy was ungrounded. The influence of deliberate management increased. But because of the imperfections in such management, the outcome was not an idyllic stability, which has to be seen as illusory in the current and foreseeable state of the economic management art. What happened rather was that the earlier bounds set by the working of automatic forces were removed.

This does not imply, as a growing number of economic sceptics allege, that the attempted cure was worse than the disease. For the test cannot be confined to the monetary sector alone. It is true, and at first sight ironical, that this half century of more active financial and monetary management in general saw greater financial instability and worse financial performance than the previous half century in which the international gold standard rested on very light official management. Exchange rates fluctuated more, prices rose much more; and in the short period of the great depression, they fell more. But at least after the early 1930s, one reason why the financial authorities did less well than the earlier automatic mechanisms in keeping money stable, is that they took on additional objectives in shielding the population at large from other shocks.

Money, in short, became more of an instrument, less of an objective. The shock absorbers that had earlier been provided by the real economy were shifted to some degree to the financial economy. Money became more accommodative. It is in this perspective that the failings of monetary control in this half century need to be viewed.

II

The period saw the virtual end of metallic money as anything more than a token instrument. The contrast with the pre-1914 period should not be overdrawn. Credit money had been expanding rapidly in the nineteenth century, not only in the form of currency notes but still more in the then less visible form of bank deposits. Paper currency and bank deposits are estimated to have accounted in 1913 for nearly nine-tenths of total monetary circulation in the world, and gold for little more than one-tenth.[1] So 'while gold was celebrating its famous victory over its honoured rival, silver, it was yearly being further outdistanced by its supposed poor relation, paper.'[2] Yet gold was at the base of the inverse pyramid of paper credit erected on it, and in that capacity continued to exercise a dominating influence on total money supply and the associated movement of prices.

These trends can be illustrated most clearly for the United States, the United Kingdom and France. In 1815, internal money supply in these countries was divided roughly equally into three components – (1) gold, (2) silver, and (3) credit money including subsidiary coin, the latter category consisting predominantly of currency rather than demand deposits. Gold and silver together accounted for two-thirds of the money supply. By 1872, this

1. Robert Triffin, *The Evolution of the International Monetary System: Historical Reappraisal and Future Perspectives*, Princeton, 1964, p. 15.
2. Fred Hirsch, *Money International*, Harmondsworth, 1969, p. 94.

TABLE 1: Structure of Money and Reserves 1815–1962 in % of Money Supply

	Three countries USA, UK, and France			Eleven major countries[1]				
End of	1815	1872	1913	1913	1928	1937	1949	1962
I Money supply	100	100	100	100	100	100	100	100
A. Gold	33	28	10	10	—	—	—	—
B. Silver	34	13	3	5	—	—	—	—
C. Credit money	33	59	87	85	100	100	100	100
1. Currency and coin	26	32	19	23	26	32	27	27
2. Demand deposits	6	27	68	63	74	68	73	73
II Monetary reserves	3	75	14	17	20	40	22	18
A. Gold	1	69	11	12	16	39	19	13
B. Silver	1	7	3	3	—	—	—	—
C. Credit reserves	—	—	—	1	5	1	3	5
1. IMF gold tranches	—	—	—	—	—	—	1	1
2. Foreign exchange	—	—	—	1	5	1	2	4

Note: 1 USA, UK, France, Germany, Italy, Netherlands, Belgium, Sweden, Switzerland, Canada, and Japan.

Source: Robert Triffin. *The Evolution of the International Monetary System: Historical Reappraisal and Future Perspectives*, Princeton University, 1964.

proportion was down to about two-fifths, with gold now taking the major share. By 1913, the combined proportion was down to 13 per cent, and 68 per cent of the money supply was in the form of demand deposits in the banking system – which remains the predominant form of money in our own day. For 11 major countries for which statistics in the later period are available – the previous three, plus Germany, Italy, Netherlands, Belgium, Sweden, Switzerland, Canada, and Japan – the proportion of metallic money in 1913 was a shade higher at 15 per cent, and so was the share of currency, but the basic trends are the same (Table 1).

Gold coin disappeared from internal circulation in all countries after World War I, and silver remained only in token amounts in subsidiary coinage. Thus the money supply was divided between currency and subsidiary coins and demand deposits, with the latter showing a general upward trend except in the years of the banking crisis during the depression of the early 1930s. By 1962, in these same 11 countries, the share of demand deposits had increased to 73 per cent, 10 percentage points higher than in 1913.

At the beginning of our period at the aftermath of World War I, therefore, the move from metallic money to paper money in its everyday use in personal and commercial transactions was virtually complete. But metallic money, and predominantly gold, retained major importance in international monetary reserves – that is to say, in monetary assets held by domestic note-issuing authorities themselves. Such monetary assets, called external or monetary reserves in modern parlance, form the ultimate base of national money supplies in any international system of market economies linked by fixed or pegged exchange rates. In their original form, they constituted the reserve that a central bank needed to keep against its liabilities in the form of bank notes and deposit claims. They consisted of gold, silver, or increasingly in the twentieth century, balances held by the central bank in the money market of another country – that is to say, foreign exchange reserves.

The development of the commercial banking system in the nineteenth century, and the need to avoid the periodic banking crises that an unregulated system fell into, led to a general move to set up central banks. These acted as bankers' banks in affording assurance of credit support in times of cash stringency. As a counterpart of this, they held part of the commercial banks' reserves.

The resulting centralisation of domestic reserve holdings at the central bank brought a growing proportion of a country's gold holdings into the hands of this central monetary authority. The culmination of this tendency came with the disappearance of gold and silver coins from

domestic circulation. The commercial banks now had no
further need to hold gold in their own tills. Accordingly, after
World War I it became the exception for commercial banks
themselves to hold gold, since such holdings took on a
speculative rather than a precautionary character. In
Switzerland, and to some extent also France, commercial
banks have continued to hold gold as part of their cash
reserve.

Gold was, on the other hand, predominant in external
reserves at the opening of our period. By 1970 its share had
been reduced to about two-fifths of global external reserves.
By 1976, although still forming a very important share of
total external assets held by official monetary authorities
in the world, gold had been demonetised in the formal sense
that there were no longer any fixed links between gold and
national currencies. Thus the period 1920–70 saw the
replacement of gold money by credit money at the official
level, following with a considerable time-lag the substitution
that had earlier taken place at the commercial level. But
the move towards international credit money was neither
uninterrupted nor smooth nor complete.

III

International monetary arrangements are a part of high
finance. Their connection with personal finance and
business transactions, through their influence on the price
level and on the availability of commercial bank credit,
remains in modern times a matter of some dispute. This
ambiguity is in itself an interesting new development in our
period. To be sure, the connection between the level of
prices and the supply of money and particularly of bank
credit had been a matter of controversy among economists
in the early nineteenth century, notably in the debates of the
English currency and banking schools. But it was not
seriously doubted that the price level bore a close relationship to the supply of gold and/or silver money. Since this
money supply was itself almost entirely autonomously
determined, with very little influence exerted by the
monetary authorities or any other centralised agency, the

causal connection between money and prices was clear enough.

This was the basis of the famous quantity theory of money, which in its general form 'has attributed the changes in prices to changes in the quantity of money'.[3] In the past half century, the more ambitious and more extensive objectives and instruments of economic policy taken on by governments and central banks have removed much of the punch of the old quantity theory. To be sure, the proximate determinant of the price level except in the very short run remains the quantity of money, as the modern 'monetarists' insist a little shrilly. But the interesting question, now that money supply is no longer given from outside but is largely determined within the system, is what determines this quantity itself.

The real dispute between modern monetarists and other economists is how accommodative money supply is – and should be – to the various pressures influencing the modern economy. These range from trade union bargaining to social expectations about living standards. If governments were confined to a single objective, such as maintaining a stable level of prices, the distinction would be without significance, since institutional and other pressures for an accommodative change in money supply could then be resisted in the cause of a stable price level. The same policy indifference to non-monetary influences would be justified if additional objectives such as increasing the level of employment and real output were accepted, but accommodative variations in money supply were powerless to further them. This is roughly the position of monetarists of the Friedman school. This position has not been accepted by any modern government nor by what almost certainly remains the majority of economists concerned with economic policy.

The practical problem for domestic monetary authorities has therefore been to regulate their domestic money supply or credit growth in the light of multiple and often apparently conflicting aims of economic policy. In the process the traditional fixed link between a country's domestic and

3. Milton Friedman, 'Money: Quantity Theory,' *International Encyclopedia for Social Sciences*, Vol. X, p. 433 (New York, 1968).

international money stocks has been loosened and even reversed. The problems associated with this are at bottom what the half century of attempted international monetary reform has been about. The loosening in turn greatly weakened the causal association between the value of world reserves, or the reserve base of national money supplies, and national price levels.

World reserves, like national money supplies, became an accommodating or endogenous element within the monetary system. In practical terms: since at least the early 1930s, insufficient gold supply has meant not a depression in world prices or in economic activity but a revaluation of gold in terms of national currencies, as well as supplementation or replacement of gold reserves by holdings of foreign exchange. The end of our period also saw the first introduction of specially created international credit assets intended as a possible eventual substitute for both gold and foreign exchange. It may be, of course, that this accommodative approach to reserve money, like the accommodative approach to the supply of national money, has helped to fuel the secular inflation that the world has experienced since at least the late 1930s, and on a more controversial interpretation, in the first three quarters of the twentieth century. But it again needs to be recalled that maintenance of price stability has been only one among several competing policy objectives.

IV

The radical change in the relationship between the international reserve base and the domestic price level represents the outcome of forces that at the beginning of our period were weak and largely unrecognised. At the end of World War I, there was a general desire among monetary authorities and business communities in all the main European countries, with the obvious exception of Soviet Russia, to restore the pre-war gold standard as speedily as possible. The purpose had little to do with the workings of the international monetary system which few people thought about in its own right. The immediate and practical concern was with domestic inflation.

Wars have always been inflationary, and World War I was no exception. Wholesale prices between 1914 and 1918 almost doubled in the United States, more than doubled in Britain, and more than trebled in France. Inflationary pressures and the primacy of government expenditure connected with the war forced a general departure from the gold standard. This took a variety of forms. Germany and other continental belligerents formally ended convertibility of their currencies into gold and suspended the free export of gold. Sweden in 1916 suspended its obligation to *buy* gold at parity, in an attempt to check the inflation of its money supply through gold imports.[4]

Britain remained formally on the gold standard by the simple expedient of declining to insure gold shipments for war risks. In addition, the Treasury supported the sterling-dollar exchange directly with the proceeds of investment sales and dollar credits. In 1919, this support policy was ended and with German submarines no longer available to hold off the normal operation of the gold points mechanism, a ban on gold exports was introduced. Sterling plunged against the dollar to a low point of $3·20, compared with its old parity of $4·86. The currencies of all the main European ex-belligerents depreciated against the dollar.

These depreciations heightened the extent of inflation in these countries in the sharp post-war boom. Wholesale prices between 1918 and 1920 rose by 37 per cent in Britain, by 45 per cent in France and by nearly sevenfold in Germany. These were unprecedented rates of inflation at the time, and were indeed above those recorded fifty years later in the inflation of 1973–75 (see below p. 672 ff).

Money appeared to be out of control. The central banks were running their printing presses virtually at the behest of governments. Mechanically, this usually took the form of the financing of government deficits through the issuing of

4. Richard A. Lester, 'The Gold Exclusion Policy in Sweden, 1916–19', in his *Monetary Experiments*, Newton Abbott (David and Charles reprints), 1970 and Princeton University Press, 1939.

short-term bills and bonds (floating debt), financed by the banking system. In addition, a further portion was financed directly by the central bank – e.g. in Ways and Means advances by the Bank of England, and in *avances extra-ordinaires à l'Etat* by the Bank of France to the French Treasury. Such direct advances were anathema to central bankers. They were seen not only as the genesis of inflation, but as the abdication of central banking control. They were an open, humiliating indication of the political subordination of the central banks.

It was in this period and under this pressure, that central bankers began to emphasise the need, as they saw it, for independence from government. The point was put in 1920 with engaging directness by H. A. Siepmann, a British financial official and future director of the Bank of England: 'The Chancellor of the Exchequer is a member of the Cabinet, and he cannot always be swayed exclusively by those considerations of sound finance . . .'[5] An official international financial conference in Brussels in 1920 recommended that 'Banks of Issue' should be freed from political pressure. The recommendation was promptly picked up by Montagu Norman in an attempt to argue his own Treasury out of any say in increases in Bank rate. Norman became governor of the Bank of England in 1920 for the then normal two-year term. By a combination of guile, the force of a strong and neurotic personality, and single-minded devotion to the interests of the City of London, Norman held down the governorship for a disastrous 24 years.[6]

However much central bankers might wish to preserve or regain their independent power, they knew in their hearts

5. 'The Brussels Conference', *Economic Journal*, 1920, p. 448.
6. Norman's official biography (Henry Clay, *Lord Norman*, London, 1957), although marred by Clay's premature death, has more information (and, between the lines, insights) than it is usually given credit for. Norman's history of mental illness, which forced him out of his merchant banking partnership in 1913, was first given prominence by Francis Williams in his *A Pattern of Rulers* (London, 1965), and then lingered over (without acknowledgement) by Andrew Boyle in his *Montagu Norman* (London, 1967).

that the democratic tide was against them. In advising his German counterparts on the need for an independent Reichsbank, Norman wrote: 'I think that what we all have in mind is . . . to make unsound finance and dangerous methods difficult though, as the State is Sovereign, not impossible.'[7] The obvious way to make unsound finance difficult was to reimpose the external discipline of the gold standard. This function played by the gold standard is often forgotten today, partly because, in the age of managed money, fixed exchange rates are a less reliable or universal guarantee of monetary stability. Countries with a low propensity to inflate, such as Germany or Switzerland, will find that their best check to inflation is to allow their currencies to float upwards. Even so, analogues to the gold standard can be found among recent blueprints for fixed rates, notably some of the proposals for European monetary union, which envisage a European currency to be issued under the control of a European monetary board independent of national governments and thereby also of national electorates.

The influential Cunliffe Committee which recommended in 1919 that the overriding aim of British economic policy in the post-war period should be to return to the gold standard at the pre-war parity emphasised also the need to restore Britain's international financial position. This ignored the questions whether restoration of the gold standard was a sufficient condition for re-establishing Britain's pre-war financial dominance in the short term; and, even if it were, whether the steps necessary to achieve this restoration would not undermine the competitiveness of British industry on which Britain's financial strength must itself depend in the long term.

The Brussels conference of 1920 recommended a general return to gold. To this end, government deficits should be eliminated; further, past borrowings should be funded (i.e. converted into longer-term debt) or be repaid. A successor conference at Genoa in 1922 again urged the re-establishment of the gold standard. To this end it suggested for the

7. Henry Clay, *Lord Norman*, p. 290.

first time co-operative measures among central banks both to co-ordinate their credit policies and to economise gold by extending the 'gold exchange standard'. This was the system under which certain central banks held their reserves not in gold itself but in a currency convertible into gold. The main currency in mind was sterling, and France in particular saw the device essentially as a means of shoring up the position of sterling – as in many ways of course it was. (In the 1960s, France was to take much the same position *vis-à-vis* the dollar.) This was the beginning of the drive in which the Bank of England, later in association with the Federal Reserve Bank of New York, sought to restore an international gold standard, under its own or else the joint leadership.

The strategy suffered from two massive defects. One was the sickly state of the leader in London. The second was the reduced room for manoeuvre which hemmed in all monetary authorities, as a result of increased pressure for maintaining stability in domestic prices and employment.[8] The whole edifice was to come tumbling down in the crash of 1931. By then, the independence of central banks was beginning to be looked on in a less favourable light.[9]

V

How then is one to account for the cavalier monetary restoration? The accepted explanation among monetary historians is that a return to gold was essentially an instinct,

8. Benjamin Strong, who played a key role in this period as Governor of the Federal Reserve Bank of New York, warned Norman: 'no "surrender of sovereignty" should be attempted under the guise or through the formalities of this expression of principles . . . the domestic functions of the bank of issue are paramount to everything . . . anything in the nature of a league or alliance, with world conditions as they are, is necessarily filled with peril.' Stephen V. O. Clarke, *Central Bank Co-operation 1924–31*, New York, 1967, p. 31.

9. 'It was a basic postulate in this period, especially in London and Washington, that central banks must be independent of government control; perhaps some thought might have been given to defending the governments against the central banks.' Edward W. Bennett, in his unjustly neglected book, *Germany and the Diplomacy of the Financial Crisis, 1931*, Harvard, 1962, p. 227.

and that the attempt to do so wherever possible at the pre-war parity was a return to known forms of financial regulation to the neglect of analytical assessment of what the new situation demanded.[10] Major changes of structure had taken place both in the world economy and in world finance as the result of World War I. The most important result was a weakening in the position of Britain. Because before 1914 Britain had been at the centre both of the network of multilateral payments and of international banking, this weakened the balancing mechanism of the international gold standard as a whole. Rather than confronting this problem head-on, the restorers of the 1920s overestimated the contribution to pre-1914 exchange stability that had been played by the gold standard itself and relied on nothing more than modest supporting credits and an array of rather thin expedients as support for what was to be the central arch of the system, the City of London.

To this traditional explanation must be added a secondary one, which has been briefly alluded to above. This involves the role of gold as a proxy for a counter-political influence. The context of the time needs to be borne in mind. The aftermath of World War I was one of the occasions, which have recurred throughout the twentieth century with forgotten frequency, when the foundation of Western civilisation appeared to many to be under threat through the soft underbelly of the economic and financial system. In newly Soviet Russia, communist expropriation had been completed by destruction of the value of money. In the early period in which Soviet power to tax directly was limited by the continuing struggle against domestic and foreign arms, the Soviet leaders had no compunction about financing their needs through the printing press. If destruction of accumulated bourgeois wealth was furthered in the process, so much the better. It was Keynes who attributed

10. This traditional view, which had its first airing in the contemporary critiques by Keynes of Britain's return to gold at the pre-war parity, is supported in the careful study by D. E. Moggridge, *British Monetary Policy, 1924–1931*, Cambridge, 1972, which has extended references to earlier treatments.

to Lenin (whether accurately or not remains a matter for contemporary dispute), the declaration that the best way to destroy the capitalist system was to debauch its currency.[11] Hyper-inflation was not deliberately designed, but its side effects were as welcome in Soviet Russia as they were dreaded in the capitalist west.[12]

Closer to home, Germany in 1923 provided a terrible example of the extent to which inflation could go when the government printing press was allowed to run free (see below). Closer still, the advent of Britain's first Labour government in 1924 persuaded new sections of establishment opinion of the usefulness of external disciplines on governmental discretion. What else is one to make of the statement by a group of Liberals led by Walter (later Lord) Layton supporting the gold standard on the ground that 'violent changes' were to be avoided when there was 'a likelihood of many changes of Government . . . and of the contingency that the Governments in power may not possess the whole-hearted confidence of the majority of the nation.'[13]

This constitutional and disciplinary function of the return to gold at the pre-war parity was in play in all the main European countries. Yet it was only in Britain that it had a decisive influence on the final decision taken. In Germany the hyper-inflation was such that stabilisation of the reformed currency could take place only at an artificial new

11. J. M. Keynes, *The Economic Consequences of the Peace*, London, 1919, p. 220. Keynes's attribution was guarded: Lenin was 'said to' have declared this.

12. Preobrazhensky, the leading economist of Trotsky's faction in the period of 'War Communism' (1918–21), observed that the printing of banknotes had been 'the machine gun of the Ministry of Finance, attacking the bourgeois system in the rear and using the currency laws of that system to destroy it.' Michael Kaser, *Soviet Economics*, London, 1970, p. 97.

13. Donald Winch, *Economics and Policy*, London, 1969, p. 92. Professor Winch adds: 'This line of thought is perhaps best summed up by the phrase used by Lord Bradbury when he said that the great virtue of the gold standard was that it was "knave-proof".' Another way of expressing this political role of gold was as a 'constitutional barrier'. See also Sidney Pollard, *The Gold Standard and Employment Policies Between the Wars*, London, 1970, editor's introduction.

parity, and Germany was in fact the first of the major European countries to return to gold, in 1924. It did so as part of an international support operation in which the Bank of England participated actively, although the Bank did not succeed in its initial attempts to enroll Germany as an effective member of the sterling area by holding its reserves substantially in the form of sterling.[14]

In France, where the high rate of inflation had brought the external value of the franc down to about one-fifth of its pre-1914 dollar value, restoration of the pre-war gold parity was still being considered in the mid-1920s, and was indeed being strongly pressed on the Bank of France by politicians. But in a remarkable reversal of the positions taken by the comparable institutions in Britain a short while earlier, the Governor of the Bank of France, Emile Moreau, insisted to the Prime Minister, Raymond Poincaré, that the desire to protect the middle classes by a return at the higher rate, could not be allowed to impoverish the French economy.[15]

France in practice showed the pragmatism that the English preached, and stabilised the franc at a decidedly undervalued rate. As a result, in the second half of the 1920s, France found itself in a continuously strong financial position. The French monetary authorities accumulated substantial reserves in foreign exchange, mainly sterling. This added a new instability to the international monetary system. For unlike the countries at the periphery of the world economy which had traditionally held their working reserves in London in the form of sterling balances, France, as noted earlier, did not regard this as a satisfactory or durable arrangement, in part at least because it appeared to cast the franc in a role subordinate to sterling.

France, not entirely without justification, saw her currency being used to shore up London's pretensions. This competitive struggle for leadership and prestige in inter-

14. Stephen V. O. Clarke, *Central Bank Co-operation, 1924–31*, New York, 1967, chapter 4.

15. Emile Moreau, *Souvenirs d'un Gouverneur de la Banque de France* (Paris, 1954), p. 573.

national finance can easily be seen to have been both frivolous and counterproductive for the result that really mattered, namely, the health of European economies. But it was not France that had invented this game. The City of London, in its determination to maintain its primacy, had rather conspicuously called the play. France merely found itself with the better cards.

The disarray among the major financial powers in this period clearly worsened the underlying strains. But to see it as the most important cause of the breakdown in the financial system that occurred in the early 1930s is almost certainly unjustified. This view, which has always commended itself to bankers and financial officials, received academic backing in the analysis published by Charles P. Kindleberger in 1973.[16] Kindleberger's view has not been generally accepted among economists. It was the weakening in the structure and the balance of the world economy that was at the source of the trouble. The lack of a financial centre with a dominance such as London had enjoyed before 1914 – and as New York and Washington were to enjoy for a briefer period for about 20 years after the Second World War – was itself an important facet of the change in the underlying economic forces.

When the crisis erupted in May 1931, with the crash of the largest bank in Austria, the Creditanstalt, it is true that an intended supporting credit from France was impeded by diplomatic considerations, leading to a quixotic loan by Governor Norman of the Bank of England of money that he did not have. But when the crisis swiftly moved to Germany and then to London itself, the sums raised in supporting credits, not only from New York, but also from Paris, were large by any contemporary standard. Their total has been estimated at $1 billion, for which no comparable precedent existed before 1914. The fact of the matter was that the underlying disequilibrium was much too large to be papered over by short-term credits. Correction of this disequilibrium could no longer be left to the automatic

16. Charles P. Kindleberger, *The World in Depression 1929-39*, London, 1973.

adjustments operating through changes in domestic incomes, employment and price levels, because governments were now under increasing pressure to resist such adjustments.

VI

The 1920s were bankers' Europe. The 1930s saw the rise of government economic controllers. When Britain was forced off the gold standard in September 1931, laissez-faire in the international economy took a severe blow. All European governments adopted positive policies to protect their external exposure. The form of the policies varied from case to case. Scandinavia as well as most British dominions and other overseas countries that had strong commercial links with Britain kept their currencies tied to the pound, which meant that they depreciated against gold and the currencies that remained tied to it. At first, the other major commercial powers did not follow Britain. In Germany, the major deterrent was fear of inflation, a fear which in retrospect seemed unreal in the context not only of high and rising unemployment but of steeply falling world prices. The hyper-inflation of the 1920s had left such deep scars that only a small and unrepresentative section of opinion advocated devaluation.[17]

The countries that now found themselves with overvalued currencies began to put up direct controls in various forms, including exchange restrictions and import quotas. Less excusably, Britain itself turned from free trade. In 1932 it introduced a general tariff for the first time, despite the protective cover provided by exchange depreciation. Thus the 1930s were a decade of competitive protectionism.

17. Characteristically, Keynes and Anglo-Saxon thought in general remained unaware of this school of German dissentient opinion. The main figure in what has been called German pre-Keynesianism was W. S. Woytinsky, statistician for the German trade union federation. His advocacy of reflation and an end to the mysticism of gold was sharply opposed by Rudolf Hilferding, the Marxist theoretician of imperialism who had been a minister of finance under the Weimar Republic. See George Garvy, 'Keynes and the Economic Activists of pre-Hitler Germany,' *Journal of Political Economy*, April 1975.

They are often said also to have been the decade of competitive devaluation, but this is much less well founded. It is true that a succession of major devaluations followed the initial move by sterling. The most important of these was the devaluation of the dollar in 1933–34. This left the gold bloc as consisting of the hard core of Latin countries – France, Belgium, the Netherlands, Switzerland, Italy – as well as Poland. Germany by this time had moved increasingly towards a controlled economy. The cycle of devaluation was completed in 1935–36, the decisive move being that of France in September 1936. As in Britain in 1931, and not for the last time either, it was a left-wing government – the Popular Front under Léon Blum – which struggled to the last to maintain its cross of sound money.

The 1936 devaluation of the franc left major exchange rates not very different from what they had been in 1931. Yet this is far from showing that the devaluations were mutually frustrating and that they served no general positive purpose. Most directly, the price of gold was raised in all currencies. This at once boosted the value of gold reserves and later the annual inflow of gold to the system. Successive downward floating of the several currencies released the monetary authorities from the earlier constrictions against reflationary policy, and thus helped recovery to get started. The most important form of such policy in this period was cheap money. The worldwide reduction in interest rates after 1931, which was clearly connected with the departures from gold, was an important factor in the modest recovery of world industrial output. This influence was especially strong in Britain, with its financial markets so closely linked to external influences.[18]

The 1931 devaluation of sterling was still regarded by many as an aberration. A world economic conference called in London in 1933 was seen by European governments and bankers primarily as a means of orchestrating an organised stabilisation of the exchanges. Not for nothing was the con-

18. Susan Howson, *Domestic Monetary Management in the U.K., 1919–38*, Cambridge, 1975.

ference housed among the relics in the geological museum (By a strange irony, the attempt at a world-wide stabilisation of the exchanges made 38 years later, in 1971, was housed in another museum, the Washington Smithsonian.) Stabilisation was torpedoed by President Roosevelt's brusque rebuff. The fact that the dollar was being depreciated by deliberate policy action, rather than by the *force majeure* of the market, was seen as especially invidious. It marks the true beginnings of managed exchange rates.

By 1936, the idea of exchange management was no longer so shocking, and the obvious need for international co-ordination was accommodated at a modest technical level. This took the form of the Tripartite Monetary Agreement, the initial purpose of which was simply to demonstrate the support of Britain and the United States for the devaluation of the franc – to make clear that no competition in devaluation was envisaged. The three powers also agreed to co-operate in smoothing out day-to-day fluctuations in the exchange markets. It was an important step forward and has rightly been seen as a precursor of the more formal international monetary co-operation established under the framework of the Bretton Woods system after World War II.

VII

Major wars normally mark a break in economic and financial evolution. World War II did not. It marked rather a continuum in the subordination of finance to economic management which had begun in embryo in the 1930s. In part, this was because World War II was, so to say, the first Keynesian war. But there was another factor. It is not only generals who fight the present war under the influence of the last. The dominating influence on financial policy during World War II, as it affected both the financing of the Allied war effort and the planning of post-war monetary arrangements, was the lesson drawn from 'last time'. Last time in this context meant the attempt to finance World War I largely on commercial terms. This had involved large-scale borrowings among the Allies which left a legacy of war

T.C.(2)

debts after the end of the war, a legacy that in turn added
pressure for the levying of large-scale reparations from
Germany. The upshot had been a chain of debt commitments that contributed to the difficulties of restoring a
smoothly functioning world economy. Much emphasis had
been given to this intrusion in retrospective analysis of the
supposed economic causes of World War II. As a result,
governments and enlightened opinion in the Allied countries
during the war were more than usually sensitive to the
need to avoid unfortunate financial legacies for the post-war
period. Beyond this, they sought to establish ordered world
monetary arrangements consistent with the domestic
policies that the academic Keynesian revolution had suggested were both possible and necessary to avoid the miseries
of the inter-war depression.

This profound turn away from the canons of orthodox
finance in World War II had a major impact on the
financing of the war. Here, in conformity with the general
Keynesian principle that finance was to be accommodative
of the needs of the real economy, governments quickly
exerted their predominance over markets. The financial
markets played an essentially passive role, as the focus of
government economic management moved to the budget
and to direct controls. Keynes played a practical as well as a
theoretical role, following his recruitment to the British
Treasury in 1940. The budget of 1941 was the first to be
drawn up on the new principles.

Secondly, and more remarkably, the principle of
accommodative finance was extended to inter-Allied
relations. The major vehicle for this was Lend-Lease, the
system under which the United States provided war supplies
to Britain and Russia for the most part without financial
repayment obligations. Between March 1941 and September 1945, Lend-Lease cost the US government $30 billion.[19]
Churchill, in the romantic atmosphere that prevailed, called
it 'the most unsordid act'. This characterisation has not
wholly withstood the test of time. Revisionist political

19. R. S. Sayers, *Financial Policy 1939–45*, HMSO London, 1956,
chapter XIII.

historians of a generation later saw Lend-Lease rather as a convenient means for the United States to purchase European manpower and industrial effort to fight the war on the terms most economical and most advantageous for the United States.[20] It was a condition of Lend-Lease that Britain first use virtually all its available resources in official gold reserves and foreign investments, and also cut down its export effort to a small fraction of its pre-war size. As a post-war American textbook put it with unconscious irony: 'The British were able to abandon their export drive and devote the resources saved to war purposes.'[21]

VIII

These wartime financial arrangements, whatever their motivation and ultimate equity, helped to ease the post-war transition by avoiding the deadweight of war debts. Inter-Allied financial co-operation also had a more direct forward influence through the preparations actively made in the war years for the post-war international financial system. These preparations were begun more or less independently in London and Washington. In London, Keynes put into operational form the plans that he had first launched in his *Treatise on Money* in 1930 (of which the first germs appeared in his *Tract on Monetary Reform* in 1923). Keynes's essential concern was to create an international safeguard for full employment policies. The internal value of the currency was not to be strait-jacketed by its external value, as had been the case under the immutable currency parities of the gold standard. Instead, the external value of the currency was to be the variable, to be adjusted to the needs of domestic policy, and above all full employment policy.

In Washington, the emphasis was rather different. The American Treasury, correctly perceiving that America was to be the major creditor of the post-war world, was concerned mainly to impose an international check on autarky and trade restriction, on trade discrimination, and on over-

20. Corelli Barnett, *The Collapse of British Power*, London, 1972.
21. Leland B. Yeager, *International Monetary Relations*, New York, 1966, p. 334.

liberal use of international credit which would in the end involve a real burden on the United States, as the inevitable major post-war creditor.

The outcome of these rather different approaches was the compromise negotiated at an intergovernmental conference at Bretton Woods, New Hampshire, in 1944, in the form of the Articles of Agreement of the International Monetary Fund. The complex provisions of the Bretton Woods agreement contained three major features:

(1) In exchange rates there was a compromise between fixity and flexibility. Currency parities were reintroduced, and were expressed in terms of gold weight (the unit being exactly the current gold weight of the US dollar, equivalent to the gold price of $35 per fine ounce that the United States had established in 1934). But these parities could be changed, on the proposal of a member country. The provisions for such a change were, significantly, phrased in negative form; a member was not to propose a change in its par value except to correct a fundamental disequilibrium. In *principle*, this gave the potential flexibility that Keynes and the Keynesians desired. For fundamental disequilibrium entailed no more than an unsustainable imbalance, irrespective of the cause of the imbalance. Thus deficits caused by expansionary financial policies were clearly eligible grounds for devaluation.

(2) The second major feature of the Bretton Woods system was provision of a pool of international credit available to member countries to finance temporary balance of payments difficulties. These credits were designed to support the exchange-rate system by enabling countries to ride out temporary speculative raids as well as to finance cyclical and other short-term payments imbalances. But under US insistence, the size of the credit pool was kept relatively small. Thus the US quota, which had special importance in marking the maximum commitments of the major creditor, was only $2¾ billion. This compared with a maximum effective US commitment of over $20 billion under the original Keynes plan, even though that plan had built into it pressures for adjustment both by creditors and

by debtors that the final IMF articles conspicuously lacked.

(3) The third major feature of the IMF agreement was provision for currency convertibility on account at least of current transactions – restrictions on capital transfers were permitted and in some cases might even be required – and prohibition of discriminatory currency practices. This was the payments analogue to non-discrimination in trade (the latter being the concern of what was to become the General Agreement on Tariffs and Trade). It was an important objective for the United States, which was anxious that the discriminatory practices that had been erected in the 1930s and in the war-time period should not become a permanent feature of the post-war system.

These three elements – limited exchange adjustment, limited balance-of-payments financing, and convertibiliy on the basis of non-discrimination – were interconnected and not entirely easy to reconcile. The smaller the credit pool, and the less use made of exchange adjustment, the greater would be the difficulty in implementing the commitments to convertibility. Also, and in the short term more important, the IMF did not provide adequately for the transitional period that would be needed to reconstruct the European economies and to dismantle the mass of trade and foreign exchange restrictions inherited from the war years. Keynes, who had negotiated the agreement on Britain's behalf, and had accepted the scaled-down compromise only under American dominance, sensed the difficulties which lay ahead. In defending the Bretton Woods agreement and the complementary American loan to Britain in 1945, Keynes told his suspicious and largely hostile Westminster audience in the House of Lords that what mattered was not the letter of the loan agreement or the IMF articles, but that America now took responsibility if things went wrong.[22]

This proved to be an exact assessment. Events in 1946–47 underlined the extent of Europe's economic disarray. A severe winter brought fuel shortages. The pound sterling was made prematurely convertible in 1947 in line with the

22. Fred Hirsch, *Money International*, p. 101.

letter of the post-war agreements, a move that marked the first major post-war sterling crisis and quickly proved a fiasco.

America's response displayed a high order of statesmanship in perceiving the extent to which its own medium-term interests demanded aid to its allies – and recent ex-enemies – on a scale without precedent in peacetime. This was the benign by-product of the Cold War. Beginning with the Marshall Plan, launched in 1947–48 under the impetus of the Secretary of State, General George C. Marshall, the United States outdid its formal IMF credit commitment many times over in grants and loans provided directly to European countries. This aid was provided not merely bilaterally, but through systematic and continued funding made available to West European countries on a regional basis. The total amounted to more than $20 billion – coincidentally, much the same as the commitment the United States had refused under the Keynes plan.

In addition, and in the same spirit, the United States accepted the continuation and in some ways the intensification of trade and payments discrimination by European countries against itself. In 1949, it actively encouraged devaluation of European currencies. Sterling was devalued by 30 per cent. This set off world-wide adjustments by the same magnitude in sterling area countries (broadly, the British Commonwealth minus Canada) and Scandinavia, and by lesser percentages in other European countries. But even at the new exchange rates, direct controls remained pervasive in nearly all European countries. The principle was accepted that liberalisation would make better progress if introduced first among the 'soft' European currencies themselves. Thus in the ten years 1948–58, west European countries gave priority within the framework of the OEEC[23] to removing quotas in intra-European trade, and to moving towards currency transferability through the vehicle of the European Payments Union. Liberalisation was extended to

23. Organisation for European Economic Co-operation, set up at US instigation to co-ordinate the distribution of Marshall Aid and the strategy of trade liberalisation in Europe.

imports from the United States, and to effective currency convertibility *vis-à-vis* all major currencies including the dollar, only in the later 1950s. The decade saw a gradual rebuilding of financial strength in Europe, within a stable global setting. The culmination of Europe's financial restoration was the successful devaluation of the French franc at the end of 1958, in the context of a financial *assainissement* ('cleansing') which was introduced by de Gaulle soon after taking power.

The year 1959, when European currencies became convertible, when most direct restrictions on non-agricultural trade had been removed by European countries, and when a healthy balance appeared to exist between European currencies and the dollar, marked the apotheosis of a successful post-war transition. At a comparable distance from World War I the year was 1932. No more had to be said to emphasise the contemporary success. From the perspective of the more troubled 1970s, it is perhaps clearer than it was twenty years earlier that this economic success owed something to the polarisation in world politics in the cold-war period. This not only gave a major impetus to the provision of American aid in such extensive amounts to its political and military allies. In addition – and the significance of this was fully appreciated only in the later period in which it was lacking – the evident need for Western political solidarity was an important help in eliciting co-operation within the financial and comm:rcial sphere, and in securing acceptance of US leadership.

In the 1960s, by contrast, the international economy was confronted with a problem that would test any system, namely a basic change in relative economic importance of the major powers. The key changes were the rise of continental Europe and Japan, at the expense of a diminution in the dominance of the United States, and of a further weakening of Britain. In the process, the world economy was left without a dominant leader. This diffusion of economic and financial strength bore obvious analogies to the ebbing of Britain's strength after 1914. Although the collectivity of the main economic powers succeeded through pragmatic co-operation in avoiding the worst errors of the earlier period, they could not painlessly adapt a dollar-centred system to the needs of a new multi-polar economic world.

On the monetary front two interconnected issues emerged and became progressively more troublesome. One was the problem of exchange rate adjustment under the par-value system. Because this entailed one-step adjustments in exchange rates of substantial size, it was inherently exposed to disruptive speculation, since operators in the exchange market merely had to guess the direction of the likely movement, and were thus provided with a one-way bet. Against these pressures, governments had only two effective means of defence – to adjust the parity at the first sign of disequilibrium (which might be challenged as contrary to the need to show a 'fundamental' disequilibrium, and also risked exciting speculation at an earlier stage next time on), or to attempt to ride out the pressures and loudly deny any intention or even possibility of exchange adjustment. In practice, it was this tactic of 'sit still and deny everything' that governments adopted. The result was that disequilibria were allowed to build up and grow, and exchange adjustments were delayed.

As a result, hedgers and speculators on the exchanges – who, contrary to popular mythology, have usually been slower than officialdom to discern the fundamentals of a situation – were eventually presented with sitting targets, and exchange rate adjustment came to be associated with an atmosphere of speculative crisis. The problem had been unobtrusive in the 1950s, partly because a still fairly restrictive network of exchange controls and the comparative underdevelopment of international banking and multinational business had limited the movement of liquid funds between countries; and partly because trade liberalisation itself provided a substitute for exchange-rate changes. Countries in relatively strong balance-of-payments positions accelerated their import liberalisation programmes. This was the partial equivalent of currency revaluation, without the financial trauma. The scope for this strategy was largely exhausted by the end of the decade.

The other related issue concerned the pattern and growth of reserves. It slowly became evident that the dollar problem, billed and analysed through the first post-war decade as a problem of severe, perhaps structural and even permanent dollar shortage, had been turned on its head. The problem now was one of US deficit or dollar glut. The heartening strength of European currencies, which had given the move to convertibility at the end of 1958 such a good send-off, was now seen to have an awkward mirror-image, in the dollar weakness.

The first dramatic manifestation of this weakness occurred in October 1960, with what then appeared as the explosion in the London gold price. (By later standards it would have appeared a hardly discernible rumble.) London maintained the world's leading gold market, which was exclusively international in the sense that it was not open to British residents. The price in that market was normally directly related to the official price of $35 an ounce, at which, with the addition of a commission of one quarter of one per cent, the US Treasury would purchase gold from any source and sell gold to central banks for 'legitimate monetary purposes'. As long as the US Treasury was freely selling and buying, an effective arbitrage link existed between the private and the official markets, since central banks could arbitrage betw en the two (though under IMF rules they were not permitted to *buy* in the private market at above the parity price).

The London gold price burst through what had been believed to be its effective ceiling of about $35·25 (equal to the New York selling price plus estimated shipment costs) to over $40 in October 1960. The underlying influence was that European central banks (e.g. Italy) had excess dollars, wanted to switch into gold, but had become shy of exercising their conversion rights in New York. The problem itself was covered over by an arrangement, at first informal and later systematised through the London gold pool, for collective intervention by the central banks in the London gold market designed to hold the price close to the official parity. The significance of the episode was its indication first that demand among central banks to convert dollars into gold was increasing; this showed that major monetary authorities no longer considered the dollar as good as gold. Secondly, the fact that the United States was discouraging other countries from exercising their gold-dollar conversion right was a telling sign that the same view had crept into the US Treasury itself.

This was to be the first in a long line of defensive expedients undertaken by the United States to 'protect the value of the dollar', i.e. to avoid or postpone a decision on the dollar/gold parity. The expedients became a rich variety. They included extensive use of short-term credits between central banks ('swaps'), and special US Treasury securities denominated in foreign currency which thereby partly or wholly removed the currency risk from the creditor.[24] The latter were called Roosa bonds, after Robert V. Roosa, who organised and orchestrated the tactical defences as Undersecretary in the US Treasury in the Kennedy administration. Neither the influential Wall Street community, nor the US Treasury nor Kennedy himself (as distinct from his more radical Council of Economic Advisers) were prepared at this stage to face a fundamental readjustment in the position of the dollar. Roosa was as adept at providing gimmicks for the restive European central banks as he was at putting down dangerous ideas from White House advisers and outside academics. The tactical objective was to minimise conversions of gold into dollars. By the mid-1960s, the US Treasury had set up a division for developing countries with the special task of leaning on potential transgressors, making it clear that Congress could be expected to take a poor view of gold conversions when making its aid appropriations.

These several devices, for which the generic name of 'ad hoccery' was coined, alleviated short-term pressures, but

24. The 'partial' removal of the currency risk refers to the little-known fact that some of these bonds carried a provision obliging the monetary authority in whose currency they were denominated to change them back into dollars before any deliberate upvaluation of its own currency.

progressively weakened the base of the system. They did so at two points, both of them impinging sharply on Europe. First, they increased rather than diminished the potential instability resulting from the co-existence of several different reserve assets – i.e. gold, dollars and sterling – in which reserves were held in a fixed-rate system. Secondly, the devices amounted to a deliberate weakening in balance of payments discipline on the United States. They thereby highlighted an asymmetry in the international financial system. The asymmetry had in a sense always been present, since in a period when US financial strength was unquestioned, the voluntary accumulation and use of dollars by the rest of the world itself relieved the United States of the kind of balance-of-payments discipline automatically imposed on other countries, when additional holdings of their currencies were presented for conversion. The difference was that the earlier asymmetry had been market-induced and was fully voluntary, while the later one was politically imposed and increasingly irksome. If credit was to be given to the United States deliberately – and that is what the devices involved – then the creditors could be expected to demand the creditors' traditional prerogative of influence or control. The fact that the continental European countries had been at the receiving end of creditor control made them especially sensitive on this point.

France, as usual, felt most deeply about the matter. This was partly because General de Gaulle saw in external finance one of the few available weapons with which to pursue his policy of asserting the independence of France, and he hoped Europe with it, from the United States. But de Gaulle reflected a more general and pervasive attitude amongst French financial officials, which, as we have seen, extends back to the 1920s.

Germany, which had been subjected to much more severe creditors' control than France after both world wars, was Washington's most amenable major partner. This was clearly linked to Germany's dependence on the US military presence for its own defence. In 1967, the United States went as far as requiring the president of the German

Bundesbank, then Dr Karl Blessing, to write a letter to the
chairman of the Federal Reserve indicating that it was the
Bundesbank's policy not to convert dollars into gold, and
referring specifically to America's financial burden in
maintaining troops in Germany in this context. There were
some behind-the-scenes doubts raised at the time in official
circles whether this letter itself transgressed the US obligation of convertibility under the IMF articles – the United
States being the one country to maintain its convertibility
obligations through the free purchase and sale of gold for its
currency, rather than through the normal method of inter-
vening in exchange markets. For the European countries
that were becoming increasingly important in the world
economy, these actions seemed to mark the silent encroachment of a full dollar standard. The anomaly was heightened
by the increasing representation of European countries in
the inner councils of monetary affairs, notably through the
medium of Working Party 3 of the OECD's Economic
Policy Committee, and through the related Group of Ten.[25]
Operational reserve management and financial diplomacy
became increasingly sensitive.

These developments raised in increasingly strident form a
basic analytical question concerning the foundations of the
reserve system. This had been brilliantly diagnosed in
1959–60 by Robert Triffin in a book that had the unusual
distinction of converting the economic middlebrows ahead
of the highbrows. Triffin's contribution was to dynamise the
gold exchange standard and to show why it was liable to
prove inherently unstable. The core of the argument was as

25. Both these groups were established in 1961. The OECD was
(and is) the successor to the OEEC, its membership extending to all
industrialised countries (i.e. the United States, Canada, and latterly
Japan, Australia and New Zealand as well as Western Europe). The
Group of Ten countries were those participating in the IMF General
Arrangements to Borrow, negotiated in 1961–62 to supplement the
Fund's resources under Article VII of the Articles of Agreement. The
membership (substantially identical with that of Working Party 3) comprised Belgium, the United Kingdom, Canada, France, Germany, Italy,
Japan, the Netherlands, Sweden, and the United States. Switzerland
was an associate eleventh member, remaining outside the IMF.

follows. In a growing world economy, countries will require a continuously growing volume of reserves. Under the gold exchange standard, reserves are held partly in gold and partly in foreign exchange convertible into gold. So long as the average price of gold in terms of currency remains more or less fixed, the system contains no mechanism assuring that the gold component will show the necessary growth – indeed, as later supplementary analysis was to point out, in a world of gradually rising prices, one must expect the accrual of gold to diminish over time. Consequently, an increasing proportion of the growing demand for reserves will be met in the form of foreign exchange balances. These balances, however, are liabilities of the reserve centre involved. As long as they are small in relation to the gold assets held by the centre, this process will proceed smoothly. But as the ratio of foreign exchange liabilities to gold assets mounts, increasing doubts will arise about the ability of the reserve centre to meet its convertibility commitment at the existing parity.

These doubts, which were evident in 1931 in the case of sterling and were just beginning to make themselves felt in the case of the dollar at the time that Triffin wrote at the end of the 1950s, then pose the system with a dilemma – later to become known as the Triffin dilemma. On the one hand, the reserve centre may respond to the financial pressures and try to strengthen its reserves: liabilities ratio. This would have a deflationary impact on the global economic climate. If successful, it would stop and perhaps even reverse the growth in world reserves, threatening either a catastrophic fall in world money supply or, more probably, a wholesale retreat from liberalised trading arrangements into bilateralism etc. On the other hand, avoidance of such a course would entail continued weakening in the external financial position of the reserve centres and particularly of the United States, thereby making the danger of a breakdown greater still. As a way out of the dilemma, and rejecting the alternative solutions of an upvaluation of gold or floating exchange rates, Triffin recommended a major reform through the substitution of credit reserves in an enlarged International Monetary Fund, to take the place of both gold and foreign exchange holdings.

Although Triffin's prescription was not accepted by any European country in the 1960s, his diagnosis – which was always the strongest element in his analysis – could be seen as a more precise version of the critique of the gold exchange standard that had long been current in France. This critique was associated particularly with Professor Jacques Rueff, who continued into the 1970s the monetary battles that he had begun in the 1920s.[26] Rueff's analysis focused both on the asymmetry of the mechanism that permitted the reserve centre to finance deficits by incurring liabilities that it was not called upon to repay, and on the progressive weakening in the reserve structure that this entailed. His proposed solution, which fitted both the psychological inclinations and the supposed national interest of France, was to remove the excrescence of the foreign exchange element and revert to a 'pure' gold standard. To do this without drastic deflationary effects, a once-for-all increase in the international gold price was necessary. The obvious trouble about this solution in itself was that it left the way open for the dynamics of the gold exchange standard to start up again. To be effective, a full gold standard solution would be as dependent as a Triffin-style IMF on rigorous suppression of countries' natural instincts and incentives to accumulate official exchange balances.

But the monetary diplomacy of the 1960s, as of most periods. was moved more by response to immediate events and by considerations of commercial or foreign policy than by theoretical consistency. In January 1965, President de Gaulle picked up Rueff's gold ideas as part of his campaign against American influence in Europe. By converting in a conspicuous manner a substantial part of France's dollar reserves into gold, and by calling for a restoration of the

26. Among Rueff's contributions to financial writing was a delicious mock simplicity of style. Thus, 'What used to be known as the gold exchange standard was a device, characteristic of colonialism, which Great Britain imposed on a number of South American countries' – Jacques Rueff, *International Currency Review*, March/April 1974.

gold standard at his famous press conference of 4 February 1965,[27] de Gaulle turned what had hitherto been a lackadaisical debate on future monetary arrangements into an aggressive if somewhat incoherent challenge to the monetary pre-eminence of the United States. The result was to strengthen American resolve not to upvalue gold. In summer 1965, the United States for the first time threw its weight behind the drive to create a new form of global reserve asset.

In many ways, this American stand was ironical. Probably no country other than South Africa would have stood to gain more than the United States from a large formal revaluation of gold at an early stage of the dollar's troubles. From the standpoint of the United States itself, gold revaluation in, say, the early 1960s would have extended the life of the gold/dollar reserve system without the necessity of defensive support measures. The gain would have come from the increased value both of the existing US gold stock and of the annual inflow of new gold to the whole monetary system. What was and remained a matter of controversy, among European governments as well as academic opinion, was whether gold revaluation could be a durable solution for reserve instability, since the prospect of its early repetition would make the gold market dominated by speculative forces. The fact that gold revaluation would rule out close administrative control over the amount of additional liquidity, as well as over distribution of windfall gains, was also seen as a severe drawback by those who wished to move 'forward' to internationally managed money. The same influence was seen, from the standpoint of the small band of gold 'realists', as a check on over-ambitious Utopian ventures. The co-authors of this survey represent, respectively, these two points of view.

The discussions and then negotiations on monetary reserves culminated in the agreement finalised in Stockholm in March 1968, on creation of Special Drawing Rights in the IMF; and in the decision a year later to activate the

27. The text of the key passage is given in Hirsch, *Money International* on p. 385.

agreement and allocate an initial $9,500 million of SDR's in the period 1970–72. This was a considerable achievement in itself, but it did not confront the central deficiencies in the reserve mechanism that had set the whole reform process going. The SDR did not replace the dollar. It did not replace gold. It did not replace anything – it was in one sense the finest product of reform by expediency, of the pragmatic principle of 'add, never take away'. Secondly, no attempt was made to link the new SDR system with an effective adjustment mechanism – and it was adjustment between the dollar and now not only European currencies but also the Japanese yen that had become the prime need.

At the beginning of the 1960s, exchange adjustment was decidedly out of fashion. Per Jacobsson, the ebullient managing director of the International Monetary Fund, whose previous career had been as central bankers' confidant at the Bank for International Settlements (an earlier spell with Ivar Kreuger was suppressed from his biographical handouts) talked about the exchange regime as a fixed rate system, to the embarrassment of some of his more enlightened staff. When Germany, accompanied by the Netherlands, upvalued its currency by 5 per cent in March 1961, this caused widespread upheaval in the exchange markets, partly in anticipation that it would be followed by devaluation of sterling. In the ensuing years, there was a growing international orchestration of defensive expedients to stop further exchange rate changes.

This was the period in which defence of exchange rate stability took on militaristic and moralistic fervour. A credit support operation mounted in New York that prevented a devaluation of the Italian lira in early 1964 was recorded in a US Treasury document under the proud heading: 'the line holds'. The fact that the lira had been 'saved' at the expense of putting a damper on the Italian economy, from which in a sense it has never recovered, was covered over in the blanket of dollar credits.

In Britain shortly afterwards, Harold Wilson maintained an overvalued exchange rate to the tune of tired quotations from the Duke of Wellington, and self-serving congratulations from the community of bankers and the American Treasury. The 'line' again held. In Washington it was plainly seen as the outer periphery of the dollar's own defences. By 1967, reality had crossed at least the English Channel. Sterling underwent its second major post-war devaluation, by just over 14 per cent to $2·40 – almost exactly half its dollar value at the pre-1931 gold parity. This time, only Denmark among European countries followed sterling; and among the traditional sterling area countries of the old British dominions, Australia also held to its old parity.

Sterling's devaluation was a reminder to the market that the earlier official pretensions to something like a fixed rate system for the major currencies could not be relied upon. Speculative pressures increased. The sterling devaluation itself triggered a wave of speculative gold buying in which some $3,000 million worth of gold (more than two years' world output at the existing price) was absorbed in three months. The US authorities responded by dissolving the gold pool, at a specially summoned meeting in Washington in March 1968. Its erstwhile members agreed to refrain for the time being from either buying or selling gold on the open market. The price there was left free to move independently of the now artificial and increasingly meaningless official peg. With official gold stocks thus hived off from market forces, speculative pressures became all the more concentrated on inter-currency relationships.

In France in May-June 1968, student uprisings, workers' strikes and a consequent wage escalation quickly led to severe pressure on the French franc, from which it had been free since the successful devaluation of December 1958. Since every European devaluation entailed some corresponding appreciation of the dollar, the US authorities saw some cause for alarm. Hitherto they had simply put their weight behind the status quo, pressuring European countries to avoid any change in their parities, in order to keep at bay suspicions that the dollar parity might be next. America now exerted active pressure for changes in relative European parities to take the form of revaluation in a surplus country rather than devaluation in a deficit country.

In specific terms in 1968, this meant revaluation of the German mark. An apparent leakage of behind-the-scenes efforts to achieve this triggered another flare-up in the exchange markets in November 1968, and a conference of the Group of Ten finance ministers was called at very short notice in Bonn. All attempts to bludgeon Germany into outright revaluation were resisted at that extraordinary meeting, essentially on grounds of what can only be called inverted prestige ('Germany now number one in Europe' read the newspaper headlines to be seen in the delegates' lounge). Instead, Germany agreed to impose a 'border tax' of four per cent on its exports, and an equivalent subsidy on its imports. The French finance minister agreed to a devaluation of the franc by 11·1 per cent, subject to agreement by General de Gaulle. The agreement, as it turned out, was not forthcoming ('devaluation would be the worst absurdity' the General announced). The world had become used to finance ministers who said they would not devalue their currency and then did. Here was the first one who said he would and then did not.[28] In 1969, this dam, too, broke. A wave of speculation into the mark occurred in May, and was followed in August/October by devaluation of the

28. The Bonn conference marked the first occasion (the Smithsonian settlement of December 1971 was the second) at which exchange rates were hammered out across an international conference table by finance ministers – the accompanying central bank governors, surely unprecedentedly, were excluded from the room, and whiled away the early hours at pingpong. Privately, France had first raised the possibility of a 15 per cent change in the franc-Deutschemark relationship, to be divided fifty-fifty between devaluation of the franc and upvaluation of the mark. At the Bonn meeting, she began by resisting devaluation altogether, but then proposed a full 15 per cent. This was considered excessive by the United States, and also by Britain which was fearful of the effect on sterling's still insecure new parity of $2·40, and the amount was whittled down in bargaining to 11·1 per cent. This was a rare semi-open instance of the role of political bargaining in setting the size of exchange adjustments under the par value system, though in this case there was not even an adjustment.

French franc and the appreciation, at first by floating, of the mark.

The bastions of the fixed-rate currency regime were falling. While lip service continued to be paid to the principles of the par value system, recognition that something was wrong was signified in the usual manner, by initiating a low-level technical study. This was set up within the IMF to examine the exchange-rate mechanism. In practice its brief was limited to pronouncing on minor extensions of flexibility within the existing par value system. Its report in 1970 bore the heavy marks of compromise. This reflected the determined attachment to fixed exchange rates (at least for presentational and negotiating purposes) by France, Belgium, and most of the primary producing countries; the main leaders of the flexibility faction were the United States and Germany. The report's recommendations were innocuous, but its significance was that it marked official recognition of *The Role of Exchange Rates in the Adjustment of International Payments*. The opponents of exchange flexibility had overlooked that the main message of the report was carried in its title. While official complacency lasted a few months longer, the Bretton Woods exchange system received its final blow in 1971, when the United States decided to force a break in order to achieve a substantial devaluation of the dollar. Reality had bridged the Atlantic.

The end of the long struggle to avoid a change in the dollar parity also involved a marked increase in variation of exchange rates among European currencies. This development was contrary to many people's expectations and still more strongly contrary to proclaimed official intentions. Those concerned with furthering economic and political integration within the European Economic Community included not only the European Commission in Brussels but an influential circle of public officials and private citizens, not only within the existing six countries of the EEC but extending also to Britain and the United States. They had as their goal a common European currency. The intermediate step to this goal was to lock together existing

European exchange rates. At the operational level, this was convenient for the functioning of the support system of the Common Agricultural Policy. It was in the 1960s that the view was often heard that changes in exchange rates within the EEC were impossible because they would disrupt the CAP (a reason which to many observers only enhanced the attractions of flexible exchange rates).

The EEC Commission exerted continuous pressure against any move towards flexibility on a world-wide scale, since it feared that this would interfere with its plans to reduce the range of fluctuation, both in daily movements within the margins and over longer periods, among the Community currencies themselves. While the Brussels Commission did not itself carry great weight, its attitude was a marginal influence reinforcing the stand of the fixed rate conservatives. In the event, when exchange flexibility arrived on the global scene, the integrationists of the Community failed in their major effort to make this the basis of a common float which would create a fixed rate bloc within the EEC. Lip service to the principle of European monetary union was intensified, receiving its biggest boost at the EEC summit conference of 1972. Divergent movements in the exchange rates of the Community countries told a different story. The technical mechanism for aligning currency movements within the EEC, which became known as the 'snake', amounted to little more than an extended DM zone. This effectively embraced Germany's major trading partners – Belgium, Denmark, the Netherlands, Norway, Sweden and, unofficially, Austria, the last three outside the Community. France was what might be called a country member, departing from the fixed link with the DM zone whenever its situation demanded.

Thus our period ends on the international monetary front with currency developments again essentially accommodative – accommodative to overriding pressures within the domestic political economy. These pressures precluded any return to the quasi-mechanical rigidities of the pre-1914 gold standard. They also precluded a tightly managed system in which decisions about exchange rates and reserves

Exchange Rates in terms of the US Dollar: Sterling, German Mark, Swiss Franc

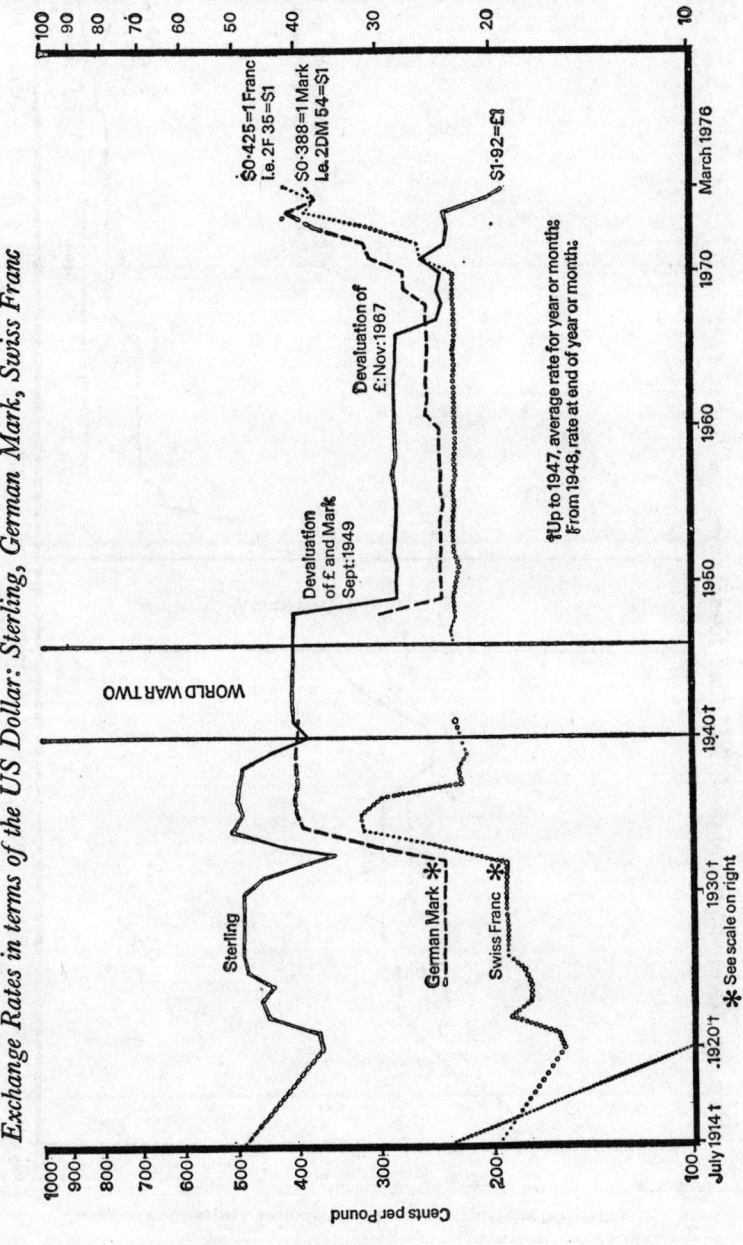

Exchange Rates in terms of the US Dollar: French Franc and Italian Lira

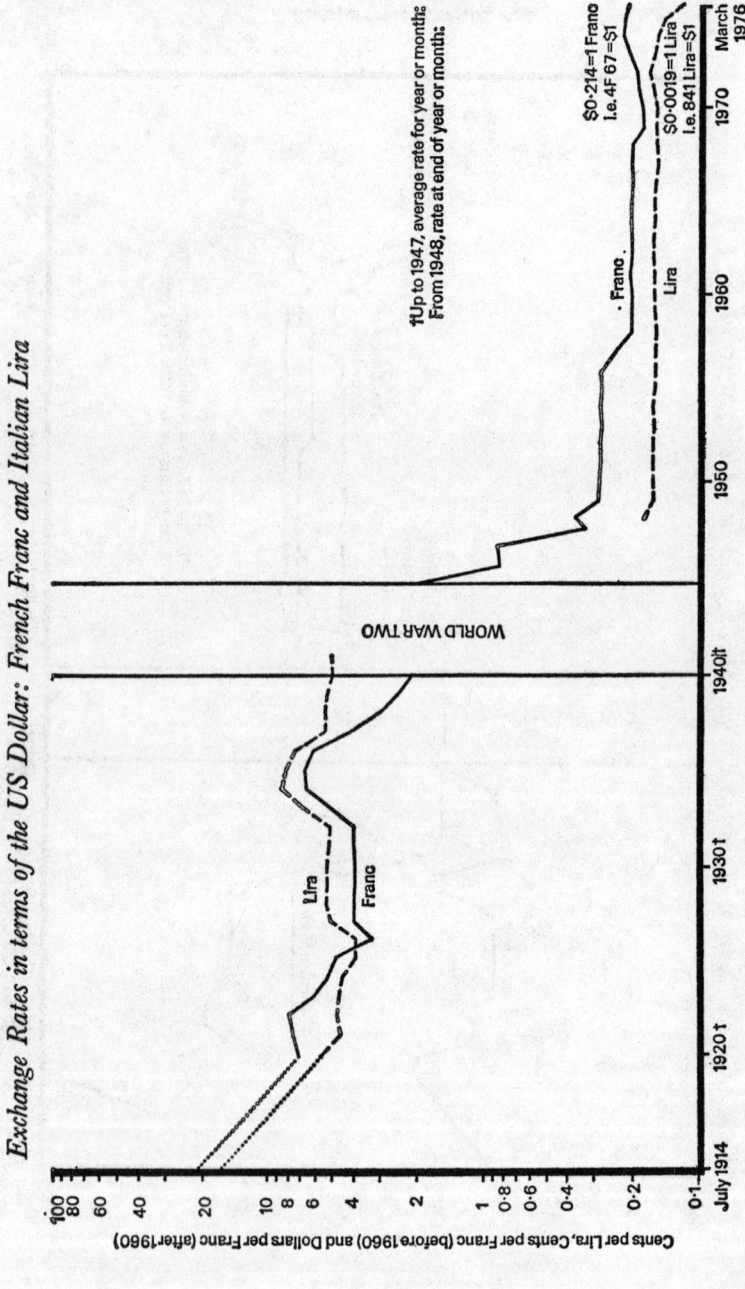

Cents per Lira, Cents per Franc (before 1960) and Dollars per Franc (after 1960)

†Up to 1947, average rate for year or month:
From 1948, rate at end of year or month:

$0·214=1 Franc
i.e. 4F 67=$1

$0·0019=1 Lira
i.e. 841 Lira=$1

would be more with supranational bodies than with nat·onal governments. This was the major change within the half century. Monetary standards no longer imposed. Rather, overriding political and economic circumstances determined monetary standards.

BANKING SYSTEMS AND CREDIT MARKETS

I

One of the hallmarks of the pre-1914 monetary order was the role of London as a world-wide credit and capital market. This position was never restored in its old form. Britain's overseas lending capacity was severely reduced in the twentieth century and, in addition, disposal of foreign assets and accumulation of foreign liabilities played an important part in the finance of two world wars. The United States took over as leading creditor nation. This was already apparent in the 1920s, when London found itself playing second fiddle to New York in the revival of international lending business. But there was another, more pervasive difference which emerged later, with the moves towards managed or accommodative money. Governments no longer took the desirability of free international capital movements for granted. Attitudes became more pragmatic. Both balance-of-payments management and real resource allocation were regarded as potentially justifying a degree of restraint on private capital transactions. The monetary collapse of 1929–31 marked the closure of international credit markets for a quarter of a century. Economic recovery and liberalisation after World War II brought a re-opening in the later 1950s, followed by massive expansion in the 1960s and 70s. But it was not a return to the straightforward liberalism of pre-1914. While international lending found wide scope, governments took care to exercise considerable influence over its volume and direction. Regulations were permissive over broad areas; but they were not absent.

This partly accounts for the institutions which functioned as the major channels for international credit in the 1960s: the Euro-currency and Euro-bond markets. Their freedom to operate stemmed initially from their 'offshore' status, which gave them exemption from a variety of national rules and restrictions. London banks doing business with non-residents in dollars were, for instance, unhampered either by UK exchange control or by US controls on bank interest rates or on capital exports. Thus, London became once again the chief centre of international finance, but now on a pure entrepôt basis, without significant participation by British capital.

These developments are discussed in context below. Meanwhile, in domestic credit systems, developments were less volatile. The 1970 structure of banking and credit within West European countries had to a large extent been established by 1920. The important changes had taken place during the previous fifty years (1870–1920), spurred by the financial requirements of general economic growth and industrialisation, by advances in communication and by commercial rivalry within the banking sector. Commercial banking became more concentrated, many small banks coalescing or disappearing into larger institutions with extensive branch networks. On balance, this probably made for greater stability, though it also meant that failure of one large bank would more readily call into question the soundness of the credit system as a whole. In Britain it was recognised that the ultimate, long-stop guarantee of banking stability was the Bank of England in its capacity as lender of last resort. This recognition was the outcome of nineteenth-century experience and Walter Bagehot's writings. Not all central banks found it easy to acknowledge responsibility of this kind. The German Reichsbank, for example, having itself operated as a major source of instability in the hyper-inflation of 1923, was hamstrung in the crisis of 1931 by memories of its earlier misdemeanour, and felt unable to engage in large-scale expansion of domestic credit (see below).[29]

29. Outside Europe, US Federal Reserve policies aggravated the

The trend towards greater concentration in banking continued at a slower rate after 1920. In England, which was pace-setter in commercial as well as in central banking, the war years of 1914–18 marked a decisive phase, leading to the domination of the banking system by the Big Five (Barclays, Lloyds, Midland, National Provincial and Westminster). A spate of mergers in 1917–18 had occasioned the appointment of a Treasury Committee on Bank Amalgamations (the Colwyn Committee), which reported that further mergers would, on balance, be undesirable from the point of view of competition and of maintenance of the capital base of the banking sector. The banks on their side had argued that larger units brought greater economies and efficiency, and were in any case necessary to keep in step with the size of industrial concerns, whose credit requirements the banks had to meet. The former argument was open to question inasmuch as mergers did not appear to lead to any reduction in the number of bank offices or branches. The latter argument was perhaps more persuasive. Certainly it has been heard at other times and places. For example, in 1872 the Swiss Bank Corporation was founded by an amalgamation of private banks in Basle, in order to create a banking unit capable of accommodating the large firms of the city's chemical industry. And in the late 1960s the establishment of international consortium banks was stimulated by the spread of multinational corporations.[30]

---

calamitous wave of American bank failures in 1931–33. Preoccupation with the external reserve position (and initially also legal provisions concerning gold cover for the note issue) led the Fed to enforce two spells of monetary tightness in autumn 1931 and early 1933. And expansionary measures in between were very half-hearted. Adherence to the gold standard took precedence over support for a domestic banking system that was thus brought to the verge of total collapse. The peculiar structure of US banking, with its dual chartering system (state and national) and its absence of branching (see next footnote) was a further complication.

30. Note, however, that extensive branch banking has never been accepted in the United States. At the time of writing (1976) inter-state branching is still whol'y forbidden, though this may change in the years ahead. Inter-state diversification of banks into non-bank financial services (consumer credit, mortgage finance etc.) has been permitted

A draft bill implementing the 1918 Colwyn Committee's recommendations was withdrawn when the clearing banks undertook to submit for approval by the Treasury and Board of Trade any future merger or joint-working proposals. A further half-dozen amalgamations did in fact take place in the 1920s and one (the District Bank with the Manchester and County) in 1935. There were then eleven London clearing banks, among whom the Big Five accounted for more than 85 per cent of deposits.

On the European continent the degree of concentration in commercial banking was generally less than in Britain. The various countries' Big Four, Five or Seven collected a lower percentage of total commercial bank deposits than the Big Five in Britain. Small regional and local banks still played a significant role. Moreover, the banking habit, and particularly the use of cheques, was less established on the continent, so that bank deposits as against currency accounted for a smaller share of the normal peacetime money stock – 50–70 per cent compared with over 80 per cent in Britain.[31]

In addition, banks other than commercial banks held – and continue to hold – a more prominent position on the continent. The main ones are the savings banks. A distinction is commonly drawn between the Post Office or National Savings Bank (in which Britain had also led the way with

through bank holding companies since 1956, and more liberally since 1970. Even within many states, bank branching was in practice fairly narrowly restricted until 1970 (though in some states bank holding companies provided a substitute some years earlier). In any case, the giant US banks which established branches throughout the world in the 1960s (Bank of America, First National City Bank of New York, Chase Manhattan and the rest) remained tied to a single area inside the United States.

31. The proportion is subject to considerable medium-term fluctuations. It appeared in the later 1950s that the UK ratio had fallen below 80 per cent, but by 1970 this could no longer be definitely stated. A clear comparison is impossible because of the altered structure of the banking system, with the ordinary deposit banks (London clearers plus Scottish and Northern Irish banks) accounting for a much lower percentage of residents' deposits than formerly. (See p. 667). This makes definition of the money supply less clear-cut.

the creation of the POSB in 1861) and others; the latter may be in either the public or the private sector. In several countries the savings banks have their own central deposit institution, which thereby occupies an important place in the capital market. Such are the *Caisse des Dépôts et Consignations* in France, the *Cassa Depositi e Prestiti* (for postal savings) in Italy, and the various *Girozentrale* in Germany; also the *Caisse Générale d'Epargne et de Retraite* in Belgium, which is a savings bank in its own right. In most continental countries the prominence of the savings banks is connected with the use of the postal giro – rather than cheques – as the standard method of money transfer. The postal giro did not exist in Britain until 1968.

The total volume of UK savings bank deposits in the 1920s was less than one-quarter that of commercial bank deposits; in the 1930s, with interest differentials favouring the savings banks, the ratio began to rise and by the outbreak of World War II was over one-third. During the war it went as high as one-half, but afterwards fell back to around 40 per cent. By contrast, many continental countries (including Finland, France, Netherlands, Sweden and Switzerland) began the 1920s with a ratio of one-third to one-half; and some (Czechoslovakia, Denmark, Italy, Norway) had a ratio of one or greater, i.e. savings bank deposits equalled or exceeded deposits at commercial banks. Austria, Germany, Hungary and Poland (and also Russia where the process had begun earlier) had their currencies destroyed by hyper-inflation in 1922–23, so the whole banking system had to start from scratch after a currency reform. In almost all continental countries deposits at savings banks built up steadily from 1925 onwards, and maintained their growth after 1930, when those at commercial banks were static or declining for six years during the slump. In Austria and Germany commercial bank deposits fell by 40 per cent from 1930 to 1932, a direct and indirect reflection of the 1931 bank failures (see below). During World War II the general pattern on the continent was for money supplies, i.e. commercial bank deposits plus note circulation, to expand rapidly, while savings banks lagged behind. Unsurprisingly, savings banks did better in the non-belligerent countries. In the post-1945 period their ability to attract funds was affected *inter alia* by regulations concerning interest rates and by the changing relative importance of personal savings. In some countries (e.g. Germany) the savings banks became even more prominent than between the wars, in others (e.g. Italy) they were less so and in yet others (e.g. France) much the same.

The contrast between Britain and the continent in the matter of savings banks should not, however, be overdrawn. In the first place, the UK government collects small savings not merely through the Post Office and Trustee Savings Banks, but also by the issue of National Savings and similar Certificates, whose amount outstanding was throughout the period 1920–70 of the same order of magnitude as the volume of savings bank deposits. Secondly, the inter-war period saw a major expansion of the UK building societies, which as a repository for personal savings are comparable to continental savings banks. Their liabilities rose tenfold between 1919 and 1939, to over £700 million, almost one-third the amount of deposits at the London clearing banks; and resumed this expansion after 1945, reaching in the mid-1970s a figure about two-thirds that of the broadly defined money supply and rather greater than the deposits of the London clearing banks.[32] Thus, when National Savings and the building societies are included, the overall structure of domestic banking and near-banking in the United Kingdom does not look at all that different from its continental counterparts.

The building societies and continental savings banks, however, must also be viewed as capital-market institutions, since their assets are largely or predominantly long-term – such as mortgages with an initial term to maturity of typically 25 years. Differences between the British and

32. In general, the broadly defined money supply includes time deposits at commercial banks. The narrowly defined money supply includes only sight deposits of the note circulation. In the British case the narrow money supply also excludes sight deposits of the public sector; and both definitions exclude non-residents' deposits. But on these latter points there are no hard and fast rules.

continental capital markets have perhaps been more marked than those between the banking systems. The salient features of the British market are the limited role of the banks in the provision of long-term finance (the deposit banks in particular do not buy equities); the much wider role, gaining greatly in importance through the period under review, of non-bank financial intermediaries, principally insurance companies, pension funds and investment and unit trusts (plus the building societies in the housing market); and highly developed securities markets, essentially the London stock exchange, with its extensive division of labour as between brokers, jobbers and issuing houses (the latter being chiefly merchant banks).

On the continent there has been much more overlap between long-term capital markets and banking systems. In Germany and Austria relations between the banks and industry have been particularly close, with banks supplying both long-term loans and equity capital, and frequently being represented on the boards of their major corporate customers. In France too the investment banks (*banques d'affaires*) and private banking houses have been a customary source of long-term and equity capital, and the deposit banks were allowed to participate in this kind of business after 1966. New security issues in the 1960s were generally higher in relation to GNP on the continent than in Britain, partly reflecting the higher volume of savings and investment. But the secondary markets in securities have been less developed. The functions of security broking and underwriting on the continent are commonly performed by commercial banks.

Various specialised institutions have been important in supplying credit to particular areas of the economy. These include, in the private sector, agricultural and other credit co-operatives; and in the public sector, especially of Belgium, France and Italy, agencies lending to medium-sized and small businesses, to manufacturing in general, to agriculture or to specific regions (notably the south in Italy). In Britain the supply of capital by state agencies and by the government itself to unviable industrial firms and projects became conspicuous after the mid-1960s and especially in the 1970s. Mortgage finance is also supplied by public bodies; in Britain local authorities became a significant source of such credit in the 1960s, besides being responsible for about 40 per cent of all residential construction. In the Netherlands, the Bank for Netherlands Municipalities raises funds by means of bond issues for on-lending to local authorities. In Sweden the National Pension Fund, established in 1960, soon rose to be the dominant capital-market lender. Compared with Britain, the importance on the continent of agricultural credit institutions is explained by the much greater share of agriculture in gross national product, especially in the interwar period and the 1950s, and by the preponderance of small and medium-sized farms.

II

Close involvement with industry contributed to the failure of the largest bank in Austria, the Creditanstalt, in May 1931, and of one of the biggest German banks, the Darmstädter und Nationalbank ('Danat Bank') two months later. The world slump, touched off by the Wall Street crash of 1929 and aggravated by the massive drop in primary-product prices which began before the collapse of industrial production, found the central European economies in a particularly vulnerable state. They had participated in the fragile prosperity of the later 1920s on the basis of large-scale foreign borrowing from America, Britain and elsewhere, mostly at short term. This applied especially to Germany, whose foreign borrowing from 1925 to 1928 inclusive was estimated at $1000m or a little under 10 per cent of her imports over those years. Funds began to leave Germany in the latter part of 1928, drawn first by the speculative orgies on Wall Street and later, in 1930–31, by worries about the German political outlook. Some of the outflow was financed by a swing from deficit to surplus in Germany's current balance of payments between 1928 and 1930 – at the cost of a sharp drop in economic activity, which severely reduced the value of bank investments in industry. With world export markets suffering from a combination of slump and rising tariff barriers, debtor countries could not in any case achieve surpluses sufficient to meet all the debt repayments sought by creditors. Continued withdrawal of funds therefore drained foreign-exchange reserves from Germany, Austria and Hungary, and reduced their internal money stocks. This worsened their slump, so undermining still further the value of commercial bank assets, while simultaneously making it more and more difficult for the banks to retain deposits. Resort to defensive or 'siege economy' tactics – devaluation and/or import barriers, plus expansion of the central bank's domestic assets to compensate for the loss of exchange reserves – was rejected at this stage because of anxiety about possible inflationary consequences and memories of 1922–23. (A few people argued that such worries were irrelevant in the prevailing circumstances – see the earlier reference to the German 'pre-Keynesians'. Their view became orthodoxy following the publication of Keynes's *General Theory* in 1936.) The spring and summer of 1931 saw the final crash.

After the Austro-German *débâcle*, sterling came under pressure. Short-term balances held in London in the late 1920s were much in excess of the sum of British banks' foreign claims plus the gold reserves – as was pointed out by the Committee on Finance and Industry (Macmillan Committee) in 1931. After World War I, UK long-term capital outflows were no longer fully matched by current-account surpluses, and the difference had to be borrowed at short term. This obliged the Bank of England to keep interest rates relatively high, despite unemployment and a low rate of industrial activity at home. Withdrawal of balances from London by the French authorities and by primary producing countries overseas began in 1929. The situation had become highly precarious by August 1931, when moratoria on German, Austrian and other debts immobilised some £70m of UK banks' overseas claims. The banks in question were not the clearers but the accepting houses (merchant banks) and British overseas banks. However, even without Bank of England assistance, enough resources were found to pay out foreign depositors and avoid bank closures. The floating rate for sterling after September put a stop to the drain of foreign balances.

Following these events, the machinery of private international finance spent twenty years in cold storage. Large capital movements among European countries and between Europe and North America during the 1930s were undertaken mainly in anticipation of exchange-rate changes or, as war drew nearer, in search of a refuge for capital. Speculation in forward exchange, along with national interest-rate policies, created opportunities for covered interest arbitrage which banks from time to time exploited. Any serious recovery in international credit business was ruled out by a variety of unfavourable influences: the depressed state of world trade, the unresolved issue of frozen debts and the exchange controls established over much of central Europe, involving official clearing mechanisms or bilateral payments agreements. Payments agreements enabled some of the UK banks' claims in central Europe to be settled; others were carried forward until after World War II, when the whole German debt question was tidied up by the London Debt Agreement of 1953. On the long-term capital market also, international loan issues all but disappeared, apart from a few in London by overseas sterling countries.

European credit systems and monetary policy in the 1930s and early 40s served mainly to meet the needs of national governments, bent first on achieving recovery from the slump and then on waging war. This was pre-eminently true of Nazi Germany. In Britain increases in government spending were modest until war broke out. But the floating exchange rate enabled credit policy to be governed by internal rather than by external considerations during the 1930s; so money was kept cheap. Bank rate remained unchanged at 2 per cent after June 1932,[33] but even at this

33. Apart from a flurry of a few weeks at the outbreak of war in 1939, when it was raised to 4 per cent and then lowered again. The decision to revert to 2 per cent was the significant one. It implied that the Second World War, unlike the First, would be a cheap-money ('3 per cent') war

level was of little more than formal significance. Gilt-edged were in strong demand. The yield on $2\frac{1}{2}$ per cent Consols declined from around $4\frac{1}{2}$ per cent in the 1920s to $3\frac{1}{2}$ per cent in 1932, when almost all the £2,000m of 5 per cent War Loan 1929–47 outstanding from World War I – 27 per cent of the entire national debt – was successfully converted at par (plus a £1 per 100 bonus) into $3\frac{1}{2}$ per cent War Loan redeemable at government option after 1952. The authorities pressed ahead with the policy of debt funding begun during the 1920s, making periodic issues of long-term bonds and so limiting the amount of both shorter-dated issues and Treasury bills. Since the volume of commercial bills financing international trade had also contracted sharply after 1931, there was a shortage of money-market paper for banks and others (including foreigners who moved balances totalling several hundred million pounds to London) to hold. Downward pressure on short-term interest rates was intensified, UK Treasury bills yielding scarcely more than $\frac{1}{2}$ per cent per annum – which was the rate on bank time deposits – from 1932 to 1938.[34] Since the banks had ample cash reserves, they were driven by the weakness of private credit demands, coupled with the shortage of bills, to enlarge their placements in gilt-edged, including longer-dated issues. By the middle of the decade about one-half of their deposits were being lent directly or indirectly to the government. Cheap money on its own was nothing like as effective in promoting economic recovery as greater spend ng by government would have been. It probably stimulated house building; but even here it was not the only factor at work. The fall in the price level raised the real value of controlled rents whose low ceiling had helped to inhibit building in the 1920s.

The public sector's role was extended in a more institu-

in Britain, with the economy managed by more direct weapons than credit policy. This bore strong testimony to the impact of Keynes's thinking after the *General Theory*.

34. Even this yield was maintained only with the help of cartel arrangements among clearing banks and discount houses to restrict competition for bills. In New York the yield on US Treasury bills fell virtually to zero in 1938.

tional manner in the thirties in Italy. The *Istituto Mobiliare Italiano* (IMI) was created in 1931, to take over medium- and long-term industrial lending from the big banks, who found many of their assets frozen at that time. Subsequently the three major banks in the private sector (Banca Commerciale Italiana, Credito Italiano, Banco di Roma – designated 'Banks of National Interest' in the Banking Law of 1936) were effectively nationalised under the state holding company, *Istituto per la Ricostruzione Industriale* (IRI); the fourth bank equal in rank to these three, the Banca Nazionale del Lavoro, had been state-owned since its foundation in 1913. Analogous measures were adopted later in France. A Bank Control Commission was created by the wartime regime in 1941 to ensure that banks' operating criteria would maintain solvency and protect depositors. After the war, more important legislation in December 1945 nationalised the four main deposit banks (Crédit Lyonnais, Société Générale, Comptoir Nationale d'Escompte de Paris and Banque Nationale pour le Commerce et l'Industrie, the last named having been reconstructed in 1932 out of the former Banque Nationale de Crédit) and created the National Credit Council as the body responsible for implementing monetary and banking policy. The membership of the Council is drawn from government ministries, the Bank of France, the banks and business, and its secretariat is provided by the Bank of France.

III

After 1945 credit policy remained in the background for several more years. This was rather different from the aftermath of World War I. Material damage was far greater in the second war, and the network of direct controls on production, consumption and trade was far wider and more systematic. Moreover, whereas the post-war task of governments in 1918 was generally seen in terms of organising a speedy return to the established liberal order prevailing before 1914, the aim in 1945 was first and foremost to *prevent* any return to the miseries of the inter-war period.

Governments accordingly took a cautious and pragmatic line. There was little rush to decontrol. Time was evidently needed to rehabilitate war-damaged economies. There was also uncertainty about how monetary policy would fit in to the wider pattern of economic responsibilities now assumed by governments.

The question of excessive money stocks left over from the closing stages of the war presented itself before there had been any serious attempt to reinstate the market economy. In West Germany a remarkably effective operation was carried out in June 1948, for which the Economics Minister, Ludwig Erhard, obtained much of the credit. A comparison with the currency reform which ended the hyper-inflation of 1923, and in which Currency Commissioner Hjalmar Schacht was the leading light, is instructive. The earlier episode, after the dizzy financial policies which preceded it, was a somewhat agonising affair, involving first an interim stabilisation from October 1923 with the issue of Rentenmark,[35] and then a fierce credit and budgetary squeeze through the spring and summer of 1924 to consolidate the new currency in the face of initial market suspicion. From August 1924 onwards the new Reichsmark was successfully established at the rate first adopted for the Rentenmark – 1 new mark = 1,000,000m old marks. In 1948, by contrast, the Germans had suffered not hyper-inflation, but three years of near-chaos due to the breakdown of both pricing and rationing arrangements which left no functioning market for bread or shoes, let alone for foreign exchange. Under Dr Erhard's chairmanship, the authorities abolished most price controls and rationing overnight, and reduced the quantity of money by substituting a new Deutschemark for the Reichsmark. Individuals were able initially to exchange RM600 for DM60, and firms were given a similar exchange per employee. All other

35. The Rentenmark issue was 'backed' by interest-bearing bonds supposedly representing a general mortgage on the country's real estate. This has been well described by Leland Yeager as 'a kind of public relations device'. The point of substance was that the quantity of Rentenmark was rigidly limited.

RM currency and bank accounts were blocked, and converted into DM later (at what turned out to be a rate of RM100 for DM6·5). Debts were converted to the new basis by being deflated to one-tenth of their RM value. (In 1924 they had also been adjusted, but mostly to only a small fraction of their original real worth.) The reform set markets for goods and services on their feet again, and proved to be a green light for the German 'economic miracle'. At the same time, the beginning of Marshall Aid provided more potent and enduring external support than the loan under the Dawes Plan of 1924 to facilitate German reparations.

The German currency reform of 1948 had no exact parallels in other countries. A few states – Greece, Hungary, Rumania – established new currencies following hyperinflation. Austria, Belgium and the Netherlands resorted to blocking some bank deposits for a time, but without currency conversion. Elsewhere there were no special measures, any excess supply of money being absorbed soon or late by the rise in GNP at current prices. In France and Italy this was allowed to happen quite swiftly, by a doubling or trebling of prices from 1946 to 1948 (on top of the massive inflation experienced in the latter part of the war). In Britain the problem was milder, but its existence was never really admitted. In fact matters were aggravated by the quixotic experiment in ultra-cheap money (attempting to force the long-term rate of interest down to $2\frac{1}{2}$ per cent) undertaken by Hugh Dalton as Chancellor of the Exchequer in 1946–47. Subsequently, absorption of excess liquidity was dragged out for well over a decade – less painful in the short-run, but ultimately more bewildering to those responsible for policy.

In the 1950s monetary policy in Europe duly emerged in its new guise, as the standard and most widespread instrument of demand management in the mixed economy. This description may surprise British readers, who are accustomed to monetary policy being overshadowed by the government budget. The British position is not, however, typical. Of course, the government sector has been a major com-

ponent of almost every western industrial economy since
1945. In west European countries the ratio of government
outlays (including transfer payments, such as pensions) to
gross national product was generally between 30 and 40
per cent in the 1950s, and then increased again during the
sixties to exceed 50 per cent in the early seventies in
some cases (Scandinavia, Netherlands, United Kingdom).
Transfer payments accounted for much of the latter increase.[36] But, over the short run, budgetary policy was unusually flexible in the United Kingdom. In many countries
constitutional, political or administrative procedures hampered speedy introduction of tax changes, so greater reliance
had to be placed on credit policy. Such differences tended
to narrow during the sixties, as monetary policy became
more prominent in Britain, and fiscal policy more available
in one or two continental countries, notably Germany.

In techniques of credit control, monetary authorities in
western Europe modified their methods from time to time,
either to strengthen official control in new circumstances or
to improve the working of financial markets. Besides the
normal weapons of open-market operations, variations in
reserve requirements and changes in the amount and terms
of central-bank rediscounting and other facilities, more
direct forms of control or 'moral suasion' were also used.
Quantitative ceilings on bank credit to the private sector
were applied at some time in all countries except Germany
and Italy. They were widespread on the continent in the
late 1960s and early 70s, when concern about inflation
and 'overheating' was strongest. A few countries also

36. For longer-run historical comparisons the British figures may be
taken as representative. UK government outlays in proportion to GNP
have been estimated as follows:

1900–1914   12½ per cent
1914–1918   35–40 per cent, with a peak of 50 per cent in 1918
1919–1939   25 per cent, rising to 29 per cent in the years of highest
            unemployment (1921 and 1931–2)
1939–1945   73 per cent
1948–1955   40 per cent
(Source: A. T Peacock and J. Wiseman, *The Growth of Public Expenditure
in the United Kingdom*, 2nd Edition, London 1967).

employed ceilings on short-term borrowing or indebtedness of local authorities (Netherlands, United Kingdom); or supplemented credit policy by quantitative controls on capital issues (France, Switzerland; also the United Kingdom in the 1950s). Special measures to control international movements of liquid funds were widespread (see p. 661).

The British authorities had particular difficulty sorting out their attitude to credit policy. When first re-activated in the early 1950s, policy was influenced by historical memories of Bank rate as a key regulator before 1914 and in the 1920s. The apparent (but not actual) contribution of Bank rate increases to resolving the 1951 balance-of-payments crisis reinforced this view. In earlier periods, however, the impact of Bank rate had been essentially on short-run international capital flows; its effect on aggregate spending or the price level was much weaker, despite what contemporary banking theorists suggested. The discrepancy between theory and practice began to be felt in the boom of 1955, when the banks had to be 'requested' to enforce a significant reduction in advances. The persistence of price and wage rises in the recession of 1957–58 increased perplexity and heightened disagreements about policy. Rumours of an impending exchange-rate realignment set off a run on the pound in the summer of 1957, the fifth external payments crisis since 1945. All three Treasury ministers (Peter Thorneycroft, who was Chancellor, Enoch Powell and Nigel Birch) resigned, when the Cabinet refused to sanction ceilings in money terms on government expenditure. In 1958 the first of four reports by the Cohen Council on Prices, Productivity and Incomes put the main blame for inflation on excess monetary demand; its opponents maintained that 'cost push' arising first from import prices and then from wages, and independent of the pressure of demand, was more important.

The Radcliffe Committee was appointed, following a well established tradition, to report on the Working of the Monetary System, which it did in 1959. Besides calling for much needed improvements in financial statistics and, by implication, in the authorities' financial analysis, Radcliffe argued that neither interest rates nor the quantity of money were important in their own right, but only as part of, and as influences upon, the 'general liquidity position', which covered all types of financial intermediation. The Report was heavily influenced by the experience of the 1950s, when the whole credit system was abnormally liquid, and by the authorities' obsessive attitude to the government debt market.

The UK national debt was, of course, exceptionally large as a result of the two world wars and the failure of British governments to finance them by hyper-inflation.[37] Its management, with continuous maturities and refinancings, was a headache. The problem was compounded by the Bank of England's reluctance to allow wide movements in gilt-edged prices. This attitude initially owed a good deal (like the Dalton cheap-money experiment) to Keynes's wartime views on the desirability of low and stable long-term interest rates. It was reinforced by the Treasury's wish to keep down the cost of debt service; but it ultimately became a kind of self-sufficient dogma of the Bank's.[38] Demand for government stocks was held to be inherently unstable because an initial fall in price was expected to be followed by a further fall; adequate marketability of stocks therefore depended on the government broker standing ready to buy at the going price whatever amount of debt the market chose to unload. Such views hampered monetary control, and, had they been valid, would have made the Bank's propaganda on behalf of the UK capital market absurd.

The policy implications of the Radcliffe analysis were vague. But insofar as it attached no special importance to the quantity of money, it was consistent with the combination of interest-rate manipulations and directives to the credit institutions which became the UK pattern in the

37. From £700m in 1914 the debt rose to £6,000m in 1918, £8,000m in 1939 and no less than £28,000m in 1952 (about twice the GNP for that year). With only modest urther increases to £32,000m in 1970, the ratio to GNP fell to 75 per cent.

38. See "Official Transactions in the Gilt-Edged Market", *Bank of England Quarterly Bulletin*, 1966.

1960s. A further change occurred, however, in the aftermath of the November 1967 devaluation, whose impact on employment and the balance of trade was slow to appear. The upshot was a shift of emphasis away from interest rates and bank credit and towards the 'monetary aggregates', (initially Domestic Credit Expansion (DCE) and later the growth of the money stock, which is equivalent to DCE but includes the monetary counterpart of any overall surplus or deficit on the balance of payments).[39] The aggregates were regarded partly as tentative targets for policy, partly as indicators. The UK authorities were influenced in their change of view not only by events but also by academic arguments and by the policy analyses of other monetary authorities, including the International Monetary Fund.[40] The shift of emphasis was confirmed by reforms of the credit system in 1971 (see below, pp. 667-8).

IV

The responsiveness of capital flows to discrepancies between monetary and especially interest-rate policies of different countries, dimly recalled by the UK authorities in the early fifties, did reappear a few years later, with the growing liberalisation of international transactions. In general, under pegged or closely managed exchange rates such responsiveness will be welcome when a country wishing

39. To be precise, DCE equals the public-sector borrowing requirement *minus* purchases of public-sector debt by private non-banks *plus* bank lending to the private sector *plus* bank lending in sterling to non-residents (net of any bank lending to residents of foreign currency for investment overseas).

40. An elegant and influential way of presenting monetary developments as a basis for policy discussion had long been adopted by the Netherlands Bank. Over any period, an increase in the volume of liquidity due to domestic credit expansion plus the balance-of-payments surplus must be absorbed either by a rise in the money value of GNP or by a change in the ratio of liquid assets to GNP. If the economy starts at full employment and wishes to hold a constant ratio of liquid assets to GNP then a necessary condition for stability of the price level is that creation of additional liquidity be kept in line with growth of the economy's real productive potential. This type of model may be described as a post-Keynesian application of the quantity theory of money.

to tighten money and curb a boom is also experiencing a deficit on its balance of payments, and when a country in recession has a surplus. In such cases, moreover, the capital flow will tend to taper off fairly soon, since the deficit country's credit-worthiness and the surplus country's willingness to export funds will encounter limits. By contrast, the process must be unwelcome if the combination of internal and external disequilibrium is the other way round, for then capital will be drawn into the country already running a surplus, thus aggravating the imbalance in international payments and also frustrating the domestic stabilisation efforts. This time, moreover, the natural limits to the flow may lie much further off. Of course, what is really indicated if such dilemmas persist is a shift in exchange rates, and speculation on this will sooner or later be unleashed. Hence the separate 'problems' of interest-sensitive and speculative capital flows tend to be conflated.

Up to a point, specific measures can be used to influence or inhibit the international movement of funds without seriously impeding free trade and current payments. Most European countries apart from Austria, Germany and Switzerland maintained comprehensive controls over short-term capital flows even in the 1960s. Non-bank residents were typically not allowed to borrow direct from banks abroad, and control was exercised over the domestic banks' net foreign position. Germany and Switzerland used more intermittent devices, such as zero or negative interest rates on non-resident-owned bank deposits and differential bank reserve requirements on home and foreign liabilities. A number of countries, including Germany, Switzerland, Italy and the United Kingdom, intervened in forward exchange markets. In short, the international banking scene in the 1960s and 70s was rather like a mini-golf course, with some hole or other always accessible, but others shut off and a variety of shifting obstacles to be negotiated.

The business and financial community became very good at playing this golf course, thanks to a major institutional development. This was the Euro-currency system together with its cousin, the Euro-bond market. Following some inter-war precedents, the accepting houses in London had begun to do business in dollars in a modest way in the mid-1950s. They took deposits from firms engaged in international trade or from east European sources wishing to keep dollar balances out of reach of the US authorities, and, when it was profitable to do so, swapped them into sterling on a three-months basis for lending to UK local authorities. The market's international take-off began in 1957, when the sterling crisis led the UK authorities to ban the use of sterling credits to finance third-country trade. The British overseas banks, who were well established in Asia, Africa and Latin America, and had been gearing themselves up to a revival of business, turned to the dollar as an alternative vehicle, bidding for deposits on terms competitive with New York and lending on terms competitive with the customer's alternative borrowing opportunities.

The return to convertibility at the end of 1958 opened the way to more rapid expansion of such business. Growth thereafter was by leaps and bounds. Dollars were supplied by central banks directly or indirectly (e.g. via swap arrangements with commercial banks, which was one form of the forward-exchange intervention mentioned above) as well as by international corporations and others. They were lent, usually by way of a series of inter-bank transactions, to businesses and governments around the world, with the main pull on funds tending to come, especially in the earlier years, from one or two countries at a time.

Besides channelling funds from original depositors to ultimate borrowers, the system provided an inter-bank money market in dollars, and soon in other currencies too, particularly Swiss francs, Deutschemarks and (in Paris and Zürich) sterling. Growing numbers of American and other foreign banks established themselves in London, and also in other financial centres both in Europe and elsewhere, such as the Bahamas and Singapore. Switzerland played a conspicuous part as an intermediary or pass-through in the Euro-markets. This resulted from its reputation for banking secrecy and security, which in turn rested partly on its political and social stability and partly on legislation passed in 1934.

The Euro-currency market was initially a market in short-term deposits, with three months the most active maturity. It was regarded at first as an offshoot of foreign-exchange dealing. The early sixties saw the beginnings of an international bond market, with banks in several countries organising mainly dollar-denominated issues of up to 15 years maturity by governments, public agencies and large corporations. The bonds were marketed to investors around the world. Interest was paid without deduction of tax, which constituted a major attraction to participants in the market.

An important stimulus to the growth of these international markets was given by US measures in force during the decade 1963–73 against capital outflows. First the Interest Equalisation Tax on foreign bond issues in the United States, and then growing restrictions on both overseas lending by US banks and transfers of funds by US corporations, had the effect of displacing a lot of the financing of these corporations' overseas activities to Europe and elsewhere. Even before 1963 some encouragement to the build-up of dollar deposits outside the United States arose from the Federal Reserve's Regulation Q, under which, until 1973, interest-rate limits on US bank deposits were imposed. No interest at all was allowed on deposits placed for less than one month. Regulation Q played a special role during the major tight-money episode in the United States in 1968–69. Together with the exemption (subsequently removed) from US bank reserve requirements of US bank borrowings from their foreign branches, it caused a large part of the intense competition for funds among US banks to take place in London rather than New York. US bank liabilities to their foreign branches reached a peak of $15,000m at that time.

The exploitation of loopholes in existing regulations or cartels was certainly part of the Euro-market's stock-in-trade, and further instances will be given in a moment. But it needs to be understood in terms of a basic economic rationale. The Euro-currency system owed its existence originally to the 'animal spirits' of banks in London who could see no other way of doing the business at which they were expert. As the inter-bank network expanded, it came to constitute a highly efficient information channel, making money-flows more sensitive than ever before to international credit demands and to divergence in monetary conditions between countries. The main banks in the various countries knew and trusted one another, and so were willing to handle huge sums on slender interest margins, leaving it to the bank at the end of the chain to 'retail' the funds out to final borrowers in its own country or locality.

As the Euro-markets developed, competitive pressures brought strategic and tactical innovations. Negotiable certificates of deposit were introduced, following the practice begun in the early sixties by New York banks. More important, longer-term loans began to be granted, up to five years or so, closing the gap between short-term credit and the Euro-bond market. Such loans were normally made on a roll-over basis, the interest rate being adjusted at intervals, commonly of six months, to maintain a certain margin over a representative short-term rate, commonly the 'London inter-bank offered rate' (LIBOR). With governments and multinational companies seeking not only longer-term loans but also ever larger amounts – frequently $200 or 300m on a five-year credit, as against $20 or 30m on a fifteen-year bond – the banks began to form consortia for medium-term lending in order to share the risks. Moreover, a new species, the consortium bank, made its appearance. This was an international bank, set up (often but not always in London) by a group of established commercial banks drawn from several countries, for the specific purpose of expanding medium-term credit facilities available to large borrowers. The first such institution was the Midland and International Bank, created as early as 1964 by the Midland Bank, Standard Bank, Commercial Bank of Australia and Toronto-Dominion Bank. For several years Midland and International was a lone horse, but from 1967 onwards the fashion took hold and by 1974 there were more than fifty banks in this category.

By the summer of 1975 the net volume of funds being transmitted through the Euro-currency market was approaching $200,000m. The market's geographical scope had also spread. Numerous developing countries became borrowers in the 1970s, a few of them, such as Brazil, Mexico and the Philippines, on a large scale. On the depositing side, some third-world states, notably the oil producers, had been in the market from an early stage. With the jump in oil prices in 1973–74 their role became much greater still. On the Euro-bond market, new issues at the end of the 1960s were running at a rate of $3,000m a year; but these figures showed signs of more than doubling in the 1970s (after a drop-off caused by the world-wide credit squeeze in 1973–74).

The spectacular expansion of the Euro-currency system and its independence of any one supervisory authority gave rise to periodic concern about its vulnerability in the face of large-scale defaults or a global political crisis. Some shocks were felt in 1974, when several important banks in the USA, UK, Belgium, Germany and Switzerland announced serious losses from foreign-exchange speculation; and one lesser institution, the Herstatt Bank in Germany, had to close its doors. The trouble stemmed from the fact that the new regime of floating, and rapidly shifting, exchange rates after 1973 provided enormous inducements to speculate, and some less scrupulous dealers inevitably burnt their (or their bank's) fingers. The episode strengthened the preference of Euro-dollar depositors for a restricted number of top 'names'. Other banks found themselves temporarily having to pay higher rates. And the consortium banks experienced a sharp contraction. Normal business was quickly resumed, but some uneasiness remained about the soundness of the international banking network. US banks especially seemed under-capitalised in the face of the massive accrual of petro-dollar deposits. And the quality of some major outstanding loan categories – on real estate and oil tankers, as well as credits to less developed countries – was questionable.

v

Besides facilitating the international movement of funds, the
Euro-currency market also injected an additional element
of competition into national banking systems. It is not easy
here to disentangle the impact of the Euro-market from that
of other factors, such as the growing importance of multinational companies. One result of these influences was a
new series of mergers among large banks. In France, the
Comptoir Nationale d'Escompte merged with the Banque
Nationale pour le Commerce et l'Industrie in 1966, to form
the Banque Nationale de Paris. In the Netherlands the Big
Four became the Big Two in 1964, the Amsterdamsche and
Rotterdamsche Banks forming the Amro Bank (a merger
first planned in 1939, but put off on account of the war),
and the Nederlandsche Handel-Maatschappij and
Twentsche Banks forming the Algemene Bank Nederland. In
the United Kingdom in 1968, following permissive hints
from the authorities, the Westminster Bank merged with the
National Provincial (which itself had acquired the District
Bank in 1961); Barclays took over Martins (but a proposed
merger of these two with Lloyds was rejected by the govern-
ment on the narrowly voted recommendation of the
Monopolies Commission); and the Three Banks Group
(Royal Bank of Scotland, Glyn Mills and Williams
Deacons) amalgamated with the National Commercial
Bank of Scotland (itself a product of merger between two
Scottish banks in 1959).

Another, perhaps more interesting result was a tendency
for existing restrictive practices and lines of demarcation in
banking to be broken down. This was the most striking
aspect of the French banking reforms of 1966–67, which
streamlined the system of reserve assets; raised the minimum
capital of banks so as to induce absorption of small units;
liberalised restrictions on deposit rates and substantially
removed the division enacted in 1945 between deposit
banks and investment banks. The former were now permitted to receive deposits of any maturity (and not merely
up to two years), to subscribe up to 20 per cent of the

capital of enterprises and to hold the counterpart of their own capital and reserves in equities. Substantial changes in the structure of French banking ensued, with much increased overlap between different classes of banks.

In Italy, a little earlier, Euro-currency lending undermined the banks' interest-rate cartel. And an analogous impact was felt in Britain. The bulk of Euro-currency business in London involved the banks in a purely international entrepôt role, with no direct repercussions on the domestic system. However, there had always been some link between the two, notably through the market in local authority and finance house deposits; and as the years passed, the British overseas and foreign (especially American) banks competed increasingly and successfully for domestic business. The ordinary deposit banks' share of total sterling deposits fell from 85 per cent in 1959 to 65 per cent in 1970 – a significant reduction, incidentally, in banking concentration.[41] The readiness of US subsidiaries in Britain to bank with local branches of US banks was, no doubt, an important factor in this development. The deposit banks responded initially to the rise of the 'secondary banking system' not by seeking to abolish the interest-rate cartel which they had maintained since 1945 (and in some respects before World War II), but by establishing affiliates to participate separately in the secondary markets. At the same time, they became willing to grant explicitly medium-term credits to business, alongside the traditional short-term overdraft. They also widened facilities available to the personal sector, notably by the introduction of credit cards after 1966. The advance of the foreign and secondary banks was not stemmed however. By the end of the 1960s the mood of the clearers had changed.[42] Moreover, with monetary policy now focused more on the monetary aggre-

41. If foreign-currency deposits are added, the ordinary deposit banks' share in 1970 was only 40 per cent.

42. An additional point of importance here was the banks' decision to declare their true profits from 1970 onwards. Hitherto they had, by permission, normally made undisclosed transfers to reserves, in order to cushion declared profits against a bad year and prevent any possible loss

gates and less preoccupied with minimising the movement of gilt-edged prices, the authorities' earlier objections to abolishing the cartel had also faded. Besides, the new diversity of the banking system was not only making selective methods of credit control increasingly problematical, but was also casting doubt on the continued efficacy of the cartel in keeping market rates down.

The clearing banks' cartel was accordingly dissolved in 1971, in conjunction with other financial reforms which included a new system of reserve-asset ratios for the credit institutions and, more significant, a more flexible approach to interest-rate and debt-management policy. Automatic support of the gilt-edged market was ended. Bank rate was replaced by 'minimum lending rate', whose level from week to week was to be market-determined (by the Treasury bill auction) unless, exceptionally, the authorities chose to override the automatic indicator.

Unfortunately, following these reforms, the authorities allowed bank credit to expand in two years by some 50 per cent. With industrial investment sluggish, this went mainly to fuel a speculative property boom, whose collapse in 1973-74 bankrupted several so-called 'fringe banks' and seriously embarrassed the financial establishment.

The usual variation of interest rates and credit conditions over the business cycle was reinforced in post-1950 Europe by the leading role assigned to monetary policy in the management of aggregate demand. Yields rose, in some cases sharply, during economic upswings and declined in the ensuing recession. Their long-run trend, however, was upward, especially after the mid-1960s, when inflation accelerated. A climax was reached in the world-wide boom and credit squeeze of 1973-74. In several European countries (including Belgium, France, Germany, the Netherlands and the United Kingdom) short-term interest rates were in the 12-15 per cent bracket for many months. The three-month Euro-dollar rate peaked at around 14 per cent at the time of the Herstatt incident in the third quarter

---

of confidence. Full profits declaration proved a strong competitive spur.

of 1974. Long-term yields generally rose somewhat less, reaching 11–12 per cent on industrial bonds. The United Kingdom was an exception, with a collapse of security prices pushing industrial bonds yields up to 18½ per cent in the autumn of 1974. At the other end of the scale, in Switzerland short-term rates rose only to 6 per cent and bond yields to around 8 per cent.

The compensation offered by higher nominal interest rates for the declining real value of money was rough and ready, and left a variety of distortions in both resource allocation and income distribution. Firstly, the adjustment of yields was by and large insufficient to produce a significant real return on money assets, especially after tax. This encouraged over-investment in real estate and dwellings, as well as a mushrooming of trade in antiques and other inflation 'hedges'. The housing market was often further distorted by subsidies and tax allowances.

Secondly, the effect, notably on income distribution, of an upward adjustment in interest rates is by no means the same as that of indexation or adjustment of capital values (with interest rates broadly unchanged). In particular, large capital losses are inflicted on holders of previously issued long-term bonds. Clever investors would, no doubt, have foreseen this and sold out in time; but this only shifts part or all of the loss to others. Furthermore, any newly incurred debt, such as a long-term mortgage, whose servicing takes the customary form of a constant stream of *money* payments (part interest and part amortisation) involves a substantial degree of 'front loading' for the debtor in real terms. To distribute the debt-service payments evenly over time in real terms would, of course, require a stream of payments rising in money terms. Again, a sensible response by the debtor to this situation might well be to meet part of the interest charge in the early years out of additional borrowing. But that imposes an additional capital risk upon creditors in the early years, which financial institutions may be reluctant to shoulder.

Thirdly, a similar problem of cash flow affects the government in its servicing of the national debt. This was most apparent in Britain, where both the national debt and the secular rise in interest rates have been large. By 1976, interest on the UK national debt was running at around £5,000m per annum, equal to about half the public sector's financial deficit. Since these interest payments were nevertheless insufficient to maintain the value of the debt-holders' capital in real terms, some observers argued that they did not represent a 'genuine' budget deficit – the implication being that the private sector could be relied upon to run a correspondingly large financial surplus in order to make good the depletion in the real value of its accumulated holdings of government debt. The argument is, however, of doubtful reliability. As already pointed out, the private sector may react to inflation not only by increasing its nominal holdings of financial assets, but by buying more residential property, consumer durables and other inventories, which sooner or later raises demand for current output. In this respect, private savings and portfolio behaviour seems to be influenced more by the economic outlook as a whole than by the specific impact of (expected) inflation on the real value of monetary assets. Unusually high levels of personal saving in the industrial countries in 1974–75 probably reflected caution and retrenchment in the face of recession as much as anything else.

Despite these various difficulties and distortions, indexation of financial assets and liabilities in western industrial countries has been employed only very sporadically. The French government and public corporations made the occasional issue of indexed bonds. Finland had indexed bank deposits from 1955 to 1967 as well as indexed mortgages, government and private bonds and insurance. The UK authorities introduced in 1975 a strictly limited scheme of indexed government debt for small savings. In western Europe that was about all.[43] Moreover, private markets showed little inclination to develop indexation schemes on their own initiative. Evidently, all such schemes involve additional risks for somebody, and this makes it difficult to strike a bargain.

43. For a full survey see *National Institute Economic Review*, Nov. 1974.

Coal and Wheat: UK wholesale prices 1920–70 (£ per ton, logarithmic scale)

PRICE MOVEMENTS

I

On a bird's eye view, the contrasts in European and world price behaviour between the nineteenth and twentieth centuries are clear-cut. Before 1914 prices were stable. In 1919–39 they fell. Thereafter they rose. These contrasts match the differences in output and employment trends: reasonably full use of resources and well-balanced growth before 1914; mass unemployment, idle resources and unbalanced markets between the wars; and full employment with rapid growth, particularly of industrial production, after 1945.

A closer examination, while not invalidating this broad picture, shows it to be considerably more variegated. Before 1914 there were not only marked cyclical fluctuations in activity and prices, but also longer-run swings from dynamic advance to relative stagnation and back again. The twenty years from the mid-1870s to the mid-1890s were labelled 'The Great Depression', before the appellation was taken over for the early 1930s. Between 1896 and 1913, wholesale prices in the major economies rose by between one-third and one-half. A period can obviously be made to look more stable than it was by taking long averages. This applies to the inter-war period, in which four phases of business activity can be distinguished: the immediate post-war years of 1919–24; the mild boom of 1925–29; the slump of 1929–35; and the short cycle of 1936–38.

The immediate post-war period began not with price declines but with a continuation, and in many cases acceleration, of price increases that had gone on through the war. Globally, there was a sharp re-stocking boom in 1919–20. An even sharper slump followed, however, in 1921–22, as commodity supplies became more plentiful and governments tightened credit. This brought prices crashing down. The sharpness of these early post-war movements was particularly conspicuous in countries whose wartime inflation had been relatively moderate, namely Britain, the Scandinavian countries (other than Finland) and the Netherlands. UK wholesale prices, having rather more than doubled from 1914 to the end of 1918, rose by a further third to March 1920 and then fell by half in the following two years. Prices of some primary products moved far more than this, especially downwards. The UK wholesale wheat price fell by nearly 90 per cent from its 1920 peak (see chart). Britain's terms of trade showed a net improvement (i.e. import prices fell relative to export prices) of some 12½ per cent from 1919 to 1923.

The 1919–20 boom was fuelled by budget deficits and credit expansion carried over from the war years. Governments were also keen to minimise the cost of debt service by keeping interest rates down. These tendencies were taken to wild excess in the countries where, for different reasons, economic and political dislocation was greatest. Large government expenditures were financed by the printing press and this, interacting with currency depreciation and spiralling wages, destroyed the national currency. Austria, Hungary, Poland, Russia and Germany all reached this stage at some point in the years 1921–23. Austria's inflation was the least of this hyper-inflation club: prices had risen a mere 14,000 times compared with pre-war. In Germany the factor was one million million times.

Following the various currency reforms and stabilisations, prices were in calmer waters during the relatively prosperous years 1925–29. Activity was not equally buoyant in all industrial countries, and was more so in the United States than in Europe. Germany was suffering from the after-effects of the 1923 inflation (in the shape of bankruptcies etc.) until mid-1926, and then her upswing lasted only two years. From 1928 onwards it was weakened by the withdrawal of foreign credits and the decline of farm prices. The United Kingdom was adversely affected by the over-valuation of sterling at its gold-standard parity after 1925. One consequence of this was the General Strike and miners' strike of the following year, as the government sought to get money wages down. UK output expanded little and unemployment remained high. But, overall, world output of manufactures rose by a quarter from 1925 to 1929, output of primary products by a tenth and world trade volume by a fifth.

In this situation the striking thing about prices was that they continued to drift lower in most countries, despite the upswing in activity. Wholesale prices fell more than retail prices; in a few cases retail prices actually rose. The lead was given by primary product prices which, after partly recovering from their 1920–22 plunge, turned down again in 1925 and reached new post-war lows by 1929. The terms of trade between primary products and manufactures had then moved at least 10 per cent in favour of the latter by comparison with 1913.[44] This happened, it may be noted, along with a smaller rise in output of primary products Demand for them was lagging, for several reasons. A slow-down in the industrial countries' population growth had been greatly accentuated by the 1914–18 war. Per capita spending on food in these countries was rising more slowly than income. And technological progress was bringing economies in the use of industrial materials.

Given the downward movement of primary commodity prices, and a continuing relative slackness in labour markets, the stage was set for stable or even declining price levels, once the domestic monetary mechanism was under control. France provides a striking illustration here. French prices rose rapidly from 1922 to 1926, wholesale prices more than doubling (see chart). The last two of these four years were marked by frequent changes of government, sizeable budget deficits and a flight from the franc, which drove its

44. The index of world primary product prices used here is that published by the London and Cambridge Economic Service in its *The British Economy: Key Statistics 1900–1970*, Table I. This is based on League of Nations data for 1929–38 and on UK import data for pre-1914. All such figures of the pre-World War II period, however, are subject to a considerable margin of uncertainty, on top of all the usual weighting problems, and should be taken only as indicating orders of magnitude. For an exhaustive study see C. P. Kindleberger, *The Terms of Trade* (New York and London. 1956).

(floating) exchange rate steeply downwards. Then in 1926 the Poincaré administration introduced firm measures to balance the budget. Confidence returned, and the government was able to fix the exchange rate (at the under-valued level which induced the big French payments surpluses of the next few years.) In 1927–29 French whole-sale prices were completely steady, and retail prices rose only 6 per cent.

II

In the great slump of 1929–35 primary product prices again led the way down, sliding as much as 60 per cent, mostly in the years 1929–32. This put them almost 50 per cent lower in dollar terms than they were in 1910–13. Prices of manufactures fell less, so the merchandise terms of trade shifted further against primary products, perhaps by an average of 20 per cent. Again, retail prices moved less than wholesale, because of their smaller primary-product con-tent. The biggest price declines in Europe occurred in the 'gold bloc' countries – Belgium, France, Italy, the Nether-lands and Switzerland, plus Poland as a fringe member – which held on longest to their fixed exchange rates. Whole-sale prices in these countries dropped 35–45 per cent and retail prices 20–25 per cent (except in Poland, where retail prices declined as much as wholesale). Germany (up to 1933), Bulgaria and Rumania also experienced price drops of this magnitude, reflecting the big fall in domestic farm prices as well as the aftermath of the 1931 bank failures. Elsewhere the decline in wholesale prices was mostly between 15 and 25 per cent, and that of retail prices between 10 and 15 per cent.

There was much talk in the early thirties about the need to raise prices in order to secure economic recovery. In some small part this made sense. Falling prices increased the burden of debt, pushed many businesses and farms into bankruptcy and drastically lowered the net worth of those that survived. Bank failures or the threat of them were in large measure a consequence of this. There was, however, also the feeling that if only farmers and other primary producers could get better prices for what they sold, they would then have more purchasing power to lay out on industrial goods, and the whole system would be raised to a higher level of activity. This line of argument was unsatisfactory, since it appeared to extract a net increase in income out of a mere transfer of income to primary producers from others. Similarly, there was an evident contradiction in the thinking behind President Roosevelt's National Industrial Recovery Act (1933) in the United States; prices were to be raised to stimulate profits and investment and simultaneously wages were to be raised to increase purchasing power. These arguments were forms of a general, ill-defined belief that higher prices could be equated with economic recovery. A modern observer puzzled by this has to remember that the concept of aggregate demand or expenditure, as something distinct from either aggregate supply or the price level, was not worked out until Keynes's *General Theory* in 1936. Much of the worry about 'low prices' in the first half of the thirties was really a worry about low aggregate demand. Higher prices would, no doubt, reduce the burden of debt. But higher expenditure at constant prices would do more to raise effective demand and employment – only this form of words was not available to contemporaries.[45]

The brief boom and slump of 1936–38 brought, curiously, a faint echo of 1919–21. An upswing in world demand, emanating from budget deficits in the United States as well as credit expansion in Europe, where the gold bloc countries finally succumbed and abandoned their fixed parities in 1936–37, encountered bottlenecks in the supply of some industrial materials, especially items subject to international cartel agreements, such as rubber, tin or copper. Commodity and wholesale prices jumped by 15–20

45. Bearing this point in mind helps one to come to grips with a good deal of pre-1936 literature on macro-economics, both professional and otherwise. Among professional literature the point is highly applicable to Keynes's *Treatise on Money* (1930). See also Bertil Ohlin, 'On the Slow Development of the "Total Demand" Idea in Economic Theory', *Journal of Economic Literature*, Sept. 1974.

per cent from 1935 to 1937. Then, however, the US budget was sharply tightened, just as commodity supplies were expanding. The upswing in activity was cut short, and in most countries prices fell back during 1938, though they remained well above their 1935 levels.

The renewed fall in prices was not, however, universal. In Germany and its economic satellites in central and south-eastern Europe prices remained stable; in Spain they rose during the civil war; and in France they continued to climb quite steeply as a result of policies pursued by a succession of Popular Front governments in 1936–38 led mainly by Léon Blum. The Popular Front episode provides a neat illustration of the fallacy involved in equating higher prices with a higher level of economic activity. On gaining power in May 1936, the Popular Front deliberately raised both wages (when cuts in the working week and other improvements are allowed for, the hourly wage is estimated to have gone up by 60 per cent) and farm prices (by 40–50 per cent). The motives were mixed: to assuage industrial unrest, to boost economic activity and to redistribute incomes in the direction of greater equality.[46] The policy's main achievement was to start a wage/price spiral and to push the franc off its gold parity, thus ushering in the end of the European gold bloc. Business confidence was shaken by the wage/price policy and by various nationalisation measures, and industrial investment remained at a low ebb. Full employment was actually restored, not by raising output (industrial production remained 20 per cent lower than in 1929) but by getting rid of labour. Working hours were reduced, immigrant foreign workers went home and many Frenchmen returned to the land.

III

The outbreak of World War II marked the beginning of an era of price inflation which continued into the 1970s and has shown no signs of ending. During the war itself many

46. The first of these motives was also that of General de Gaulle in raising French wages after the riots of 1968; but not the second and third.

countries, including Austria, Denmark, Germany, the Netherlands and the United Kingdom, suppressed or disguised price increases by direct controls and rationing. Hence there was less outward price inflation than in World War I, despite the great economic dislocation. As pointed out earlier, this left countries after the war with a problem (one among several) of money-stock adjustment, which they handled in varying ways and with varying degrees of promptness. Apart from the hyper-inflation in Greece, the European countries that had the worst price inflation during the war were France, where prices rose by a factor of about 4 from 1939 to 1945; and Italy, where they rose by a factor of 10 from 1943 to 1945. In both cases the momentum of inflation persisted for a further three years after the war, raising prices another $2\frac{1}{2}$ times.

Various factors brought a respite to European inflation in 1948–49, including the American recession, the beginnings of Marshall Aid and the gradual restoration of peacetime production, which avoided the boom and bust of the immediate post-1918 period. Then came, however, the European devaluations of 1949, followed in 1950–51 by the global stockpiling boom, triggered by the outbreak of the Korean War. The United States played the leading role in the scramble for primary commodities. It was the dominant economy in the West and the principal allied belligerent in Korea, and was also at this time building up official stockpiles against feared future shortages of some key minerals. In the 12 months from first-quarter 1950 to first-quarter 1951 world primary product prices increased by about 50 per cent. Wholesale prices in the United Kingdom and the countries that had devalued in line with sterling rose by 40 per cent in the space of two years; in Austria they doubled; in Belgium and France they rose by 25–30 per cent and in other countries by smaller percentages. Retail prices generally went up somewhat less than wholesale prices, as in earlier such episodes.

Recession followed in 1952, and by the following year primary product prices were back to their 1948 level. Thereafter they remained fairly stable for five years, then fell another 10 per cent from 1957 to 1961. Part of this ground was regained later in the sixties; but only in the 1970s did primary commodity prices again undergo really substantial movement.

In contrast to the inter-war period, however, it was not primary product prices that set the tone for the behaviour of prices in general in the 1950s and 60s. This was an era of persistent inflation throughout the world (though the United States had a spell of almost stable prices in the first half of the 1960s). With primary product prices showing no net tendency to rise, the main inflationary impulse evidently came through the price of domestic value-added in the industrial countries; or, more precisely, of value-added in the secondary and tertiary sectors. Retail prices therefore moved more than wholesale prices; and within retail prices, the biggest increases were recorded by services and construction costs, and the smallest by manufactures. This pattern of price increases reflected differential productivity gains, combined with a tendency for pay rises to be led by the rate of productivity increase in the most dynamic sectors. Hence, the sectoral dispersion of productivity growth rates had an inflationary impact in its own right.[47]

The inflation was at a moderate ('creeping') pace for most of the 1950s and 60s. There was a slight tendency for it to accelerate, but not in a uniform way across countries. For instance, the United Kingdom's peak inflation rate (before 1970) occurred in 1956, France's in 1957–58, Germany's in 1961–62, Italy's in 1962–64 and the Netherlands' in 1964–66.[48] After 1965, Europe was again subjected to inflationary winds from across the Atlantic, attributable in large part to stepped-up military outlays on the Vietnam war (unmatched by higher US taxation). Only by 1970, however, did the acceleration of price rises become general and pronounced, with price levels in Western Europe increasing by a minimum of 5 per cent year-on-year. Before

47. This point has been made in different ways by Paul Streeten (*Kyklos*, 1962), Bela Balassa (*Journal of Political Economy*, 1964) and Messrs. G. Edgren, K-O. Faxen and C-E. Odhner, *Wage Formation and the Economy* (London, 1973).

48. See OECD, *Inflation: the Present Problem* (1970).

that, if one takes the sixteen years 1953–69, countries can be classified into three groups, according as the average compound rate of increase in retail prices (the cost-of-living index) was below 3, between 3 and 4, or above 4 per cent per annum. The first, low-inflation group contains Belgium, Germany, Portugal and Switzerland; the second, Austria, Greece, Ireland, Italy, Netherlands, Norway, Sweden and the United Kingdom; and the third, Denmark, Finland, France, Iceland and Spain.

The persistence of inflation through the 1950s took observers by surprise. Up to the middle of the decade there was a widespread presupposition that, with post-World War II adjustments out of the way, price stability would return. The Korean War had merely delayed matters by causing an aberrant fluctuation in commodity markets. Books and articles were written with titles like *The Great Inflation 1939–51*[49] suggesting implicitly that these things were now over and done with. Naturally, therefore, the nature and causes of the continuing price spiral became the subject of debate from the late 1950s on.

The main division of opinion was between those who believed that the inflation was solely due to excess demand for labour (so that demand restraint, and perhaps a slight rise in unemployment, was a necessary and sufficient condition for bringing inflation to a halt) and those who believed that there was also an element of 'wage push' independent of demand pressure but susceptible to moderation through some form of 'incomes policy', i.e. direct influence over, or reform of, collective bargaining procedures. The terms of the debate were initially Keynesian in the sense that explanations of price rises were all couched in terms of the short-run behaviour of real (i.e. non-financial) variables, such as the pressure of demand on productive capacity or the attitude of trade unions. Financial variables such as the stock of money or the budget deficit were brought in only as factors affecting real demand.[50]

49. A. J. Brown (Oxford, 1955).
50. See the reference on p. 658 to the Cohen Council and its critics in Britain. One of the first attempts at a comprehensive analysis of post-1951

This changed, however, in the late sixties and early seventies under the combined impact of academic debate and accelerated inflation. The simple demand-pull hypothesis became difficult to defend, because faster inflation was occurring in some countries together with wider margins of unemployment.[51] This was taken to reflect inflationary expectations, which had gradually taken root and which would keep the wage/price spiral going for years (though not indefinitely) after the disappearance of excessive demand pressure. Long-term price stability, it was argued, could be assured only by limiting the long-run growth of the money stock to that of the economy's productive potential. This revived quantity-theory or 'monetarist' view became increasingly influential in the 1970s, though its influence was more visible in discussion of the issue than in the actions of governments. Meanwhile, the wage-push hypothesis had not been disproved – it had, rather, broadened out into a general view about interest clashes and decision-making conflicts within the mixed economy; but the inflation problem was becoming more serious, and there was no certainty that incomes policy could in the longer run contribute much to solving it.

The rate of inflation, after slowing down slightly in 1971, reached a crescendo in 1972–73. For the first time since the Korean War a cyclical upswing was synchronised right across the western industrial world. In 1973 OECD industrial output rose nearly 10 per cent in one year. Moreover, also for the first time since the 1950s, the chief input bottlenecks occurred not in the domain of skilled man-

---

inflation was the 1961 OEEC report, *The Problem of Rising Prices*, by Messrs Fellner, Gilbert, Hansen, Kahn, Lutz and de Wolff. This took an eclectic view, but placed considerable emphasis on the wages problem. The establishment of the committee in 1959 to make the study owed much to the influence of Sir Robert Hall, Chief Economic Adviser to the UK Government.

51. Admittedly, one might seek to explain this by saying that the significance of unemployment, and of unemployment statistics, had changed, causing excess demand to be felt at higher levels of recorded unemployment than formerly. This was, in fact, part of the story in some countries (e.g. the United Kingdom).

power or advanced manufacturing capacity, but at the basic materials end of the chain. This owed something to a long cycle in the pattern of investment. During the 1950s there had been major investment both in raw-material extraction (stimulated by the high prices reached in the Korean boom) and in the early stages of processing (steel mills, smelters, paper mills etc.). In the 1960s, with capacity in these basic sectors now adequate or even excessive, and with primary commodity prices having fallen considerably, emphasis shifted to the lighter end of industry. By the early seventies the wheel had turned full circle. Investment was needed in basic materials production; but it was being held back by political uncertainties in the third world, and also by environmentalist pressure in the industrial countries (since smelters and paper mills pollute). The situation was aggravated by stockpiling of materials, due partly to the outpouring of dollars from the United States in 1970–72. The Japanese authorities organised the placement of their excess dollar reserves in wool, copper, etc. And poor harvests, notably in the Soviet Union, put pressure on international grain supplies. The result was that from 1971 to the end of 1973 primary product prices trebled. Inflation rates in Western Europe soared well above 10 per cent. Wholesale prices once more rose faster than retail.

A new dimension was added with the quadrupling of oil prices by the OPEC cartel at the end of 1973. This helped to prolong the wage/price spiral while also directly and indirectly intensifying the incipient cyclical downturn in activity. The 1974–75 recession was much the deepest since 1945. Inflation, however, continued at a disquieting pace. At the end of 1974 consumer prices in Western Europe were nearly 15 per cent higher on average than a year earlier. The country figures ranged from 5·9 per cent for Germany to 51·3 per cent for Iceland. The worst performers of the major countries were Italy (24·5 per cent) and Britain (19·1 per cent and still rising; a peak of 26·7 per cent was reached in September 1975). Deceleration was slow in coming. In the spring of 1976 consumer prices in Europe were still 11 per cent up over twelve months. Primary product prices in the recession lost some but by no means all of the ground which they had gained in 1971–73; and turned sharply upwards again when a recovery of world industrial output became apparent in 1976.

Thus, at the end of our period, as in 1950–51, a burst of rapid inflation was associated with a substantial terms-of-trade shift in favour of primary producers. During the inter-war period, on the other hand, the terms of trade moved substantially against primary producers mainly in the more violent spells of price deflation (1920–21, 1929–32). These associations are what economic analysis would lead one to expect. The reason is that, making due allowance for cartels, buffer stocks and other attempts to control markets, prices of primary products are more readily mobile in the face of market disequilibria than prices of manufactures and services, which tend to be 'administered' or cost-determined. For cost-determined items, a larger share of short-run adjustments occurs on the side of volumes or quantity, through changes in inventories, order books and sub-sequently output and unemployment. Because of input-output relationships and other interconnections between markets, the result is that the general price level moves faster (in either direction) when the major disequilibria (over-supply or excess demand) occur in the primary-producing sector.[52] For much of the 1950s and 60s, by contrast, a moderate rate of industrial inflation went to-gether with little change in primary product prices.

Over the long run things tend to even out. In the primary sector the volume of output responds to price movements. And in the rest of the economy, not only do prices alter, but the nature of quantity adjustments alters too. Changes in inventories or in the amount of unemployment give way to changes in the composition of output. What happens in

---

52. Input-output effects are, of course, additional to the purely statistical effect on overall price indices of rapid movement in one particular group of prices.

The importance of excess supply of primary products as a cause of the violent price deflation between the wars was stressed by W. Arthur Lewis in his masterly *Economic Survey 1919–39* (London, 1949).

the long run to the terms of trade between primary products as a whole and industrial goods as a whole depends on long-run changes in demand patterns and technology and on the response of producers to them. For example, if productivity in agriculture is growing more rapidly than demand for foodstuffs at given prices, the terms of trade will be tending to move against agriculture, unless an offsetting shift of labour into other sectors is already in progress. Such long-run trends, however, are no longer specifically related to any upward or downward movement of the price level as a whole.

T.C.(2)

Wholesale prices, 1920-70 (logarithmic scale, 1950=100):
Netherlands, Switzerland, United Kingdom

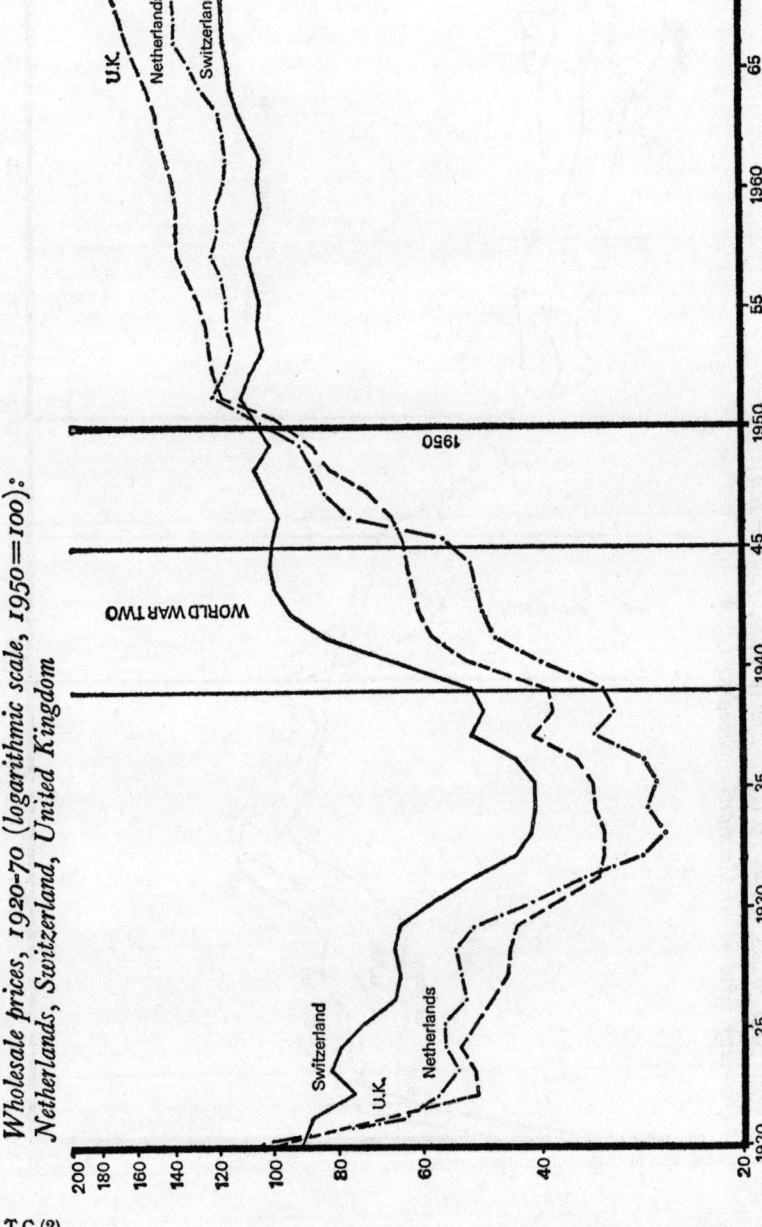

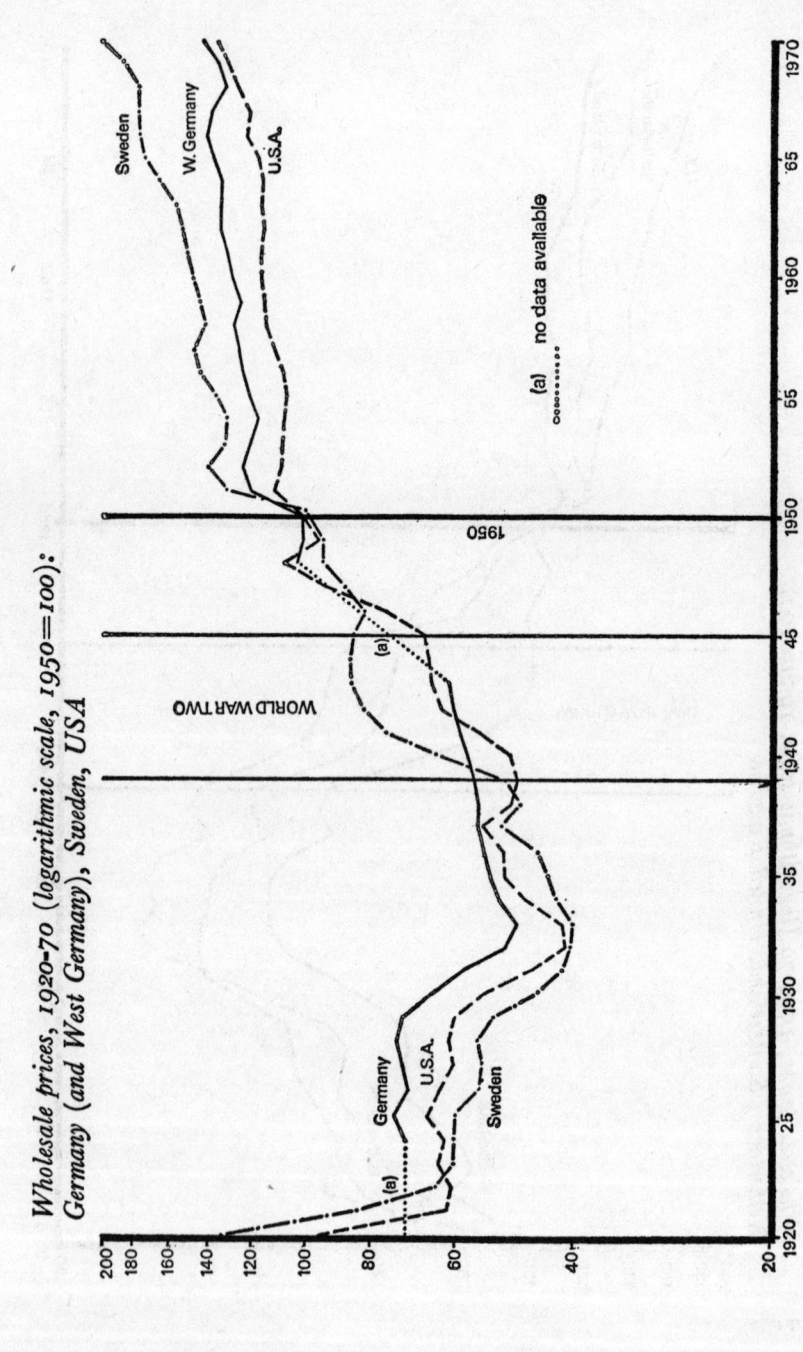

Wholesale prices, 1920–70 (logarithmic scale, 1950=100): Germany (and West Germany), Sweden, USA

Wholesale prices, 1920–70 (logarithmic scale, 1950=100): France and Italy

Wholesale prices, 1920–70 (logarithmic scale, 1950=100): Belgium

CONCLUSION

There seems little doubt that the twentieth century will be styled by historians as a century of secular inflation: perhaps as *the* century of secular inflation, replacing the sixteenth century in that capacity – unless, of course, our current tendencies have been carried so much further by the 2000s as to make recent inflation look innocuous. By all past standards, inflation in our century has been strong and especially, since the late 1930s, sustained. Why?

As with any complex phenomenon embedded within a wide social process, satisfactory explanations are unlikely to be simple or certain. Indeed, the more definitive and unicausal the proffered explanation of price inflation, the less it is likely to tell us. To say that inflation has resulted from too much money, so that responsibility rests with the governments that created this money, is true but trite. It is not far removed from saying that people die of alcoholism because they drink too much. The interesting question is what has driven governments – or drinkers – to their excessive indulgence. Is it ignorance? Or expediency? Or a change in 'real' circumstances? Or more or less deliberate choice, at least among alternative evils?

These general explanations are not mutually exclusive, and each of them has something to tell us. The extent to which inflation has been exacerbated by governments not knowing what they were doing has probably been insignificant in the broad sweep of inflationary experience over the period as a whole. The behaviour of the German Reichsbank in 1923, and to a lesser extent of the British Treasury in the cheap-money period after 1945, are the main examples. More significant has been the increased technical ease of operating and sustaining, at least for a time, an inflationary financial mechanism: the expedient was more available than before. To be sure, the possibility of governmental inflation had been present for many centuries: witness the currency debasements of sixteenth-century monarchs and the massive over-issue of the first French Republic's *assignats*. But as long as the bulk of the business world adhered to an undebased metallic standard, the scope for these local departures from that standard was limited: in the end, it was the good money that drove out the bad, in an inversion of the short-period Gresham's Law. That is why the demise of metallic money has been significant. It unhooked the money supply and thereby also the price level.

The evolution to a virtually complete paper standard had much less to do with deliberate intellectual or governmental choice than with the natural dynamic of the banking process. Metallic money is costly to hold and to transfer; paper money created as debt obligations of banks is a source of earnings for them, besides yielding interest to the holder. In the nineteenth century, that basic commercial incentive led to the then partly unrecognised replacement of metallic money by paper money in business transactions. In the twentieth century, the same commercial incentive has helped complete the process at the level of monetary assets held internationally by the monetary authorities themselves. So the base, as well as the superstructure, of money has become paper-made.

Money has in this way become more manageable, which is the same as saying more manipulable. Yet this still provides insufficient explanation of why the manipulation has been so pervasively in the inflationary direction. The expedient has been easier to use; but since its use involves evident costs, something remains to be explained.

What then of the influence of changes in 'real' economic forces? Have there been in this period significant changes in the structure of the world economy that have themselves tended towards inflation, or made inflation more difficult or costly to avoid? It was noted in the last section that no such general influence is to be found in the relationship between the major sectors of primary commodities and manufactures, although the progressive tendency for a larger share of economic activity to take the form of services, where productivity gains are less, probably had some net inflationary impact. Another structural influence of obvious importance has been war. Wars have been inflationary from the beginnings of the money economy, and the two world wars of the twentieth century had no counterpart in the century after 1815. Writing twenty years ago, we would obviously have given major importance to this factor. Yet the continuation of creeping inflation through the first quarter century after World War II, advancing to a near-gallop in the early 1970s, points (Korea and Vietnam notwithstanding) fairly decisively to wider and more enduring influences.

These influences are surely to be located in the broad thrust of the political economy of the time. The period has seen a progressive widening of effective political participation among national electorates and economic groups. Economic demands made on the state have in consequence greatly increased. Not surprisingly, the sharpened political and bargaining weapons have been seen by the worse off as a means of improving their economic position – following the well-travelled route of the nineteenth-century middle classes. A strong politico-economic drive for improvement in the absolute and relative positions of organised groups, whether of industrial workers or farmers, has been a marked feature of our times. Yet explicit provision for income redistribution has rarely been made in a way that reconciles competing demands, partly, no doubt, because agreement to redistribution from those at the paying end is notoriously difficult to obtain.

Inflation, at the deepest level, can be seen as the expression of this distributional struggle. It expresses the fact that societies, and not just governments, are unable or unwilling to resolve that struggle by direct confrontation; and yet are unable or unwilling to put it aside. It is in this sense that inflation can be seen as a matter of more or less deliberate choice; and given the political constraints, not necessarily irrational choice.

The four influences that have been outlined here are

clearly interconnected. Twentieth-century inflation has not
been, for the most part, a mere ignorant lapse on the part of
governments. It has been facilitated by the ease of money
creation that ultimately results from perfection of the
banking process. It received a particular boost from two
world wars. But more generally, our inflation has been a
by-product, damaging and wasteful in itself, of major
economic advance coexisting with an unresolved political
struggle over its fruits.

BIBLIOGRAPHY
(See also works cited in the text)

The literature on international and domestic monetary developments since World War I is vast; the selection here is made with the non-specialist in mind. For the broad sweep, see Robert Triffin, *The Evolution of the International Monetary System: Historical Reappraisal and Future Perspectives* (Princeton, 1964); and Fred Hirsch, *Money International* 1969: Harmondsworth, particularly chapter 4). On World War I finance and the immediate aftermath, a wealth of material is in John Maynard Keynes, *Collected Writings*, Vol. XVI, 1914–19. For international developments in the 1920s, an outstanding source is Stephen V. O. Clarke, *Central Bank Co-operation 1924–31* (New York, 1967). Charles P. Kindleberger, *The World in Depression 1929–39* (London, 1973) takes the story up to 1939. Works on Montagu Norman have been cited in the text. Hjalmar Schacht, *My First Seventy-Six Years* (London, 1955), is an interesting if characteristically self-serving memoir of a great survivor.

Milton Friedman and Anna Jacobson Schwartz, *A Monetary History of the United States, 1867–1960* (Princeton, 1963) is a major source, although detailed, specialised, and in its extreme monetarist interpretation, controversial. Excellent analytical treatment of the inter-war period is in Leland B. Yeager, *International Monetary Relations* (New York, 1966). This reinterprets, in a way broadly favourable to flexible exchange rates, the classical and still valuable League of Nations, *International Currency Experience* (1944), which was written by Ragnar Nurkse, and had an important influence on post-war planning. W. Arthur Lewis's masterly *Economic Survey 1919–39* (London, 1949) has not been superseded as a general account of the inter-war period. The basic text on British war finance is R. S. Sayers, *Financial Policy 1939–45* (London, 1956).

The post-war international financial institutions are covered in the main basic texts. An excellent analytical treatment from the perspective of the 1970s is in John Williamson, *The Failure of International Monetary Reform*

(London, 1976 forthcoming). A good supplement covering the Bretton Woods negotiations, is Richard N. Gardner, *Sterling-Dollar Diplomacy* (Oxford, 1957), which remains probably the best treatment of an international financial negotiation. The official three-volume history of *The International Monetary Fund, 1945–65* (IMF, 1969) contains the main documents as well as an invaluable narrative by J. Keith Horsefield and others. Its limitations are a deluge of details and a misleading concentration on the significance of the IMF executive board (as distinct from the home governments issuing the instructions, and to a lesser extent the IMF staff).

For the post-World War II period until 1969, the best single source is probably Robert Triffin, *Europe and the Money Muddle* (Yale, 1957). For analysis of the problems of the international financial system that emerged in the 1960s, key texts are Robert Triffin, *Gold and the Dollar Crisis* (Yale, 1960); Milton Gilbert, *The Gold-Dollar System: Conditions of Equilibrium and the Price of Gold* (Princeton, 1968); Emile Despres, Charles P. Kindleberger, and Walter S. Salant, 'The Dollar and World Liquidity – A Minority View', *The Economist*, February 5, 1966; and Harry G. Johnson, 'Theoretical Problems of the International Monetary System', in Richard N. Cooper (ed), *International Finance* (Harmondswith, 1969). For a conspectus of views on exchange rate flexibility, see George N. Halm (ed), *Approaches to Greater Flexibility of Exchange Rates* (Princeton, 1970). Jacques Rueff, *Balance of Payments* (Macmillan 1967) and the same author's *Le Péché Monétaire de L'Occident* (The Monetary Sin of the West) (Plon, 1971), contain perhaps more than the reader would want to know about the undoubtedly influential writings of this French political economist between the 1920s and the 1960s. For a more sophisticated exposition of the positive role of gold, see, besides the Gilbert reference noted above, Peter M. Oppenheimer, 'The Case for Raising the Price of Gold', *Journal of Money, Credit and Banking*, August 1969.

European monetary integration has attracted an uneven literature, befitting its status as part-problem, part-slogan.

The best single coverage is perhaps in Lawrence B. Krause and Walter S. Salant (eds), *European Monetary Unification and its Meaning for the United States* (Brookings, 1973). See also Peter M. Oppenheimer, 'The Problem of Monetary Union' in D. Evans (ed), *Britain in Europe*; and Fred Hirsch, 'The Political Economics of European Monetary Integration', *The World Today*, October 1972.

Increasing information becomes available from official sources as the period wears on. The annual reports of the *Bank for International Settlements* are an outstanding source from their beginning in 1931, largely because they were inspired first by Per Jacobsson, and after 1960 by his successor, Milton Gilbert. From 1964 onwards they are also the main official source of facts and figures on the Euro-currency market. The annual reports of the *International Monetary Fund*, by contrast, are rather formal documents, representing what can be agreed as the common view of the IMF executive directors. The six-monthly reports of US Federal Reserve and Treasury Operations, published in the March and September issues of the *Federal Reserve Bulletin* since 1962, are a prime source, for operations affecting European countries as well as the United States. The annual and monthly reports of the *Deutsche Bundesbank* (before 1957, the *Bank Deutscher Laender*) are outstanding. From about the mid 1960s the quarterly *Bulletin* of the Bank of England, which was started in 1960, also reached high quality.

Historical analysis of international finance continues to lean unusually heavily on contemporary press coverage, partly because central banks have never accepted the same obligation as governments to release records on a systematic basis, other than to their own favoured historians. Thus, detailed treatment by Susan Strange of *International Monetary Relations, 1959–1971*, in Andrew Shonfield (ed), *International Economic Relations of the Western World, 1959–71* (Oxford, 1976), is somewhat limited by reliance on contemporary press accounts, though it is selective in its references and is a valuable chronicle of events and contemporary attitudes. Gerald M. Meier, *Problems of a World Monetary*

Order (Oxford, 1974), is an ingenious and highly readable compilation of contemporary press reports and official statements on major episodes from Bretton Woods to the post-1971 reform exercise. The numerous books by Paul Einzig, which flowed in a gushing stream from the 1920s to the 1970s, and stemmed from Einzig's work as a journalist on the pre-war *Financial News* and after World War II on the *Financial Times*, contain much interesting information but have to be used with considerable discrimination.

On domestic banking systems a valuable compendium covering the twenties (up to 1928) is H. P. Willis and B. H. Beckhart (eds), *Foreign Banking Systems* (London, 1929). Its post-1945 successor is R. S. Sayers (ed), *Banking in Western Europe* (Oxford, 1962). T. Balogh, *Studies in Financial Organisation* (London, 1945) is a useful source on the inter-war period in Britain; Edward Nevin and E. W. Davis, *The London Clearing Banks* (London, 1970) a specialised but very readable account; and D. K. Sheppard, *The Growth and Role of UK Financial Institutions, 1880–1962* (London, 1971), a major statistical source. Continental European capital markets in the 1960s are described in the Segré Report, *The Development of a European Capital Market* (EEC, Brussels, 1966). Well worth sifting is the multi-volume *OECD Capital Markets Study*, Vols. I–IV (1967–68). Current developments in banking and financial markets are reported and discussed in *The Banker*, *The Banker's Magazine* and *Euromoney*, all of them monthlies.

Literature on the Euro-currency system is substantial and rather diffuse. E. W. Clendenning, *The Euro-Dollar Market* (Oxford, 1970) is a straightforward and comprehensive account up to the mid-1960s. A more selective and analytical treatment, also containing a full bibliography, is John Hewson, *Liquidity Creation and Distribution in the Euro-currency Markets* (Lexington Books, 1975). A number of interesting and sometimes controversial articles on Euro-currencies appeared during the late 1960s and early 70s in the *Banca Nazionale del Lavoro Quarterly Review*. See in particular W. D. McClam, 'Credit Substitution and the Euro-Currency Market' (1972). The relations between liberalised international transactions and national economic policies in the 1960s world of fixed exchange rates are the subject of Richard N. Cooper's *The Economics of Interdependence* (New York, 1968).

The classical account of Germany's inflation in 1923 is C. Bresciani-Turroni, *The Economics of Inflation* (London, 1937). A distinguished analytical study is Phillip Cagan, 'The Monetary Dynamics of Hyper-inflation' in M. Friedman (ed), *Studies in the Quantity Theory of Money* (Chicago, 1956). Among the textbooks on inflation, R. J. Ball, *Inflation and the Theory of Money* (2nd edn, London, 1974) is impressive for its combination of depth and readability (though it ignores international aspects). D. Laidler, 'The Current Inflation – Explanations and Policies', *National Westminster Bank Review*, 1972, and Erik Dahmén, 'Inflation: Economics or Politics?', *ibid*, 1973 represent divergent views on the causes and cures of European inflation in the 1960s and 70s. A comprehensive account of this inflation is G. Maynard and W. van Ryckeghem, *World of Inflation* (London, 1976).

12. National Economic Planning and Policies in Twentieth Century Europe 1920-1970[1]

Benjamin Ward

The rise of planning is one of the central themes in the history of twentieth-century Europe. Nowadays governments everywhere recognize a responsibility to use their powers to control a variety of important aspects of economic behaviour, and there is even a measure of such control in the international sphere. A century ago no country was seriously engaged in economic planning. This dramatic change is in large measure a product of three interacting factors. In the first place there has been a rise in the size of governments which was much more rapid than the increase in the level of economic activity. As a result, variations in government behaviour have a far greater effect on the rest of the economy than had been the case; willy nilly, governments were forced to consider the consequences of their actions over a broader area.

Secondly, there has been considerable progress by economists towards understanding economic processes which are relevant for government policy. Much of this progress has been forced by the pressure of events, particularly of the consequences of the rise of big government; but by the turn of the century economics as a science had already acquired a more or less autonomous life of its own, and further progress was in part conditioned by the nature of economics itself. The final factor has been the tremendous increase in the amount of information available about the performance of economies. Stimulated by both the above factors, but also by technical changes which have greatly cheapened the cost of collecting and processing information, and by the need for information to control the newly risen bureaucracies of business and government, almost every

1. The author would like to thank Gregory Grossman, Richard Roehl and the editor, Carlo Cipolla, for many helpful comments and criticisms.

generation of this century has seen a manifold increase in the quantity of economic statistics available.

Each European country has its own planning story to tell. Britain perhaps succeeded throughout the twentieth century in retaining her status as Europe's most reluctant planner. Russia, Czarist and Soviet alike, perhaps was Europe's most planned country. These two countries' positions at the extremes of the spectrum no doubt partly account for the fact that during the twenties the world's most exciting economics was being done in Cambridge and Moscow, and that economics was centrally concerned with problems of planning the economy. Later on the great developments in planning come not from the great countries but from such places as Holland, Scandinavia and Yugoslavia, as some sort of middle way between the extremes of planning is sought. But developments in one country are usually quickly diffused elsewhere, and the three great catastrophes of the twentieth century, two world wars and a depression, have strong and rather similar impacts on all. Consequently there is a coherent story to be told of European planning in the twentieth century. We will follow first one country and then another through this period, and will not cover every country, but there is an important sense in which each can speak for all.

THE TRANSITION TO PLANNING, 1910–1940

GREAT BRITAIN, 1910–1939

On the eve of World War I the British government was already familiar with certain aspects of planning. Government revenue and spending had long since been put on a relatively unified accounting basis so that the annual budget gave considerable insight into the nature and purposes of money flows through the government. Defence expenditures absorbed about forty per cent of the budget; the magnitude of this expenditure, rapid change in military technology, and the rather long lead times for construction (i.e. from the decision to build until the date of effective operation), especially for the navy, combined with the highly competitive international military environment, forced at least the rudiments of a comparison of benefits to costs on both parliament and the departments. And the creation of an embryo set of welfare provisions had introduced policy-makers to the intricacies of design of such things as income support and health delivery systems. Monetary policy was being used effectively to protect the nation's gold reserves against excessive outflows and inflows. And, as with all governments everywhere, there was considerable concern over the effect on the population of variations in the kinds and levels of taxation.

Outside government the problem of planning aroused only limited interest among economists. The theory of taxation far outstripped the theory of public expenditure, while monetary theory tended to concentrate on the blessings of automatic adjustment under the gold standard and the evils of bimetallism. However, the Fabians, often called 'the sewer socialists', constituted a major exception, and their efforts played no small role in the establishment of municipal amenities as well as of that embryo welfare state. Still farther from the centre of economic discussion the voice of John Hobson was faintly heard calling for public measures to relieve a tendency in the economy towards underconsumption. But on the whole economists were not ahead of government in their understanding of coming needs, and those few who were tended to be unconvincingly vague in their analyses. This was not entirely a fault to be laid at their doors, since statistics were few and far between and economic theory owed more to the 'principle of right reason' for its plausibility than to any firm empirical base.

That this package of policies and theories did not add up to anything like a clear picture of the interaction between government and the national economy emerged clearly during the war years. After some initial measures in the autumn of 1914 to control a financial panic, and which amounted *de facto* to going off the gold standard, the government attempted to follow its usual practices as the means of financing the war. It went on the uncontrolled market in competition with other buyers to obtain the goods it needed and tried to finance the purchases with modest increases in existing tax rates. As a result, a year into the war there were severe shortages, and the tentative budget proposed revenues that amounted to less than 20 per cent of proposed expenditures. From this point the government backed, step by step, into a much more substantial set of controls. Taxes were increased substantially, though over the war years as a whole they covered less than a third of total spending, the remainder being obtained by borrowing on the market at high rates of interest. Price controls were introduced piecemeal, though the range of covered goods expanded steadily. Import controls were introduced, shipping capacity rationed. The history of food policy typifies developments in other areas. Price controls came first; when they did not suffice and long queues began to form in 1917, a number of local governments introduced rationing. Months later the government, prompted at least in part by fears of industrial unrest, finally imposed a widespread rationing system. Government spending rose from 15 to 75 per cent of national income, and by the end of the war a comprehensive system of direct and financial controls was functioning. But this system arose as a series of isolated responses to individual bottlenecks, was never administered from a unified control centre, and was dropped almost immediately after the end of the war. That is to say, it was never viewed by the actors as a comprehensive system.

From the point of view of planning, the interwar years were transition years between the belief in the viability of a self-regulating market system, both at home and abroad, and the recognition that a substantial, deliberate policy of economic control was essential to stability. War controls were dropped, to be followed by a brief but intensive boom and bust, and then by a policy of deliberate deflation so as to permit a return to the gold standard at prewar parity. This policy in itself required considerable management, though, given the state of knowledge of policy-makers, the actual achievement may well have been a product of luck rather than skill.

The immediate policy goal was achieved in 1925 when Britain returned to the gold standard at an exchange rate of $4.86 to the pound. But in a broader sense economic policy was a failure. The periods of reconstruction and deflation brought with them massive unemployment. Over 40 per cent of the budget was being devoted to servicing the public debt. Despite all efforts at retrenchment, the budget rose to a level equal to about a third of national income or twice its relative level of the last prewar years. London returned to its position as a great world centre of finance, but no longer could dominate the New York money market. And, the final blow, the international gold standard could not be made to work and was finally and definitely left behind·in the crisis of 1931.

Big government, massive and chronic unemployment, the failure of automatic regulation: these three unavoidable facts destroyed the vision of the economic world that had informed policy-makers and economists alike in previous times. But there was at first no new vision to put in its place, and the piecemeal approach to policy continued to be the norm. Montagu Norman, the dynamic director of the Bank of England, apparently felt that bank rate should only be used to defend Britain's international position and that consequently he had no responsibility for the state of the domestic economy. Balanced budgets were believed essential to the preservation of confidence in government, and this was considered a decisive answer to those who would do more for the millions of distressed families. But even this rule could not be followed consistently, and welfare expenditures rose sharply in bad years; income support for the poor, for example, rising from £34 million in 1923 to £85 million a decade later.

As with all revolutions, the Keynesian revolution too was a product of many forces. Monetary theory had not yet been successfully adapted to the neoclassical mode of analysis epitomized in the work of Alfred Marshall. The twenties were a period of great ferment in this area of economics, this was precisely the area of research in which Keynes was most deeply engaged, and it was from this vantage point that Keynes jumped off into the new economics. The central notion of the new theory, namely that an economy could stagnate indefinitely because of a lack of sufficient effective demand, had appeared a number of times, though in garbled form, in the works of earlier unconventional economists such as Hobson. In fact, Keynes in the twenties was advocating 'Keynesian' policies long before he had developed his theoretical defence of them. World War I and the great Soviet experiment, whose progress was followed with keen interest in British intellectual circles, had opened men's eyes to the possibility of a 'managed' economy. All these factors played their role. But none was more persistently before the eye than the contrast between the Edwardian and the interwar economic situations and the consequent pressures to find some way out of the present trap.

The story of the emergence of Keynesian theory is told elsewhere in this volume. It was the central theoretical advance that provided the basis for modern indirect planning and control of a market economy. But despite the need, despite the prestige of the Keynesian voice, despite the rather quick acceptance of the basic ideas by many British economists, Keynesianism does not seem to have had any significant impact on interwar British economic policy. In fact, two other ideas seem to have had far wider support. One was contra-cyclical public works spending for the purpose of providing employment *directly*, which had been advocated by the Webbs before the war and in both Labour and Liberal circles was widely believed to be the most effective way to combat unemployment. The other was the idea of planning, in the special form in which, in Britain and Germany and elsewhere, it developed among progressive industrialists. The basic idea was co-operative regulation of supply and price of many goods, a substitution of 'industrial self-government' for the no longer self-regulating market system. Among the leading supporters of this idea in Britain was the young Harold Macmillan. The early thirties saw public works spending being used as an anti-depression policy in Sweden and a progressive variant of supply regulation adopted as the key measure of the early New Deal in the United States. In Britain a deeper understanding of the nature of economic depression was developing, but her government's actual policies throughout the thirties remained piecemeal and traditional.

GERMANY IN TWO WARS

On the eve of war in 1914 German heavy industry was far more concentrated than British industry, from scale of enterprise to cartelization to industrial association. Though German, and especially Prussian, bureaucracy was a by-word of efficiency, it was still a bureaucracy with all the limitations of that organizational form, and German civilian government was probably less cohesive and less able to exert effective control over economic processes from the centre. Finally, the armed forces operated a massive instrument of war by means of a relatively well organized system of central control and, by the nature of the German geo-political situation, were relatively sensitive to the relation between economics and war.

Out of this combination of circumstances the first war's model set of economic control institutions developed. The key step was taken already in August 1914 when the industrialist Walter Rathenau convinced General von Falkenhayn that a system of raw materials controls was essential to military success, and the *Kriegsrohstoffabteilung* was set up with Rathenau at its head. Operating under army control but operated by industrialists and their representatives. and dealing with key bottleneck goods of the war economy, this organization combined basic political and economic ingredients for the successful control of a war economy. Essentially, goal or mission determination was in the hands of the military, the allocation of orders among factories and the control of non-essential uses was in the hands of the nation's economic leadership, and attention was focused on dealing with the most important bottlenecks. As the war wore on the need to develop systematic priority criteria in granting allocation of scarce materials forced a certain amount of thinking ahead, of planning of the structure of future consumption. The fact that this was being done by the agency that possessed the most potent means for controlling economic outcomes lent immediate force to the planning itself.

In practice, of course, there were many difficulties. Army procurement officers were insensitive to the problem of lead times for changeovers to new types of production. Industrialists could not easily be convinced that highly profitable but militarily inessential production really was inessential. As new bottlenecks emerged, new agencies emerged to deal with them, as with food and manpower control, and coordination was not always achieved. And the interaction between the system of direct controls and the financial system was not effectively controlled or even understood. Compared to some ideal of planning, the German system in World War I was badly flawed, but compared with other countries faced with a similar problem at the time, the Germans were the first to establish an effective system, and the system they established was probably the most effective one in operation.

The German collapse and the rise of Weimar socialism ended this system of controls; but much of both the personnel and the ideas survived. When in the thirties a new regime, oriented towards war, came to power, one might have expected that this tradition would once again flourish; but such was not to be the case.

Politically speaking, the New Germany was essentially an alliance among three groups: the industrialists, the army, and the Nazi Party. Compared with the eve of the previous war, the industrialists remained powerful, but the army was in a relatively weaker position and the Party exerted rather more influence than had the prewar civilian government. Though allied, the groups had substantially different aims and were mutually suspicious; close co-operation among them was virtually impossible. Furthermore, the new notion of war that Hitler brought with him seemed to change the nature of war economic needs. A series of Blitzkriegs required a series of short-term build-ups of goods whose mix would vary with the name of the opponent. Strict overall planning need not be a part of such preparations, and wars of short duration too could be met without any fundamental economic transformation. Whatever its merits as a strategic notion, this idea fitted the domestic political requirements of a party that felt it had to deliver consumer goods to its clientele in addition to national regeneration. It also fitted the strong aversion to inflationary policies that the great inflation of the twenties had imprinted on many German minds.

As a consequence, a table of organization of German planning institutions before 1942 would be extremely confusing. There was an economics ministry, presided over much of the time by the finance minister, and endowed with planning authority which in practice was largely nominal. The High Command possessed a War Economy and Armaments Office which seemed to be the inheritor of the old Rathenau organization; but its chief, General Thomas, reported that even during the war it was supplied neither with strategic plans nor even with overall material requirements. Goering's Four-Year Plan Office, established in 1936, seems to have had more power, but even so did not take a serious interest in economic control. Much of the latter was in the hands of decentralized committees, staffed largely from industry, who were much more like 'industrial self-regulators' than planned controllers of a war economy. This system was responsive to the Führer's commands, but the process of implementation was decentralized. The armed forces translated the command into orders for goods which entered the economy essentially as ordinary tenders of contracts, allocated among firms by the rules of the cartelized, regulated industries. Direct planning, such as the Four-Year Plan itself, had little to do with the outcomes.

The transition to a full war economy came in Germany later than in Britain or the Soviet Union, and resulted in an increase in armaments production during 1942-4. This came as an unpleasant surprise to allied officials who, apparently taking the earlier Nazi propaganda about total war at face value, thought that a full war economy had long since been established. Economic controls were centred in the office of Albert Speer and resources were obtained by a variety of devices, from the sharp restriction of domestic consumption to the import of forced labour from occupied territories. There appear to have been no great novelties in this system of controls, nor this time does the performance of the German war economy stand out as a model of success when compared to the systems of its opponents. One can say, however, that Germany's failure in the war could not reasonably be laid at the door of its economic planners.

RUSSIA, 1917–1937

Lenin and the Bolsheviks came to power without a blueprint of the society they were committed to build. Indeed, none of the top leadership had any managerial experience that could serve as a practical guide. They had a vision of a society in which the power of privately owned capital no longer guided economic decisions, and in which the state was operated in the interest of the working class. They believed that in advanced capitalist countries, especially in Germany, economic concentration had already reached the point at which the cartel leaders effectively planned the economy, and that the system of war controls in Germany constituted a sort of keystone to the arch of planning. Thus, in Germany at least, the institutions of a planned socialist society already existed; they merely needed to be brought under proletarian control. But they were also aware that this process of concentration had proceeded much less far in Russia.

The Bolsheviks came to power in a Russia that was already on the edge of chaos. The army had ceased to function, transport had broken down, runaway inflation and shortages were already forcing the beginning of a mass exodus from major cities, including especially Petrograd, the capital. As a result, central government power was transferred with very little violence, but, also as a result, the new government was less powerful and more constrained merely to react to events. As the German pressure increased and civil war began in earnest, the economy came perilously close to shutting down. Industrial output in particular dropped to less than a fifth of previous levels and regional autarky at a level barely above, and sometimes below, subsistence became the norm.

Inspired no doubt by their vision of Germanic efficiency as well as by the desperate needs of the moment, the Bolsheviks installed a paper system of thoroughgoing central control of the economy, organized both by branches of production and by regions, under a Supreme Council of the National Economy (Vesenkha). But this organization was mostly made of nothing but paper, and actual control consisted more of piecemeal interventions with commands aimed at such things as continuing some production of locomotives and some supply of food to the troops and the depopulated cities. This *ad hoc* system sufficed to keep the armies in the field, but clearly could not be used to keep the economy in order.

By 1920–1 the issue of survival had shifted from the realm of military activity back to the economy and the needs of reconstruction. War Communism gave way to NEP. Agricultural land was largely in the hands of peasant freeholders who sold their produce on the market or consumed it themselves. Large-scale industry was state owned and controlled, but though there was some control of prices and outputs and inputs, there was a considerable measure of autonomy for enterprises, and they were even encouraged to make a profit. Much of small-scale industry and the distribution system, aside from the railroads, was in private hands. How should a socialist state control such an economy?

Lenin, perhaps impressed by the failures of overall control under War Communism, did not feel that comprehensive planning was the answer. The only real enthusiasm he expressed in this area was for a programme of electrification of Russia, inspired by a wartime book by a German engineer, and which resulted in the first large-scale investment planning project, the famed Goelro. Though he permitted the establishment of the State Planning Commission (Gosplan), he prevented Trotsky and Larin from putting it in the central position as chief economic controller, continuing to prefer planning as a series of *ad hoc* projects. The planners also ran afoul of Narkomfin, the finance ministry, whose officials preferred themselves as operators of the economy, and also disagreed as to the role of agriculture in the continuing economic reconstruction. Ironically, it was not until 1924–5 that Gosplan and its allies finally won the political battle for recognition of planning as a central institution of socialism.

All during the time that these political battles were being fought, the planners were hard at work developing the tools needed to operate this first socialist economy. Some developments were relatively pedestrian, though even these often took long years to become the general property of the world's economists. For example, Strumilin, as early as 1921, recognized the functional nature of the division between short and longer run planning. The term for the former was fixed at a year because crops were mainly produced on a yearly basis, and difficulties in estimating the harvest were immediately translated into planning difficulties. State budgets had long been annual in nature for just this reason. The strength of a short run plan, based on solid information as to the size of this year's harvest, lay in its prospects as the base for direct control of the process of simple reproduction, that is, of the process of conversion of materials and labour into outputs using only the already existing plant. But when investment entered the picture, a several year period would have to be used, which allowed for the gestation period of new investment before it could be used in producing new goods. By the mid-twenties Gosplan was producing both these types of plans.

Short-run planning, as embodied in the volumes of so-called 'control figures' published by Gosplan during 1925–8, was a close relative of wartime planning in Germany.

Special balances of sources and uses were constructed in a variety of areas, for example for grain, energy, transport, construction, foreign trade, the state budget, and money and credit, as well as a balance of incomes and expenditures of the population. Each of these was balanced separately, but there was a growing recognition of their essential interdependence, as reflected in the fact that now one balance and now another turned out to deal with the key commodity that controlled the prospects for balancing all the others. There was a movement beyond the mere control of individual bottlenecks, but this was still limited, as the planners themselves put it, to 'an attempt scientifically to forecast only the principal directions of economic development and plan basic lines of economic policy'.

These balances could not be used by themselves to determine policy, because the statistics were still too poor in quality and incomplete. In addition, there was reliance on consultations with experts in each industrial field, and their informed judgments helped determine effective capacity limits and input requirements for the various sectors. Substantial efforts at data collection were steadily improving the statistics, but 'the informed judgment of experts remains central to economic planning down to the present day' (1926). In the Soviet Russia of the twenties, agriculture remained the area in which the statistical base for planning was weakest and, unfortunately for the planners, agriculture was emerging as the key bottleneck to further development, in terms both of the grain balance with its orientation towards feeding the cities, and the financial balances with their orientation towards 'determinng the market equilibrium between the goods masses of industrial and agricultural origin'.

But the planners' vision had already extended well beyond their current operational capacities. A section of Gosplan economists was at work on a 'balance of the national economy' which would depict in one grand tableau the relations among the partial balances of the control figures and provide a basis for integrated planning of the entire interdependent system. Balance tables of figures were actually constructed, and might well have seemed to the planners, as they did to Trotsky, to be the 'glorious music of the rise of socialism'. But they could not be used effectively in practice until they were supported by a theory of inter-dependence which could tell the planner by how much other sectors of the economy would be affected by a change in one place. This was not to come for another decade, when a Russian emigré at Harvard, Vassili Leontiev, developed the theory, and the balance of the national economy remained an adjunct not a centrepiece of Soviet planning.

Longer term planning came into its own in the late twenties. Under Strumilin's editorship a volume of 'perspectives for development' covering 1926–31 was published in 1927. But the attention of the entire world was caught by the initiation of the five-year plans a year later. The first five-year plan, also edited by Strumilin, was the product of a great deal of discussion and political struggle and was a good deal more optimistic than his earlier version. The planners had become caught up in the great debate over the proper strategy for the country's further economic development. This debate marked perhaps the first time in history in which planners and politicians together fought out the process of developing principles of theory and practice for modernizing a developing country. The process of struggle was messy, and though theory did not choose a winner, politics did, and the Soviet Union under Stalin's leadership embarked on its great and terrible adventure of developing a modern socialist economy.

The winning strategy favoured very rapid transformation, with investment apparently absorbing an unheard of proportion of national income and with primary emphasis on the growth of heavy industry. The principal losing strategy called for a more balanced development of industry and agriculture, with an emphasis in industrial production on goods that could be traded with the peasants for the produce with which to sustain the growing cities. We will never know whether this strategy would have worked. The one chosen was successful in the sense that output grew very rapidly for a decade, but the costs were very heavy too. The forced collectivization of agriculture produced the grain needed to feed the cities, but at the cost of a substantial deterioration in diets as meat products almost disappeared, and also at the cost of the death or incarceration of many millions.

Not all this was contained in the three-volume five-year plan document. Though much more optimistic than the Strumilin plan, its targets were still further increased for steel and a number of other goods during the first year or so of its operation. The plan called for considerable movement in the direction of collectivization but did not envisage the forced draft campaign that actually occurred. And when the final year of the first plan came around in 1932 there were vast areas of underfulfilment, especially in the production of consumer goods, but many important producer goods too were underfulfilled. As a forecast the first five-year plan could not be considered a success.

Nevertheless it is surely one of the half-dozen most important documents in the history of planning. Its 1700 pages contain detailed surveys of the situation in each sector and each region of the economy. These appraise the potential over the five-year plan period in terms of past achievements, prospective productivity increases and the completion of new investment projects. A detailed list of the factories to be built is provided, together with key measures of their expected impact both during and after their construction. Two alternative variants are worked out for most indices, so that the planners can react systematically to unexpected changes in the environment. Clearly much attention was given to interdependent impacts of key changes, even though no theory was available to assist the planners' experience and intuition.

The Soviet First Five-Year Plan remains a model exercise, setting a standard of care in construction that has since been met by very few planning agencies right down to the present time. One could hardly blame the planners for failure to foresee the great depression or the political decision to collectivize the countryside; such dramatic changes as these were major causes of the forecasting failures. The second plan, which ran to 1937, achieved much better success at forecasting, and revealed more fully the potential possessed by the longer run planning instrument.

By the mid-thirties the new institutions of the 'Soviet-type economy' had become firmly established in a form whose basic elements have remained visible down to the present. Short-run planning had been developed considerably beyond the scope of the control figures. One major change resulted from the steady decrease in market relations among industrial enterprises, and farms as well, and the substitution of a complex system of priorities and quotas for it. From the planning point of view this increased greatly the amount of work that had to be done at the centre; but most important it stimulated the development of a new system for dealing with problems of interdependence among sectors.

The new system, which seems to have emerged from practice and without assistance from more theoretically minded planners, many of whose voices had already been silenced by purges, was astonishingly simple. To idealize the system, assume the central planners assign initial targets to enterprises and ask them to report back their requirements in order to fulfil these assignments, using norms of input use per unit of output to make their calculations. The planners then add these requirements to the initial targets and go back to the enterprises with this revised plan. As less efficient enterprises come into operation norms can be revised upward, and various *ad hoc* adjustments made to deal with a few fixed capacity constraints. The odd thing about this system, which in practice was far less neat than this brief description suggests, is that it does in principle converge with continued revision; that is, the additional requirements at each revision become steadily smaller and result finally in a consistent plan. Neither theoretical acumen nor massive calculation was required to operate this system in practice and, though it had many problems, some of which are discussed below, it finally accomplished the job that the planners of the twenties were never able to get the 'balance of the national economy' to do.

The operational plan was at the centre of this system, with finance playing a supporting role and the five-year plan serving essentially as a massive guide to investment policy. The short-run planners essentially issued the orders that enterprise managers were expected to execute and provided them with the allocations of materials that were supposed to make the orders feasible. Control of enterprise performance was tied to the plan through the system of orders that were derived from the plan itself. Thus plan, implementation and control were tied together into one package, an instrument that could be effectively used to bring about, at the level of the enterprise, the changes desired at the highest levels of political economic control. The planned economy had become a reality.

KEYNES AND THE SECOND WORLD WAR

In Britain at least some partial lessons were learned from World War I. Though again the economic requirements for a major war were at first underestimated and the machinery not immediately set in motion, recognition came quickly and the necessary machinery even more quickly. More important, there was, this time, some ability to foresee the process of development of economic requirements and so to develop a more ophisticated style of planning. A leading economist-participant in the wartime effort, E. A. G. Robinson, suggests that there are four economic stages to the war effort. In the first the main problem is to create the capital equipment, factories and machinery, of the munitions industry. Then this capacity is used to build up the initial equipment for the armed forces. The third stage is one of reduction in activity to the level necessary to cover losses and maintain appropriate strength. In the final phase, with the end in sight, consumption can be increasingly out of inventories rather than new production, and serious attention can be given to postwar reconversion.

These are, of course. rough and ready categories. but they give one a kind of vision of the process of development of needs and provide a starting-point for the anticipation of bottlenecks. The bottlenecks, in fact, varied from one stage to another. In the first stage gold and currency reserves were the prime bottleneck, then the problem shifted to production capacity, and from 1942 onwards the key problem was finding enough manpower. But it was also recognized that discussion of bottlenecks at this level conceals as much as it reveals. At times the acute shortage was not an overall one, but the lack of a particular kind of tool or skill to do the required job. Hence the pyramiding of responsibility, with basic issues of strategy being settled by a small War Cabinet, large economic questions being handled by the Lord President's Committee under Sir John Anderson, and the problems of particular areas being handled by more specialized groups. Of special note among these was the Directorate-General of Planning, Programmes and Statistics of the Ministry of Aircraft Production, the co-ordinating body for aircraft procurement planning, because of the sensitivity to the problems and opportunities inherent in this form of planning with which one of its leading members, Ely Devons, has reported his experiences.

The operation of the wartime system of direct controls revealed that considerable learning had occurred as compared with the past, at all levels. Examples abound, from recognition of the need for a small super-agency to decide basic issues of policy at the top to the need for a strong co-ordinator of production programmes which was not itself responsible for production operations at the ministerial level. The further experience gained in operating this system no doubt had its effects on postwar organization, both in government and industry, but these do not seem to be traceable at the moment.

However, there was another development that was to have a far more obvious effect on the postwar world, namely the acceptance within government of the basic lines of the Keynesian argument in considering financial policies.

Ironically this key step in the integration of theory and practice dealt not with the problem of unemployment in a stagnant economy, but with the issue of control of inflation in a wartime boom. In his 1940 pamphlet, *How to Pay for the War*, Keynes made his argument for avoiding the great policy errors of the previous war. The basic argument was very simple: First, by comparing expected demands for wartime production, and the accompanying civilian demand for goods, with the available production capacity measured in terms of aggregate output, it could be seen that demand far outstripped supply. The levels of taxation necessary to bring about balance were so great that they would destroy incentives to work. So substantial borrowing would once again be necessary to finance the war, but to avoid another massive postwar debt servicing obligation, borrowing would have to be at low interest rates. Direct control of the export of capital would be used to prevent a capital flight. Workers would be given part of their pay in the form of deferred payment coupons, which would be released at the first sign of the postwar slump.

This was the basic Keynesian technique of relating aggregate supply and demand categories in order to understand the appropriate monetary and fiscal policies, and was now for the first time being presented to a government whose leadership was actually listening. Much of the proposal was adopted as policy. Furthermore, under the stimulus of these new ideas and needs, a statistician, Richard Stone, began developing the national income accounting system that was to provide the data base for Keynesian policy formation in all West European countries after the war. These two strands came together as the basis on which the 1941 budget was prepared, which makes that a historic document indeed. The approach was a basic success during the war. One measure of this was proposed by the participant-historian of wartime finance, R. S. Sayers: 'Those responsible for organizing Britain's war effort were never forced to feel that financial policy was important.'

GROPING FOR THE OPTIMAL PLAN

WESTERN EUROPE SINCE THE WAR

By the end of World War II there were two kinds of planned economies in existence, and two ideal types of planning. The centralist ideal type left all major decisions to the top leadership and planned by direct means, using quotas and targets. Initiative at lower levels was to be devoted to increasing productivity and quality. The Keynesian ideal type forswore direct controls, relying on the market to produce the right kinds of goods and to supply factories with the right inputs, while the planners used their instruments of monetary policy and levels of government taxing and spending to keep overall output at the full employment level. Roughly speaking, these ideal types remained at the centre of attention; in fact, in academic circles they acquired increasing interest over the postwar period as the theory of functioning of each type of economy underwent rapid development.

However, in practice neither the Soviet nor the British systems proved satisfactory, and both within these countries and elsewhere there was much experimentation with variants on the basic themes. The story of postwar planning is partly a story of the spread of these two basic systems and of their further elaboration, and partly the story of political economic groping for improved versions. The latter aspect will be emphasized in what follows; it is probably the more interesting, but is also revealing as to important aspects of the spread and development processes.

The Labour government that took over in Britain at the end of the war had a three-fold strategy of economic control. In J. C. R. Dow's words: 'Unemployment could be cured by the management of total demand, inequality by redistributive taxation. and monopolistic restrictions by selective nationalization.' Neither the Labour Party leadership nor the Conservative governments which were to come felt any pressing need for a central planning agency to assist in designing and implementing this policy and, aside from occasional and abortive flirtations with such things as 'Neddie' (National Economic Development Council) and the Department of Economic Affairs, none was forthcoming.

Furthermore, it is not unreasonable to say that in practice each of these three instruments was a failure. Nationalization did not prove to be an efficient means for removing inefficiency. Parliament found itself unable to construct social performance criteria which could be made sufficiently operational to permit appraisal of nationalized industry's performance on the basis of those criteria. And the transformation from private to social control did not seem to affect the productivity of workers or the behaviour of managers very significantly; indeed, there was often not even much change of managerial personnel. Among the nationalized industries there were examples of both effective and ineffective operation. It just did not seem to make much difference.

Nationalization lost much of its appeal throughout Western Europe in the fifties as a result of rather similar experiences on the Continent as well. Of course, part of the problem was political. A major reason why socialists wanted to nationalize was to reduce or eliminate the economic power of the capitalist class. But under régimes of parliamentary, interest group politics no socialist party had the votes to carry out this political programme. Efficiency was about the only politically feasible ground for nationalization, and it became increasingly evident that piecemeal nationalization had little discernible effect on efficiency.

Income redistribution measures faced a similar fate. Interest group politics, operating in the environment of affluent welfare state capitalism in the fifties and sixties, seems to have produced relative stability in income distributions. Socialists often felt that the existing distribution remained excessively skewed, but they were powerless to effect substantial change while operating within the system.

There is one exception to this charge of ineffectiveness of income redistribution policy, namely the widespread adoption of incomes policies, that is, of policies of controlling prices and wages with a view to controlling inflation while meeting some criterion of equity in distributing the burden. However, in practice this was very much a marginal operation. Market and political pressures permitted incomes policies to have at best only marginal impact and even then for only a short period of time. As a short-run policy they could have some effect; if there was also a long-run impact it has yet to be measured.

Finally, there is the management of aggregate demand to maintain a stable and growing economy at or near full employment. It is true that Britain's unemployment rate was far lower throughout the postwar period than it had been interwar. The problem is not with this aspect of performance but with causation. Close analysis of government policy during 1945–60 leads Dow to conclude: 'As far as internal conditions are concerned, then, budgetary and monetary policy failed to be stabilizing, and must on the contrary be regarded as having been positively destabilizing,' while the successor study for the sixties concludes in a similar vein.

What went wrong with the Keynesian vision? The answer has a political, a technical, a statistical and an economic side. The first problem consisted in getting the government to respond quickly once the need for action was established by the experts. The British had better luck than many countries on this dimension, the government being given considerable discretionary authority, for example, to vary some tax rates in support of economic stability. Nevertheless, there was a significant and variable time lag between perception and action. Time lags are, of course, important because Keynesian policies are supposed to affect the short run.

The technical problem had to do with special properties of the various instruments. For example, even if a shopping list of public works projects had been prepared in advance, the immediate employment and spending effects of the go-ahead decision might be very small for some months, and might then continue well beyond the transformation of slump into boom. Monetary policy also had its lags before becoming effective, and often was highly concentrated in its impact; for example. high interest rates had a major impact on housing construction, but might affect other capital spending sectors only marginally. In other words, it turned out not to be technically possible to design a programme of variation in fiscal and monetary policy that had the right impact, both by time and by sector, on the economy; the desideratum, a policy with immediate and sectorally neutral impact, was clearly unattainable.

The lack of adequate statistics was a serious hindrance to policy in the late forties, but this situation underwent steady and vast improvement in the succeeding two decades. National accounting systems made their appearance everywhere, the data becoming available on a quarterly basis, and in some cases even monthly. The time lag in obtaining results was also much reduced. But two problems still remained. First there still was a lag, to be measured at least in weeks, between the ending of a time period and the generation of a solid estimate of the values of the key variables. Secondly there was no way to quickly distinguish between a downturn and a mere squiggle on the curve of economic activity. Over the years this problem of interpretation came to be more serious than that of obtaining the data promptly.

Finally there was the problem of the theory itself. Conceptual difficulties with the variables, the problem of aggregation, of lumping differently behaving time series together into a single catchall variable, and the problem of the changing structure of the economy, all set upper limits to the quality of the economic models to which the statistics were to give specific shape. And the theory itself said that a government would frequently have to make the hard choice between international economic strength and domestic full employment.

Each of these areas provided a challenge which was widely recognized and studied, and the last two decades have seen much progress. Basically three kinds of variation on the British approach were tried out on the Continent. In Holland a more integrated system of central planning within the Keynesian framework was tried. In France a relatively detailed scheme of investment planning was introduced into the market economy. And in Sweden government policy attempted to restructure some key markets, especially those for investment and labour, so as to get a better adjustment to equilibrium. Each of these attempts requires a brief comment.

The name Jan Tinbergen deserves a place alongside that of Keynes as one of the founders of modern, Western style planning. Tinbergen made two central intellectual contributions. In a 1939 study he integrated Keynesian and other ideas into an econometric model which characterized the business cycle in the United States and estimated the quantitative effects of various alternative courses of action. After the war in a seminal book he reoriented the then burgeoning literature on aggregative economics towards direct assistance in solving planning problems. In this work he distinguished particularly between target variables, such as the employment level, for which the planners wanted to achieve some desired level, and instrument variables, which the planners had under their control. He then constructed a series of models which displayed key properties of the operation of regulating an economy's target variables by means of the available instrument variables. These two notions, econometric models of the whole economy and the target-instrument structure, when put together spelled central plan.

Tinbergen was closely associated with the development of planning in Holland, and in particular led in constructing the planning models that were actually used, beginning in 1950. Very roughly the process of planning went as follows. On the basis of the plan model, Tinbergen was able to show what the implications for the Dutch economy of any particular set of policies would be. The political process of policy determination was quite centralized, with government, business and labour each represented in the decision making. By providing relatively hard evidence of the consequences of alternative policy, the process of reaching agreement was simplified, because a variety of policies desired by one or another influential group could be shown to have rather unpleasant consequences. The effectiveness of this system was enhanced by another feature, namely the national wage bargain. Individual wages were tied to the national wage by a formula, which enhanced both the meaningfulness of the national bargain and the usefulness of the rather high level of aggregation of the variables in the model. This system functioned so effectively that it was at one point possible to convince the Foundation of Labour, an association of employee and employer unions, that a reduction of real wages was in the workers' interest.

The famous French indicative planning grew out of government involvement in postwar reconstruction and recovery. Development of key sectors, such as electric power, steel and transport, on a national basis was a key aspect of recovery policy and required a good estimate as to the national demand for these goods a few years hence. Out of this grew the peculiar combination of direct planning of investment in considerable sectoral detail, joint consultations especially with business, but also with labour, on their roles in making and executing the plan, and an incentive system based on the government's taxing and lending powers to keep businesses in compliance with the plan. Because of the latter, which was used in practice when necessary, French planning was by no means entirely 'indicative' but involved considerable elements of coercion. The economy did grow rapidly under the first few plans, and the planning had considerable influence on the changing structure of the economy; but perhaps its chief contribution was in developing investor expectations to a state of confidence that others were in fact doing the things that would make one's own project viable.

There is a third type of planning which was very frequently used by European governments in the postwar period and which may well have had more impact on the economies than macroeconomic and investment planning. This was the design of social systems to support the welfare state policies. A good example is the British National Health System. Though government health plans came to

Britain before World War I, the early systems were very narrow in coverage. Under the stimulus of the Beveridge Report in 1944, however, the new Labour Government assumed responsibility for designing and putting into operation a scheme that would provide guaranteed medical service to anyone who needed it, at the level demanded by the patient's medical needs, and without any regard for the patient's ability to pay. This required a massive restructuring of the organization of medical care, considerable investment in new facilities and personnel, and the design of an incentive system which would ensure some adequate level of quality in the health service delivered. Furthermore, the amount of service delivered was not under control; that is, the system must deliver the goods whenever there was genuine need, so that supply must be adaptable to 'real' demand.

Economists had no grand theories to offer practitioners in areas like this, which included other systems, such as social security, education and, even, defence. Beveridge was the nearest thing to a Keynes this area had; but Beveridge's great contribution was not theoretical acumen but practical concern. When conventional economists participated in this form of planning, they brought with them cost-benefit analysis and the tools of microeconomics, which by and large in practice offered not a vision of the system as a whole with supporting theory, but piecemeal insights into how to make parts of the system operate more effectively.

Indeed, the history of the last twenty years might easily be read to show that the principal practical accomplishments of planning lay in this area rather than in the development of monetary-fiscal policy, that it was due to progress in this area that vast segments of Europe's population had their situations dramatically improved, and perhaps even that it was a more important stabilizer of demand and stimulator of growth than monetary-fiscal policy.

Support for this argument comes from such things as the above-mentioned studies which show that British monetary-fiscal policy was usually destabilizing, results which can easily be duplicated for many instances of policy application on the Continent as well. Support also comes from another and rather peculiar feature of this period, namely a tendency towards convergence in policy and the organization of planning among countries simultaneously with deteriorating performance. For example, in several countries, of which the Netherlands was the archetype, a quite centralized system of political bargaining had developed to produce a compromise agreement among labour, business and government as to the amount of change in prices and wages to be permitted in the plan. In the middle and later sixties these centralized bargaining systems broke down as inflation became a more serious and less predictable problem. French indicative planning since 1965 has put decreasing emphasis on the detailed design of the investment programme and increasing emphasis on conventional monetary and fiscal instruments of control. Short-term planning has become more controversial, with the multiplication of planning models for a given country, each producing somewhat different results and often becoming a basis for advocacy by a particular interest group. Britain became a bit more planning-conscious while most countries on the Continent moved substantially closer to the relatively loose British system of indirect controls.

But this convergence was not the product of a pull towards a demonstrably more effective procedure. Rather it was the result of a push away from systems that were no longer politically feasible. The sixties were an era of stop-go, of inflation followed by controls followed by slowdown until balance of payments or internal demand pressures eased off, followed once again by growth. The existing theory and experience as of 1970 did not provide a basis for substantial improvement of this deteriorating situation. The problem had not yet reached crisis proportions, but had substantially eroded the enthusiasm of the early Keynesians.

EASTERN EUROPE SINCE THE WAR

By the terminal date of this essay the basic Soviet type planning system had been in operation for thirty-five years. There were of course many changes during this period which reflected the growing understanding of and experience with the system. Moving to Soviet type planning was a far larger structural change than moving towards Western style planning, and so there was a great deal more to be learned.

Probably the underlying force behind most of these developments was the need for the top leadership, both at the Council of Ministers and Gosplan levels, to make fewer and less detailed decisions. There is a tendency in a hierarchy for conflicts to move up, and many conflicts occur in a large and rapidly growing economy. The response has been in several directions. The Soviet Union returned to consumer rationing during World War II, but the experience once again demonstrated that the quasi-market system they had instituted before the war, roughly speaking with outputs planned and prices adjusted to keep demand just a touch ahead of supply, was a more effective system. Price reforms were initiated with a view to obtaining prices that reflected costs more accurately. Enterprises were given somewhat greater autonomy, from being assigned fewer directives regarding product mix to being given some flexibility, especially with respect to new goods, to being given somewhat more control over wages and employment. Enterprises were also given more stimulus to control costs, among others by means of changes in the structure of managerial bonuses, through pressures towards more inter-enterprise contracting, and towards more concern for the fate of goods after they had been produced. The plan making process has also been rationalized somewhat through the use of input-output analysis and other techniques for analysing the vast quantity of data that flows into Gosplan. All these measures have had their effect, as is suggested by the continued development of the economy and the improvement in the quality of many goods over the years.

However this is not the whole. story. There are certain respects in which informed participants in this sort of planning system believe that the system is seriously flawed. Despite improvements the quality and mix of Soviet output remains inadequate and departs substantially from the planners' desires. Incentive problems remain, as do inadequacies in the price structure. Innovativeness seems rather narrowly concentrated in the highest priority sectors and is not always adequate even there, as witness the disappointing developmental history of the Soviet computer industry.

As a consequence, in Eastern Europe, where at one point, say around 1950, there were a half-dozen or so essentially Soviet type planning systems in operation, there are now several deviants, and there is also a great deal of diversity even among those economies that have remained with essentially the Soviet type of system. We turn now to a brief look at three directions in which groping towards a substantially different planning system has occurred.

In the early fifties Yugoslavia embarked on the first large-scale venture into a new form of socialism. Interpreting the Soviet Union's hostility as having a basis in Marxist theory, the Yugoslav leadership concluded that a new class had arisen in the Soviet Union. This class consisted of the bureaucracy which controlled the Soviet production apparatus and so, assertedly, operated the Soviet economy in their own interest. The message seemed clear: to avoid the rise of a similar class at home the economic bureaucracy would have to be dismantled. This they proceeded to do in a dramatic and thoroughgoing revolution from above.

The new economic system that emerged had two new bases: worker management of enterprises and a socialist market to mediate relations between firms. The means of production remained in social ownership, but the workers in a given enterprise paid taxes to the state based on the factory's income and assets. Workers shared in the after tax profits and investment was made from profits and loans, the latter having to be paid off with interest. Within these limits (and much sharper limits for foreign trade) enterprises were free to make contracts with other firms regarding prices and deliveries and to decide for themselves the rate of output and the mix of goods.

What role was there for planning in such a system? Essentially the Yugoslav economy passed through two phases. In the first, the state continued to make five-year plans that provided a detailed schedule of capital investment projects for the next five years, in much the same way as the Soviet type plan. The annual plan, of course, was much' more substantially affected. It now consisted primarily of an overall analysis of the expected performance of the economy, primarily in terms of aggregates, combined with the government's budget. The instruments of control of the economy were somewhat different from those in a Western style planning system however. For one thing there was more direct control over short-term credit grants. Secondly there were instances of direct intervention to freeze various accounts of enterprises during periods of unusual inflationary pressure. Also there was on average a far more extensive system of price controls.

In the second phase, beginning in 1965, a substantial further decentralization occurred. The federal government no longer took a major direct hand in investment and so the five-year plans lost their detailed programming. There was also a substantial reduction of direct intervention both in individual enterprises and in the control of credit. This system began to look very much like its Western counterparts. For example, in the first phase the ratio of investment to consumption was largely under direct control, while in the second phase indirect instruments were the major control device. However, beneath the surface substantial differences remained. For example, because there is no capital market where factories are socially owned, since the state is the sole owner of capital goods, and very little voluntary savings by the consumers in this still developing economy, Keynesian policies could not be clearly distinguished from monetary policy. A budget deficit or surplus was bound to be reflected in changes in the supply of money, and the two could not easily be separated. Nevertheless, on balance Yugoslav planners now had more to learn about how to control their economy from capitalist planners than from socialist ones.

Though Yugoslavia had a very good growth record, and the quality of her goods has improved greatly over the years, the planning system has yet to demonstrate its superiority over its competitors. Inflation has been a very serious problem and relatively strong stop-go cycles occur regularly. Price controls remain a major instrument of policy. And it is still not clear that the government can, within the framework of the decentralized system, effectively control the rate of investment so as to maintain relatively stable growth.

The Hungarian way developed as a carefully prepared programme of structural change, the product of several years of political economic search for a controlled but decentralized socialist system. Its flavour is captured in the phrase 'managerial market socialism'. By 1970 it had only had two years of operation so appraisal was really not possible. The new system grew out of a feeling that the standard Soviet planning model could be substantially improved by dividing incentives better between the central planners and the operators of the economy. The Hungarian solution provided for a modest number of quite large enterprises, each run by a manager possessing considerable autonomy. He was subject to quotas on only a very few inputs, was allowed to make his own contracts, both at home and abroad, and even had some initiative power with respect to investment. He was controlled by an incentive system that rewarded growth and higher profits according to a formula worked out at the centre, by the modest rationing scheme, and by a number of remaining controls on foreign trade. However because of the relatively small size of the Hungarian economy and relatively small number of enterprises, there is room for a great deal of informal control of the manager from the centre. How this system will fare remains to be seen; clearly it is a substantial departure from Soviet practice.

In the years after the ideological thaw following Stalin's

death, a major transformation occurred in Soviet economics. Mathematics once again became an acceptable tool in working both theoretically and at the applied level on problems of planning. Since this was also the era in which the computer began to play a major role in assisting the planners, the two factors have a highly interdependent history. The computer held out the vision of a fully automated economy and, in fact, so did the mathematical theory of central planning.

These developments have probably had a far greater impact on Soviet planning than appears on the surface. This is because the impact seems to have been more on the minds of the participants than, so far at least, on actual practice. Since 1961 each year has produced a new cohort of economists who, as graduates of the university programmes in mathematical economics, are trained to think in ways that are very different from those of their older colleagues. They tend to pose problems in ways that make them accessible to the mathematical and statistical techniques that they have learned, using such tools as input-output, linear programming and control theory in thinking about how to plan the delivery of cement from producers to construction sites in next year's plan, or how to fix the capacities and locations of ceramic construction materials factories for the next five-year plan. Having all learned this same language they communicate easily with one another, and outsiders no doubt find it very difficult seriously to counter the arguments made by these technical means. The intellectual quality of these younger economists seems very high and as they move up the various bureaucratic ladders they could easily come to dominate the planning 'techno-structure'.

These new technical ways of dealing with planning problems have opened practitioners' minds to the feasibility of designing alternative planning systems based on the new techniques and a massive use of computers. L. V. Kantorovich spelled out, somewhat imprecisely, one such system in 1959 which was not unlike the famous model of market socialism which Oscar Lange developed in the thirties.

And in the early sixties there was serious appraisal of the possibility of creating a fully centralized economy in which millions of goods would be planned by means of an integrated system of mathematical plans supported by an integrated national computer system. Still others in this group found the introduction of essentially market relations among production units to be an interesting possibility.

These visions may have great significance for the future. However they had had rather limited practical impact by 1970. On closer examination the available mathematical plans proved to be flawed in several ways that were crucial for very large-scale applications. The development of computer capacity proceeded at too modest a pace to support even existing data processing requirements, and accurate solution of million-variable problems was not yet feasible in practice. And as study continued it became clear that the design of a system of incentives to support implementation of the plan, assuming it could be computed, had not yet been developed.

The marketeers could not seriously obtain the ears of the political leadership. This left in the field the new style practitioners who were content to use the new techniques to bring about piecemeal improvements in the existing system. This, in fact, was done in a variety of areas. The effort was further encouraged by the situation in computers; the available stock by 1970 was of most use in dealing with the kinds of problems that in fact came up at the enterprise level, or the level of specific and partial problems of broader gauge planning. The new combination of mathematics, computers and technical economists, it turned out, could be put to good, perhaps even to maximal, current use by supporting improvements in the existing system rather than by concentrating on more dramatic transformations.

CONCLUSION

A great deal of scholarly work has been devoted to appraising aspects of planning organization and performance in particular countries over various time periods. There has also been a great deal of work devoted to developing theories of planning. However, overall appraisal of the twentieth century experience with planning is still in its infancy, so that many of the remarks in this paper should be treated as speculations rather than as established facts. Furthermore, our account has entirely omitted international planning, which has in fact undergone substantial development as the impact of the international environment on domestic economies has increased. However the narrative does seem to revolve around two key issues, namely the relation between theory and practice and the extent of convergence, which we now discuss briefly by way of conclusion.

Planning history suggests three areas in which there may be an inadequate appreciation of the relation between theory and practice. In the first place, there is some reason to believe that the role of economic theory in the development of applied planning is often greatly exaggerated. Conventional economic theory may actually have been a hindrance to the application of effective full employment measures in Britain in the twenties, and elsewhere as well. The vast elaboration of complex mathematical planning schemes in the last two decades of our period seems to have had almost no impact on practical planning schemes. Even aggregative forecasting models, which have proved their usefulness, owe a great deal of that usefulness to the economic intuition and experience of the builders and users, possibly as much as to theoretical acumen. The thorough and percipient reader of the economic press still has considerable standing both as expert and as forecaster. as he did in the days of the Soviet control figures planning.

Not only has theory played a relatively limited role in the development of practical planning, but basic theoretical insights have not infrequently come from the world of policy rather than from the corpus of theory itself. The notion of interdependence captured in the Soviet 'balance of the national economy' provided the firm basis on which input-output theory was to be developed a decade later. Of course the idea that economic activities were highly interdependent was well known to economic theorists; the novelty of the practitioners' specific insight was that it made the idea a matter of direct empirical relevance. And of course the basic Keynesian notion of stagnation due to lack of sufficient effective demand was, in one form or another, circulating among 'underworld' and policy oriented economists for decades before the *General Theory* made it analytically respectable.

Thirdly, there may have been a considerable distortion of priorities in analysis and in the appraisal of performance because of the semi-autonomous development of economic theory. The heavy emphasis on central planning, both Western and Soviet styles, diverted attention away from the design of service delivery systems at the sectoral level, such as health, education, defence and income support, where possibly the more important events were taking place. This point is strengthened by the distinct possibility that the theoretical support for neither type of planning has played much of a direct role in practice. One recalls especially in this connection the evidence that government monetary and fiscal policy in the postwar period has tended to be destabilizing.

There has been a great deal of discussion about the convergence of the two systems, capitalism and socialism, in recent years. Of course, in the perspective of the entire twentieth century, a very notable feature has been divergence, that is, the creation of the Soviet Union and its survival for more than half that century as a strikingly different form of economic organization. Furthermore, we have noted other lesser kinds of diversity such as the experiments in Holland and France in Western Europe, and Yugoslavia and Hungary in the East. Nevertheless, there are also some respects in which convergence is noticeable.

In the first place Western style planning converged strongly in the sixties after the various experiments of earlier years. A rather loose system of monetary and fiscal policy, periodic price and wage controls and foreign trade controls, and some limited variation in sectoral spending combined with quite limited direct controls, are the heart of nearly all Western stabilization and growth programmes. Even the sectoral service delivery systems are coming to resemble each other more and more.

Secondly, the Soviet style of planning seems to be under steady pressure to carry decentralization further. The younger technicos seem largely committed to this direction of movement, even more so in the smaller East European socialist countries than in the Soviet Union. And the example of Yugoslavia, and possibly even of Hungary, suggest that once this sort of change has been carried so far, the pressures to adopt essentially Western style planning, with the accompanying decentralization and corresponding institutional development, become overwhelming. This is by no means to claim that the Soviet system is not viable, or even that it is less effective at performing desired tasks than a Western system would be, but only to assert the fact of these pressures.

But, as noted in the narrative, there is little reason to believe that these convergent trends are towards some sort of optimal planning régime. What has been dominant is the pressure caused by inadequacy in the existing system, whatever that system may be. The move towards more decentralization may have been more a product of politicians' desires to escape direct responsibility for failures than of planners' knowledge that the change would make planning more effective. Indeed, the later sixties were quite generally a time of deteriorating planning performance.

This situation could produce the general adoption of a similar form of planning, one which meets the demands of both politicians and the economically active citizenry, *faute de mieux*. But it also could presage a new hunt for more substantial changes, and more experimentation. It would be unfortunate if, in such an event, the history of past failures were simply allowed to repeat itself.

SELECT BIBLIOGRAPHY OF ENGLISH
LANGUAGE WORKS

GENERAL WORKS

Friedmann, W., *Law in a Changing Society*, Berkeley, 1959.

Keynes, J. M., *General Theory of Employment, Interest and Money*, London, 1936.

Kirschen, E. S. and L. Morissens, *Economic Policy in our Time*, 3 vols., Amsterdam, 1964.

Mayne, Richard, *The Recovery of Europe*, London, 1970.

PEP (Political and Economic Planning), *European Organizations*, London, 1959.

OECD (Organization for Economic Co-operation and Development), *Country Studies*. (An annual pamphlet is published on each country surveying economic policy, planning and performance.)

Rimlinger, Gaston V., *Welfare Policy and Industrialization in Europe, America and Russia*, New York, 1971.

Shonfield, Andrew, *Modern Capitalism, the Changing Balance of Public and Private Power*. London, 1968.

Tinbergen, Jan, *An Econometric Approach to Business Cycle Problems*, Paris, 1939.

——, *Economic Policy, Principles and Design*, Amsterdam, 1956.

United Nations, Economic Commission for Europe, *Economic Survey of Europe in 1962, Part 2, Economic Planning in Europe*, Geneva, 1965. (The annual economic surveys provide generally useful accounts of developments in planning and economic policy in both Eastern and Western Europe.)

COUNTRY STUDIES

United Kingdom

Ashworth, William, *An Economic History of England, 1870–1939*, London, 1960.

Chester, D. N., ed., *Lessons of the British War Economy*, Cambridge, 1951.

Cohen, C. D., *British Economic Policy, 1960–1969*, London, 1971.

Devons, Ely, *Papers on Planning and Economic Management*, Manchester, 1970.

Dow, J. C. R., *The Management of the British Economy, 1945–1960*, Cambridge, 1964.

Hicks, Ursula K., *British Public Finances, 1880–1952*, London, 1954.

Pollard, Sidney, *The Development of the British Economy, 1914–1950*, London, 1962.

Sampson, Anthony, *Anatomy of Britain Today*, New York, 1965.

Winch, Donald, *Economics and Policy, A Historical Study*, London, 1969.

Germany

Brady, Robert A., *The Spirit and Structure of German Fascism*, New York, 1937.

Feldman, Gerald D., *Army Industry and Labor in Germany, 1914–1918*, Princeton, 1966.

Klein, Burton H., *Germany's Economic Preparations for War*, Cambridge (Mass.), 1959.

Milward, Alan S., *The German Economy at War*, London, 1965.

Speer, Albert, *Inside the Third Reich*, London, 1970.

Wallich, Henry C., *Mainsprings of the German Revival*, New Haven, 1955.

France

Balassa, Bela, 'Whither French Planning', *Quarterly Journal of Economics*, Cambridge (Mass.), 1965.

Denton, Geoffrey, *et al.*, eds. *Economic Planning and Policies in Britain, France and Germany*, London, 1968.

Hackett, John and Anne-Marie, *Economic Planning in France*, Cambridge (Mass.), 1963.

Sheahan, John, *Promotion and Control of Industry in Postwar France*, Cambridge (Mass.), 1963.

Wellisz, Stanislaw, 'Economic Planning in the Netherlands, France and Italy', *Journal of Political Economy*, Chicago, 1960.

Scandinavia and the Low Countries

Abert, J. G., *Economic Policy and Planning in the Netherlands, 1950–1965*, New Haven, 1969.

Bjerve, P. J., *Planning in Norway, 1947–1956*, Amsterdam, 1959.

Childs, Marquis W., *Sweden, The Middle Way*, rev. ed., New York, 1947.

De Wolff, Peter, *et al.*, *Governmental Planning and Political Economy*, Berkeley, 1967.

Netherlands, Planbureau, *Scope and Methods of the Central Planning Bureau*, Amsterdam, 1956.

Soviet Union and Eastern Europe
Bergson, Abram, *The Economics of Soviet Planning*, New Haven, 1964.
Carr, E. H., *The Bolshevik Revolution, 1917–1923*, vol. 2, London, 1952.
——, *Socialism in One Country, 1924–1926*, vol. 1, London, 1958.
Dobb, Maurice, *Soviet Economic Development since 1917*, New York, 1948.
Horvat, Branko, 'Yugoslav Economic Policy in the Post-war Period: Problems, Ideas, Institutional Developments', *American Economic Review*, Supplement, 1971.
Montias, J. Michael, *Central Planning in Poland*, New Haven, 1962.
——, 'Planning with Material Balances in Soviet-Type Economies', *American Economic Review*, 1959.
Nove, Alec, *An Economic History of the USSR*, London, 1969.
Spulber, Nicholas, ed., *Foundations of Soviet Strategy for Economic Growth, Selected Soviet Essays, 1924–1930*, Bloomington, 1964.
US Congress, Joint Committee Print, *Economic Developments in Countries of Eastern Europe*, Washington, 1970.

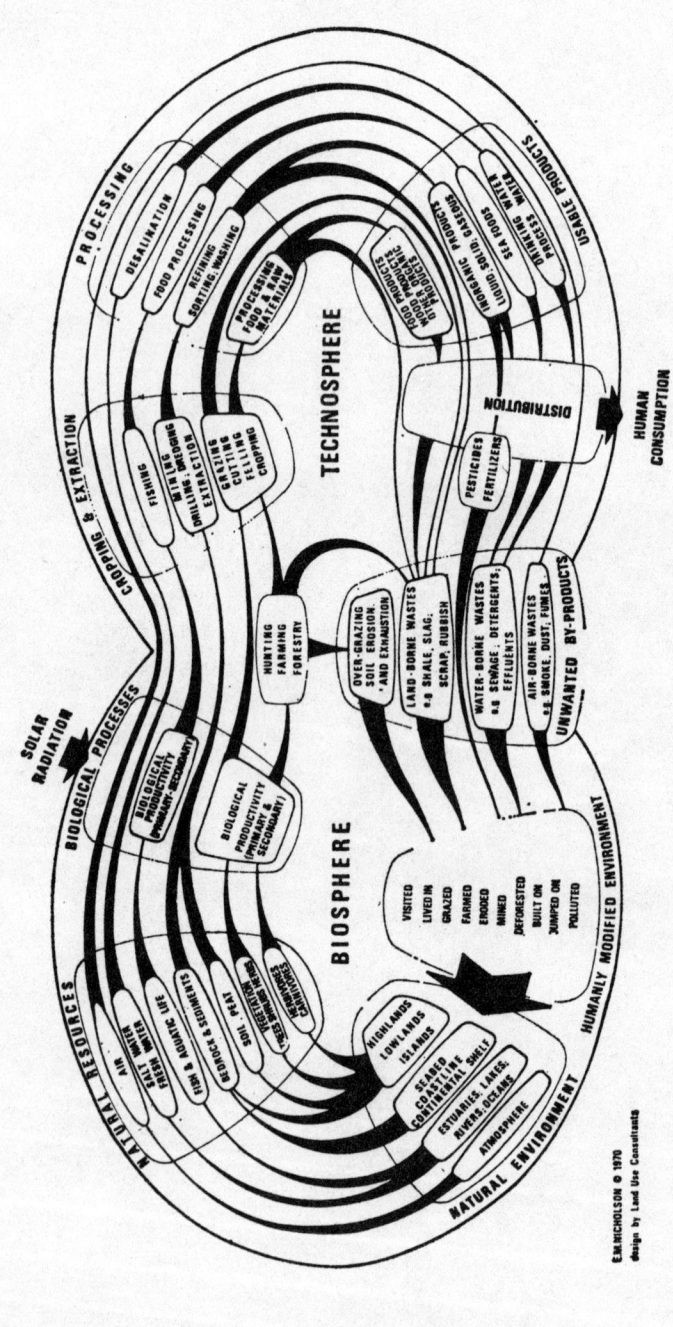

E.M.NICHOLSON © 1970
design by Land Use Consultants

13. Economy, Society and Environment 1920-1970

Max Nicholson

PREAMBLE

A fundamental dilemma confronts us at the outset in treating as if it were a single subject the complex interplay of the natural Biosphere with man's expanding modern Technosphere.[1] It consists of a dynamic, fluid and intricate set of processes, in which the repercussions are mutual and involve continuous feedback, giving warning of impending collisions and seeking to avert or mitigate their impacts through spontaneous adaptations on both sides. The early warnings obtainable from ecology on the one side and economics on the other may or may not be received, understood and acted upon in time to avert damage or even disaster. Much depends upon the degree of flexibility built into the relevant ecosystems and technologies, and the extent of elbow room which exists in time and space for groping about until an answer is found. A substantive treatment of these interrelations, which must be closely integrated with analysis of the present stage of their evolution, inevitably runs counter to the conventional approach for students of breaking down a subject into well-defined successive periods and distinct aspects. The function of this preamble is to provide such a structural representation, so far as possible without too much distortion of the open-

1 The terms *Biosphere* and *Technosphere* relate to the physical processes involved in the total activities on the earth of nature and man respectively, divested of any philosophical, ethical, economic, social, aesthetic or other value judgements. The *biosphere* converts solar radiation and inorganic elements into a world of living matter, or biomass, sustained by continuous processes of biological productivity. It is primarily responsible for the growth of vegetable matter and secondarily, through vegetation, for the growth of animal matter. The *technosphere* extracts from, or crops, the biosphere by mining, farming, fishing, hunting and other methods, to acquire elements which are processed into 'usable' products. Most of these are immediately distributed to human consumers or users while a few, such as pesticides and fertilisers, are chan-

ended dynamic interplay with which we are essentially concerned.

In chronological terms, human impacts on nature have emerged only during the very latest stages of an immensely longer evolution of other forms of life on earth. In the course of that evolution natural selection has enabled a high proportion of the planet's natural resources to be put to effective use by plants and animals exploiting the results of such physical processes as climate and geomorphological occurrences. Biological productivity, both primary by plants and secondary by animals, has been accompanied by a vast diversification of organisms, interacting and largely stabilising their numbers and impacts by a series of mechanisms functioning none the less effectively despite their blindness.

The advent of man injected into this unconscious system of control a slowly unfolding and increasingly potent discordant element of conscious intelligence and will. For hundreds of thousands of years human numbers and capabilities remained too insignificant to exert measurable effects on the operation of natural forces. The discovery how to trigger off extensive forest and grassland fires, and how to trap and eventually domesticate and exploit large animals started man, however, on his way to building his Technosphere as a rival system to the Biosphere in which he originated. The oar, the sail, the wheel, the axe, the plough and countless other inventions led to the emergence, first locally, then regionally and later more widely, of

---

nelled back into the biosphere by being spread on the land. In addition to these 'usable' products. however. vast quantities of wastes, effluents and gases are either leaked or dumped back into the biosphere. These latter processes, like extraction and cropping, conver the land and natural resources affected from a natural to a humanly modified environment (See p. 738)

The significance of this form of presentation is to place natural and human activities within the total environment on a comparable physical basis. bringing out their dynamic nature and consequences and their many interrelations. It warns against being misled by such crude and tendentious terms as 'raw materials'. 'waste' and 'pollution'. It cannot however, express the great relative growth in scale and importance of the technosphere as against the biosphere.

artificial systems in conflict with the natural. Only in modern times, however, has the relative scale of these systems on the planet and the power of their technology seriously begun to challenge the management of the planet's resources by natural forces and processes. Until the last few years most people assumed that 'the conquest of nature' followed inevitably and smoothly from man's 'progress'. The thought that a vast and painful adaptation would be demanded, and that this adaptation would call for fundamental rethinking of man's role on the planet occurred to very few. The belated recognition of this truth proved even more traumatic because during the mid-twentieth century shallow thinking and widespread crude materialism had been allowed to harden and reinforce pre-existing trends to a point, not quite of no return, but at least of the utmost embarrassment and difficulty in retracing steps and changing course. During the mid-twentieth century therefore, the growing impetus of expansion of population and of economic activity, fuelled by technological advance, held mankind on a collision course with the biosphere, and with the unalterable conditions of man's survival on the earth. The strength and prestige of this vast vested interest, and the inertia which it had created, hindered and delayed reception of warnings over its perils until, when at last they had to be heard, reactions of impending doom became widespread. The resulting confusion and loss of confidence, and the shortage of leaders trained to cope with such realities threw the Western world in particular into grave disarray, which affected every activity, from religion to military strategy. It is against that background of disarray that we have to do our urgent rethinking of the fundamental issues, and of their immediate application to world problems.

In the remainder of this preamble an outline structure of the subject will be presented under two main heads, first chronological, and secondly in terms of the main distinguishable aspects for separate study.

A chronological structure involves a breakdown into six main phases. The first approximate date to be estimated must be that until which human numbers and capabilities were nowhere significant in modifying the functioning of the biosphere as it had evolved in the ages before man. Recent discoveries and studies are rapidly changing the picture as we know it, but, if we are guided especially by the acquisition of capacity to use fire and to organise co-operative hunting of large animals, rather than simple tool-making on a small scale and in crude terms, we are led to a period some 450,000–500,000 years before the present as the critical point where the total control of the planet by natural forces began to be challenged and gradually modified.

The next and decisive step was the capacity to make specialised tools, weapons and clothing and to construct huts, closely followed by domestication of animals, metal-working, agriculture and the first cities. These advances distinguished the era between 35,000 and 5,000 years before the present as the second phase during which man's exploitation of the biosphere became systematic and significant, if still on little more than a token scale. It was during this period that the extermination of the Mammoth first gave clear warning of the shape of things to come. During the ensuing third phase, roughly between 5,000 and 1,000 years ago, civilisation became organised, confident and profusely aggressive, not least in its attitude towards nature, the primary target of man's obsession with achieving power. The hold of tradition, of customs, hierarchies and established religions provided some sort of curb on some of the most important cultural groups. This, however, gradually weakened during the fourth phase of pre-industrial small technology, persisting until the Industrial Revolution gathered strength some 200 years ago, ushering in the age of modern technology. It could well be argued that this fifth phase still continues, and there is a strong case for this view in many parts of the world. For our present purpose, however, it seems preferable to identify a sixth phase, starting after the first quarter of the twentieth century – a phase when Big Technology began to overreach itself and to show signs of toppling, even before its confrontation with the champions of the environment became conspicuous.

On this view we have to consider an ever shortening series of six main phases in the relationship of Man and Biosphere, which may be listed as;

I   B.P.   c. 450,000–35,000   Impact of fire and simple tools
II   c. 35,000–5,000   Impact of pastoralism, agriculture, urbanism &c
III   c. 5,000–1,000   Impact of highly organised societies
IV   c. 1,000–200   Impact of pre-industrial technology
V   c. 200–50   Impact of organised large-scale technology
VI   c. 50–now   Collision between Big Technology and the Biosphere. Crisis of fundamental readjustment.

Such a chronological table, inevitably over-simplified and approximate, may need to be modified to some extent in the light of further discoveries. It does not fully coincide with a chronology of human development considered without regard to its main environmental impacts. It is based on a wide range of sources in interpreting which Professor J. Z. Young's *An Introduction to the Study of Man* (Oxford 1971) has been taken as the arbiter, and is strongly recommended as an ideal counterpart to works based on the natural environment, such as the present writer's *Environmental Revolution* (Hodder and Stoughton 1970).

The recent emergence, only within the past quarter of a million years of *Homo sapiens*, and the concentration within a mere one and a half million generations of virtually all specifically human experiences presents tremendous problems of adaptation at a pace consistent with the demands of survival for a dominant species such as man has so rapidly become. Qualities and attributes developed by selection during some four-fifths of man's existence have had to be intensively modified during the remainder. The immediate challenge is to develop further modifications, perhaps as great as all those of the past quarter-million years put together, within the next few decades. This presupposes that intelligent conscious change in man's fundamental make-up and basic attitudes to fit him for the role into which he has blundered must be the overriding commitment of this and the next generations. It is accordingly necessary to outline next the main fields in which adaptation is mandatory, within a very brief period.

Looking briefly at the main distinguishable aspects of the subject for purposes of study in depth the obvious starting point is the multiplication of human numbers, both absolutely and in terms of rate of increase. In our phase I, world human population according to present knowledge probably ranged between 100,000 and 5 million; during phase II it may have roughly doubled to around 10 million and by the end of III it could have exceeded 200 million, of whom more than a quarter were in China. The take-off point in multiplication came near the end of phase IV, when it headed for the first billion (thousand million), and the previous net annual increase of around 0.04 per cent turned up rapidly towards the 2 per cent overall average attained in phase VI, producing a current total of 4,000 millions. There has therefore been a fairly close parallel between the acceleration of population growth and the rising human numbers with the progress to successive phases of relationship between man and the biosphere. It may safely be predicted that the crisis phase (VI) will not be over until zero population growth has at least been attained, and probably succeeded by orderly reduction of the human biomass on the planet. Although the ecological and cultural elements in each phase are so complex and immeasurable the recent elucidation of their corresponding demographic levels provides a welcome yardstick for assessing human impacts on the environment. The contrast between fewer than a billion persons increasing at around 0.64 per cent per annum and more than four billion increasing at an average 2 per cent, rising locally to more than 3 per cent, is self-evident. Before long it may be possible to estimate with some approach to accuracy the human carrying capacity of the planet earth on various assumptions concerning acceptable limits of rundown of non-renewable resources and of pollution and other pressures, and acceptable standards of life involving different mixes of material and non-material components.

This leads us to the second main aspect – itself forming an immense subject of specialist studies – the evaluation of natural resources, quantitatively, qualitatively and in terms of the different options for their recovery, use and re-use. Until quite recently economists and technologists generally, and also many scientists, combined to maintain the assumption that any limits there might be to natural resources were either so distant or so readily countered by technological innovation that there was no overall global problem to worry about. Even now that the falsity of this view has been so overwhelmingly demonstrated by environmentalists there is considerable drag in rethinking economics and public policies in the light of our new understanding of the situation. The Club of Rome forced the issue by initiating the well-known M I T computerised exercise extrapolating present trends in a crude but stimulating manner, which for the first time compelled the main establishment of economists, social scientists, administrators and politicians to face the unreality of their own assumptions regarding the comparatively near future.

The resulting spate of critical reassessment, which it was the object of the Club of Rome to release, has begun the long gradual process of developing a firmly based world view of the scale, nature and intractability of the total budget of resources within which mankind must live, and the consequent requirements for their conservation, extending to the whole terrestrial mass, to the depths of the oceans and to the atmosphere up to the stratosphere and beyond. Logically we must expect that in time resource economists will replace monetary and other more traditional types as the key group in assisting in the formation of public policy. An indicator of this trend is given by the abrupt and widely unexpected emergence of energy budgeting as a key factor in economic planning. Under traditional economics practices which were absurdly prodigal of energy were permitted and even encouraged to grow up during the middle years of the twentieth century. Thanks to the dramatic and effective gestures of the OPEC states under Arab stimulation a confrontation was brought about between the long-term planetary requirements and the briefly fashionable regime based on squandering 'cheap' energy, in the nick of time to compel the start of drastic readjustments before all tolerable options for the future had been closed. Here again the significance of money as a yardstick has been strongly qualified by the greatly enhanced role of energy as a factor in deciding what can and should be done for the future in terms of what is loosely called development. We may accordingly class energy as the third great distinguishable aspect of the subject, which is also a subject in its own right of enormous significance for Europe and the whole world.

A fourth main aspect, only very recently perceived as such by the managers of the planet and its national jurisdictions, is that of pollution of the air, water, land and the quality of human environment. Here again the Club of Rome has done great service by emphasising the need, long neglected in economics, for studying and bringing into account the relevant social costs, and consequently for appropriating adequate resources to research and to preventive and remedial measures. While the immediate threat posed by pollution in all its manifestations is vast and severe it is arguable that, given vigorous prosecution of the measures now belatedly devised, pollution may be the first of these cosmic problems to be brought effectively under control, perhaps as early as the first half of the twenty-first century.

Closely related to the foregoing main aspects is that which has come to be called conservation. Conservation has been variously defined, but for our present purpose it embraces the total conduct of the permanent relationship of man to his physical environment. Therefore, quite apart from its many practical and technical manifestations, conservation is an essential field of study for modern civilisation, because it gives rise to new concepts and approaches no less revolutionary and dynamic than those of natural science and politics.

Eventually, if conservation is to succeed, it must cease to be a thing apart and become inextricably interwoven with the fabric of a renewed civilisation. This fact has been more fully appreciated within wide areas of public opinion than in government, the professions and business, where there is still a tendency to treat it as a separate and extraneous factor, often tacked on as an afterthought to policies and projects already worked out on different and often incompatible lines. It is, therefore, not enough to consider the goals and methods of conservation; we have also to look at it as a major guiding element in public affairs, having its own approach which needs to be fully absorbed throughout the processes of education, training, management and operations. No more need be said at this stage, since the topic is integral to the following discussion.

Finally, and as a counterpart to the preceding subject, it is necessary to regard the future socio-economic pattern of modern cultures as a further major aspect of study in its bearing on the relations between Man and biosphere. Environmental impacts are not fortuitous and unpredictable. They flow logically and inevitably from the kind of society and economy prevailing, and the relative values which it holds. That is why the environmental movement could not be content with seeking superficial changes in treatment of the environment, but has been compelled to challenge the entire philosophy and mystique of materialist technological civilisation, with consequences which must be felt in every field. The serious study of this confrontation, its origins, its course and its influence has hardly yet begun, but it must form a substantial item on the agenda of scholars towards the turn of the century.

GENERAL

Environmental problems arising from man's impact on the biosphere can be traced back for thousands of years. During the past fifty years or so, they have, however, assumed a new and much more serious character, as they have grown in scale and complexity. The reasons are fairly clear. Early man, even within historical times, was only locally numerous and busy enough to convert a primary 'natural' habitat into a secondary managed or adapted landscape. Still less frequently could he go the full length of virtually replacing its given ecological pattern by an artificial substitute of his own. The pressure and the capability for such takeovers from nature have become dominant over wide areas only during the past century, and especially since about 1920. Before that, fire had had the greatest impact on natural vegetation, whether forest or open heath and grassland, followed, wherever climate and soil permitted, by grazing, the axe and the plough. Regulation of rivers, hydraulic engineering, drainage and pollution of air and water remained strictly local manifestations of human ingenuity. Mining and other extractive workings, defence structures and transport facilities were even more concentrated.

By contrast reservoirs of plant and animal genes in their full variety were still copious and widespread, enabling rapid recolonisation of areas temporarily or marginally affected by human impacts. These were generally less powerful, less persistent, less artificial and less mutually reinforcing than their current successors. Man's technosphere[2] formed only small intrusive islands in nature's biosphere, where today the biosphere in its pristine integrity is confined to islanded *refugia* within man's technosphere.

The half-century from around 1920 to 1970 has seen this secular process come to a head in diverse and dramatic ways, especially in populous and affluent Europe. The confrontation during these decades between economy, society and environment began largely unperceived, except

2. For definitions see pp. 5-6.

by a few ecologists and conservationists, during the World War I period. By the turn of the half-century enlightened leaders of public opinion had recognised some of the emerging problems, but viewed them naïvely in terms of a need for wise restraint against over-exploiting man's undoubted conquest of nature. Only during the last decade did it become widely appreciated that the conquest of nature was a mirage, and that the much abused and despised biosphere would soon call an abrupt halt to the ruthless runaway expansion of the technosphere at its expense.

Issues which had been complacently regarded as local and secondary or trivial were suddenly seen to be cosmic and fundamental, demanding a full, immediate and agonising rethinking of man's attitude towards his tenure of the earth, and towards himself as the earth's feckless temporary tenant. Many misgivings in various quarters of the values of the new affluent society, which had hitherto been felt largely in terms of cultural stresses, were suddenly discovered to reflect basic ecological distortions and errors. For a brief moment the amazed ecologist found himself thrust on a stage in the role of the prime seer and the voice of human conscience – a role traditionally held by the priest, the philosopher and the artist in literature and the visual arts, who found themselves for the moment at a loss. It is the evolution of this triangular confrontation between economics, society and environment, as it now appears at this moment of truth and full awareness, with which we are here concerned.

THE ECONOMIC ASPECT

Despite its ostensible maturity the economy of early twentieth-century Europe was spread through a remarkably long series of phases of evolution even within particular regions, with correspondingly diverse social and environmental conditions. At one extreme, especially in southern Britain and the lower Rhine basin, a megalopolitan stage of urban growth was beginning to emerge, with great conurbations and urban regions reaching out across their immediate suburbs to develop commuter belts, shopping catchments and commercial-industrial relations involving new social and environmental patterns over large areas. At the other there were still island, upland and outlying communities whose economic, social and environmental conditions had changed little since the eighteenth century or earlier. In between these extremes, mildly modernised peasant agriculture, family farming and fishing, local individual carriers and boat operators, and even fragmented units of mining and manufacture were very widely prevalent. Over wide regions the economy, as the Americans expressed it, was still not on wheels.

Over such regions it followed that demands on the environment were mainly shaped by the needs of self-sufficiency. Little attempt was made to exploit the great new markets for primary products created by the industrial revolution, which thrived increasingly on food and raw materials carried from new economies far beyond Europe. These great new sources of supply long cushioned the impact on Europe's landscape of Europe's rapid but patchy and localised industrial expansion, with its corresponding growth of population.

Yet over large regions, and in many ways, the hard-pressed peasantry and their rural fellows pressed more heavily on their environment than ever before or since. Ever since landscape painting became popular in the seventeenth century hundreds of faithful pictures attest the mangled and maltreated state of the trees in populated European countrysides. Any other usable wild plants were ruthlessly exploited, and edible animals snared, shot, massacred or persecuted. Such trades as sale of fashion plumage, cage-birds and rarities or oddities bore down heavily on the affected species. Where peat existed it was cut in vast quantities; reed was harvested for thatch, and the stripping of marram grass led to sand-dunes losing their stability and advancing over adjoining land. The thinning of rural population through emigration and movement to the towns accordingly lifted a grave burden off the country environment and permitted many plants and animals to recover from it during the later twentieth century.

In the closely-built urban settlements nineteenth-century experience had shown how vital are good sanitation, paving and water supply to the maintenance of public health. The movement which carried through this sanitary revolution more than a century ago was the precursor of the modern environmental movement, using similar methods to achieve similar aims. Above all it demonstrated the ease with which anti-social practices, once publicly identified, could be tackled by well-directed legislation backed by a firm and efficient administrative service. The speed with which cholera was converted from a public menace to a memory demonstrated that the penalties of environmental abuse, although severe, are readily remediable.

While such progress was being made in public hygiene the path of nineteenth-century technology was unfortunately creating many types of pollution of air and water which industrialists were encouraged by classical economics to regard as externalities which could properly be unloaded on the community.

By World War I the chemical industry, first in Germany, and later in other industrial countries, became developed in large close-knit units run by experienced scientists and technologists who had the training to appreciate and the resources to start preventing part of the more severe pollution which clinging to nineteenth-century practice would have involved. Stimulated by wartime demand, and assisted for reasons of national defence, the industry was largely emancipated from economic dogmas, and was moreover eager to cultivate the support of public opinion. Its readiness to study and to assist in eliminating grossly injurious pollution helped to bring about a new view of what could reasonably be expected from users of industrial processes damaging to the quality of air and water.

About the same time the powerful angling interest was advised of the long neglected power of the English Common Law to put a stop to the shameless poisoning of rivers by irresponsible industrialists. Through a series of test cases injunctions to desist from discharging toxic effluents were given by the Courts against a number of large firms and at least one local authority. Having blithely assumed that they could make such discharges indefinitely with impunity these firms found themselves subjected to the equivalent of immense fines in the form of requirements to instal suitable remedial measures in quick order. The right of the citizen to pure water and of the angler to surviving fishes was strikingly vindicated, but it was to be several decades before economists could be persuaded to face and study the full implications of the community's insistence that such so-called externalities must form part of the costs of industry.

Although it was apparently only in England that the existing law could provide drastic and effective remedies against industries disregarding their obligations to the common interests of their fellow citizens this unloading of objectionable substances into air and water, and the encouragement given to it by economics, represented a retrograde step in the historically well-marked care shown by most European peoples for their inheritance. Perhaps the greatest and worst example was formed by the combined activities of Swiss pharmaceutical firms, French mining and power interests, the German chemical industry and others to convert the Rhine into Europe's largest open sewer, culminating in the poisoning disaster of 1970 when a sudden fishkill in the middle Rhine was followed by an emergency affecting the water supplies of Rotterdam and other parts of the Netherlands.

In this grey area between public law and industrial management and environmental conservation the difficulty of establishing what should not be done has been more than matched by the difficulty of ascertaining and regulating what in practice is being done. It became generally accepted that effluents destructive of life and injurious to the interests of other water users ought not to be discharged into rivers untreated. But which effluents, in which conditions and amounts possess that property, and in what types of river flow? What if two effluents, each tolerable in itself, combine to form an inacceptable element lower down? The setting of tolerances, the monitoring of water quality and the management of rivers and waterways so as to achieve the most workable and acceptable regime have bristled with technical difficulties, even when economic and legal responsibilities have been settled.

Almost throughout the mid-century decades most seamen and inland water crews clung stubbornly to the age-old practice of disposing of anything unwanted by throwing it or releasing it into the water. Statutes could be enacted, solemn undertakings given and instructions issued, but only with the utmost vigilance and exertion over many years was it found possible to enforce them. The task was doubly difficult in international waters, or where different nationalities were involved. Here enforcement tended to be no one's business, and where it was attempted it tended to meet a wall of resistance and an utter dearth of information.

In addition to the deep-seated practice of unloading waste products and letting others worry over the consequences, there was an equally stubborn refusal to admit that the very much greater volume of shipping, carrying far larger and more hazardous cargoes and bunkers at increased speeds on tighter schedules, called for drastic revision of navigation practices and freedoms handed down perhaps since the days of Homer. By the end of the period a state was reached in which peaceful navigation, aided by the most costly and sophisticated instruments, was involving actual losses of shipping worldwide greater than the World War II sinkings in the Battle of the Atlantic. Pleas to have at least the narrow waters brought under something comparable with air traffic control, and to have some agreement that ships moving in a certain direction should follow in the same lane, went for years unheeded by international and national authorities, the resulting environmental damage being matched by the waste of ships, investments and in some cases valuable lives.

Such experiences led ecologists and conservationists,

especially after the middle 1950s, to cease merely tracing the proximate cause of, for example mass mortality among seabirds through oil spillages, or among birds of farmlands through concentrations of lethal chemicals in the fields, and to begin to look critically at the underlying reasons why parts of the economy were so operated as to lead to such effects. The widespread tendency to shrug them off as trivial or inevitable, and to represent them as the price of progress, became increasingly irksome to conservationists, whose studies deepened their suspicion that such careless-ness and irresponsibility towards the environment reflected a similar carelessness and irresponsibility towards wider social obligations, and not infrequently even towards shareholders themselves. Some private industries proved sufficiently co-operative and open to lend confirmation to such views while amicably revising their practices to remedy the abuses without any ill results to themselves.

One example of this was the British agricultural chemical industry, which found itself on a collision course with conservationists when many wild birds and mammals were found dead or dying on farms early in 1960. Fortunately discussions had been opened in anticipation of such problems some years earlier under official auspices, and much preparatory investigation and technical communica-tion had been carried through. With the possible exception of oil pollution of the sea, no other example so well illus-trates both the threat posed by the economy to the environ-ment and the means of resolving it to the satisfaction of all parties. The story therefore merits a summary here. Even during the nineteenth century minor incidents had been created by the use of toxic substances on the land for agricultural, game-preserving or other purposes. By the 1940s, however, escalation set in owing to three fresh developments. The expanding chemical industry now had the capability, and saw the commercial attraction of developing large-scale production of substances able to destroy wholesale on the land invertebrates held to be injurious to crops, livestock and human health. Larger and more modern units in farming, backed by official agencies at national and international level, saw the advantages, both commercially and in public relations, of a spectacular war against pests. At the same time, especially in the medical field, substantial public funds became available for campaigns to eradicate such diseases as malaria. Extra impetus to all three of these developments was given by World War II and its aftermath, at a time when the environmental conservation movement was particularly weak.

Nevertheless environmental scientists gave early, clear and soundly-based warnings of the dangers, not only from parts of the United States which were feeling the main impact, but from Sardinia and other parts of Italy, and from England and elsewhere. The hazards of blind use of DDT and of indiscriminate commercial or private spraying, and the need for research, selectivity and control were convincingly stated at the first International Technical Conference on the Protection of Nature, organised by the International Union for the Protection of Nature (then only a few months old) and UNESCO at Lake Success, New York in August 1949. Three specialised agencies of the United Nations, represented at the meeting, were requested to establish a joint permanent Commission on Pesticides, but they neglected to do so, and the warnings also fell on deaf ears at national level, with a few exceptions.

In the United Kingdom, where some of the earliest fatalities had fortunately been human, there was sufficient concern to secure investigation by a strong and well-balanced official Working Party under Sir Solly Zuckerman on 'Precautionary Measures against Toxic Chemicals used in Agriculture'. Its Report, issued in 1955, was of greater significance than was realised at the time, seven years before Rachel Carson's *Silent Spring*. While it was too early, so far as Great Britain was concerned, to find any dramatic or massive evidence it set a standard for comprehensive scientific treatment, ranging from effects on operators to repercussions on bee-keeping and wild life. Its acceptance by the Ministry led to the immediate appointment of an Inter-Departmental Advisory Committee, representative both of the trade and of conservation interests, and to the issue within a year of a revised leaflet for public guidance (APS/1) containing useful practical advice such as:

'The prevention of spray drift, either by the use of boom covers or by not spraying in wind, will do much to prevent losses of livestock and wild life. Many domestic, farm, and wild animals have been killed by spray poisoning their food or drinking water.'

'When dinitro weedkillers are used on cereals, they should be sprayed as early in the season as possible, before wild life starts using the crop for cover, and artificial water points, away from the corn, should be provided for game.'

It was pointed out that there is scope 'for fruitful co-operation between the contractor and the farmer and their men, and also between the farmer and the bee-keeper, who should be warned of spraying whenever possible'.

In the spring of 1957 the Advisory Committee completed arrangements with the Industrial Associations concerned for a voluntary notification scheme for pesticides. It provided for safeguards in the use of chemicals formulated as insecticides, fungicides, herbicides, rodenticides or similar products used in agriculture or food storage which could constitute a threat to the health of workers, consumers or wild life. The industry agreed not to market a product with fresh properties which could cause new or increased risk without first informing the Committee of the nature of the product, and their reasons for believing that it will be effective and safe, and obtaining the Committee's approval of its use. Provision was also made for recommended precautions to be printed on labels of products where appropriate.

Several novel principles were embodied in these arrangements. Competing manufacturers waived their prized commercial secrecy in putting their cards openly on the Committee's table, and agreed quite voluntarily to accept its rulings. Conservationists became committed to share responsibility for formulating tests to be taken as authoritative in determining, subject to fuller information in due course, the toxicity of agricultural chemicals to wild life. For this purpose it was agreed by eight leading naturalist societies to collaborate with the industry in monitoring field trials and operational uses under a Wildlife Panel. These and other provisions plainly presupposed a climate of rationality, mutual trust and avoidance of emotional confrontation which contrasted sharply with the situation in the United States and elsewhere. Admittedly this climate had been made possible by the relatively slow and cautious adoption of hazardous chemicals both by the industry and by farmers, and the consequent fewness at that time of gross examples of impacts on the biosphere in Britain.

Unfortunately the implied reliance on scientific manpower and funds proved optimistic in the circumstances, and it was two years before the Wildlife Panel could be set up, consisting of two scientists nominated by the Inter-Departmental Advisory Committee, three by the trade and three from the Nature Conservancy. One of the first examples of detailed teamwork at all levels between government, industry and conservationists on an important environmental issue of international concern had got off the ground before the close of the 1950s.

Its test was soon to come. During 1959 the Nature Conservancy continued to appeal for any reliable evidence 'where it is believed that chemicals have caused the death of birds, mammals or beneficial insects'. A few months later such a plea was dramatically outdated by widespread mortality of wild mammals and birds in areas where spraying was taking place. Not only seed-eating finches and wood-pigeons, but such game birds as pheasants were badly hit, together with their predators and carrion feeders. There was an embarrassment of material, aggravated by the lack of proven techniques for determining such causes of death, and the high cost of post mortems for each body analysed, which was comparable with that for a human corpse. An unexpected factor was the heavy mortality among foxes during late 1959 and 1960, which brought into action the little-known but immensely strong capabilities of the Masters of Foxhounds, who preside over the peculiarly British institution of hunting the fox across country. Long viewed with some hostility by many animal-lovers, the Masters reacted instantly and threw their full weight behind the effort to determine beyond question what had destroyed no less than 1,300 of the animals which it is their pleasure to pursue.

The ensuing confrontation strongly illuminated the emerging issues between the economy, society and the environment. From the angle of the economy it was argued that the world food shortage and the British balance of payments required an expansion of home food production at all costs; that this could not be achieved without un-inhibited use of pesticides and herbicides to minimise crop losses and to control scourges of livestock, and that if an incidental consequence was to inflict injuries upon wild life and the environment that must be recognised as a small price worth paying. Some agricultural scientists went further, claiming that the environmental losses attributed to the use of toxic chemicals could be due to other natural causes, and that ecologists who contended otherwise were being unscientific. In these circumstances it would have been natural for the manufacturers of agricultural chemicals, members of the immensely powerful oil and chemicals industries, and the farmers who had adopted their products and techniques to come out strongly against environmental conservation. Indeed this happened not only in the United States but in such European countries as the Netherlands where the dominant Royal Dutch element in the international Shell Group reacted publicly in that sense.

In Britain, however, the years of patient preparatory teamwork between the interested parties paid off, and the will to find a mutually acceptable solution enabled wiser counsels to prevail. The Wildlife Panel produced its first Report setting out a basis for further co-operation with the industry on treatment of data to fill the many gaps in knowledge. At the Annual Dinner on 18th May 1960 of the Association of British Manufacturers of Agricultural Chemicals, the principal guests were the Minister of

Agriculture and Lord Hurcomb, President of the Council
for Nature and also a leading figure in the Nature Conservancy – as was said then it was 'the first time that anyone
from "over the fence" has been present at an ABMAC
dinner.' The Chairman expressed the industry's view on
this 'very complex problem depending as it does on ecological studies' and referring to the Council for Nature and
the Nature Conservancy added 'We want to establish this
as a real working partnership . . .' The industry was as
good as its word, and while Rachel Carson across the
Atlantic was moved to pen her classic indictment in *Silent
Spring* scientists of the Nature Conservancy and the chemical
manufacturers, aided by the Government Chemist and the
veterinarians, were engaged in an all-out effort to trace the
paths by which toxic elements employed in agriculture
entered and affected wild life populations, and how to
modify pesticides and herbicides so as to retain their
specific effectiveness for their function while so far as
possible eliminating their harmful side-effects in use.
Volunteers provided prompt and accurate information and
sent in corpses for analysis. In this task the Game Research
Association and the Masters of Foxhounds, representative
of landowners concerned with field sports, played an
invaluable part, not only practically but in averting a
confrontation publicly between farmers and naturalists.
The divided views and interests of countrymen, which
might have been exploited in the media to blow up controversy and kindle emotion, were happily conciliated while
the inevitably slow work of the scientists went ahead.
Meanwhile a meeting at the Ministry of Agriculture in
June 1961 involving the manufacturers, the distributors,
the farmers, the country landowners and the scientific and
conservation bodies, had reached an interim voluntary
agreement, which was widely publicised, restricting the use
of seed dressings containing suspect chemicals. Underlying
tensions created persistent difficulties, and it took years
before the scientific data were sufficiently complete to
convince all doubters of the basic diagnosis, but the work
was successfully carried through, the farmers continued to

expand production, with increasingly sophisticated aid from the chemical producers and distributors, and from the official advisory ervice, but the birds and mammals which had been so hard-hit at the outset were making an encouraging recovery by the end of the 1960s, and the battle ended without leaving any group or disgruntled losers.

The principles thus successfully applied were equally applicable to many other issue between the economy and society and the environment, but unhappily this has proved over Europe generally the exception rather than the rule. For that two reasons were perhaps all-important. The problem here was so highly technica that scientists had to be given a central role, and were thus enabled to explore in depth whether the various aims and interests were basically irreconcilable, or only fortuitously appeared so. Also there was a sufficient potential conflict of interests, cutting across normal loyalties, to keep responsible leaders anxious for a tolerable compromise, and ready to make it work voluntarily, without fresh laws. Some foreign commentators, reflecting on this case, have wryly remarked that it is inapplicable in their countries since it rests on a gentleman's agreement, and they have no gentlemen. In this they do themselves an injustice. Insofar as gentlemanliness is involved at all it is quite secondary to the fact-finding approach and to scientific analysis inspired and firmly supported by enlightened self-interest. It is the failure to adopt such an approach, and to recognise the dictates of enlightened self-interest, which has put managers of the economy on a collision course with environmental conservationists in so many instances in every country. Environmental extremists are created and maintained by thoughtless or predatory interventions against the environment; they disappear where thoughtfulness and restraint is the rule.

This is well illustrated by experiences in reclamation of wetlands. The greatest of all, the conversion of the old Zuider Zee into the modern freshwater Ijsselmeer, has been conducted by the Netherlands Government on broadly acceptable lines embracing a wide diversity of land uses, including agriculture and forestry, recreation and nature conservation. In contrast to the situation elsewhere, reclamation in the Netherlands is strategically a defensive operation against successive historical encroachments of the sea and the great rivers upon the land. It is therefore deeply embedded in the national culture, and correspondingly mature and sophisticated, attuned to a highly complex series of forces and natural sequences, and to unceasing effort tempered by opportunism and compromise. Only in the great Delta Plan, necessitated by the disastrous tidal flooding of 1953, is there some approach to the more grandiose and aggressive attitudes characteristic of a number of other large reclamation projects elsewhere. It is probably no coincidence that the Delta Plan has led to more conflict between various sectors of the economy – fishing, agricultural and commercial – and also conservation and local community interests.

In other parts of Europe reclamation from the sea has been no more than a localised secondary affair, but reclamation of wetlands, and of standing water or delta and estuarial lands, has not infrequently created conflicts between environmental and other interests. The conversion of tracts of the Camargue in the Rhône Delta into ricefields, especially during the 1940s, has been a particular cause of international concern. This outstanding European wilderness area embraced some 60,000 hectares around 1830, which was reduced by some 5,000 ha during the ensuing century, but between 1939 and 1967 the loss was more than tripled, from 55,000 to a residue of only 38,000 ha. By that time the adjoining Marseilles urban region had grown to 1,350,000 inhabitants, with a forecast 3,000,000 by the end of the century, much of the growth being around its nearest corner, amid the steel, chemical, fertiliser and refinery plants of Fos. This new complex of threats has dwarfed those already faced through the encroachment of rice-growing to the extent of 75 per cent of France's requirements, and massive workings of salt-pans. These, like the vineyards, have not proved entirely incompatible with the needs of wild life, whereas the explosion of industry and population has been uniformly destructive.

To mention only a few examples, interference with watercourses has, in the case of navigation works to reduce the turbulence of the Rhône, also reduced oxygenation and called for costly purification plants to restore capacity for handling sewage. The extensive Berre Lagoon, originally saline, was transformed to fresh water by a canal from the River Durance, but this has again been modified by creation of a large underground reservoir in which five million cubic metres of fresh water are dissolving large natural deposits of salt which discharge into the lagoon. The location here also of an immense hydrocarbon refining industry has added pollution which detracts from the recreational value of the lagoon, and ruins its hitherto pure air. Bauxite, the raw material for aluminium, is named from the neighbouring Les Baux, and its exploitation led to deposits of the noxious red mud at a site near the airport at Vitrolles, which has been chosen for a new town, necessitating the removal of this toxic material, which should never have been put there in the first place.

The non-tidal nature of the Mediterranean and intense sunshine complicate the problems of pollution and of population pressure. These date back to before World War II, when drainage of unpurified sewage towards the colony of Herring Gulls on islets off Marseilles led to multiplication of the birds which later began feeding *en masse* on household refuse deposited by the trainload on the Crau to the northwest. This flight-line led large flocks across the approach to the Istres airbase, involving grave accidents. It also encouraged the birds to start roosting in the nearby Camargue, where they took opportunities of devouring eggs of the very rare Flamingos whenever these were disturbed by the same aircraft which were themselves imperilled by birdstrikes on the gulls. These few examples illustrate the diversity and complexity of the repercussions on both human and natural environment through rapid and massive expansions of industry and population. Even the material benefits are by no means clear-cut; in the Department of Bouches-du-Rhône the 6 per cent of the active population engaged in environmentally acceptable agriculture were producing in the 1960s one quarter of the value of the whole output of industry, against which so many offsetting social costs have to be admitted.

The urbanisation of Berre/Fos, occurring as it does close to areas of the highest natural and tourist value is widely recognised as one of the most important test cases of the ability not only of France but of Europe to reconcile economic growth with environmental quality. Owing to many scientific and technical studies data on the problems and on what has occurred are plentiful and good. (A number mentioned above are well summarised in the Documentation of the ECE Symposium at Prague in 1971 on Problems relating to Environment, in A Study of Environmental Conditions and Problems encountered in a Metropolitan Region and Zone; Metropolitan Region of Marseilles-Aix-Fos, submitted by France; published by the United Nations, New York 1971.) The question arises whether in such cases modern Europe is proving any more successful in avoiding capital errors and irreversible injuries than the Europe of the initial Industrial Revolution. It would be difficult, on the record up to 1970, to give any reassuring verdict.

How far would other cases confirm or modify such doubts? The example of Venice and the destruction not only of its environmental quality but of its actual fabric by the industrialisation of its lagoon, centred on Mestre, has been widely reported, and is of long standing, although the problem has come to a head since about 1950. There is a remarkably close parallel between the vulnerability to oil and air pollution and to ill-judged interference with a finely balanced water regime of the Camargue as a natural wetland wilderness and the city of Venice as a superb human achievement. Venetians, like flamingos, are dependent for their survival on the continuance of successful functioning of a peculiar delicate habitat and water regime, which modern industry rudely disturbs and encroaches upon, heedless of consequences. The necessary remedies and safeguards indicated by technical studies are fairly similar, but up to 1970 efforts to put them into practice had been largely ineffectual, insofar as they required action and sacrifices outside the immediate area of deepest concern.

Perhaps the most closely comparable example from northern Europe is the creation of Europoort and the partial fusion of Rotterdam in a new megalopolis based on the lower Rhine. This development during the 1950s involved the absorption and blotting out of a major bird sanctuary named De Beer, compensation for which, although promised, has proved largely illusory, being confined in effect to better protection of some small bird islands already in being. The design and layout of the new industrial and port area constructed after World War II was disappointing, whether viewed in terms of convenience, of landscaping and visual amenity or of effective steps to minimise pollution, especially from petro-chemicals. The best that can be said is that no such injury was threatened as those to the Camargue or Venice, because no such treasure of European significance was there to spoil.

Turning to a last example, the industrial development of Southampton Water in southern England after World War II affords an interesting comparison. During the preceding decades this favoured waterway had been the European terminal of passenger liners larger, as it proved, than any built before or since. Among the requirements of post-war reconstruction was the building up of oil refinery capacity less remote and vulnerable than that in the Persian Gulf and other producing areas. The choice fell upon Fawley, fronting the Water in the narrow zone between it and the unspoilt Crown Land of the New Forest, equivalent to a National Park in other countries. Under public pressure a real effort was made to avoid giving offence, in terms of design and pollution. The Fawley Smell was much spoken of, but proved a relatively mild nuisance. During the 1960s an adjoining site was used for a large but excellently designed oil-fired power station, whose stack rose above 200 m high, with correspondingly high demands on cooling water. Despite these and other large developments, including an earlier big power station farther up, monitoring showed that water quality nearby, and the populations of marine animals and plants, were indistinguishable from what would have been expected in the absence of an oil refinery and a power station. A rational and environmentally tolerable co-existence had been achieved. Much the same was true in the model oil port of Milford Haven, created under four separate Acts of Parliament from 1958. Here, under the guidance of a leading Welsh landscape architect, even the large oil tank farms were discreetly screened by rising land, and after many initial difficulties oil spillages were reduced to a negligible level.

During the half-century therefore the capability for harmonising economic projects with the conservation of environment just about kept pace with the rapid advance of technology and industrial expansion. Unfortunately, under political and commercial pressures, aggravated by the excessive rate of population growth and by public apathy, the application of this capability proved patchy and commonly inadequate, especially where one or more economic interests came into intense competition for sites and resources with the requirements for conserving environments of special value. The worst and least manageable problems arose where such a natural resource as a sheltered deep harbour or rich mineral deposit more or less coincided with the nucleus of a large labour force and market, or with a gateway to a distribution network, giving rise to pressures for rapid and ill-prepared development. Projects involving abrupt changes in hitherto remote areas also presented special threats and difficulties. The nature of these however varied greatly with differing cultural, social and political backgrounds, forming the element termed Society to which we now turn.

SOCIETY

Considered in relation to impacts on environment Society

has three distinct facets. First there is the general pattern of cultural values and priorities governing the relative attractions of urban and rural living, the appreciation of or indifference to landscape, wilderness and wild life, the reverence or callousness towards other living creatures, and the tendency towards husbanding or indiscriminately exploiting natural resources. Each nation, and within it each regional, cultural or religious group, tends to present a somewhat different profile in such matters, and that profile in turn is reflected, and can be read by the experienced observer, in its pattern of landscape and land use.

These special characteristics are often crystallised in custom, law and institutions, which partly reflect but partly distort or obstruct their free expression. Among the most obvious and widespread are land tenure and inheritance, social dispersal or grouping in village and town, and the degree and nature of community initiative, intervention or ownership. During the half-century under review more widespread and drastic changes have occurred in this field than in any previous period, with correspondingly intense repercussions on the environment.

The third facet consists of the current range of uses and activities affecting the environment, not only in the course of work but for leisure, defence and other purposes. It is here that society bears most directly on environment, and here that the most rapid and significant changes are manifest.

Taking the cultural facet first it is obvious that during the past few millennia man's subordination to natural imperatives and his close continuity of exposure to natural elements have progressively been lessened, while the ingrained tendencies to resist the dominance of nature and to strive to replace it by human mastery over nature have persisted. The outcome has however been very different as between inhabitants of northern Russia, the Mediterranean coasts, or islands in the Atlantic. Stay-at-home groups view their environment differently from outgoing or nomadic peoples; pastoralists differently from cultivators, foresters or seamen; villagers differently from scattered peasants, and catholics differently from protestants. These factors are vividly illuminated in America, where states which were colonised largely by Scandinavians or Germans show land use and landscapes conspicuously different from those colonised by an English squirearchy, as in Virginia, which again differ radically from those originally settled by the English middle-class Puritans. Such sidelights indicate that the actual landscapes of a region arise from a blend of physical characteristics, economic and social convenience at a given level of political evolution and technology, and also a stamp of fashion or style, derived perhaps by historical accident from the initiative of a minority, which the majority will readily forget or repudiate if they emigrate or in the event of drastic social change. The whole subject, fascinating as its implications are, has hitherto been little studied, and we must be content here to note that in the background of all the more concrete and readily defined influences bearing upon the environment there stands a host of imponderables, all the more elusive because of their protean and continuously transitional nature. In the end they are the arbiters of what will be done and what will not be done to conserve or exploit the environment, and their judgement will be determined by their understanding and evaluation of the significance of what they see happening to it. Turning next to the institutional facet only the most superficial observer in flight over Europe can fail to notice the contrast between the landscape of primogeniture and that of equally shared inheritance, the landscape of strongly capitalised estates with tenant farmers and that of peasants or smallholders, or the tracts of State forests and those belonging to communes or private owners. Many important changes in land tenure occurred during our half-century in various parts of Europe, ranging from total nationalisation in eastern countries to rationalisation and reallocation of farmlands, for instance in the Netherlands, and to the breakup of large estates in some other areas.

In conjunction with the growth of centralised State power much land was publicly acquired by various means, and was often placed under the management control of an agency preoccupied with a single function such as water supply, defence, afforestation or agrarian reform. The result was to build up a class of neglected land which happened to have been acquired together with land appropriate to the functions of the agency concerned, but which itself was unsuitable and of no interest.

Growing demands for land for an ever increasing range of purposes threw into relief the contrast between countries in which there was a free market in land and those in which it was governed by tacit social constraints affecting both availability and price, among which Great Britain was notable, especially during the earlier decades of the period. Another important background influence, also particularly significant in Britain, was that of town and country planning, with its implications for the restraint of urban sprawl, for the artificial creation of new towns, and for the enforcement of appropriate zoning, including the prohibition of further industrial or office development in areas held to be already overdeveloped.

In the Netherlands physical planning was more comprehensive and more centralised, being closely integrated with economic planning. In France stress was laid on planning by regions on a basis of thorough technical studies, taking a more positive initiative than in Britain, and being backed where necessary by massive new supporting investment. In Italy the partial regional autonomy accorded to Sardinia and Sicily after World War II was not extended to the mainland regions until the end of the period; in Britain also the degree of effective devolution to regions remained minimal.

In these and many other ways, changes in institutions and laws lagged behind the evolution of public opinion and new values on the one hand, and the actual pattern of activities and land use on the other. In terms of legislative programmes and administrative reforms the environmental revolution became conspicuous only late in the 1960s. Yet, despite this timelag, the growth of public opinion and the increasing effectiveness of voluntary environmental bodies made itself felt both nationally in a number of countries and internationally through such organisations as the International Council for Bird Preservation, from the 1920s, the International Union for the Protection (later Conservation) of Nature, from the late 1940s, and the World Wildlife Fund, from 1961. All three covered the world but all three were run from Europe, and all worked closely together in their respective fields. Dealing largely with governments of sovereign states, they thought and acted in terms of one earth, with a dedication, an intelligence and research network, and a grasp of strategy and tactics which eventually converted them into a formidable influence.

Under their stimulus and leadership many public-spirited people who had been alienated by political parties, churches and other conventional groupings came to find common cause in a broad movement, which they readily perceived to have rewarding implications not only for nature but for the quality of human living. Thus the prod and stimulus of the rejuvenated conservation movement achieved during the later 1950s and the 1960s much more action on behalf of the environment, often by interventions behind the scenes, than would have been supposed on the basis of the rather modest legislative record.

Included in this was the series of national laws in support of the successive International Conventions for the Prevention of Pollution of the Sea by Oil, the first of which was initiated by the International Council for Bird Preservation in 1950 and concluded in London in 1954, although not effective until some years later. This widespread and often deliberate pollution, obviously injurious to tourism, fisheries and other major interests, was allowed to continue unchecked until the ornithologists, backed by the wider conservation movement, insisted upon action. Mass popular support was demonstrated only much later, after the carelessness of the master of the large tanker *Torrey Canyon* exposed to crude oil pollution the coastlines of south-west England and north-west France, in attempting to save half an hour on his schedule which had been wasted by faulty navigation. Behind that disaster, and many others less publicised, lay a fundamental issue. Given that the so-called law of the sea had evolved in response to conditions of navigation and to types and scales of cargo infinitely less hazardous to environment than had now been substituted, was it reasonable that effective international regulation of activities carrying such hazards should be refused or evaded, and that masters of vessels should continue to be accorded a discretion even in narrow waters which the record showed them to be incapable of exercising acceptably? In reporting to Parliament in December 1961 the Nature Conservancy had

> 'raised the question whether safety margins for the movement of oil ought not to be as strictly defined and as thoroughly policed as those relating to aircraft and mining hazards, and whether the good intentions of the authorities and oil companies concerned were being adequately fulfilled by those actually carrying out the operations.'

These highly relevant questions were not faced by the national and international authorities until the decade was nearly over. Once more they clearly illuminate the role of the nature conservation movement as a pacesetter and expositor of reforms which society clearly should have made in the interests of its own good government, even if abuses to the natural environment had not also been involved.

While those pursuing activities which impinge on the environment continued to content themselves with regarding one aspect of one sector of it by a kind of tunnel vision, environmentalists used their ecological approach to view these impacts as a whole. It thus came about that governments and international agencies with responsibilities for the total management of their countries and the planet were forming and applying fragmentary, mutually inconsistent appraisals and prescriptions while environmentalists, although still an obscure minority group with little status in political and administrative spheres, were already seeing the problems whole and proposing soundly integrated courses of action.

It is only against this background that the meteoric rise

in the influence of environmentalists on European public opinion during the 1960s can be understood. In a situation which called for a rethinking of basic principles and a reappraisal of rapidly changing situations they alone, through historical accident, had the intellectual equipment and outlook to view the complex of problems as a whole, and the motivation to press for action. To the delight of some, and the consternation of others, the tail began to wag the dog.

This point is perhaps most aptly illustrated by the Chart of Human Impacts on the Countryside prepared as an annex to Paper No. 2 for the Duke of Edinburgh's Study Conference on 'The Countryside in 1970' held in London in November 1963. The Chart grouped all human activities on the rural landscape in 23 sectors within six main groups – reshaping the land, cropping the land, mining the land, construction on the land, activities on the land and letting the land alone. It distinguished more than 160 activities or operations, and for each of these outlined the area or land-type affected, the nature of the effects; their incidence in time, space and degree; the parties interested, and examples of the problems and possible solutions, with references to specific reviews and treatments. The parties identified ranged from landowners, farmers and industrialists to developers, highway and harbour authorities, water boards, aviators, soldiers, yachtsmen, anglers, golfers, mountaineers, potholers and boy scouts. For the first time it became possible at a glance to discover for any type of land how many competing interests would be concerned, and how far they might be conflicting or complementary. To some, such a comprehensive and scientifically based tool of analysis seemed indispensable to a rational approach to the many conflicting claims on land, and to its varying needs for conservation. The reaction of others was expressed by a highly intelligent civil servant in this field whose comment was the question 'What kind of mind would be interested in something like that?'

Nevertheless the Study Conference and its two successors in 1965 and 1970 had a profound influence not only in

Britain but throughout Europe. They were indeed the inspiration for European Conservation Year 1970, and for the sustained efforts in this field of the Council of Europe, which led on to the United Nations Stockholm Conference on the Human Environment in 1972, remarkable among other things for the fact that it was held, on Swedish initiative, in Europe rather than North America. A further influential example of this holistic approach, springing to life in Europe at the same stage was the Club of Rome, initiated as a result of a meeting in the Accademia dei Lincei (which goes back to the days of Galileo) in 1968. Its statements on the predicament of mankind, notably in *The Limits of Growth* 1972 leapt the remaining fences and carried the approach of the environmentalists into the ideological strongholds of economics and politics.

The timing proved excellent. While the 1920s and 1930s in Europe had been dominated by an abortive effort to reconstitute in viable form a modified regime of nationalist sovereign states under Great Power hegemony, learning as little as possible from the experience of World War I, it might equally be suggested that the 1950s and 1960s had been dominated by ideas of economic growth, of aid to the Third World, of social welfare and equality of opportunity and of military containment which had been embraced in reaction against the disillusionment of the interwar period, but which postulated a quite unrealistic carrying capacity for a vastly expanded human population at an enormously improved standard of living. During the earlier stage of applying high technology to tapping hitherto unexploited sources of non-renewable types of energy and dwindling reserves of land and other natural resources this line seemed practicable to economists, engineers and others lacking in ecological background. To those who had this background the immediate necessity to defend an irreplaceable natural heritage from irreversible destruction led quickly to perception that the whole politico-economic drive of the period was taking Europe and the world into a blind alley, catastrophic for man as well as for the biosphere.

Two of the clearest and largest factors were population increase and energy. It may be salutary here to quote from an analysis of these published in London in 1955 by a group of which the present author was a member:

World Population and Resources. A Report by PEP
'Modern Western civilisation contains exceptionally strong and varied inhibitions against facing the idea that a serious population-resources problem can and does exist. An optimistic materialism grew naturally out of the vast nineteenth-century success in both technological and geographic expansion. This materialism permeated equally strongly the Marxist-Communist, the liberal-capitalist and the social-democratic political creeds.'

'. . . too often development plans are made on the wrong assumption that development will not increase the rate of population growth or that population changes are of no consequence in calculating the effects of development projects. In reality the two factors – population and economic development – are engaged in a race which will last many years, and which the supporters of development cannot be sure of winning, because the practical difficulties are very substantial. Moreover, no government or international agency is yet taking sufficient account of the problem of conserving the world's natural wealth, a problem which has ethical, economic, political and strategic implications. There seems also to be a danger of taking excessive risks in order to push ahead fast enough with new technical discoveries, such as nuclear energy.'

Those general warnings were worked out in some detail in the Report; they indicate that the bombshell effect of such concepts on governments and public opinion in the late 1960s cannot be attributed to their being either unforseeable or unforseen. (Other similar cautions were issued even earlier on both sides of the Atlantic.) Yet they were nowhere more blatantly ignored than by successive international conferences promoted by the United Nations and its agencies. For example, that on the Application of

Science and Technology for the Benefit of the Less Developed Areas held in Geneva in 1963 as part of the United Nations Decade of Development was, in the words of Professor Lynton K. Caldwell:

'almost totally concerned with the exploitation of the natural environment for human material needs . . . The conference's underlying assumption was clearly stated when its president began it by declaring, "the air, the earth, the oceans and the sun contain riches which can support increases in population at higher and higher standards of living" . . . The world as perceived by the conference was one of unlimited possibilities only awaiting the application of science and technology to make the possible actual . . . In the relatively short retrospect of less than a decade it would appear that the assumptions of the conference were inconsistent with the conditions of the real world; and the optimistic and ambitious projections of the future advanced by its participants and by heads of government in messages to the conference, were fundamentally in error. It should not be surprising that at the end of the First United Nations Development Decade the general condition of humanity throughout the world was worse rather than better.'

In Defense of Earth. International Protection of the Biosphere. Bloomington 1972.

The copious record of thought and action concerning the environment shows in essence that during the initial quarter-century of our period the true relation of environment to the economy and society was only beginning to be perceived in partial and distorted perspective by a small peripheral minority of opinion-formers. During the following two decades more and more opinion-formers arrived at a more balanced but still incomplete and inadequate interpretation, but it was only during the final five years up to 1970 that any understanding of the implications began to illuminate public opinion, and to filter through to its ostensible leaders.

The extent to which informed opinion responded ahead

of all but a few leaders in politics, administration, business management, higher education and the main media calls for explanation. In part it was no doubt due to the over-centralised and intellectually incestuous pattern of government and public affairs in the mid-century, and to the tenacity with which it clung to its myths. Much was also due to the talented band of naturalists and enthusiasts for the countryside and open-air pursuits who wrote, lectured, broadcast and pictured their experiences so persuasively, to thousands and eventually millions released from urban or parochial bondage, and enabled to travel far and wide by the internal combustion engine and later by the flying jet. They not only threw open doors but invited participation in a wide diversity of shared leisure experiences, offering escape and fulfilment to many who had felt themselves thrust into the position of outsiders, or mere cogs in the machine. Walking tours, cycling and railway outings had started the movement in various forms in different parts of Europe, notably in Germany and the Alpine lands. After 1920 however it ramified out into countless fresh forms, including sailing, canoeing, angling, rock-climbing, gliding, skiing, bird-watching, riding, music festivals, field archaeology, camping, caravanning and many other activities in the open air, often transcending national frontiers. Divorced from inherited local, church, political and vocational loyalties, many found in such activities something more than a leisure outlet. The thought that they could not be pursued indefinitely unless the environment could be successfully conserved, and that success was possible whether the authorities cared about it or not, began to take roots after the middle of the century. Once that point was passed the fact that those who cared for the future of the environment so largely coincided with those who were more actively in contact with it all over Europe gave the movement a peculiar authenticity and practicality.

Nevertheless the very multiplicity of the outdoor interests concerned, and the amateur and sketchy nature of most of their organisations made for difficulties in developing a coherent, constructive approach, and bringing it to bear on the right occasions and in the right ways. Conflicts and divisions between tourist and recreational, amenity and preservationist and nature conservationist bodies and schools of thought were often serious, leading in a number of cases to major deadlocks or defeats. Such divisions were doubly crippling where major commercial interests were involved, such as the firearms industry behind the *chasse* or *caccia* in Mediterranean lands, and the resort and hotel developers and travel industries eager to expand tourism regardless of the callous ruin of thousands of kilometres of Europe's finest sea coasts and mountain valleys.

CHANGES IN THE EUROPEAN ENVIRONMENT

Around 1920 the European environment had already lost a larger proportion of its primary natural elements than that of any other continent. Such elements remained substantial only in arctic-alpine, steppe, northern coniferous forest and tundra regions, and more narrowly on islands and coastal strips and in some of the larger wetlands, by lakes and along watercourses.

Virtually all lands of gentle slope, favourable exposure, easy drainage and cultivable soils had passed into the secondary phase of managed forest or pasture, or substituted farm crops, and a sizeable although minor part of these areas had reached the stage of tertiary landscape consisting of or dominated by such artefacts as buildings, highways, railways and artificial waters. These encroachments, however, were only locally extensive and out of scale or harmony with the traditional landscape. Highly industrialised zones, such as the Ruhr and the English north and midlands, remained unusual, as did great conurbations such as metropolitan Paris and London. Grossly polluted waters were equally uncommon, and even within fifty kilometres of large cities it was still the rule to find a self-sufficient and not visibly much altered countryside.

Leisure resorts such as spas and seaside towns were highly compact, and circuits for tourists and holiday-makers were well-marked and formed beaten tracks, to deviate from which was still something of an adventure. Control over and management of the environment remained overwhelmingly in the hands of descendants of people who had exercised it for generations, or were at least deeply imbued with local traditions.

During the following half-century much of this was to be drastically changed. Even the widespread destruction and damage caused directly by World War II was dwarfed by the repercussions of economic and social trends. Wilderness areas, mountainous, forested or coastal, were invaded by ever more restless, mechanised and demanding tourists or pursuers of outdoor leisure, bringing in their train a formidable array of hotels, highways, second homes and assorted services and facilities, even in locations previously rated as uninhabitable.

Competing to encroach upon wilderness were vast hydro-electric projects, military establishments and training areas, motorways and tunnels, new mines, pipelines, powerlines and other far-flung ancillaries of technology serving the expanding urban networks. Dictatorships such as Mussolini's in the 1920s and Hitler's in the 1930s have been especially prone to embark on spectacular prestige projects such as motorway networks and large-scale reclamation of wetlands for agriculture or to eliminate malaria. These fashions eventually spread to the most respectable democracies, the elements of utility and of prestige being often inseparable. Engineers in particular, once having tasted the delights of indulging in some form of prestige technology have often sought for further openings to apply it regardless of genuine requirement.

A much publicised case is that of the proposed reclamation of the Waddensee as a successor to the conversion of the Zuider Zee into the Ijsselmeer. Recent trends within the European community have checked and partially reversed earlier expectations of a pressing requirement for additional agricultural land in the Netherlands, and an increasing proportion of the more lately reclaimed polders has become available for recreation, nature protection and urban development, including one of Europe's largest planned new towns (Almere in South Flevoland for 250,000 plus inhabitants). Simultaneously the importance of fishing has much increased, yet engineers have looked with covetous eyes on the opportunities of converting the vast recreational, fishing and nature conservation area of the Waddensee into a dull and unwanted tract of reclaimed land. On a smaller scale the practice of transforming curving natural watercourses into straight canal-like channels constricted between steep stone embankments has developed in some parts of Europe in a manner more readily explained in terms of engineering fashion trends than of social necessity. For example in Switzerland, where the practice has a long history, well illustrated by the early projects for regulation of the River Aare between Berne and Solothurn.

Among the most recent additions to major engineering works across country have been the international oil pipelines from the Mediterranean into central Europe during the 1960s. So far as is known however, such pipelines, once laid, have involved little interference with environment. Among other major intrusions large airports have assumed great importance, on account of noise and traffic accompanying them, but until the Maplin site was selected for London's third airport conflicts involving conservation of nature have been less significant in Europe than in other parts of the world. In one way or another, however, the direct or indirect impact of engineering has made itself felt during the period over a substantial area of the European rural environment.

American ecologists have long been interested in an opposite trend, due to the withdrawal of human occupancy of lands previously developed not only for farming but for mining and other uses, either because their resources have become exhausted or spoilt by misuse, or because better opportunities elsewhere have drained away the economically active adult population. In Europe since 1920 the second type of influence has become widely operative from the Celtic fringe of Atlantic islands, uplands and peatlands through the more elevated parts of France and into the centre of the continent. At a transitional stage, in certain Departments of France, the native inhabitants were at first replaced in part by even poorer peasants from Italy and elsewhere. More recently, in the sunnier and more fortunate regions, the ruined farmhouses and even outbuildings have been colonised, largely as second homes, by enterprising incomers from the northern centres of population in search of tranquillity and recreation.

Either way, as in the United States, extensive areas once grazed or even cultivated, including former vineyards are left undisturbed, to revert to a wild state. Ecologically, however, there is a vast difference between the reversion of abandoned farmlands in America through a phase of rough grassland and juniper scrub to something very like the primitive forest, and the situation in Europe where much longer exploitation, the extinction of so many indigenous plants and animals and the introduction of exotics arrest the process at a mongrel intermediate stage, at least so far ahead as can be foreseen.

As the regions affected are *ipso facto* poor and ill-equipped to face such complex types of decay and transition, and the incoming ex-urbanites seek nothing but the unorganised simple life, the gradual withdrawal of hill and other marginal farmers has begun to create a novel major problem of rural derelict land which is no longer thought worth managing, but which stands urgently in need of comprehensive ecological rehabilitation. In isolated instances tourist or other local investment has helped to solve the employment and some of the social problems involved, while neglecting or even aggravating those of the environment. In more fortunate areas landowners and others have kept up the traditional landscape, but as preservationists of a kind of landscape museum rather than as conservationists able to adapt it to a new style expressive of modern land uses and modern ecological knowledge. In summary, the changes in the environment of Europe since 1920 have been more extensive and drastic than in any previous half-century, partly owing to direct impacts of projects designed to transform it, partly owing to the indirect effects of changing distribution and density of human settlement and visitation, and partly owing to the influence of new attitudes towards the environment, tending to supersede satisfactions in mastering nature by values embracing harmonious co-existence with nature.

Being intangible these new values are not easy to define or to trace in action. Perhaps the best indicator is the appearance and mass dissemination of expressions previously unknown. For example in 1920 such terms as 'protection of nature' were tolerably familiar in limited circles, and laws for the protection of birds existed in a number of European countries. Movements for National Parks, for Nature Reserves and for rural preservation were beginning to make some mark in some countries, but incipient international co-operation was still very weak, and remained so until after World War II. Fresh impetus was given by the experiences of many during wartime, and the expanded interest in travel. In Britain in 1949 the then Lord President of the Council, Herbert Morrison, launched a new type of government organisation for the scientific conservation of the natural environment for which he chose after careful reflection the title 'Nature Conservancy', reviving a little-used word from the past. Five years later, at Edinburgh, under American persuasion the new International Union for the Protection of Nature changed its name to 'for the Conservation of Nature and Natural Resources', thus proclaiming acceptance of a much broader mission. Misgivings were expressed not only over the substance but over the word conservation, which French-speaking members feared would prove untranslatable and likely to lead to confusion with jam-making. Not until 1960 was 'conservation' used willingly in Britain by either the British Broadcasting Corporation or the serious press, although it had long been familiar in the United States. For some years further the term 'environment' was not in general use, 'countryside' being generally preferred. Similarly the word 'wildlife' or 'wild life' was unfamiliar in Europe prior to the launching in Zurich in 1961 of the

World Wildlife Fund, and once more there were difficulties over French translation. (In France the rendering is *Fonds Mondial pour la Nature* and in Italian *Fondo Mondiale per la Natura*.) A semantic stumbling-block is formed by the inclusion in 'wildlife' of not only plants but landscape, soil and water.

Systematic scanning of the files of leading European newspapers would show the gradual adoption of these and other key terms in the vocabulary of the environment, and also the immense expansion in the number of mentions of such words as 'ecology' and 'pollution' during the 1960s, when pressure of public interest claimed a vastly greater number of column-inches for the subject generally.

Compared with most other cultural subjects, such as the arts and recreation, the environment as a topic was distinguished by a remarkably hybrid character, bracketed at one time with engineering projects, at another with leisure pursuits and again often with governmental decision-making. This was largely due to the defensive posture in which environmentalists found themselves, and to the fact that even positive and long-term initiatives towards environmental harmony presupposed a partnership with some other economic or social interest. There was however a more fundamental reason. The world of the early twentieth century had fashionably been dominated by specialists, whose very success and limitations had inevitably generated a reaction, especially among intelligent laymen. Ecologists, conservationists and environmentalists themselves sprung from specialist disciplines and relied heavily on technical and scientific studies, but the holistic character of their problems early led them to move over towards the then unpopular role of the generalist, which, as the event showed, found a ready and eager response from public opinion.

As it developed the movement therefore found itself on a course converging with that of important intellectual and emotional currents which were independently gaining strength in Europe, and which found in it, at least temporarily, a welcome and constructive focal area. It may

T.C.(2)

be here that the explanation for the sudden rise of interest and support for it is to be sought. Reactions against many unsatisfying features of contemporary European life were leading or driving thoughtful people into a state of mind demanding some concrete apolitical and disinterested expression, which was slow to crystallise except in terms of conserving the environment, to which cause therefore many naturally gravitated. If such a diagnosis proves tenable it follows that the growth of the environmental movement between 1920 and 1950, and its relation to economic and social trends, may prove to merit a place in the history of twentieth-century European thought and attitudes.

Notes on the Authors

HERMANN PRIEBE
was born in Berlin in 1907 and educated at the universities of Göttingen, Königsberg and Berlin. He did practical work in agricultural extension from 1934-42, and after the war began lecturing at Giessen University. Since 1958 he has been Professor of Economics in Frankfurt/M and Director of the Institut fur Ländliche Strukturforschung (Institute for Rural Structural Research) connected with the university. From 1958 to 1970 he was economic advisor to the EEC Commission in Brussels. His main fields of activity are European agricultural policy, regional policy, and agricultural problems in the developing countries. Recent publications: *Landwirtschaft in der Welt von Morgen*, Dusseldorf 1970, *Fields of Conflict in European Farm Policy*, London 1972, and *Der Ländliche Raum – eine Zukunftsaufgabe*, Stuttgart 1973.

ANGUS MADDISON
is the author of *Economic Growth in the West*, *Economic Growth in Japan and the U.S.S.R.*, *Economic Progress and Policy in Developing Countries*, *Class Structure and Economic Growth*, and a number of articles on economics and economic history in academic journals. He was educated in Cambridge, in the USA and Canada, and has held academic posts in Scotland, the USA and Canada. He was formerly Head of the Economics Division in OEEC and a Fellow of the OECD Development Centre. He has worked as an economic advisor to governments in Ghana, Greece, Brazil, and Pakistan. He is currently head of the group on economic analysis and resource allocation in the Department of Scientific Affairs of OECD.

CARLO ZACCHIA
was born in 1920 and studied at the University of Pisa. In

1947 he joined the Research Department of the Banca Nazionale del Lavoro in Rome, and, in 1956, moved to the Secretariat of the United Nations Economic Commission for Europe in Geneva, where he still works as a senior economist.

FRED HIRSCH

is a Professor of International Studies at Warwick University. He graduated in economics at the London School of Economics in 1952. He worked as a financial journalist on *The Banker* and the *Economist*, where he was financial editor from 1963-66. From 1966-72 he was a Senior Advisor in the International Monetary Fund. Between 1972 and 1974 he was a Research Fellow of Nuffield College, Oxford.

Professor Hirsch is the author of *The Pound Sterling: a Polemic* (Gollancz, 1965), *Money International* (Penguin and Doubleday, 1969), *Newspaper Money* (with David Gordon: Hutchinson, 1975). and a forthcoming book, *Social Limits to Growth*, being published for the Twentieth Century Fund. He has been a consultant to a number of official institutions and is the author of several pamphlets and numerous articles.

PETER OPPENHEIMER

who has been a Student (Fellow) of Christ Church, Oxford since 1967, was born in London in 1938 and educated at Haberdashers' Aske's School and The Queen's College, Oxford, graduating in 1961. He arrived at Christ Church after three years on the staff of the Bank for International Settlements in Basle, and another three as Research Fellow of Nuffield College, Oxford. He broadcasts (willingly) and writes articles (reluctantly), his main professional interests being in international economics and public policy issues.

BENJAMIN WARD

born in 1923, completed his studies at the University of California, Berkeley, in 1956 and has taught in the economics department of that institution since 1959. His publications include *Studies of Greek Regional Development* (1962), *The*

Socialist Economy (1967), and *What's Wrong with Economics* (1972).

MAX NICHOLSON
is a graduate of Oxford and an Honorary Doctor of Aberdeen University and of the Royal College of Art, London. His career began as an ornithologist, but during the 1930s he took charge of the social and economic research organisation PEP during its early formative years, leaving it for a wartime assignment in shipping. He then headed the Office of the Lord President of the Council, who was at that time Deputy Prime Minister, before switching back to applied ecology as Director-General of the Nature Conservancy, then one of the official Research Councils. He has been closely concerned in the growth of environmental conservation internationally.

Index of Persons

Index of Places

General Index